Excel® Workbook FOR DUMMIES®

by Greg Harvey, PhD

WILEY

John Wiley & Sons, Inc.

Excel® Workbook For Dummies®

Published by
John Wiley & Sons, Inc.
111 River Street
Hoboken, NJ 07030-5774
www.wiley.com

Copyright © 2006 by John Wiley & Sons, Inc., Hoboken, New Jersey

Published by John Wiley & Sons, Inc., Hoboken, New Jersey

Published simultaneously in Canada

For general information on our other products and services, please contact our Customer Care Department within the U.S. at 877-762-2974, outside the U.S. at 317-572-3993, or fax 317-572-4002.

For technical support, please visit www.wiley.com/techsupport.

Wiley publishes in a variety of print and electronic formats and by print-on-demand. Some material included with standard print versions of this book may not be included in e-books or in print-on-demand. If this book refers to media such as a CD or DVD that is not included in the version you purchased, you may download this material at http://booksupport.wiley.com. For more information about Wiley products, visit www.wiley.com.

ISBN 978-0-471-79845-3 (pbk); ISBN 978-0-470-04410-0 (ebk); ISBN 978-0-470-19842-1 (ebk)

Manufactured in the United States of America

10 9 8

1B/TR/QY/QW/IN

WILEY

About the Author

Greg Harvey has authored tons of computer books, the most recent being *Excel Timesaving Techniques For Dummies* and *Roxio Easy Media Creator For Dummies,* and the most popular being *Excel 2003 For Dummies* and *Excel 2003 All-In-One Desk Reference For Dummies.* He started out training business users on how to use IBM personal computers and their attendant computer software in the rough and tumble days of DOS, WordStar, and Lotus 1-2-3 in the mid-80s of the last century. After working for a number of independent training firms, he went on to teach semester-long courses in spreadsheet and database management software at Golden Gate University in San Francisco.

His love of teaching has translated into an equal love of writing. *For Dummies* books are, of course, his all-time favorites to write because they enable him to write to his favorite audience, the beginner. They also enable him to use humor (a key element to success in the training room) and, most delightful of all, to express an opinion or two about the subject matter at hand.

Greg received his doctorate degree in Humanities in Philosophy and Religion with a concentration in Asian Studies and Comparative Religion last May. Everyone is glad that Greg was finally able to get out of school before he retired.

Dedication

To Chris, my partner and helpmate in all aspects of my life, and to Shandy, the newest addition to our family.

Author's Acknowledgments

I'm always very grateful to the many people who work so hard to bring my book projects into being, and this one is no exception. This time, preliminary thanks are in order to Andy Cummings and Katie Feltman for giving me this opportunity to write in this wonderful workbook format.

Next, I want to express great thanks to my project editor, Linda Morris (a more knowledgeable person about the *For Dummies* series and better editor you'll never find), and to my partner in crime, Christopher Aiken (I really appreciate all your editing, additions, and comments on this one). Thanks also go to Mike Talley for the great technical edit, Maridee Ennis for coordinating its production, and everybody at the Wiley Publishing Composition Services department for their proofreading and indexing work.

Publisher's Acknowledgments

We're proud of this book; please send us your comments through our online registration form located at www.dummies.com/register/.

Some of the people who helped bring this book to market include the following:

Acquisitions, Editorial, and Vertical Websites

Project Editor: Linda Morris

Acquisitions Editor: Katie Feltman

Copy Editor: Linda Morris

Technical Editor: Mike Talley

Editorial Manager: Jodi Jensen

Vertical Websites Specialists: Angela Denny, Kate Jenkins, Steven Kudirka, Kit Malone, Travis Silvers

Vertical Websites Coordinator: Laura Atkinson

Vertical Websites Project Supervisor: Laura Moss

Vertical Websites Manager: Laura VanWinkle

Editorial Assistant: Amanda Foxworth

Cartoons: Rich Tennant (www.the5thwave.com)

Composition Services

Project Coordinator: Maridee Ennis

Layout and Graphics: Lauren Goddard, Denny Hager, LeAndra Hosier, Stephanie D. Jumper, Melanee Prendergast

Proofreaders: Melissa D. Buddendeck, Jessica Kramer

Indexer: Estalita Slivoskey

Publishing and Editorial for Technology Dummies

    Richard Swadley, Vice President and Executive Group Publisher

    Andy Cummings, Vice President and Publisher

Mary Bednarek, Executive Acquisitions Director

    Mary C. Corder, Editorial Director

Publishing for Consumer Dummies

    Kathleen Nebenhaus, Vice President and Executive Publisher

Composition Services

    Debbie Stailey, Director of Composition Services

Contents at a Glance

Table of Contents

Introduction

Excel is the most sophisticated spreadsheet program available in the world of personal computing. As such, this program is much more than just an electronic version of an accountant's familiar green sheet for crunching numbers. For millions of users the world over, Excel is also their number one forms designer, their interface to the corporate database, as well as their premier charting program.

Given Excel's indisputable versatility, it should come as no surprise that mastering the basics of the program, not to mention its finer points, is no small undertaking. My experience, however, in teaching adults to use all manner of Excel's capabilities has convinced me that this mastery is greatly accelerated with just a modicum of hands-on experience judiciously applied to rather simple *but* realistic data-related problems.

About This Book

As its name suggests, *Excel Workbook For Dummies* is designed to give you the kind of hands-on experience with all the major aspects of the program you need to start using the program for business or home with a certain degree of confidence and efficiency. As you'd expect from this type of book, the workbook is primarily composed of questions and exercises that give you plenty of opportunities to experience the purpose and benefits of Excel's many features.

It's my hope that as a result of doing the exercises in this workbook, you'll not only be in firm command of the basic skills necessary to work with confidence in the Excel spreadsheet but also have a good idea of the overall power of the program through experience with its features beyond the spreadsheet.

Conventions Used in This Book

By convention, all the text entries that you type yourself appear in bold. In addition, all filenames appear in italicized type even though they are not italicized when you see their names in Windows Explorer or the Excel Open dialog box.

When it comes to instructions in the exercises throughout the workbook, you'll notice two conventions:

- Menu commands are introduced by the word "choose" followed by the menu sequence separated by the ⇨ symbol, as in "Choose File⇨Save As."
- Selections in dialog boxes are most often introduced by the word "select" followed by the name of the option name or button, as in "Select the Alignment tab" or "Select the OK button."

In both cases, you must decide on your own whether to select the menu command or dialog box option or button with the mouse or with the keyboard. In the case of menu commands, you can choose among clicking the menu and menu items with the mouse, activating the menu by pressing F10 and selecting the menu and menu items with the cursor keys, or pressing the

Alt key and then pressing the menu's and menu items' hot keys. In the case of dialog box options, you have a choice between clicking them with the mouse or pressing their hot keys. You can also select default buttons in a dialog box (indicated by shading around the button) by simply pressing the Enter key.

The method you use for selecting commands and dialog box options is completely up to you and should be dictated by your comfort level with the mouse or keyboard as well as which method is most efficient. For example, pressing the Enter key to select the default OK button in a dialog box is often the most efficient method when the next step you take is entering or editing in the current cell or range.

One other convention that you'll notice used throughout the text is the display of the names for Excel menu commands, toolbar buttons, and dialog box options in the title case, wherein all major words are capitalized except for prepositions. The title case is used to make these names stand out from the rest of the text. Often, however, especially in the case of dialog box options, Microsoft does not always follow this convention, often preferring to capitalize the first letter of the option name.

Foolish Assumptions

I assume that you're a new Excel user motivated to master its essentials either for work or at home. Further, I assume that you're someone who learns by doing as least as well, if not better than, by reading alone.

To complete most of the exercises in this workbook, you only need to have Microsoft Excel installed on a computer running a version of Microsoft Windows. For some of the printing exercises, you will benefit from having a printer installed on your system (although you can complete most of their steps and get the gist of the lesson without actually printing the sample worksheets). For a few of the Web exercises in Part VI, you *will* need to have access to the Internet in order to complete them.

The workbook is designed to be used with various versions of Excel; from Excel 2000 up to and including Excel 2003. There are, however, a few exercises that are designed primarily for users of Excel 2003, whose specific steps require slight modification in order to be accomplished on earlier versions. Only in the rarest of cases will you encounter an exercise that cannot be completed with all three versions. If you are a user of Excel 97, you can complete the majority of the exercises in the workbook, although you may find some of the steps confusing as they reference toolbar buttons or task pane commands that haven't yet been invented as far as your edition of Excel is concerned.

How This Book Is Organized

This workbook is organized into eight parts, each of which contains two or more related chapters. Each of the chapters follows a similar pattern of introductory text followed by exercises. In some of the chapters, you'll also encounter question and answer sections that are designed to stimulate your thinking regarding the features you're about to practice in the subsequent exercises. Note that although the exercises within any given chapter do build on one another, you're certainly not expected to complete them in strict chapter order. Feel free to work on the exercises in any order that feels comfortable and fits your learning needs.

Part 1: Creating Spreadsheets

This part contains the most exercises of any in the workbook. It is made up of four chapters designed to give you practice in all the spreadsheet basics, all the way from starting Excel to editing a completed spreadsheet:

- Chapter 1 enables you to practice creating a new spreadsheet.
- Chapter 2 runs you through formatting spreadsheet data.
- Chapter 3 gives you training in all aspects of printing the completed spreadsheet.
- Chapter 4 gives you plenty of experience with making modifications to the completed spreadsheet.

Part 11: Using Formulas and Functions

This part gives you all the practice you need with creating and using formulas in the spreadsheet. Chapter 5 introduces you to formula-making just as Chapter 6 introduces you to the all-important topic of formula copying.

Because of the importance of Excel's built-in functions in formula building, the remaining seven chapters in this part concentrate on building formulas using a particular category of functions:

- Chapter 7 gets you up and running on date and time formulas.
- Chapter 8 trains you in the use of financial formulas.
- Chapter 9 gives you practice creating formulas using Excel's Math functions.
- Chapter 10 concentrates on exercises in creating formulas using Statistical functions.
- Chapter 11 introduces you to the creation of formulas using Lookup functions.
- Chapter 12 runs you through the creation of formulas using the Logical functions, the performance of which depends upon prevailing conditions in the spreadsheet.
- Chapter 13 introduces you to the creation of text formulas that manipulate and change text entries in the spreadsheet.

Part 111: Working with Graphics

This part takes you into the graphical aspects of Excel, the most important of which is its rich and versatile charting capabilities covered in Chapter 14. In addition to charts, in Chapter 15 you get practice in working with other types of graphics in the spreadsheet, both those that you generate with the program's own drawing tools and those that you import from other sources such as clip art and digital photos.

Part 1V: Managing and Securing Data

This part is concerned with the management and security of the vast amounts of data that you accumulate in your worksheets. Chapter 16 gives you practice in creating, maintaining, sorting, and querying database tables and data lists in the worksheet. Chapter 17, on the other hand, gives you practice using Excel's various methods for protecting your data and worksheets from illicit viewing and unwanted changes.

Part V: Doing Data Analysis

This part takes you to the next step of using the Excel spreadsheet by introducing you to two different kinds of data analysis. Chapter 18 gives you practice in doing various types of what-if analysis that enable you to look at different potential outcomes in the spreadsheet. Chapter 19 concentrates on training you in the use of pivot tables, a dynamic type of data table that you can use to summarize vast amounts of data.

Part VI: Excel and the Web

This part gives you experience with Excel's Web capabilities in two forms. Chapter 20 gives you experience converting Excel spreadsheets to Web pages, both in static and dynamic formats. Chapter 21 trains you in the use of hyperlinks in spreadsheets that connect you to different sheets in the same workbook, different documents on the same computer, as well as to different pages and e-mail addresses on the World Wide Web.

Part VII: Macros and Visual Basic for Applications

This part introduces you to the topic of creating and using macros to both streamline and customize your work in Excel. Chapter 22 introduces you to recording your actions as Excel macros and then playing them back in the worksheet. Chapter 23 gives you practice using Excel's Visual Basic Editor to edit macros and extend macros you've recorded as well as to create your own user-defined functions.

Part VIII: The Part of Tens

This part gives you tips for using Excel on your own after you complete the exercises in this workbook. Chapter 24 is full of tips on using some of the many features you've practiced using in the workbook like a professional. Chapters 25 through 28 are full of various and sundry keystroke shortcuts designed to save you keyboard enthusiasts out there all sorts of time as you work in Excel.

Using the Practice Material on the CD-ROM

The CD-ROM that comes with this workbook is an integral part of the workbook experience. It contains not only the practice material that you need to complete most of its exercises but lots of third-party utilities that you may be able to put to good use as you start to work with Excel on your own.

All the practice material for the book is located in a single Excel Workbook folder on the CD-ROM. This Excel Workbook folder contains 22 chapter folders (Chapter 1 through Chapter 21 and Chapter 23 — the exercises in Chapter 22 don't require any practice files), plus a Templates folder.

Before you start working through the exercises in this workbook, I suggest that you copy this Excel Workbook folder to the My Documents folder on your computer's hard disk and then rename the Excel Workbook folder to My Practice Spreadsheets as follows:

1. Insert the CD-ROM into your computer's CD/DVD drive.

2. Click the Start button on the Windows taskbar and then click My Computer on the Start menu to open My Computer in Windows Explorer.

3. Right-click the icon for your CD/DVD drive and select Explore to open its contents in the Windows Explorer window.

4. Click the Excel Workbook folder icon and then press Ctrl+C.

5. Click the My Documents link in the left pane of the Windows Explorer window and then press Ctrl+V.

6. Right-click the Excel Workbook folder and then select the Rename option on its shortcut menu.

7. Replace Excel Workbook by typing **My Practice Spreadsheets** and then press Enter.

8. Click the Close button in the upper-right corner of the Windows Explorer window to close it.

9. Open the My Practice Spreadsheets folder in My Documents on your hard disk and then open the Templates folder. Select all the files by pressing Ctrl+A and copy them to the Windows Clipboard by pressing Ctrl+C.

10. Open the Microsoft Templates file on your computer's hard disk by double-clicking the My Computer icon on the desktop and then double-clicking the Local Disk (C:) icon followed by the following folders: Document and Settings⇨Your personal folder (as in Greg) ⇨Application Data⇨Microsoft⇨Templates.

    If the Application Data folder icon does not appear in your personal folder, you need to choose Tools⇨Folder Options and then select the Show Hidden Files and Folders option button on the View tab before you select OK.

11. Paste the copied template files into the Templates folder by pressing Ctrl+V.

You are now ready to tackle any of the exercises in the workbook using the practice files saved in the My Practice Spreadsheets folder inside the My Documents folder on your hard disk.

When you're finished doing the exercises and no longer need access to the practice files, go ahead and delete the My Practice Spreadsheets folder and all its contents by dropping it in the Recycle bin on the Windows desktop.

Icons Used in This Book

Icons are sprinkled throughout the text of this workbook in high hopes that they draw your attention to particular features. Some of the icons are of the heads-up type, while others are more informational in nature:

This icon indicates the start of a question-and-answer section in the workbook.

This icon indicates that the question that follows is a little more difficult and its answer a little less than obvious than the others in the question-and-answer section.

This icon indicates a hint that can help you perform a particular step in the exercise.

 This icon indicates that the file referred to in an exercise or some part of it is supplied to you on the CD-ROM that comes with this workbook.

 This icon indicates a tidbit that, if retained, can make your work somewhat easier in Excel.

 This icon indicates a tidbit that is essential to the topic being discussed and is, therefore, worth putting under your hat.

 This icon indicates a bit of trickery in the topic that, if ignored, can lead to some real trouble in your spreadsheet.

Where to Go from Here

This workbook is constructed such that you don't have to start working through the exercises in Chapter 1 and end with those in Chapter 23. That being said, it is still to your benefit to complete all the exercises within a particular chapter, if not in a single work session, at least in a short time period.

If you're a real newbie to Excel and have no experience with the program, I urge you to complete the exercises in Part I, Chapters 1 through 4, before you take off in your own direction. The exercises in this part are truly fundamental and are meant to give you a strong foundation in the basic features that all Excel users need to know.

Please keep in mind that I designed the exercises in this workbook to work with my Excel companion books, *Excel For Dummies* and *Excel All-In-One Desk Reference For Dummies* (published by Wiley). They can therefore provide you with additional information about the Excel features you're using either at the time you go through the workbook exercises or afterward. To facilitate this crossover usage, I have, wherever possible, used the same example files in the exercises of this workbook as you see illustrated and explained at length in these references.

Whatever you do next and wherever you go in this workbook, just be sure that you enjoy yourself!

Part I
Creating Spreadsheets

The 5th Wave   By Rich Tennant

"Unless there's a corrupt cell in our spreadsheet analysis concerning the importance of trunk space, this should be a big seller next year."

In this part . . .

The chapters and exercises in Part I form the core skills on which all spreadsheet users rely. These skills run the gamut from basic data entry to more complex data editing with cell formatting and worksheet printing in between. When you have these skills under your belt, you are well on your way to mastering Excel.

Chapter 1

Entering the Spreadsheet Data

Data entry is the bread and butter of any spreadsheet you create or edit. The exercises in this chapter give you a chance to practice launching Excel, moving around a new spreadsheet, the many aspects of data entry, and, most importantly, saving your work.

Launching Excel

Excel is only one of the many application programs included as part of Microsoft Office. In order to be proficient in its use, you need to be familiar with all the various ways of launching the program.

Q. What are the different techniques I can use to start Excel?

A. You should be familiar with all these methods:

- Click Start on the Windows taskbar and then highlight All Programs and click Microsoft Office Excel (2003 users need to select the Microsoft Office item before clicking Microsoft Office Excel).

- Double-click an Excel workbook file in any folder on any drive to which your computer has access.

- Double-click the Excel program icon on your computer's desktop.

- Click the Microsoft Excel icon on the taskbar's Start menu.

- Click the Excel icon on the Quick Launch toolbar.

Exercise 1-1: Launching Excel

The last three methods listed previously for launching Excel are available only if you've added the Excel program icon to the desktop, the Start menu, and the Quick Launch toolbar, respectively. For this exercise, add the Excel program icon to your computer if you still need to and then launch Excel using each of the five methods.

✔ Add an Microsoft Office Excel shortcut to the Windows desktop by right-clicking the Microsoft Office Excel item as it appears on the Start⇨All Programs⇨ Microsoft Office submenu and then highlighting Send To before you click Desktop (Create Shortcut) on the Send To submenu.

✔ Add Excel to the Start menu by right-clicking the Microsoft Office Excel desktop shortcut and then clicking Pin to Start Menu on its shortcut menu.

✔ Add Excel to the Quick Launch toolbar on the Windows taskbar by holding down Ctrl as you drag and drop the Microsoft Office Excel desktop shortcut on to its place in the toolbar.

Q. How do I make Excel launch automatically each time I start my computer?

A. Copy the Microsoft Office Excel item to the Startup submenu on the All Programs menu.

Opening a New Workbook

Each time you launch Excel (using any method other than double-clicking an Excel file icon), a new workbook containing three blank worksheets opens. You can then build your new spreadsheet in this workbook, using any of its sheet pages.

The blank workbook that opens with Excel is given a temporary filename such as Book1, Book2, and so on that appears after Excel's name on the program window's title bar. If you want to start work on a spreadsheet in another workbook, click the New button on the Standard toolbar.

When Excel opens a blank workbook upon launching the program or after clicking the New button, the new workbook follows the general Excel Worksheet template (which controls the formatting applied to all its blank cells). You can also open new workbooks from other, specialized templates or from a workbook that you've already created. To do this, choose File⇨New. If you're running Excel 2002 or 2003, the program opens the New Workbook Task pane, where you can click the template or file to use. If you're running Excel 2000 or earlier, the program opens the New dialog box, from which you can open the template.

The Templates folder in the Excel Workbook folder on the workbook CD-ROM (which you copied to the Excel Workbook Templates folder on your hard disk) contains a couple of template files that you can use and modify for your own use. To take a peek at them on the General tab of the Microsoft Templates folder, click the On My Computer link under Templates on the New Workbook task pane.

Q. What's so special about an Excel template?

A. A template is a particular type of Excel file designed to automatically generate new workbooks that use both its data and formatting. Each time you open a template, Excel opens a copy of the template file rather than the original (by appending a number to the template's original filename). Excel template files use the filename extension .xlt to differentiate them from regular Excel workbook files, which carry an .xls filename extension.

Q. How can I create templates out of my own Excel workbook files?

A. Build a spreadsheet in a new or existing workbook file. To this spreadsheet add all the stock text and data, calculating formulas, and formatting required in all the files

Q. What's the difference between opening a new workbook file from an Excel template file rather than an existing Excel workbook file?

A. None, provided that you open the new file using the From Existing Workbook under New or the On My Computer link under Templates in the New Workbook Task pane, rather than in the Open dialog box. (Doing this opens not a copy of the template or workbook file but the original file for editing.)

you will generate from its ensuing template and then save this file with the File⇨Save As command. Select Template (*.xlt) in the Save As Type drop-down list box and edit the dummy filename (without removing the .xlt filename extension) before you click the Save button.

Try It

Exercise 1-2: Opening a New Workbook

Launch Excel and then open a new workbook (Book2). Switch to Book1 (notice the change in the Excel program title bar) and then back to Book2 and close this workbook. Notice what happens to Book1 when you close Book2. Leave Book1 open for the next exercise.

To switch from Sheet1 of Book2 and make Sheet1 of Book1 active, click the Book1 icon on the Windows taskbar or press Ctrl+Tab (to switch back to Book2, click the Book2 icon on the taskbar or press Ctrl+Tab again so that Sheet1 of Book2 is selected).

To close a workbook file, choose File⇨Close or click the workbook's Close Window button. (The Close Window button is the one with the black X, which is immediately beneath the program's red Close button, which has a white X.)

Exercise 1-3: Opening a New Workbook from a Template

Open a new workbook from the Hourly Wages template that you copied from the Templates folder on the workbook CD-ROM to the Microsoft Templates folder (see "Using the Practice Material on the CD-ROM" in the Introduction for details). Switch back and forth between the Book1 and Hourly Wages1 workbook files. Then, close the Hourly Wages1.xls workbook file, leaving open the Book1.xls file for the next exercise.

To open a new workbook from a template file, you click the On My Computer link under Templates on the New Workbook task pane, and then click the .xlt file to use in the General tab of the Templates folder before you select OK.

Moving around the Workbook

The key to doing both data entry and data editing in any spreadsheet is selecting the cell or cells you want to fill or modify. Selecting a cell almost always entails moving the cell cursor (or pointer) to another part of the current worksheet. Sometimes, it also involves activating a different worksheet in the workbook file.

Excel gives you plenty of choices in techniques for moving the cell cursor: Some use the mouse and others are keyboard driven.

Moving within the displayed area

Here's a recap of the most important ways to move the cell cursor to a new cell within the area of the worksheet that is currently displayed on-screen:

- ✔ Click the target cell with the white-cross mouse pointer.
- ✔ Press the arrow keys until the cell pointer is in the target cell.
- ✔ Click the Name Box with the current cell reference at the very beginning of the Formula Bar, enter the reference of the target (by column letter and row number as in D12), and press Enter.

Try It

Exercise 1-4: Moving the Cell Cursor within the Displayed Area

Make Sheet1 of the blank workbook, Book1, active and then practice moving the cell cursor to different cells in the displayed area using the mouse, arrow keys, and Name Box:

1. **Move the cell pointer to cell F9 with the mouse.**

2. **Move the cell pointer to cell C13 using just the down and left arrow keys.**

3. **Move the cell pointer to cell A1 using only the Name Box.**

Keep in mind that you can always move the cursor to cell A1 (also known as the Home cell) of any active worksheet simply by pressing Ctrl+Home.

Moving to a new area of the worksheet

Many times you have to make cell entries in areas that aren't currently displayed in the active worksheet. One of quickest ways to do this is by entering the reference of the cell you want to go to in the Name Box. You can also use any the following techniques to scroll to new parts of the current worksheet:

- ✔ To scroll up and down rows of the worksheet by windows, press Page Up or Page Down or click the blank area above or below the scroll box in the vertical scroll bar.
- ✔ To scroll left and right columns of the worksheet by windows, click the blank area to the left or right of the scroll box in the horizontal scroll bar.
- ✔ To quickly scroll through rows or columns of the worksheet, hold down the Shift key as you drag the scroll box up or down in the vertical scroll bar or left and right in the horizontal scroll bar.

✔ If you use a mouse with a wheel button, scroll up and down the rows of the worksheet by rotating the wheel button forward (to scroll up) and backward (to scroll down).

✔ If you use a mouse with a wheel button, pan through the rows and columns of the worksheet by clicking the wheel button and then dragging the triangular mouse pointer in the direction you want to scroll.

Don't forget that scrolling is not the same as selecting! After scrolling to a new part of the worksheet in view, you still have to select a cell by clicking it to set the cursor in it.

Try It

Exercise 1-5: Moving the Cell Cursor to Distant Parts of the Worksheet

Practice moving the cell pointer to cells in unseen parts of Sheet1 in the Book1 workbook by doing the following:

1. **Move the cell cursor to cell C125 with the Name Box on the Formula Bar.**

2. **Move the cell cursor to cell CA125 using the horizontal scroll bar.**

3. **Move the cell cursor to cell CA63560 using the vertical scroll bar.**

4. **Move the cell cursor directly to cell A1 (the Home cell) in a single operation.**

Hold down the Shift key to scroll quickly through columns and rows by dragging the scroll box in the horizontal or vertical scroll bar.

After scrolling into view the region with the cell you want to select, you still need to click the cell to select it.

Q. What's the most efficient way to move between ranges of data that are spread out across a worksheet?

A. Use the Ctrl key in combination with any of the four arrow keys to jump from occupied cell to occupied cell in a particular direction.

Try It

Exercise 1-6: Moving the Cell Cursor from Entry to Entry

Practice moving the cell pointer around a blank worksheet and between data entries with the Ctrl key and the arrow keys in Sheet1 of Book1 by doing the following:

1. Press Ctrl+→, Ctrl+↓, Ctrl+←, and Ctrl+↑ in succession to jump the cell cursor from A1 to IV1, IV1 to IV65536, IV65536 to A65536, and A65536 to back to A1 (when there are no occupied cells in a particular direction, the cursor jumps right to the border of the worksheet).

2. Move the cell cursor to cell A18, type **Stop**, and press Ctrl+Home. Next, press Ctrl+↓ (the cursor stops in A18 rather than A65536 because A18 is now occupied).

3. Move the cell cursor to cell AB18, type **Stop Again**, and press Home. Next, press Ctrl+→ (the cursor stops in cell AB18 rather than IV18 because AB18 is now occupied).

4. Press the Delete key, and then press Ctrl+← followed by the Delete key to remove the two dummy cell entries. Press Ctrl+Home to put the cursor back in cell A1.

Moving to a different sheet in the workbook

Each new workbook you start uses the general Excel Worksheet template that automatically includes three blank worksheets that you can fill with data. If you need more space for a particular spreadsheet, you can add additional worksheets with the Insert➪Worksheet command. If you want all new workbooks you open to have more worksheets, enter a new value in Sheets in a New Workbook text box on the General tab of the Options dialog box (Tools➪Options).

Each sheet in a workbook is automatically given the next available numeric name such as Sheet1, Sheet2, and the like, but you can easily replace these generic names with something descriptive: Double-click the tab you want to rename, type the new sheet name, and press Enter. You can also color-code a sheet tab by right-clicking it, clicking Tab Color on the shortcut menu, and then selecting the color Format Tab Color dialog box before you select OK.

Of course, you must know how to move between the sheets in order to be able to add and edit data in them. The most direct way to select a new worksheet is to click its sheet tab, although you can also use the shortcut keys Ctrl+Page Down to select the next sheet and Ctrl+Page Up to select the previous sheet.

If you add so many worksheets to your workbook that all their sheet tabs can't all be displayed at one time, you can use the Tab scroll buttons to the immediate left of the sheet tab to bring into view the tabs you want to select. You can also display more tabs by reducing the width of the horizontal bar (by dragging to the right the split bar that appears when you position the mouse pointer on the vertical bar at the beginning of the scroll bar).

Try It

Exercise 1-7: Moving to Different Worksheets

Practice moving the cell cursor to specific cells in different worksheets of Book1 by doing the following:

1. Move the cell cursor to cell J25 on Sheet2 (whose cell reference is Sheet2!J25).

2. Move the cell cursor to cell CC1000 on Sheet3 (Sheet3!CC1000).

3. Move the cell cursor to cell Sheet 3:J25 on Sheet3, and then activate Sheet2 (note the difference in the worksheet view despite the fact that you've moved to the same cell on an earlier worksheet).

4. Rename Sheet1 to **Spring Sale**.

Selecting Cell Ranges

When entering, editing, or formatting a single cell, all you have to do is move the cell cursor to it as you practiced in the earlier exercises. You can also enter the same data as well do the same type of editing and formatting in a bunch of cells at one time, but to do so, you must first select the cells where all this is going to happen.

Most of the time when selecting multiple cells in a worksheet, you select a discrete block of cells of so many rows high and so many columns wide. Such a block is known as a *cell range* in the parlance of spreadsheet software.

A cell range is most often described by the reference of its first and last cell (that is, the cell in the upper-left corner and the lower-right corner of is block, respectively). When written, a cell range is separated by a colon, as in B15:F20, for a six-row and six-column cell range whose first cell is B15 and last cell F20. To select this cell range, you move the cursor to cell B15 and then hold down the Shift key as you use the ↓ and → keys to move the cursor to cell F20.

Excel, however, does not limit you to selecting a single cell range for data entry, editing, or formatting. You can select as many cell ranges (even those as small as a single cell) by holding down the Ctrl key as you add a new range to the cell selection.

Always think of the Shift key when you want to select a single range of cells and the Ctrl key when you want to select more than one cell range at one time.

Q. How do I select cell ranges that include complete rows and columns of the active worksheet?

A. Click the letter of the column or the number of the row whose cells are to be selected in the column and row header, respectively. To select multiple columns or rows, hold down the Shift key as you drag through them, if they are consecutive, or click them as you hold down the Ctrl key, if they are noncontiguous. Press Ctrl+A or click the box at the junction of the column and row header to select all the columns and rows in the active worksheet (in other words, the entire worksheet).

Q. How do I select cell ranges that span different worksheets of the active workbook?

A. Click the tab of the first worksheet and then hold down Shift as you click the last sheet before you select the cell range or ranges on the active sheet.

Try It

Exercise 1-8: Selecting Various Cell Ranges

Practice selecting cell ranges in the Spring Sale worksheet of Book1 by doing the following:

1. Select the cell range A2:E2, and then click the Fill Color drop-down button on the Formatting toolbar. Click the Gray-25% square in the pop-up color palette.

2. Select the cell ranges A3:A9 and B3:E3 as a single cell selection (I'm sure you can ConTRoL it) and then assign Light Turquoise to it using the Fill Color drop-down button.

3. Select the cell range B4:E9 and then assign Light Yellow to this range using the Fill Color drop-down button. Next, move the cell cursor to cell A1 (Home).

Making Cell Entries

As you are probably already aware, Excel recognizes only two types of cell entries, text (label) and number (or value). Numeric cell entries are those that consist solely of numbers or calculable formulas. Text entries are those that consist of all letters or a combination of letters, numbers, and punctuation on which Excel can perform no sort of calculation.

Anything you enter into a cell or cell selection is immediately analyzed as either being a number or text entry. Because the general Excel Worksheet template automatically left-aligns all text entries and right-aligns all numeric ones, you can often tell immediately how your entry has been classified by noting how it's aligned in its cell.

When you make a numeric entry in a worksheet, Excel not only right-aligns the value in its cell but also assigns the General number format to it. In this format, only significant digits are displayed. This means that all trailing zeros are dropped. Also, if the number you enter contains more that can fit within the current column width, Excel automatically converts the value to scientific notation (as in 5.00E+09 for 5,000,000,000).

Sometimes you have to override Excel's number/text assignment in order to obtain the desired cell entry. The most famous example of this is a ZIP code or all numeric part or item number that begins with a zero, as in 00105. If you try to enter this ZIP code into a cell simply by typing its five digits, Excel will interpret it as a numeric entry and in assigning the General format to it, retain only the value 105 in the cell. In order to retain the preceding zeros, you need to force the entry to be recognized as text by typing an initial apostrophe as in **'00105** (this apostrophe does not appear in the cell although you can see it on the Formula bar).

Entering data in a single cell

Most cell entries are made by typing from the keyboard (although later versions of Excel do support voice and ink text entry). After typing the characters, which appear both in the cell and on the Formula bar, you must still complete the entry.

Anytime prior to completing the cell entry, you can press the Esc key to clear the cell of all characters you typed there.

Q. How many methods can I use to complete an entry in the current cell?

A. You should be familiar with all these methods:

- Click the Enter box on the Formula bar (the one with the check mark).

- Press the Enter key.
- Press one of the arrow keys.
- Press Tab, Shift+Tab, Home, Ctrl+Home, Page Up, Page Down, Ctrl+Page Up, Ctrl+Page Down, or any of the other cursor-movement key combinations

Click the Enter box on the Formula bar when you want the cell cursor to remain in the cell where you just made the entry (so that you can format it in some fashion). Press Enter when you want to move the cell cursor to the next row in order to make another entry.

Try It

Exercise 1-9: Making Simple Data Entries

Complete the data entry for the simple Spring Sale table shown in Figure 1-1 by doing the following:

1. Enter the table title **Spring Sale Furniture Discounts** in cell A2.

2. Enter the column headings in row 3 as follows:

   - **Code** in cell A3
   - **Description** in cell B3
   - **Retail Price** in cell C3
   - **Discount** in cell D3
   - **Amount** in cell E3

3. Enter the code numbers in column A as follows:

   - **02-305** in cell A4
   - **02-240** in cell A5
   - **04-356** in cell A6
   - **01-234** in cell A7
   - **03-003** in cell A8
   - **01-240** in cell A9

4. Enter the furniture descriptions in column B as follows:

   - **36-inch round table** in cell B4
   - **72-inch dining table** in cell B5
   - **Hutch** in cell B6
   - **Side chair** in cell B7
   - **Arm chair** in cell B8
   - **Armoire** in cell B9

5. Enter the retail prices of the furniture in column C as follows:

   - **1250** in cell C4
   - **1400** in cell C5
   - **2500** in cell C6
   - **350** in cell C7
   - **500** in cell C8
   - **1750** in cell C9

6. Enter the discount percentages in column D as follows:

   - **25%** in cells D4, D5, and D6
   - **15%** in cells D7 and D8
   - **25%** in cell D9

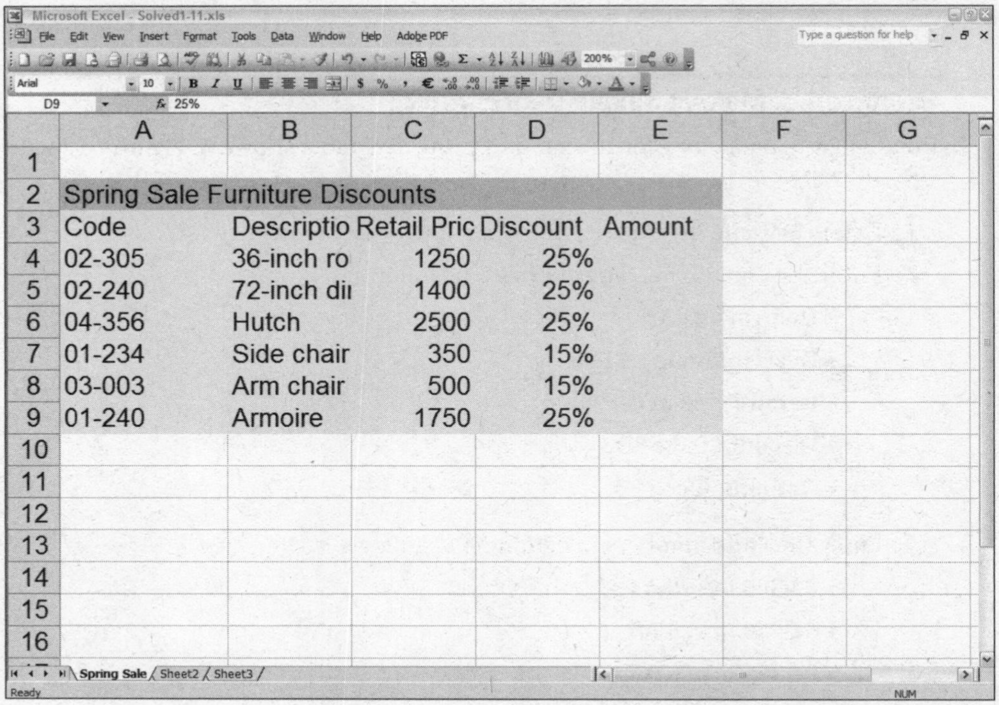

Figure 1-1:
The Spring
Sale table
after com-
pleting the
data entry.

	A	B	C	D	E	F	G
1							
2	Spring Sale Furniture Discounts						
3	Code	Descriptio	Retail Pric	Discount	Amount		
4	02-305	36-inch ro	1250	25%			
5	02-240	72-inch dii	1400	25%			
6	04-356	Hutch	2500	25%			
7	01-234	Side chair	350	15%			
8	03-003	Arm chair	500	15%			
9	01-240	Armoire	1750	25%			
10							
11							
12							
13							
14							
15							
16							

Check your completed spreadsheet table against the one in *Solved1-9.xls*. (Open this
workbook in the Chap1 folder inside the My Practice Spreadsheets folder that you've
created in your My Documents folder your hard disk, or in the Excel Workbook folder
on the CD-ROM that came with this book.)

Entering data in a cell range

Sometimes you want to make the same entry in several different cells in the same
worksheet. To do this, select all the cells and cell ranges and then press Ctrl+Enter to
both complete the entry you make in the active cell and simultaneously insert it into
all the other selected cells.

Filling in a data series with the Fill handle

The tiny black square in the lower-right corner of the cell cursor is known as the Fill
handle. The Fill handle is your key to the AutoFill feature that makes it super-easy
either to fill in a continuous range with the same entry or with data series (such as
Monday, Tuesday, Wednesday, and so on, or 101, 102, 103, and the like).

To create a sequential series that increments by one unit (day, hour, month, widget
number), you enter the first entry in the series in a blank cell and then drag the Fill
handle in the direction you want the series to appear (down or to the right are the
most common directions). To create series that increments by other units (every
other day, every third month, every fourth hour, every tenth widget), you enter the
first two entries in the series (that serve as an example of the increment to be used) in
two adjacent blank cells and then drag the Fill handle in the appropriate direction.

Instead of filling in these recognized data series with AutoFill, you can force Excel to copy the entry you've made in the current cell by holding down the Ctrl key as you drag the Fill handle. Excel indicates that it copied rather than filled a range by displaying a tiny plus sign to the side of the Fill handle mouse pointer.

Exercise 1-10: Entering the Same Entry and Using AutoFill

Open a new blank workbook, Book2, and then practice making the same data entry in multiple ranges and using the Fill handle to create various data series in its Sheet1:

1. Enter today's date, following the date format *Oct-25-06*, in the cell selection A1, D3:F3, and B4:B6.

   - Don't forget to hold down the Ctrl key when you're selecting the three ranges in the cell selection.

   - Be sure to complete the current date entry into all the cells of the selection by pressing Ctrl+Enter.

2. Use AutoFill to create a data series with all 12 months in the cell range A8:A19 starting with **January**.

3. Use AutoFill to create a data series with the names of all the days of the week in cell range C8:I8 starting with **Monday**.

4. Use AutoFill to create a data series with hours that go from **8:00AM** to 8:00PM in cell range C10:C22.

5. Use AutoFill to create a data series in cell range E10:H10 containing the headings **Qtr1**, Qtr2, Qtr3, and Qtr4.

6. Use AutoFill to create a series in cell range E12:E21 containing **1st Team**, 2nd Team, 3rd Team, and so on all the way up to 10th Team.

7. Use AutoFill to create a data series in cell range G12:L12 that contains the name of every other month starting with **November** and ending with September.

   - Don't forget that you need to indicate the every-other-month increment to Excel (by entering January in cell H12 and then selecting the range G12:H12) before using the Fill handle to create the data series.

8. Use AutoFill to copy the data entry **Item 1** to the entire cell range G14:G19 (don't let this one get out of ConTRoL).

Copying a formula with the Fill handle

AutoFill is not only useful for filling in a data series or copying a static data entry to a continuous cell range but also for copying a formula across a row or down a column of a data table. When you copy a formula, Excel automatically adjusts the column and row references in the copies so that they refer to the right data.

Don't forget that Excel automatically uses the so-called relative column and row references cell addresses in all formulas you create. If you ever need to override this so that all or part of a cell reference is not adjusted in the copied formulas, you enter a $ (dollar sign) before the cell's column letter or row number (you can have Excel do it for you by pressing F4 while building the formula on the Formula bar).

Try It

Exercise 1-11: Copying a Formula with AutoFill

Complete the Spring Sale table by using the following steps to enter the formula that calculates the discount amount in cell E4 and then use AutoFill to copy that formula down the cell range E5:E9. (Check your results against those in the Spring Sale table shown in *Solved1-11.xls.* You can find this workbook in the Chapter 1 folder in the My Practice Spreadsheets folder in the My Documents folder on your hard disk or in the Excel Workbook folder on the CD-ROM that comes with this book.)

ON THE CD

1. Switch to the Spring Sale sheet of Book1 and then move the cell cursor to cell E4.

2. Type = (equal) to start the formula for calculating the sale price of the 36-inch round table (all Excel formulas start with the equal sign).

3. Click cell C4, and then type * (asterisk), which Excel uses as the sign of multiplication, before you click cell D4 (the formula now reads =C4*D4 on the Formula bar).

4. Click the Enter box on the Formula bar and then drag the Fill handle of the cell cursor in cell E4 down to E9 and release the mouse button to make the copies of the formula.

Saving the Spreadsheet in a Workbook File

Now all that remains to do is to save the spreadsheets you created while performing the exercises in this chapter before exiting Excel. As you know, all work that you do in between the times you save the worksheet is at risk because you immediately lose it if your computer experiences even the briefest power interruption.

The first time you save your spreadsheet in a workbook file, the Save As dialog box appears, giving you the opportunity to rename the file (replacing the Book1, Book2 monikers with something more descriptive) in the File Name text and indicate the folder in which it should be saved in the Save In drop-down list box. After that, you can use the Save command to save all additional changes to the same file without opening any dialog box.

TIP

Excel saves the current position of the cell cursor in the worksheet when you save its workbook. Therefore, always position the cursor in the cell you want to be current when you next open the workbook for editing before doing the final save of your work session.

EXAMPLE

Q. How many different techniques can I use to save changes to my workbook file?

A. You should be familiar with all these methods:

- Click the Save button on the Standard toolbar (the one with the disk icon).

- Choose File⇨Save on the Menu bar (choose File⇨Save As if you want to open the Save As dialog box again so that you can rename or save a copy in a new folder).

- Press F12 (Shift+12 to open the Save As dialog box).

Try It

Exercise 1-12: Saving a Spreadsheet

Save the Spring Sales table in a new My Spreadsheets folder inside the My Documents folder on your hard disk:

1. With the Spring Sales table displayed on-screen, select cell A2 before you open the Save As dialog box and then click the New Folder button in the Save As dialog box.

2. Type **My Spreadsheets** (or **My Practice Spreadsheets** if you already have a My Spreadsheets folder inside the My Documents folder) as the folder name in the Name text box of the New Folder dialog box and select OK.

3. Replace Book1.xls in the Name text box by typing **Spring Furniture Sale** and then clicking the Save button.

4. Close the *Spring Furniture Sale* workbook and then switch to Sheet1 of Book2. Save this spreadsheet in the My Spreadsheets folder with the filename **AutoFill Practice** after positioning the cell cursor in cell A1.

5. Close the *AutoFill Practice* workbook and the *Hourly Wages1* workbook by exiting Excel (File⇨Exit or Alt+F4) — don't save your changes to the *Hourly Wages1* workbook.

Chapter 2

Formatting the Spreadsheet

● ●

In This Chapter

▶ Resizing columns and rows in a worksheet

▶ Formatting cells with the Formatting toolbar

▶ Formatting cells with the Format Cells dialog box

▶ Formatting tables with AutoFormat and ranges with Format Painter

▶ Using Conditional Formatting

▶ Hiding columns and rows in a worksheet

● ●

*I*n Excel, formatting means formatting cells of the worksheet. Therefore, the formatting you assign a cell not only affects the cell's current contents, but any contents you enter into it. Performing the exercises in this chapter gives you a chance to practice widening and narrowing the columns of rows of a worksheet to suit the formatting and contents of its cells. You also discover a full array of techniques for assigning formatting to cells in a worksheet, including using the Formatting toolbar and the Format Cells dialog box and the AutoFormat and Conditional Formatting features.

Resizing Columns and Rows

In all new workbooks generated from the general Excel Worksheet template, all the columns of its worksheets are a standard 8.43 characters or 64 pixels wide, and all the rows are 12.75 points or 17 pixels high. You can, if you need, change this default column width for an entire worksheet by clicking its sheet tab to select it before choosing Format⇨Column⇨Standard Width on the Excel menu bar. Then, you enter the new default width in the Standard Column Width text box (in characters) before you select OK.

Note that Excel does not provide any way for setting a new row height default in a worksheet. The 12.75-point default value is universal for all worksheets unless you manually override this height. This is probably because Excel always automatically increases the height of all rows to suit the formatting of its cell entries. Column widths, on the other hand, are automatically widened only under certain circumstances (when applying certain AutoFormat styles and building data tables with later versions of Excel).

Making column widths suit the data

Resizing particular columns to suit the data they contain is one of the most common formatting tasks you perform in creating and editing a spreadsheet.

You need to widen a column in a worksheet whenever it contains cells with numerical data having too many digits to be displayed in the current column width (indicated by a string of pound signs (#) in the cells) or text data with characters cut off (because they spilled over into cells in columns to the immediate right that were then truncated by entries made in the adjacent column).

Q. How many different ways should I know for resizing particular columns in a worksheet?

A. You should be familiar with all the following methods:

- Drag the column's right border in the column header to the left (to narrow) or right (to widen). To resize several columns at once, drag through their column letters in the header or Ctrl+click them before dragging right border of one of them.

- Double-click the column's right border in the column header to resize it with AutoFit. To resize several columns at once, drag through their column letters in the header or Ctrl+click them before double-clicking the right border of one of them.

- Select the column or columns to resize and then choose Format⇨Column⇨ Width. Enter the new width (in characters) in the Column Width dialog box before you select OK.

- Select the cell range or selection whose columns need resizing and then choose Format⇨Column⇨AutoFit Selection. (Excel widens or narrows the columns in the cell selection to display all the digits and text in the cells in the selection.)

- Select the column or columns to resize to standard column width (of 8.43 characters) and then choose Format⇨ Column⇨Standard Width and select OK in the Standard Width dialog box.

Try It

Exercise 2-1: Modifying Column Widths in a Spreadsheet

Launch Excel and then open the *Spring Furniture Sale.xls* workbook you created in doing the exercises in Chapter 1 and saved in the My Spreadsheets (or My Practice Spreadsheets folder). If you didn't do these exercises, open the *Exercise2-1.xls* file in the Chapter 2 folder.

✔ If you're using Excel 2002 or 2003, look for the *Spring Furniture Sale.xls* on the Open Task pane and, if you find it, click its name to open the file. If you're using an earlier version, open the File menu and then type the number of *Spring Furniture Sale.xls* if it's listed among the four most recently used files at the bottom of the File menu.

✔ If *Spring Furniture Sale.xls* is not listed as one of the four most recently used files, click the Open button on the Standard toolbar. Next click the My Documents button on the left pane and double-click the My Practice Spreadsheets folder to display the Chapter 2 folder (which contains the *Exercise 2-1.xls* file). After displaying the file to open, click its icon and then select the Open button.

After you open this workbook file, make the following changes to the widths of the columns on the Spring Sales worksheet:

1. Use the AutoFit feature to widen Column B containing the furniture descriptions sufficiently so that none of these descriptions are cut off.

2. Drag the right border of Column C to the left until the column is 33 pixels wide and then release the mouse button (note the appearance of ### indicators in all but two cells in the Sale table). Next, use AutoFit to widen Column B so that all the entries in this column are displayed.

3. Use the Column Width dialog box to set column E to a width of 10 characters.

4. Narrow column A to 7.14 characters or 55 pixels wide (use any method that works).

5. If you've been modifying your *Spring Furniture Sale.xls* file, click the Save button on the Standard toolbar or press Ctrl+S to save your changes. If you've been modifying the *Exercise 2-1.xls* file, choose File⇨Save As or press F12 to open the Save As dialog box and then rename *Exercise 2-1.xls* to *Spring Furniture Sale.xls* in the File Name text box. Make sure that the My Practice Spreadsheets folder inside My Documents is selected as the location in the Save In drop-down list before you select Save.

Manipulating the height of certain rows

You don't find yourself having to resize the rows of a worksheet all that much. Most of the time, Excel does all the work for you by automatically resizing them just right to accommodate any and all formatting changes you make to their cells.

About the only time you might want to increase the height of a row on your own is when you want to increase the space between the contents of one row and the contents of the row immediately above without going through the trouble of inserting a blank row as a spacer between them.

Q. How can I manually modify the height of selected rows in a worksheet?

A. You should be familiar with both of these methods for changing row height:

- Drag the lower border of the number of the row to modify in the row header either up (to shorten the row) or down (to heighten the row). To modify multiple rows at one time, select the rows (by dragging through or Ctrl+clicking their

row numbers in the row header) and then drag just the lower border of just one of the selected rows.

- Position the cell cursor in any one of the cells in the row to be modified, and then choose Format⇨Row⇨Height, and then enter the number of points in the Row Height text box before you select OK. To modify multiple rows at one time, select the rows before opening the Row Height dialog box.

Try It

Exercise 2-2: Modifying Row Heights in a Spreadsheet

In the *Spring Furniture Sale.xls* workbook, practice modifying row height by doing the following:

1. Increase the height of Row 2, which contains the table title, to 26.25 or 35 pixels by dragging the row's border.

Note how the spreadsheet title sinks down when the row height is increased.

2. Restore the height of Row 2 to its original height with AutoFit.

Double-click the lower border of a row in the row header to modify its height using AutoFit or place the cell cursor somewhere in the row and choose Format➪Row➪AutoFit.

Cell Formatting Techniques

Cell formatting can run the gamut from changing the font, color, attribute, and/or alignment of a cell entry to the color, borders, and protection status of the cell itself. You can accomplish much of the formatting in a typical spreadsheet with the buttons on the Formatting toolbar. The rest you can accomplish with the options available on the various tabs of the all-important Format Cells dialog box.

The first rule of formatting is to remember to select all the cells that need formatting before you select the desired button on the Formatting toolbar or an option on one of the tabs in the Format Cells dialog box.

Formatting cells with the Formatting toolbar

The Formatting toolbar shown in Figure 2-1 contains the tools you most often need when formatting your average spreadsheet. These tools are arranged into six groups of buttons (from left to right across the toolbar):

- Font and Font Size drop-down buttons
- Bold, Italic, and Underline attribute buttons
- Left, Right, Center, and Merge and Center alignment buttons
- Currency, Percent, and Comma Style buttons along with Increase Decimal and Decrease Decimal buttons
- Decrease Indent and Increase Indent buttons
- Borders, Fill Color, and Font Color buttons

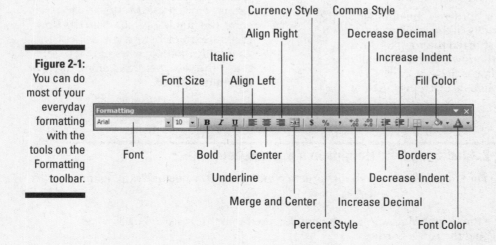

Figure 2-1:
You can do most of your everyday formatting with the tools on the Formatting toolbar.

To make it easier to find the tool you need while you're first learning Excel and, especially, while using this workbook, be sure that Excel always displays the Standard and Formatting toolbars on separate rows (ensuring instant access to all their buttons) and that the full Excel menus are always displayed. To do this, choose View⇨Toolbars⇨Customize to open the Customize dialog box. Then, put a check mark in the Show Standard and Formatting Toolbars on Two Rows and Always Show Full Menus check boxes on the Option tab before selecting the Close button.

Try It

Exercise 2-3: Formatting Cells from the Format Toolbar

In the *Spring Furniture Sale.xls* workbook, practice modifying formatting cells from the Formatting toolbar:

1. Center the title of the table in cell A2 over the range A2:E2 and make it bold.

   Click the Merge and Center button after selecting the range of cells over which you want to center the text that's entered in the first cell of the range (the range A2:E2, in this case).

2. Make the column heading entries in cell range A3:E3 bold and italic and center them in their cells, and then increase the height of row 3 to 17.25 points (23 pixels) to put some space between the table title and the column headings.

3. Right-align the code numbers in the cell range A4:A9.

4. Increase the indent of the furniture descriptions in the cell range B4:B9 one tab and then use AutoFit to widen column B sufficiently to display all the descriptions.

5. Apply the Comma Style number format to the retail prices in the cell range C4:C9.

6. Center the percentages in the cell range D4:D9.

7. Apply the Currency Style number format to the sale prices in the cell range E4:E9.

8. Add a thick line border around the entire Spring Sale table.

   To draw a border around a block of cells, select its cell range (A2:E9 in this case), and then click the Borders drop-down button and click the Thick Box Border on the pop-up palette (the one in the lower-right corner).

9. Put borders between all the cells in the table in the range A3:E9.

   Select this range and then click the All Border swatch on the Borders pop-up palette (the one divided into four quadrants).

10. Check your fully formatted table against the one entered on the Spring Sale sheet in the workbook file, *Solved2-3.xls*, and then when everything checks out, save your formatting changes in the *Spring Furniture Sale.xls* workbook file.

Formatting cells with the Format Cells dialog box

You rely on the Format Cells dialog box for applying more complex formatting than provided by the buttons on the Formatting toolbar. This includes applying any number formats other than the standard Currency, Percent, and Comma number formats from the Number tab as well as for applying alignment changes that involve modifying the vertical alignment and wrapping, orientation, or direction of the text from the Alignment tab. You can also use its options on the Font tab for selecting more font attributes, the Patterns tab for applying patterns along with fill-in colors for cell backgrounds, and the Protection tab to change locked or hidden status of cells that goes into effect as soon as you protect the worksheet (see Chapter 17 for details).

Press Ctrl+1 (that's the Ctrl key and the number 1 on the top row of the QWERTY keyboard) to quickly open the Format Cells dialog box.

The options on the Number tab for applying the various and sundry number formats that Excel has to offer as well as for creating your own custom number formats are possibly the most important in the Format Cells dialog box (see Figure 2-2). This tab organizes the ready-made number formats by category from General, the default for all cells in a new worksheet, which retains only significant digits, to Custom, where you can create your own number formats. Here's a quick rundown on the other ten categories of number formats that you will probably use more often:

- **Number** applies a number format to numeric entries in which you determine the number of decimal places to display, whether to use the comma as a thousands separator, and the appearance of negative numbers (either with a negative sign or enclosed in parentheses in black or red).

- **Currency** applies a number format to numeric entries in which you determine the currency symbol (the dollar sign is the default), the number of decimal places to display, and the appearance of negative numbers (either with a negative sign or enclosed in parentheses in black or red).

- **Accounting** applies a number format to numeric entries in which you determine the currency symbol (the dollar sign is the default) and the number of decimal places to display (the difference between Accounting and Currency is that Accounting always uses two decimal places and aligns the currency symbol and decimal points in their cells).

- **Date** uses a new date format for numeric entries that Excel recognizes as representing dates of the year (because it was entered following one of these date formats).

- **Time** applies a time format using either a 12- or 24-hour clock for numeric entries that Excel recognizes as representing times of the day (because it was entered according to one of the time formats).

- **Percentage** multiplies the numeric entries by 100 with a percent sign and the number of decimal places you designate.

- **Fraction** selects a fractional number format for the decimals in your numeric entries.

- **Scientific** applies scientific notation to numeric entries by applying an exponent and the number of decimal places you designate.

- **Text** formats numeric entries as though they were text entries.

- **Special** formats numeric entries following the Zip Code, Zip Code + 4 (with leading zeros retained), Phone Number (with parentheses added to the first three digits as the area code and dashes between the third and fourth digits of the next seven indicating the prefix and main number), or Social Security Number (with dashes between the third and fourth and fifth and sixth digits of the nine-digit number).

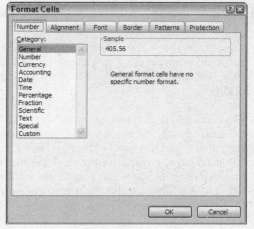

Figure 2-2:
The Number
tab of the
Format Cells
dialog box
gives you
access to a
wide variety
of number
formats.

Try It

Exercise 2-4: Formatting Cells with Number Tab on the Format Cells Dialog Box

Open a new spreadsheet on Sheet1 of a Book1 workbook and use it to practice applying the following number formats using the Number tab on the Format Cells dialog box:

1. Format the cell range B2:B5 using the Accounting number format with two decimal places, and the dollar sign.

2. Enter the following values in the cell range with the Accounting format:
   - **1234.75** in cell B2
   - **23500** in cell B3
   - **-1450.5** in cell B4
   - **100.345** in cell B5

3. Apply the Text format to cell B7 and then enter **200.25** in this cell. Note how Excel left-aligns the value and the appearance of the Number Options drop-down button in later versions of Excel (the diamond with the exclamation point in the upper-left corner of cell B7).

4. Create a formula in cell C7 that adds B5 and B7 together and then apply the Accounting format to the cell. Note that despite the application of the Text format, Excel still uses its value to return the correct sum (real text entries such as Paris or Budget all carry a zero value in terms of arithmetic calculations).

5. Enter the date **02-15-05** in cell B9 (note how Excel automatically converts this entry to 02/15/2005). Format this cell with the Date format that follows the pattern March 14, 2001.

6. Format cell B9 with the General number format (note the appearance of the date serial number 38398, indicating that this date represents the 38,398th day since the dawn of the twentieth century). Click the Undo button on the Standard toolbar to restore the previous date formatting.

7. Enter the number **00401** in cell B11 and then format it with Special Zip Code format (note what happens to the dropped zeros).

8. Enter the number **4155051122** in cell B13 and then format it with the Special Phone Number format.

9. Enter the number **20012551** in cell B15 and then format it with the Special Social Security Number format.

10. Check your results against those on Sheet1 in the workbook file, *Solved2-4.xls*, and then when everything checks out, save your practice workbook in your My Practice Spreadsheets folder inside My Documents under the filename *Number Formatting Practice.xls*. Close the workbook.

The options on the Alignment tab of the Format Cells dialog box, as you can see in Figure 2-3, give you control not only over the horizontal alignment of cell entries (that is, between the left and right borders of their columns) but over vertical alignment (between the top and bottom borders of their rows) and the orientation (direction of the text with regard to a horizontal baseline of 0 degrees) as well. In addition, its Text Control options (Wrap Text, Shrink to Fit, and Merge Cells) enable you to accommodate longer cell entries to restricted column widths.

Figure 2-3:
The Alignment tab of the Format Cells dialog box gives you access to more complex text alignments.

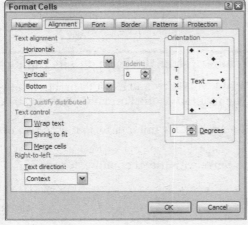

Try It

Exercise 2-5: Formatting Cells with the Alignment Tab on the Format Cells Dialog Box

In the *Spring Furniture Sale.xls* workbook, practice modifying the alignment of various cell entries using the options on the Alignment tab of the Format Cells dialog box:

1. Increase the height of row 2 from 12.75 points (17 pixels) to 30 points (40 pixels) and then change the vertical alignment of the table title in cell A2 from Bottom to Center.

2. Apply the Wrap Cell control to the cell range B4:B9 with the furniture descriptions and then narrow Column B to 12.71 (94 pixels). Then, use AutoFit to increase the height of rows 4:9 to accommodate the wrapping of the text in cells B4 and B5.

3. Change the vertical alignment of the cell ranges A4:A5 and C4:E5 from Bottom to Center.

4. Change the orientation of the column headings in the cell range A3:E3 from 0 degrees to 60 degrees counterclockwise (don't forget to use AutoFit to increase the row height so that all the text in the now-diagonal column headings are displayed).

Entering positive numbers in the Degrees text box on the Alignment tab of the Format cells dialog box moves the orientation of the text up, counterclockwise to the baseline; whereas entering negative numbers in the Degrees text box moves the text orientation down, clockwise from the baseline.

5. Remove the Gray-25% fill color from the merged super-cell A2 by selecting the merged cell (A2 in this case) and then clicking the No Color button on the Patterns tab of the Format Cells dialog box.

6. Remove the borders from the merged super-cell A2 by clicking the None button under Presets on the Border tab of the Format Cells dialog box.

7. Unmerge cell A2 and return it to left horizontal and bottom vertical alignment.

   To unmerge a super-cell, select it and then remove the check mark from the Merged Cells check box on the Alignment tab of the Format Cells dialog box.

   To restore left horizontal and bottom vertical alignment, select Left (Indent) on the Horizontal drop-down list and Bottom on the Vertical drop-down list on the Alignment tab.

8. Return the height of row 2 to its default height and then move the table title in cell A2 to cell A1 by clicking the empty sample called None in the Presets section on the Border tab of the Format Cells dialog box.

9. Place a top line border back on top of the skewed column headings in the cell range B3:E3 by selecting the cell range and then clicking the sample with a line at the top in the Border section on the Border tab of the Format Cells dialog box.

10. Move the cell pointer up to cell A1, and then check the changes you've made to the formatting of your Sale table against those shown in the *Solved2-5.xls* workbook file in the Chapter 2 folder. When everything checks out, save your work as a new workbook called *Spring Furniture Sale – fmt01.xls* in your My Practice Spreadsheets folder inside My Documents on your hard disk and then close the workbook.

Using Format Painter and AutoFormat

Excel's Format Painter and AutoFormat features are designed to make quick work of applying complex formatting to large regions of the worksheet. Format Painter enables you to copy the formatting you've applied to a single cell to many ranges, whereas AutoFormat enables you to apply formatting to an entire table of data.

To use Format Painter, you put the cell cursor in the cell containing the formatting you want to copy (formatting that you've already applied with the tools on the Formatting toolbar or the options in the Format Cells dialog box). Then click the Format Painter button (the one with the paintbrush icon) to copy the formatting in the current cell (indicated by a marquee moving around inside the cell's borders) and drag the mouse pointer (now equipped with a paintbrush icon) through the range of cells to be formatted. As soon as you release the mouse button, all the formatting in the cell where you originally clicked the Format Painter button is now transferred to the selected range you painted.

Format Painter normally turns off the moment you release the mouse button after dragging through the cell range to be painted. If you need to paint multiple ranges, you need to turn on Format Painter by double-clicking its button on the Standard toolbar. This enables you to paint as many ranges as you want by dragging through them. When you finish copying the formatting, you must, however, remember to click the Format Painter button on the Standard toolbar again to turn Format Painter off.

Exercise 2-6: Formatting Cells with the Format Painter

Open the *Exercise2-6.xls* workbook file in your Chapter 2 folder inside the My Practice Spreadsheets folder in My Documents on your hard disk (or in the Excel Workbook folder on the workbook's CD-ROM) and then practice using Format Painter to quickly add formatting to its unformatted Production Schedule for 2006:

1. Apply the following formatting to cell B2 containing the first column heading:

- Light Yellow fill color

- Italic text attribute

- Outside Borders all around the perimeter of the cell

2. Use the Format Painter button to copy the formatting you applied to cell B2 to all the other column headings in the cell range C2:J2.

3. Apply the following formatting to cell B3 containing the production value for Part 100 in April, 2006:

- 9-point Arial type

- Number format with zero decimal places

- Gray-25% fill color

- Outside Borders all around the perimeter of the cell

4. Use Format Painter to copy all this formatting to all the rest of the production values in the table in the cell range B3:J6.

When copying the formatting and/or entry from the first cell in a block to all the cells in that block, you need to include the cell with the formatting or contents to copy as part of the copy-to range

5. Apply the following formatting to cell A3 and then use Format Painter to copy it to the cell range A4:A7 and the range B7:J7:

- Right alignment

- Number format with zero decimal places

- Light Green fill color

- Outside Borders all around the perimeter of the cell

When you need to use Format Painter to copy formatting to more than one cell range in a worksheet, double-click its button — when you're finished painting all the ranges, click the Format Painter button again to turn it off.

6. Move the cell cursor to cell A1 and then check your fully formatted Production Schedule table against the one shown in *Solved2-6.xls* in the Chapter 2 folder. When everything checks out, save your work as a new workbook called *Production Schedule 06 – fmt.xls* in your My Practice Spreadsheets folder inside My Documents on your hard disk and then close the workbook.

As fast as Format Painter is for copying complex formatting from one to many cells in the worksheet, its speed is nothing compared to that of AutoFormat. With AutoFormat, you can dispense complex formatting to an entire table of data in just a single operation.

All you have to do to use AutoFormat is put the cell cursor in any one of the cells in a table of data (that is, a block of data bounded by the borders of the worksheet or empty cells), and then open the AutoFormat dialog box (Format⇨AutoFormat). Now select the style of table formatting to apply to the table from the samples shown in this dialog box.

Exercise 2-7: Formatting a Table with AutoFormat

Open the *Exercise2-7.xls* workbook file in your Chapter 2 folder inside the My Practice Spreadsheets folder in My Documents on your hard disk (or in the Excel Workbook folder on the workbook's CD-ROM) and then practice using AutoFormat to format another copy of the unformatted Production Schedule for 2006 table, this time in one operation:

1. Open the AutoFormat dialog box and then double-click the Classic 1 sample.

2. Click the Undo button or press Ctrl+Z to remove this table formatting and then open the AutoFormat dialog box a second time. This time, double-click the List 3 sample.

3. Apply the Number format with zero decimal places to the cell range B3:J7.

4. Move the cell cursor to cell A1 and then check your Production Schedule table formatted with AutoFormat against the one shown in *Solved2-7.xls* in the Chapter 2 folder. When everything checks out, save your work as a new workbook called *Production Schedule 06 – autofmt.xls* in your My Spreadsheets (or My Practice Spreadsheets) folder inside My Documents on your hard disk and then close the workbook.

Using Conditional Formatting

Conditional Formatting enables you to set up a particular type of formatting that goes into effect only when a condition or a series of conditions that you define actually go into effect in the spreadsheet. This type of formatting is useful when you want to apply a special type of formatting (such as a red fill color or underlining) to a cell to alert when its calculated data entry reaches a particular (high or low) value.

Try It

Exercise 2-8: Formatting Cells with Conditional Formatting

Open the *Exercise2-8.xls* workbook in the Chapter 2 folder and then use its Income Statement to get practice in applying and using Conditional Formatting by doing the following:

1. Put the cell cursor in cell B10 containing the formula for calculating the total operating loss and then open the Conditional Formatting dialog box.

2. Click the drop-down list button in the box to the immediate right of the one that says Cell Value Is and select Greater Than or Equal To on its drop-down menu.

3. Click the empty text box to the immediate right of the drop-down list box that now says Greater Than or Equal To and then type **100000** (1 and five zeros).

4. Click the Format button to open the Format Cells dialog box where you select the following formatting:

- Bold as the Font Style and Yellow as the Color on the Font tab

- Red as the Color and 6.25% Gray as the Pattern on the Patterns tab

5. Select OK to close Format Cells. After checking the preview of the conditional format, select OK again to close the Conditional Formatting dialog box.

6. Reduce the Product Costs in cell B6 from the current -12,175 to **-2175** (note that cell B10 now uses your yellow-on-red conditional formatting because the Operating Income (loss) in this cell has risen to 109,440, 9,400 above 100,000 condition you set).

To replace an existing entry with a new entry, simply select the cell and enter the new entry as though the cell were still blank.

7. Click the Undo button on the Standard toolbar or press Ctrl+Z to return the Product Costs and Operating Income (loss) cells in this spreadsheet to their original values. (Note how the conditional formatting immediately disappears when the value in cell B10 returns to its original 99,440.)

8. Click the Redo button or press Ctrl+Y to undo your undo in step 7, restoring the -2175 entry in cell B6 and 109,440 calculated value in cell B10. (Note how the conditional formatting for Operating Income (loss) cell returns.)

9. Check your Income Statement with conditional formatting against the one shown in *Solved2-8.xls* in the Chapter 2 folder. When everything checks out, save your work as a new workbook, *Income Statement 06 – condfmt.xls* in your My Practice Spreadsheets folder inside My Documents on your hard disk, and then close the workbook.

Hiding Columns and Rows

Excel enables you to hide entire columns and rows in your worksheet. You can use this facility to conceal sensitive data (such as salaries and the like) in a spreadsheet that are used in formula calculations but that are not for everyone's eyes.

Hiding columns and rows is a lot like modifying their width and height (in fact, if the truth be known, a hidden column is just one whose width is reduced to zero and a hidden row is one whose height is shrunk down to zero). Select the column or columns to hide and then choose Format⇨Column⇨Hide or the row or rows to hide and Format⇨Row⇨Hide.

To redisplay concealed columns, you select the remaining columns on either side (left and right) of the hidden columns and then choose Format⇨Column⇨Unhide. To redisplay concealed rows, select the rows on either side (above and below) the hidden rows and then choose Format⇨Row⇨Unhide. Excel then redisplays all the formerly hidden columns or rows, which are automatically selected, and all you have to do is click a single cell anywhere in the worksheet to deselect them.

Q. Is there any way to hide individual cell entries in the worksheet rather than entire columns and rows?

A. Although Excel does not provide a command for hiding individual cells or cell ranges, you can accomplish this by creating a Custom number format and then applying it to their cells. This Custom number contains only the codes ;;; (three semicolons in a row with no spaces between). Be aware, however, that applying this ;;; Custom number format hides only the entries as they appear in the worksheet itself but does nothing to cloak their appearance on the Formula bar when the cell cursor is in them. This limits the usefulness of this method to the distribution of printed copies of the spreadsheet as all the entries in electronic copies are vulnerable via the Formula bar.

Exercise 2-9: Hiding Columns and Rows in a Worksheet

Open the *Exercise 2-9.xls* workbook file in the Chapter 2 folder located in the My Practice Spreadsheets folder inside My Documents on your hard disk (or in the Excel Workbook folder on the workbook's CD-ROM) and use its 12-month Regional Income table to practice hiding columns and rows:

1. Hide the column ranges B:D, F:H, J:L, and N:P and then put the cell cursor in cell A1 so that only columns A, E, I, M, Q, and R are displayed at the far left of the Income Analysis worksheet.

2. Select the column range A:Q and then choose Format⇨Column⇨Unhide. Click cell A1 and then verify that all the erstwhile hidden columns of the spreadsheet are redisplayed.

3. Hide the row ranges 4:8, 12:16, and 20:24 and then scroll up to verify that only rows 1, 2, 3; 9, 10, 11; 17, 18, 19; and 25 are displayed at the top of the Income Analysis worksheet.

4. Select the row range 3:25 and then redisplay all the hidden rows by choosing Format⇨Column⇨Unhide. Click cell A3 and then verify that all the missing rows are now redisplayed in the worksheet.

5. Close the *Exercise 2-9.xls* workbook file without saving your changes and exit Excel.

Chapter 3

Printing Spreadsheet Reports

*P*rinting easy-to-read and well-organized reports from your spreadsheets is one of the most important tasks you do in Excel. The exercises in this chapter give you a chance to practice printing many types of spreadsheet reports using Excel's Print Preview, Page Break Preview, headers and footers, and print title features. Don't worry if you don't have access to a printer while completing these exercises: In almost all cases, you can use the Print Preview feature to get an idea of how the report would appear on the printed page.

Previewing the Printed Report

Print Preview is your first line of defense against wasting paper on useless reports that contain bad page breaks, which separate columns and rows of the spreadsheet with data that need to appear together on a page. In Print Preview, all the information, both text and graphics, within the current *Print Area* (that is, the section of the worksheet included in the printout) is displayed as it appears on the printed page. Along with this spreadsheet data, any headings that you've assigned to the pages of the report also appear.

Always use Print Preview to check your report before sending it to the printer, unless it's one that you've already successfully printed from the spreadsheet.

Exercise 3-1: Previewing a Printed Report

Open the *Spring Furniture Sale.xls* workbook in your My Spreadsheets (or My Practice Spreadsheets) folder inside the My Documents folder and use it to practice using Print Preview:

1. Click the Print Preview button on the Standard toolbar to open it in the Print Preview window.

2. Click the Margins button on the toolbar at the top of the Print Preview window to display the markers for the left, right, top, and bottom page margins along with those indicating the current column widths.

3. Click somewhere in the displayed Sale table with the magnifying glass mouse pointer to zoom in on the table and its data.

4. Click the Setup button on the Print Preview toolbar to open the Page Setup dialog box and then select the Horizontally and Vertically check boxes in the Center on Page section on the Margins tab.

5. Select the Page 1, *Spring Furniture Sale.xls* heading in the Header drop-down list box on the Header/Footer tab and then select the OK button.

6. Click the Print button on the Print Preview toolbar to close the Print Preview window and open the Print dialog box. If you have a printer installed on your system, make sure that its name is displayed in the Name text box and then select OK to send the one-page report to it. Otherwise, click Cancel to close the Print dialog box without printing the report.

7. Close the Spring Furniture Sale workbook and save the changes when an alert dialog box appears asking you to do so (your changes to the print settings, including the header, are then saved as part of the file).

Adjusting Page Breaks

Whereas Print Preview alerts you to all sorts of potential problems in the printed report by showing you everything on the page as it will print, Page Break Preview only shows you where the page breaks occur. Page Break Preview does this by drawing lines between columns and rows in the worksheet that indicate the limits of each page in the report. You can then manipulate the page breaks by dragging these lines to new columns and rows.

Try It

Exercise 3-2: Paging a Report with Page Break Preview

Open the *Exercise3-2.xls* workbook in the Chapter 3 folder in your My Practice Spreadsheets folder in My Documents on your hard disk (or in the Excel Workbook folder on the workbook CD-ROM) and use it to practice using Page Break Preview:

1. Select View➪Page Break Preview on the Excel menu bar to put the Income Analysis worksheet into Page Break Preview mode and then select OK or the Close box to close the Welcome to Page Break Preview dialog box. Note that Page Break Preview automatically sets the worksheet zoom factor to 60% (indicated by the 60% in the Zoom combo box in the Standard toolbar).

2. Click the Zoom combo box, type **48**, and press Enter to increase the zoom factor to 48% (just a little below half-size) so that the entire Income Analysis spreadsheet is displayed on the screen.

3. Remove the first bad page break that occurs between rows 28 and 29 where the Northern region Net Income in row 28 on pages 1, 3, and 5 of the report is separated from the other regions on pages 2, 4, and 6.

Return the spreadsheet to 100% (by clicking 100% on Zoom drop-down list on the Standard toolbar), scroll down until you see the break between rows 28 and 29, and then drag the page break line between rows 28 and 29 up two rows so that the break now occurs between rows 26 and 27. The heading Net Income and Northern region income figures are now printed on pages 2, 4, and 6 of the report.

4. Adjust the page break between pages 1 and 3 and pages 2 and 4 so that only the Qtr 1 income figures are printed on pages 1 and 2 and all the Qtr 2 income data are together on pages 3 and 4.

   Scroll up so you can see the column header in the worksheet and then drag the page break line between columns G and H to the left so that the break now occurs between columns E and F, putting all the Qtr 2 figures on pages 3 and 4 of the report.

5. Adjust the page break between pages 3 and 5 and 4 and 6 so that only the Qtr 2 income figures are printed on pages 3 and 4 of the report.

6. Adjust the page break between pages 5 and 7 and 6 and 8 so that only the Qtr 3 income figures are printed on pages 5 and 6 of the report.

7. Choose View⇨Normal to get out of Page Break Preview mode. Note that the page breaks continue to appear as dotted lines in normal spreadsheet view.

8. Verify the pages of the report in Print Preview.

9. Center the printing between the left and right margins on each page of the report.

   Select the Horizontally check box in the Center on Page section on the Margins tab of the Page Setup dialog box to center the printing between the left and right margins.

10. Remove the column and row gridlines from the report by removing the check mark from the Gridlines check box on the Sheet tab of the Page Setup dialog box.

11. Preview all eight pages of the final report using the Page Down key to advance to the next page and the Page Up key to return to the previous page (make sure that you've zoomed out on the previewed page before pressing these keys, or you only end up scrolling around the same page).

12. When you're sure that all the pages of the report are okay, print the report if you have access to a printer; otherwise, close the Print Preview window and then save the revised Income Analysis workbook file as *Solved3-2.xls* in the Chapter 3 folder before you close the workbook.

Adding Custom Headers and Footers

In Exercise 3-1, you added a canned or ready-made header to your simple one-page report. This header centered the page number between the left and right margins and aligned the name of the workbook file with the right margin inside the top margin of the printed page. In addition to these types of ready-made headers and footers, Excel enables you to create custom headers and footers for your reports.

To add a custom header or footer to a report, you insert codes (selected from buttons like those that appear in the Header dialog box shown in Figure 3-1) that retrieve information about the report or workbook file that you can mix with stock text (such as the company or department name) in one of three sections:

✔ **Left Section** for information to be left-aligned against the page's left margin

✔ **Center Section** for information to be centered between the left and right margins

✔ **Right Section** for information to be right-aligned against the page's right margin

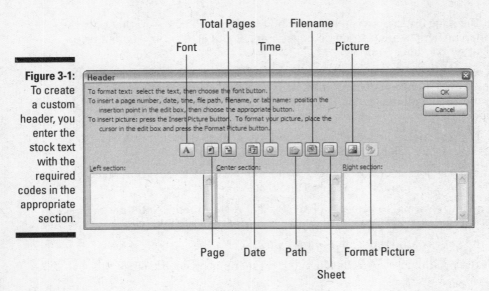

Figure 3-1:
To create
a custom
header, you
enter the
stock text
with the
required
codes in the
appropriate
section.

Q. How do I add a ready-made header and footer to my report?

A. Select it from the Header or Footer drop-down list box on the Header/Footer tab of the Page Setup dialog box (choose the File⇨Page Setup menu command or click the Setup button in Print Preview).

Q. Can I customize a ready-made header or footer?

A. Yes, you can: Simply select the ready-made header or footer you want to customize from the Header or Footer drop-down list box on the Header/Footer tab of the Page Setup dialog box. Then click the Custom Header or Custom Footer button and insert the codes and stock text you want to add to it in the Header or Footer dialog box.

Try It

Exercise 3-3: Creating a Custom Header and Footer for a Report

ON THE CD

Open the *Exercise3-3.xls* workbook in the Chapter 3 folder of your My Practice Spreadsheets folder in My Documents on your hard disk (or in the Excel Workbook folder on the workbook CD-ROM) and use this new copy of the Income Analysis worksheet to practice creating a custom header and footer for a report:

1. Open the Print Preview window, open the Page Setup dialog box, and select the Header/Footer tab.

2. Select Page 1 of ? in the Footer drop-down list box (Page 1 of 8 appears in the Footer preview area at the bottom of the Page Setup dialog box).

3. Click the Custom Header button to open the Header dialog box and then insert the date and time codes in the Left Section and make their text 9-point bold Times New Roman.

When inserting codes in a custom header or footer, you need to insert spaces between the codes and any stock text if you don't want their text to all run together.

To change the font or assign an attribute to the codes or stock text you add to a section of a custom header or footer, drag through them, and then click the Font button. Choose the font, font style, and attributes in the Font dialog box.

4. Insert the filename in the Center Section of the custom header and make its text 9-point bold italic Arial.

5. Insert the stock phrase **PRELIMINARY** (in all caps) in the Right Section of the custom header: Make this stock text 9-point Times New Roman and then select OK to close the Header dialog box.

6. Make the ready-made footer with the current page and total page numbers 10-point bold Arial.

To customize the font settings for a ready-made header or footer, open the Header or Footer dialog box with the Customize Header or Customize Footer button, respectively, and then select the codes or stock text before you click the Font button.

7. Close the Footer dialog box and the Page Setup dialog box and then check out your custom header and footer in the Print Preview window.

8. If the header and footer check out, close the Print Preview window and then save the revised Income Analysis workbook file as *Solved3-3.xls* in the Chapter 3 folder and close the workbook.

Adding Print Titles to a Report

In Excel reports, you use Print Titles to print the column and row headings from the worksheet on each and every page. If you don't bother to add Print Titles to multi-page reports, only the first pages of the report contain the headings that identify the related data, and your readers have no way of identifying the data on the later pages of the report.

Exercise 3-4: Adding Print Titles to a Report

Open the *Exercise3-4.xls* workbook in the Chapter 3 folder in your My Spreadsheets (or My Practice Spreadsheets) folder or on the workbook CD-ROM and use it to practice adding Print Titles to a report:

1. Open the Bo-Peep Client List in the Print Preview window and then preview each of its four pages. Note that page 2 lacks the spreadsheet title and the column headings with the field names, page 3 lacks the row headings with the case numbers, and page 4 lacks the spreadsheet title as well as the identifying column and row headings.

2. Close the Print Preview window and then open the Page Setup dialog box (File⇨Page Setup) and select the Sheet tab.

You can only assign rows and columns of the spreadsheet from the Sheet tab of the Page Setup dialog box when you open this dialog box in the normal worksheet window. The Rows to Repeat at Top and Columns to Repeat at Left text boxes in the Print Titles section on the Sheet tab are grayed out and unavailable when you open the Setup dialog box with the Setup button in the Print Preview window.

3. Click the Rows to Repeat at Top text box and then click row 2 of the Client List. Note that the Page Setup dialog box temporarily collapses down to just Rows to Repeat at Top text box as you click row 2 in the worksheet. A marquee now appears around this row in the worksheet and that its row range, $2:$2, appears in the text box on the Sheet tab.

4. Click the Columns to Repeat at Left text box and then click somewhere in column A in the Client List — a marquee now appears around column A in the worksheet and the column range. $A:$A appears in this text box on the Sheet tab.

5. Click the Print Preview button on the Sheet tab in the Page Setup dialog box and then page through each of the four pages in the Print Preview window. Now the column headings with the field names for the list and the row headings with the case numbers appear at the top and at the left of every page in the report.

6. Close the Print Preview window and then save the revised Bo-Peep Client List workbook file as *Solved3-4.xls* in the Chapter 3 folder and close the workbook.

Modifying the Print Setting for a Report

Regardless of what type of printer you use, Excel has a number of default print settings that it automatically puts into effect when you first print a spreadsheet. These print settings include

- ✔ Portrait rather than landscape orientation for the printing (so that the printing runs with the shorter width of the page rather than with the longer length)

- ✔ Printing at 100% of normal size

- ✔ Print quality medium (on printers that support different print quality modes)

- ✔ Letter (8.5 x 11 in.) paper size

- ✔ Top and bottom margins of 1 inch

- ✔ Left and right margins of 0.75 inch

- ✔ Header and footer margins of 0.5 inch (with no header or footer defined)

- ✔ No printing of the column and row gridlines that define the cells in the worksheet

- ✔ No printing of the column letters and row numbers associated with the cells within the Print Area in the worksheet

- ✔ No printing of the comments attached to cells included in the Print Area (see Chapter 4 for more on comments)

- ✔ Printing of error values returned by formulas as they appear in the worksheet (see Chapter 5 for more on error values)

- ✔ Paging order down the rows of the Print Area and then across the columns

- ✔ Printing a single copy of all the pages generated from a Print Area that includes all the data in the active worksheet(s)

Many times you may find that you can solve minor paging problems in a report simply by modifying the orientation of the printing, the percentage of normal size on the Page tab of the Page Settings dialog box, or the margin settings on the Margins tab.

If your intention is simply to produce a facsimile of the worksheet for reviewing its data, you should include the worksheet gridlines and column and row headings in the printout. To do this, you select the Gridlines and Row and Column Headings check boxes on the Sheet tab of the Page Settings dialog box. If you also want to print the comments, select the At the End of the Sheet or As Displayed on Sheet option on the Comments drop-down list box on this tab.

Try It

Exercise 3-5: Changing the Print Settings for a Report

Open the *Exercise3-5.xls* workbook in the Chapter 3 folder in your My Practice Spreadsheets folder in My Documents on your hard disk (or in the Excel Workbook folder on the workbook CD-ROM) and use it to practice changing various print settings:

1. Open the Print Preview window and check out the page breaks for this three-page report that prints all the data in the Total Sales worksheet in portrait mode.

2. Open the Page Setup dialog box from the Print Preview window and then select the Page tab.

3. Click the Landscape option button under Orientation and then select OK to close the Page Setup dialog box.

4. Check out the page breaks for printing the report in landscape mode. Note that the third page now contains an "orphaned" column with the annual total sales.

5. Open the Page Setup dialog box again and then click the Page(s) Wide text box to the immediate right of the Fit To option button in the Scaling section of the Page tab. Replace the 1 in this text box with a **2** so that the Fit To option button is selected with the setting 2 pages wide by 1 page tall.

Using the Fit To Scaling option to constrain the printing to a particular number of pages rather than Adjust To option to set a specific scaling percentage is often a much more effective way to eliminate pages with orphaned columns or rows of data.

6. Close the Page Setup dialog box and then check out the paging in this now two-page report. Note that the column with annual total sales is no longer orphaned.

7. Close the Print Preview window and then select Qtr1 worksheet.

8. Open the Print Preview window for this second worksheet in the *Exercise 3-5.xls* workbook and then click the Margins button to turn on the margin and column markers in Print Preview.

9. Turn on the gridlines and row and column Headings with the Page Setup dialog box in the Print Preview window.

The display of the gridlines and row and column headings are controlled from check boxes located on the Sheet tab of the Page Setup dialog box.

10. Zoom in on the preview of page 1 of the report by clicking the Sales table with the magnifying glass mouse pointer.

11. Narrow column B to somewhere between 14.43 and 14.39 characters wide, column C to somewhere between 14.29 and 14.22, and column D to somewhere between 14.22 and 14.20 characters wide. Note the addition of the Qtr1 totals in column E and the reduction of the report to a single page.

Refer to the Width display indicator on the left side of the status bar in the Print Preview window when you manipulate the column markers (this indicator changes to Left Margin, Right Margin, Top Margin, Header Margin, Bottom Margin, and Footer Margin when you move their respective markers).

12. Turn off the gridlines and row and column headings in the Print Preview window; add a footer that prints the page number centered and the worksheet name right-aligned.

13. If you have access to a printer, print this worksheet; otherwise, just close the Print Preview window and then save the workbook as *Solved3-5.xls* in the Chapter 3 folder in your My Practice Spreadsheets folder before you close the workbook.

Printing All or Part of the Workbook

As noted in the previous section on default print settings, the Print Area that defines which cell ranges are included in the printout consists of whatever worksheet or worksheets that you've selected at the time of printing. Many times you need to reduce the Print Area to just a range of cells within the active worksheet or to increase it to include the data on all the worksheets in the entire workbook. The exercises in this section give you practice in printing not only Print Areas of different sizes but also printouts that include the contents of formulas in the spreadsheet (as opposed to their calculated values) and charts that you've created (see Chapter 14 for practice on charting spreadsheet data).

If you want to print all the data on the active worksheet using the print settings currently in effect for that sheet, simply click the Print button on the Standard toolbar: Excel then sends the print job directly to the default printer without ever opening the Print dialog box.

Printing a range of cells

Many times you only need to print a particular table or list of data on the active worksheet (as opposed to all the data on the sheet). To do this, select the cell range or ranges that encompass this data in the active worksheet and then click the Selection option button in the Print What section in the Print dialog box (File⇨Print or Ctrl+P). Then send the print job to the printer by selecting OK.

If you have a table or list in a worksheet whose updated data you need to print regularly, name the range and use the Go To feature (as covered in Chapter 4) to quickly select it for printing.

Try It

ON THE CD

Exercise 3-6: Printing a Particular Range of Worksheet Data

Open the *Exercise3-6.xls* workbook in the Chapter 3 folder in your My Practice Spreadsheets folder in My Documents on your hard disk (or in the Excel Workbook folder on the workbook CD-ROM) and use it to practice printing just a table of data:

1. Select the cell range A1:R15 (note that several of the rows and columns in the worksheet are hidden) and then open the Print dialog box.

2. Click the Selection option button and then click the Preview button at the bottom of the Print dialog box to verify that only the Sales table, and not the embedded column chart immediately beneath it in the 2006 Sales worksheet, will be printed.

3. Center the printing of this sales table both horizontally and vertically on the page.

4. Add a footer that prints the page number centered at the bottom of the printout.

5. Add a custom header that prints your name or your company name in the Left Section, the current date in the Center Section, and type the word **CONFIDENTIAL** in the Right Section.

6. If you have access to a printer, print this worksheet; otherwise, just close the Print Preview window and then save the workbook as *Solved3-6.xls* in the Chapter 3 folder in your My Practice Spreadsheets folder before you close the workbook.

Printing the entire workbook

Printing all the data in the entire workbook is a snap: Simply open the Print dialog box (File➪Print or Ctrl+P) and then select the Entire Workbook option button in the Print What section before sending the print job to the printer by selecting the OK button.

Q. How can I print data on multiple worksheets without printing the entire workbook?

A. Select the tabs for all the worksheets in the workbook that contain data you want printed (remember to Ctrl+click to select multiple sheet tabs) before sending the job to the printer.

Try It

Exercise 3-7: Printing the Entire Workbook

Open the *Exercise3-7.xls* workbook in the Chapter 3 folder in your My Practice Spreadsheets folder in My Documents on your hard disk (or in the Excel Workbook folder on the workbook CD-ROM) and use it to practice printing all the sheets in a workbook:

1. Open the Print dialog box and then select the Entire Workbook option button in the Print What section before selecting Preview to open the Print Preview window.

2. Check out all three pages of the report in the Print Preview window. Note the orphaned column of data on page 2 and the landscape orientation of the printing of the column chart on page 3.

3. Select page 1 of 3 in the Print Preview window and then change the orientation of the printing of this page from portrait to landscape. Check out the paging again in Print Preview.

4. Center the printing of the Production Schedule on page 1 between the left and right margin.

5. Add a footer to the report that prints the current page number and total pages centered at the bottom of the page.

6. Preview the two pages of the report. Note that the page number footer only appears at the bottom of page 1 with the data table and not on page 2 with the column chart.

The footer isn't displayed on page 2 with the chart because by default Excel prints all charts on their own Chart sheets Full Page, leaving no room for a header or footer (see Exercise 3-8 to see how you go about changing this setting).

7. If you have access to a printer, print this two-page report; otherwise, just close the Print Preview window and then save the workbook as *Solved3-7.xls* in the Chapter 3 folder inside your My Practice Spreadsheets folder before you close the workbook.

Printing charts in the spreadsheet

Charts that you create from the data in your spreadsheets are either embedded in the same worksheet that contains the data or on a separate Chart sheet (see Chapter 14). In Exercise 3-6, you saw that embedded charts are printed as part of the worksheet unless you select just the data ranges they're created from as the print selection. In Exercise 3-7, you saw that charts placed on their own Chart sheets are not printed unless you select their sheets as part of the print selection.

What you didn't see is that when you print a chart placed on its own Chart sheet, Excel adds a Chart tab to the Page Setup dialog box. The Chart tab contains options for scaling the chart instead of printing it full page and for printing the chart in black and white instead of color. You get experience using these options in Exercise 3-8 that follows.

Try It

Exercise 3-8: Printing a Chart in a Report

Open the *Exercise3-8.xls* workbook in the Chapter 3 folder in your My Spreadsheets (or My Practice Spreadsheets) folder or on the workbook CD-ROM and use this copy of the 2006 Production Schedule workbook to practice printing a chart saved on its own Chart sheet in a workbook:

1. Select the Column Chart sheet in the *Exercise3-8.xls* workbook and then open the Page Setup dialog box.

2. Change the Printed Chart Size option from Full Page to Scale to Fit Page and select black-and-white printing for the Printing Quality. Next open the chart in the Print Preview window.

3. Display the margin markers in the Print Preview window and then add a header with the sheet name centered in the top margin and the current page number in bottom margin.

4. Close the Print Preview window and return to the Column Chart sheet in the *Exercise3-8.xls* workbook.

5. If you have access to a printer, click the Print button on the Standard toolbar to print this Chart sheet; otherwise, just make the Schedule sheet active before you save the workbook as *Solved3-8.xls* in the Chapter 3 folder in your My Practice Spreadsheets folder, and then close the workbook.

Printing the spreadsheet formulas

When you print a worksheet, Excel prints the entries exactly as they appear in their cells of the worksheet. As a result, when you print a section of a worksheet that contains formulas, the printout shows only the results of the calculations performed by the formulas, not the contents of the formulas themselves. In addition to a printout showing the results, you may also want to print a copy of the worksheet showing the formulas by which these results were derived. You can then use this printout of the formulas when double-checking the formulas in the worksheet to make sure that they are designed correctly.

To help you identify the cell reference of each formula in your printout, be sure to include the gridlines and column and row headings as part of the printout.

Exercise 3-9: Printing the Formulas in a Spreadsheet

Open the *Exercise3-9.xls* workbook in the Chapter 3 folder in your My Practice Spreadsheets folder in My Documents on your hard disk (or in the Excel Workbook folder on the workbook CD-ROM). Use this copy of the Income Analysis spreadsheet to practice printing the formulas in a table of data in a workbook:

1. Display the formulas in the cells of the Income Analysis spreadsheet by selecting the Formulas check box on the View tab of the Options dialog box (Tools⇨ Options). Note how turning on the formula display enlarges the columns to accommodate all the formulas.

2. Press Ctrl+~ (tilde) to turn off the formula display and return to the normal worksheet display.

The tilde key is located on the ` key (accent grave) that is usually located to the immediate left of the 1 key on the top row of the QWERTY keyboard.

Ctrl+~ (tilde) is a toggle key combination: The first time you press it, it turns on the formula display and the second time turns it off.

3. Press Ctrl+~ (tilde) again, this time to turn the formula display back on and then change the following settings in the Page Setup dialog box:

- Change the orientation of the printing from portrait to landscape.

- Add a centered header that contains the text **Formula Check** and a centered footer that displays the current page number and total pages in the report, both in 10-point Arial Black.

- Make the row 3 the Rows to Repeat at Top and column A the Columns to Repeat at Left.

- Add the gridlines and the row and column headings to the printout.

- Change the page order from Down, Then Over to Over, Then Down.

4. Close the Page Setup dialog box and then display the Income Analysis worksheet in the Print Preview window. Note that the report now contains 18 pages.

5. Constrain the pages to 9 pages wide by 1 page tall and center the data on each page horizontally between the left and right margins; then close the Page Setup dialog box and return to the Print Preview window.

6. Turn on Page Break Preview mode and then dispense with the Welcome dialog box.

7. Move the page markers so that page 1 contains only Qtr1 figures; page 2 only Qtr2 figures; page 3 only Qtr3 figures, and page 4, the Qtr4 figures with the grand totals.

8. If you have access to a printer, click the Print button on the Standard toolbar to print the four-page report showing all the Income Analysis formulas; otherwise, use Print Preview to verify the layout and contents of these pages and then return to the Normal worksheet mode.

9. Hide the display of the formulas in the cells.

10. Save the workbook as *Solved3-9.xls* in the Chapter 3 folder in your My Practice Spreadsheets folder and then close the workbook file.

Chapter 4

Modifying the Spreadsheet

· ·

In This Chapter

▶ Finding and opening a workbook for editing

▶ Selecting the cell ranges that require editing

▶ Finding data entry errors with Text to Speech

▶ Inserting and deleting cell ranges

▶ Moving and copying cell ranges

▶ Using comments in the spreadsheet

▶ Finding and replacing cell entries and spell-checking the spreadsheet

▶ Editing worksheets as a group

· ·

Some of the spreadsheets you work with require constant updating, whereas others need only the occasional revision. Whichever is the case, being able to revise an existing spreadsheet without disturbing either its underlying structure or its current contents is essential. The exercises in this chapter give you a chance to practice all aspects of basic editing, including locating the workbook file to open, finding the area in the worksheet that needs editing, and making all the necessary editing changes.

Finding and Opening the Workbook for Editing

You can't edit a spreadsheet if its workbook is not open in Excel, and you can't open its workbook in Excel if you don't know where it's saved on your computer. The secret to locating the workbook files that need editing (aside from sticking to a clear and consistent system for naming your files and deciding where to save them) is to make them eminently searchable. And the key to making your workbook files super-searchable is to add summary information that you can then use in doing a file search to each and every new workbook you save.

Adding summary information to a workbook

The Properties dialog box (File⇨Properties) contains all sorts of vital statistics about the workbook, such as its size, location, the name of its creator, as well as the date it was originally created, last modified, and last opened (accessed). In addition to this information that's automatically kept on the file (as listed on the General and Statistics tabs), you can add your own information to its Summary tab. You can then use any and all of the statistics, both those automatically recorded and those you add, when doing a file search to locate the file for editing.

Figure 4-1 shows the Summary tab of the Properties dialog box for the *Exercise4-1.xls* workbook you use later in a related exercise. As you can see, this tab contains a number of fields that you fill in. Although you may not want to add all this summary information to all the workbooks you create, you would do well to develop a system whereby you consistently fill in those fields you routinely use when doing a file search.

Figure 4-1:
You can search for a workbook using the information you enter on the Summary tab of its Properties dialog box.

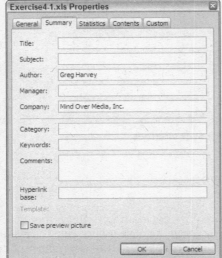

Be sure to check the Save Preview Picture check box at the bottom of the Summary tab if you want to be able to use the Preview viewing mode in the Open dialog box to later identify it. When you select Preview on the Views drop-down list, a snapshot of the upper-left part of first worksheet in the workbook appears in a pane on the right side of the dialog box whenever you select its filename in a list in a pane on the left side. If you don't select this check box, all you see is a Preview Not Available message when you select the workbook's filename.

Try It

Exercise 4-1: Adding Summary Information to a Workbook

If Excel's not already running, launch the program. Then, open the *Exercise4-1.xls* file in the Chapter 4 folder inside your My Practice Spreadsheets folder in My Documents on your hard disk. You will use this workbook to practice adding summary information:

1. Open the Exercise4-1.xls Properties dialog box (File➪Properties) and then select the Summary tab.

2. Enter the following information into the designated fields:

- **Hourly/Wages – February, 2006** in the Title field
- **Monthly payroll** in the Subject field
- **Payroll** in the Category field
- **Array** in the Keywords field

3. Select the Save Preview Picture check box and then select OK to close the Properties dialog box.

4. Open the Save As dialog box (F12). If My Documents folder is not already shown in the Save In drop-down list box, click the My Documents button and then create a new folder name Lost Spreadsheets inside this folder.

To create a new folder in the Save As dialog box, click the Create New Folder button on the Open dialog box toolbar (the one with the star-burst on its folder icon) and then enter the folder name in the New Folder dialog box.

5. Rename the workbook *Exercise4-1.xls* to *Hourly Wages 02-06.xls* and then select the Save button.

6. Close the *Hourly Wages 02-06.xls* workbook.

Searching for workbook files

The file search feature available from Excel's Open dialog box is one of the program's better-kept secrets. To use this very important feature, you open the File Search dialog box by selecting the Search item at the very top of the Tools drop-down list. (Open the drop-down list by clicking the Tools button at the end of the Open dialog box toolbar on the right.)

The File Search dialog box contains two tabs:

✔ **Basic,** where you can search for workbook files by entering all or part of their filenames in the Search Text box

✔ **Advanced** (shown in Figure 4-2), where you can search for a workbook by selecting the property (including automatically kept stats and information you add to the Summary tab fields) and then designating the value it should contain

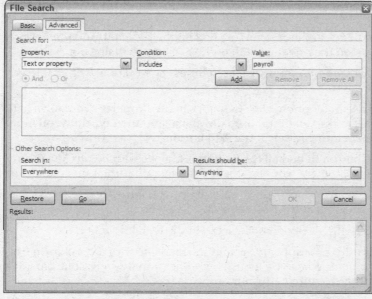

Figure 4-2: The Advanced tab of the File Search dialog box enables you to search for workbooks using summary information.

Try It

Exercise 4-2: Searching for the Workbook to Edit

This exercise gives you practice finding workbook files using both the Basic and Advanced tabs on the File Search dialog box:

1. Display the Open dialog box (Ctrl+O) in Excel, click the My Documents button to make this folder current, and then open the File Search dialog box (click Search on the drop-down list attached to the Tools button).

2. Type **Exer** in the Search Text box on the Basic tab of the File Search dialog box and then set up the following Search Options:

- My Computer and all its subfolders as the location to search in the Search In drop-down list box

- Excel Files as the type of files to find in the Results Should Be drop-down list box

- To restrict the location of the file search to My Computer and its subfolders, click the Everywhere check box on the Search In drop-down list to deselect it and all the other locations, and then click the My Computer check box (the Search In drop-down list box will then read Selected Locations).

- To restrict the type of files to be searched for to Excel files, click the Anything, Outlook Items, and Web Pages check boxes to deselect them and their associates and then click only the Excel Files check box under Office Files. (The Results Should Be drop-down list box will then read, "Selected File Types.")

3. Select the Go button to begin searching for all the Excel files that contain Exer in the filename within your My Computer folder and its subfolders.

When the file search stops, you will see a whole list of all the Exercise workbook files that you copied from the workbook CD-ROM and that you created in doing the exercises in previous chapters in the Results section at the bottom of the File Search dialog box.

4. Delete the text Exer in the Search Text box on the Basic tab and then click the Restore button on the Advanced tab of the File Search dialog box.

5. Using the Advanced tab, set up a Search for every workbook with a Category that includes payroll:

To set up this search option, click Category in the Property drop-down list, select Includes in the Condition drop-down list, and then type **payroll** in the Value text box before you select the Add button.

6. Select the Go button to find all the Excel workbooks within your My Computer folder and its subfolders whose Category summary information contains payroll.

When the File Search stops, you should see your *Hourly Wages 02-06.xls* file listed in the Results section at the bottom of the dialog box.

7. Click the *Hourly Wages 02-06.xls* file listed in the Results section.

Note that a border now appears around the filename with a drop-down list button on the right. When you mouse over this drop-down list button, a ToolTip displaying the file's entire path name appears.

8. Select the Properties item on file's drop-down list to open the *Hourly Wages 02-06.xls* Properties dialog box and then click its Summary tab.

Note that this tab contains all the summary information you entered there when you created this file as part of Exercise 4-1.

9. Select the OK button to close the *Hourly Wages 02-06.xls* Properties dialog box. Next click the OK button while *Hourly Wages 02-06.xls* is still selected in the Results section to close the File Search dialog box and return to the Open dialog box. (Leave this dialog box displayed in Excel for Exercise 4-3 on using the Open options.)

Exploring the Open options

Normally you don't think twice about opening workbooks that you located and selected in Excel's Open dialog box. However, just opening the original file for editing by selecting the Open button is not your only option. In addition to the normal Open option, the drop-down list attached to the Open button gives you the following other options:

 ✔ **Open as Read-Only** to open the workbook file in read-only mode in Excel so that you can't save changes to the original file.

 ✔ **Open as Copy** to open a copy of the workbook file in Excel so that you can't save changes to the original file.

 ✔ **Open and Repair** to have Excel attempt to repair a damaged workbook file before opening. (Use this option when you're unable to open a workbook file that has somehow become corrupted using the normal Open option.)

`Try It`

Exercise 4-3: Using the Various Options for Opening a Workbook

Use the *Hourly Wages 02-06.xls* file that you located with File Search and selected in the Open dialog box in Exercise 4-2 to get practice with using the different Open options:

1. Click the drop-down list button attached to File Name combo box in the Open dialog box and then click the path name of the *Hourly Wages 02-06.xls* at the top of this drop-down list.

 Excel responds by selecting the Lost Spreadsheet folder that you created for the *Hourly Wages 02-06.xls* file in the last lesson.

2. Click the *Hourly Wages 02-06.xls* file icon in the Open list box to select it.

3. Click the drop-down button attached to the Open button and then select the Read-Only option on its drop-down list.

 Excel opens a copy of the *Hourly Wages 02-06.xls* workbook in read-only, indicated by [Read-Only] appended to the filename on the program window's title bar.

4. Increase Michelle's hourly wage from $25.00 an hour to $40.00 in cell A4 and then save the changes (Ctrl+S).

 To replace one value with another, enter the new value in the cell just as though it were blank — as soon as you complete the entry by clicking the Enter box or pressing the Enter key, Excel replaces the original value with the new one, using the formatting assigned to the cell.

5. Select OK in the alert dialog box informing that this workbook is read-only and then save your changes in the Lost Spreadsheets folder under the filename *Hourly Wages 02-06-rev1.xls* and close this workbook file.

6. Display the Open dialog box again (Ctrl+O) and this time open a copy of the *Hourly Wages 02-06.xls* file icon in the Lost Spreadsheets folder.

To open a copy of a workbook, select its file icon in the Open list box and then select the Open as Copy option on the Open button's drop-down list — Excel opens the a copy of the original file indicated by the Copy (1) of text that precedes the filename on the program window's title bar.

7. Redisplay all the hidden columns in the Feb 06 sheet of this workbook (see Chapter 2 if you've forgotten how to do this), and then select cell A1 before you save your changes (Ctrl+S) and close the workbook.

Finding and Identifying the Region that Needs Editing

As you're already well aware, an Excel worksheet represents an extremely large space in which to work. Often the biggest challenge in editing a spreadsheet is just finding and identifying the data ranges in the worksheet that are in need of revision. To help in this endeavor, you can often use the following three features to good advantage:

 ✔ **Zoom** to gain an overview of the worksheet and its data ranges by zooming out on the worksheet and then using it to gain a close-up view of the particular range in the sheet you need to edit

 ✔ **Freeze Panes** to prevent the rows and columns containing the column and row headings from scrolling so that these headings remain visible at all times while you are scrolling through their data entries

 ✔ **Custom Views** to name and save a combination of different worksheet display settings (including frozen panes and various magnification settings) so that you can put them into effect by simply selecting them

Q. What is the range of zoom settings I can select for my worksheet display?

A. You can set the worksheet display magnification setting anywhere in the range of 10% to 400% of normal by entering the value of the new magnification percentage directly into the Zoom combo-box in whole degree increments.

Try It

Exercise 4-4: Using Zoom, Freeze Panes, and Custom Views

Open the *Exercise4-4.xls* workbook file in the Chapter 4 folder inside your My Practice Spreadsheets folder or on the Excel Workbook CD-ROM. This file contains a copy of the now-familiar Regional Income worksheet that you can use to practice using the Zoom, Freeze Panes, and Custom Views features to find and identify ranges for editing:

1. Select 50% on the drop-down list attached to the Zoom combo-box.

Excel reduces the magnification of the worksheet display to half the normal size. Note, however, that even at one-half, not all of the data ranges are visible on-screen.

2. Click the Zoom combo-box that reads 50% on the Standard toolbar and then type **45** and press Enter.

At a magnification setting of 45% of normal, you can now see all the data entered in the Income Analysis worksheet.

3. Select the cell range J20:M25 by carefully dragging through this range in the worksheet (not so easy to do when the cells are so small), and then click Selection at the bottom of the drop-down list attached to the Zoom combo-box.

Excel responds by setting the magnification setting to something over 200% so that all of the cells in the selected range J20:M25 are visible in the display. Note, however, that without the row and column headings, it is impossible to identify these entries in this range.

4. Put the cell cursor in cell A1 (Ctrl+Home) and move it to the empty cell B3 so that the cursor is in the row immediately beneath the one with the table's column headings and the column immediately to the right of the one containing the row headings.

5. Select Window⇨Freeze Panes.

Excel draws a horizontal line between rows 2 and 3 and a vertical line between columns A and B indicating the limits of the frozen panes — any entries above the horizontal line and to the left of the vertical line remain on screen as you scroll through their columns and rows.

6. Use the Tab key to scroll new columns on the right into view.

Note how the column headings in row 2 as well as the table title in row 1 remain displayed as you move to columns of the table into view.

7. Use the Page Down key to scroll new rows lower in the worksheet into view.

Note how the row headings in column A remain displayed on the screen as you move new rows of the table into view.

8. Repeat steps 2 and 3 in this exercise. Select the cell range J20:M25 and then set the magnification to the display of this selection.

Note that this time with the addition of the frozen panes that retain the associated row and column headings, you can tell right away that you're looking at the 3rd Qtr operating expenses for all the divisions.

9. Return the Zoom setting to 100% and then position the cell cursor in cell B3, which you used to freeze the row and column headings.

10. Open the Custom Views dialog box (View⇨Custom Views) and then select the Add button to open the Add View dialog box.

11. Type **100% w/ Row & Col Headings** in the Name text box and then select OK.

12. Hide the column ranges B:D, F:H, J:L, and N:P. Next, select cell B3 and then, following steps 10 and 11, name this view **100% 4 Qtrs Display**.

13. Open the Custom Views dialog box and double-click the 100% w/ Row & Col Headings view in the Views list box.

14. Open the Custom Views dialog box and select the 100% 4 Qtrs Display view and then hide the following row ranges: 4:8, 12:16, 20:24, and then select cell B3. Save this view under the name **100% 4 Qtrs Total Display**.

15. Return the worksheet to the 100% w/ Row & Col Headings view, and then choose Window⇨Unfreeze Panes to remove the panes.

16. Position the cell cursor in cell A1. Save this version of the Income Analysis worksheet with the custom views under the filename *Solved4-4.xls* in the Chapter 4 folder and close the workbook.

Selecting the Ranges to Edit

Selecting occupied cells in the worksheet for editing is very much the same process as selecting blank cells for preformatting or data entry with one important exception. Because the cells already contain data, in addition to dragging through the ranges and clicking the first and last cell while holding down the Shift key, you can use a technique known as AutoSelect to quickly select an entire block of occupied cells in a couple of mouse clicks.

Moreover, you can use Excel's Go To and range name features to combine locating a cell range that needs editing and selecting its cells all at the same time!

Try It

Exercise 4-5: Selecting the Range of Cells for Editing

ON THE CD

Open the *Exercise4-5.xls* workbook file in the Chapter 4 folder inside your My Practice Spreadsheets folder or on the Excel Workbook CD-ROM. This file contains a copy of the 2006 Production Schedule worksheet that you can use to practice selecting cell ranges for editing beginning with the AutoSelect feature:

1. Position the mouse pointer on the bottom edge of the cell cursor in cell A2, hold down the Shift key, and then when the Arrowhead mouse pointer appears, double-click the bottom edge.

AutoSelect extends the selection down to row 7, the last occupied row in the data table.

2. Continue to hold down the Shift key as you double-click anywhere on the right edge of the extended cell cursor.

AutoSelect extends the cell selection to column J, the last occupied column in the data table, effectively selecting all of its cells in the range A2:J7.

3. Click cell A15 in the worksheet to position the cell cursor in this cell while at the same time deselecting the cell range A2:J7.

Now you will practice selecting the cells in the data table using Excel's Go To feature, which is normally used to position the cell cursor in a new cell in the worksheet.

4. Press F5 or Ctrl+G to open the Go To dialog box and then type **A2** (it's all right to enter the reference as **a2**) and press Enter.

The Go To dialog box disappears and the cell cursor jumps to cell A2, making it current.

5. Press F5 or Ctrl+G to open the Go To dialog box again and then type **J7** (or **j7**). This time, however, hold down the Shift key as you press Enter.

Excel jumps the cell pointer to cell J7 and, because you held down the Shift key, the program also selected all the cells in between (if you didn't hold down Shift key, the program just moves the cursor from A2 to J7).

6. Position the cell cursor in cell A1 and use AutoSelect on your own to select the cell range A1:J7.

Note that this time it takes an extra double-click on the bottom edge of the cell cursor to extend the cell selection down to row 7. Next, you're going to name this cell selection.

7. Click the Name Box on the Formula bar that currently displays A1, and then type **prod_table** (with an underscore and no space) and press Enter.

Excel assigns the range name prod_table to the cell selection, A1:J7.

8. Use the Go To feature to move the cell cursor to cell IV4000 on the other side of the worksheet.

9. Click the drop-down button attached to the Name Box on the Formula bar and then click prod_table on its drop-down list.

Excel responds by selecting the range A1:J7 and repositioning the worksheet so that this range is in view.

10. Click cell A1 to deselect the range A1:J7, and then save this workbook with the prod_table range name with the filename *Solved4-5.xls* in your Chapter 4 folder inside the My Practice Spreadsheets folder and close the workbook file.

Editing Data Entries

In the previous exercises in this chapter, the sole technique you've used to modify the entry in a cell is to replace it completely by entering the new value into that cell as though it were still blank. This method is fine as long as the replacement entry is short and easy to type. It is not, however, the preferred method when you only need to make slight corrections to a long text entry or a complex formula. Rather than replace the original entry, you need to put Excel into Edit mode so that you can edit its contents as you would a word or phrase in a word-processing program such as Microsoft Word.

Excel gives you a choice of techniques for putting the program into Edit mode:

- ✔ Click the I-beam cursor at the place in the current cell entry that needs editing on the Formula bar and then edit its contents on the Formula bar.

- ✔ Double-click the white-cross mouse pointer at the place in the cell entry in the worksheet that needs editing and then edit its contents in the cell.

- ✔ Press F2 to place the Insertion point at the end of the current cell entry in the worksheet and edit its contents in its cell.

After you've placed Excel in Edit mode and positioned the Insertion point somewhere in the entry, you can then use the ← and → to move the flashing pointer in front of or immediately after the characters to modify. Press the Delete key to remove characters to the right of the Insertion point or the Backspace key to remove characters to its left. To insert new characters at the insertion point and move existing characters out the way and to the right, just type them.

After you finishing modifying the contents of the entry, you still need to complete the edit as you do a new entry. Only in this case, you need to rely on the Enter box, Enter key, Tab, or clicking another cell as you can't use any of the arrow keys ($\uparrow$, $\downarrow$, $\leftarrow$, or $\rightarrow$). In Edit mode, these cursor keys only move the Insertion point within the characters of the entry.

If you need to abandon an edit without entering the changes you've made in the cell or on the Formula bar, press the Esc key. If you complete a mistaken editing change, click the Undo button on the Standard toolbar or press Ctrl+Z to undo the change (and keep in mind that Excel supports multiple levels of undo).

Exercise 4-6: Editing Cell Entries

Open the *Exercise4-6.xls* workbook file in the Chapter 4 folder inside your My Practice Spreadsheets folder or on the Excel Workbook CD-ROM. This file contains a copy of the CG Media 2006 Sales worksheet that you can use to practice making simple editing changes to the contents of particular cells in the spreadsheet:

1. Click the I-beam pointer in front of the C in Category, and then type **Media and** on the Formula bar and click the Enter box to insert this text in the spreadsheet title in cell A1.

   The edited title in cell A1 now reads, CG Media – 2006 Sales by Media and Category.

2. Double-click the white-cross pointer after the *s* in Discs in the row heading in cell A3, and then remove this extraneous *s*.

   The edited row heading in cell A3 now reads, Compact Disc Sales.

3. Position the cell cursor in cell A14, press F2 and then replace Cassette in the row heading with **Tape** and press Tab to complete the edit.

   The row heading in cell A14 now reads, Total Tape Sales.

4. Select cell A1 again and save your editing changes in a new file named *Solved4-6.xls* in your Chapter 4 folder inside the My Practice Spreadsheets folder, and then close the workbook file.

Catching Errors with Text to Speech

If you're using Excel 2002 or 2003, you can use the Text to Speech feature to catch data entry errors by listening to them. Text to Speech reads the entries in a data table or list out loud, enabling you to check their accuracy by keeping your eyes focused on the printed source from which they were originally entered.

Exercise 4-7: Verifying Data Entries with Text to Speech

If you have Excel 2002 or 2003 installed on your computer, open the *Exercise4-7.xls* workbook file in the Chapter 4 folder inside your My Practice Spreadsheets folder or in the Excel Workbook folder on the workbook CD-ROM. This file contains a copy of the Spring 2006 Furniture Sale spreadsheet that you can use to practice using Text to Speech to verify the accuracy of entries in a data table:

1. Choose Tools⇔Speech⇔Text to Speech on the Excel menu to open the Text to Speech toolbar (see Figure 4-3).

   If this is the first time you've used Text to Speech, Excel must install the program before it can display this toolbar. Follow the prompts to install the program and then after you have it installed proceed to the next step of the exercise.

2. Click the Speak Cells button on the Text to Speech toolbar and listen to the entries in cell A1 and then across the column headings in the row. After you hear the entry Sale Price in cell E2, click the Stop Speaking button.

3. Click the By Columns button and then click the Speak Cells button again and listen to the entries in the cell range A3:A7.

Notice how the mechanical voice, called LH Michael (LH stands for Lerner & Hauspie, the folks who created the voice), pronounces the contents of cell A3 as "twelve to three hundred five" rather than "twelve dash three hundred five" (the program interprets the dash as indicating a range).

4. After LH Michael finishes speaking "retail price one thousand three hundred ninety-nine" in cell C7, click the Stop Speaking button again.

5. Click the Start button on the Windows taskbar and then click Control Panel on the Start menu.

6. Click the Sounds, Speech, and Audio Devices link followed by the Sound link (if your Control Panel is in Classic view, simply double-click the Speech icon) and then click the Text to Speech tab to display its options in the Speech Properties dialog box.

7. Select LH Michelle in the Voice Selection drop-down list and listen to her voice preview before you select OK.

8. Click the Speak Cells and listen to LH Michelle say the remaining entries in the data table. When she's finished speaking, click the Stop Speaking button.

In addition to listening to entries already made in a spreadsheet, you can have Text to Speech read back each entry as you make it. Try this in a scratch worksheet in a blank workbook.

9. Open a new blank workbook by clicking the New button on the Standard toolbar.

10. Click the Speak on Enter button on the Text to Speech toolbar (upon which LH Michelle tells you that "cells will now be spoken on Enter." Make the following entries down column A:

- Northeast Consortium in cell A1.
- Alfred E. Neuman in cell A2
- -89.45 in cell A3
- CD-ROM in cell A4
- 95-11-0034 in cell A5
- 415-555-0023 in cell A6
- 3678.6 in cell A7
- May 12, 2006

11. Close the blank workbook without saving your Speak on Enter text entries to the scratch worksheet; then click the Speak on Enter button to turn off this feature before you close the Text to Speech toolbar. Close the *Exercise4-7.xls* workbook without saving your changes.

Figure 4-3:
The Advanced tab of the File Search dialog box enables you to search for workbooks using summary information.

Speak Cells

Speak on Enter

By Rows

By Columns

Stop Speaking

Deleting and Inserting Data and Cells

Deletions in a worksheet are a little more complicated than in other software programs. This is because Excel gives you a choice between deleting only the cell entry, leaving intact the cell structure and all assigned formatting attributes; clearing the cell of all its contents without disturbing its structure; and removing the cell structure along with everything its contains, causing remaining cell entries in neighboring cells to adjust to fill in the gap:

- Press the Delete key to remove only the entry in the current cell.

- Choose Edit⇨Clear⇨All to remove the entry in the current cell plus all formatting attributes and comments.

- Choose Edit⇨Delete and then choose between the Shift Cells Up and the Shift Cells Left options to remove the cell along with all its contents, formatting, and comments and to adjust remaining cells in rows below up or in columns on the right to the left.

The Insert⇨Cells command is the opposite of Edit⇨Delete. You use it to insert blank cells in regions where you need to squeeze in data entries that were somehow left out. In the process of squeezing in these blank cells, you can have Excel shift existing entries down to rows below or to columns to the right.

You can delete and insert entire rows and columns from the worksheet by selecting the Entire Row and Entire Column option in the Delete or Insert dialog box or by selecting the rows and columns in the column and row header in the worksheet and then selecting Edit⇨Delete or Insert⇨Columns or Insert⇨Rows commands.

Be very cautious about deleting *or* inserting entire rows or columns in any worksheet, especially one that you didn't create or are not that familiar with. You can easily take out vital data in tables and lists located in unseen regions of the worksheet when doing a deletion. Inserting new columns and rows can be almost as dangerous, however, as your insertions can just as well corrupt the accuracy or even disrupt the functionality of the formulas in these unseen tables and lists. To stay on the safe side, constrain your cell deletions and insertions to just the cell ranges in the region you're working in.

Try It

Exercise 4-8: Deleting and Inserting Cells in the Spreadsheet

Open the *Exercise4-8.xls* workbook file in the Chapter 4 folder inside your My Practice Spreadsheets folder or in the Excel Workbook folder on the workbook CD-ROM. This file contains a copy of a House Sales table that you can use to practice deleting and inserting cells and cell entries.

1. Select cell C4 with the selling price of the house on Elm Street and delete just this entry by pressing the Delete key.

2. Enter **1250000** in now blank cell C4.

Because you only deleted the contents in cell C4, Excel applies the remaining Currency style number format with no decimal places to the new entry you made so it immediately appears as $1,250,000 in the cell.

3. Delete everything in cell C4 by choosing Edit⇨Clear⇨All.

4. Enter **735000** in the now blank cell C4.

This time, Excel does no number formatting to the 735000 value because you cleared the cell of formatting plus contents.

5. Use the Format Painter to restore the Currency style number format with no decimal places to cell C4.

Position the cell cursor in cell C5 that still contains this Currency number formatting. Click the Format Painter button on the Standard toolbar and then click cell C4 to copy just the formatting from cell C5.

6. Select the cell range A5:C5 listing a house sale on Apple Drive.

7. Choose Edit➪Delete and then leave the default Shift Cells Up option button selected as you choose OK.

Excel removes the cells in the selected cell range A5:C5 while at the same time pulling up the data in the rows below so that there are no gaps in the table.

8. Click the Undo button on the Standard toolbar or press Ctrl+Z to restore the deleted cell range.

9. Leave the cell range A5:C5 selected and then choose Insert➪Cells. Leave the default Shift Cells Down option button selected as you select OK.

Excel inserts three blank cells above the Apple Drive sales information, shifting the remaining entries in this table down. If you're using Excel 2002 or 2003, you'll note the appearance of the Insert Options button at the Fill handle in the lower-right corner of the extended cell cursor: You display its drop-down button by positioning the mouse pointer over the button and then use its options to copy cell formatting from the cells in the row below (it automatically uses the formatting in the cells in the row above) or to clear all formatting from the newly inserted cells.

10. Make the following entries in the new, empty cell selection, A5:C5:

- The address, **500 King Street,** in cell A5
- The selling date, **4/2/2006,** in cell B5
- The selling price, **820000,** in cell C5

11. Select cell A1 and then save your editing changes to the House Sales table in a new workbook named *Solved4-8.xls* in your Chapter 4 folder inside the My Practice Spreadsheets folder.

Moving and Copying Data and Cells

Excel provides two methods for moving and copying a cell selection (along with their contents and formatting) to a new place in the same worksheet. You can either use

- ✔ Drag-and-drop to manually take the selection or a copy of it with the mouse pointer and drop it into its new place in the sheet
- ✔ Cut and paste to cut or copy the selection to the Windows Clipboard and then paste it into its new position after moving the cell cursor to the first cell of that range

Keep in mind that you must use the cut-and-paste method to move or copy cell ranges from one worksheet to another in the same workbook or from one workbook to another.

When using the cut-and-paste method, you can select what part of the cut or copied data is transferred when pasting it into their new position in the worksheet or workbook. You do this by selecting the Edit⇨Paste Special command and then selecting the appropriate Paste option in the Paste Special dialog box (see Table 4-1).

Table 4-1	The Paste Options in the Paste Special Dialog Box
Paste Option	**What It Does**
All	Pastes all types of entries (numbers, formulas, and text), their formats, and comments from the selection in the paste area
Formulas	Pastes only the entries (numbers, formulas, and text) from the selection in the paste area
Values	Pastes only numbers and text from the selection in the paste area, converting all formulas to their current calculated values so they're pasted into the worksheet as numbers
Formats	Pastes only the formats from the selection into the paste area
Comments	Pastes only the comments from the selection into the paste area
Validation	Pastes only the entries in cells that use data validation into the paste area
All Except Borders	Pastes everything but the borders assigned to the cell selection into the paste area
Column Widths	Pastes everything into the paste area and adjusts the column widths in this area to match those of the original cell selection
Formulas and Number Formats	Pastes only the formulas and number formatting (omitting all text and numeric entries) from the cell selection into the paste area
Values and Number Formats	Pastes only the numbers and number formatting (omitting all text and converting all formulas to their calculated values) from the cell selection into the paste area

Use the Transpose check box in the Paste Special dialog box to transpose the data in the table so that data that used to run across the columns now run down the rows, and vice versa.

Try It

Exercise 4-9: Moving and Copying Cells in the Spreadsheet

Open the *Exercise4-9.xls* workbook file in the Chapter 4 folder inside your My Practice Spreadsheets folder or in the Excel Workbook folder on the workbook CD-ROM. This file contains a formatted copy of the Production Schedule table that you can use to practice moving and copying cells and their data entries. Note that this copy of the spreadsheet contains the range name prod_table assigned to the cell range A1:J7 that you can use to select its cells:

1. Select the table's cells (A1:J7) and then use drag-and-drop to move it so that it now occupies the range B8:K14.

Position the white-cross mouse pointer somewhere on the bottom edge of the extended cell cursor and then when the pointer changes to an arrowhead, drag the selected range of cells to its new position.

When the ToolTip at the bottom of the outline representing the cell selection you're moving reads B8:K14, release the mouse button to drop it in place.

2. Use AutoFit to widen columns B, E, and H so that their column headings can be displayed in their cells.

3. Use drag-and-drop to copy the table you've just moved to the cell range B8:K14 to the cell range B19:K25.

Hold down the Ctrl key as you drag the outline of the copy of the selected cell range to its new position in the worksheet.

4. Cut the copy of the Production Schedule table in the cell range B8:K14 to the Clipboard by clicking the Cut button on the Standard toolbar, or press Ctrl+X.

Excel responds by putting a marquee around the cell selection B8:K14 and displaying Select Destination and Press ENTER or Paste on the status bar.

5. Make Sheet2 active, and then move the cell cursor to cell B2 and press Enter.

The moment you press the Enter key, Excel moves the table to the cell range B2:K8 on Sheet2 of the workbook.

6. Switch back to the Schedule sheet and select cell A1.

Excel deselects the cell range B8:K14 on the Schedule sheet that used to contain the table you moved to the B2:K8 on Sheet2.

7. Select the cell range B8:K14 containing the original Production Schedule table by selecting its range name, prod_table, on the Name Box button's drop-down list.

Note how a range of cell entries retains its range name even after you've changed all of its cell references in a workbook.

8. Click the Copy button on the Standard toolbar or press Ctrl+C to copy the cell selection, B8:K14 to the Windows Clipboard.

9. Select cell B17, and then choose Edit⇨Paste Special to open the Paste Special dialog box. Select the All Except Borders Paste option in this dialog box and then select OK.

Excel makes a copy of the table without the borders that divide the table's row and column headings from their data.

10. Select the range B22:K22 with the Part 103 units in the copy of Production Schedule table.

11. Use drag-and-drop to move this cell range up three rows (so that the row with the Part 103 units is in row 19, right below the column headings in row 18).

Excel displays an alert dialog box the moment you release the mouse, asking you if you want to replace the contents of the destination cells.

12. Select the Cancel button in the alert dialog box to abort the move.

13. Repeat the move of the cell selection B22:K22, this time holding down the Shift key as you drag upward.

Holding down the Shift key as you drag a cell selection ensures that Excel automatically shifts existing cell entries out of the way so that you don't inadvertently replace them. Excel indicates that the range will be inserted by representing the moved range as a horizontal or vertical I-beam rather than as an outline.

14. When the extended horizontal I-beam appears between rows 18 and 19 and the ToolTip reads B19:K19, release the mouse button.

This time Excel inserts Part 103 data entries at the top of the table without any warnings.

15. Use drag-and-drop with the Shift key to complete the reordering of the rows of data in the copy of the Production Schedule table so that cell range B20:K20 contains the Part 102, B21:K21 the Part 101 data, and B22:K22 the Part 100 data.

16. Relocate the two Production Schedule tables that now exist on the Schedule Sheet up so that the original table now in cell range B8: K14 occupies the cell range A1:J7 and the copy you made in cell range B17:K23 occupies the range A10:J16.

17. Select cell A1, and then save your work in a new workbook in your Chapter 4 folder in the My Practice Spreadsheets folder with the filename *Solved4-9.xls*. Close this workbook.

Using Notes in the Spreadsheet

Excel makes it easy to attach notes to the cells of a spreadsheet. You can use these notes (officially called comments in the program) to remind yourself or your coworkers of changes that need to be made in the spreadsheet or data that needs to be reviewed and verified.

The key to adding and managing notes in a worksheet is the first section on the left side of the Reviewing toolbar. This section (identified in Figure 4-4) contains all the buttons you need to add, edit, delete, display and hide, and move from comment to comment in the worksheet.

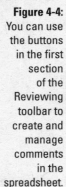

Figure 4-4: You can use the buttons in the first section of the Reviewing toolbar to create and manage comments in the spreadsheet.

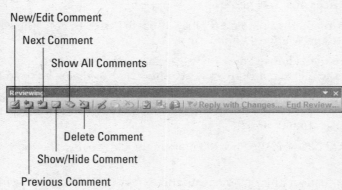

New/Edit Comment
Next Comment
Show All Comments
Delete Comment
Show/Hide Comment
Previous Comment

Try It

Exercise 4-10: Adding Comments to the Spreadsheet

Open the *Exercise4-10.xls* workbook file in the Chapter 4 folder inside your My Practice Spreadsheets folder in My Documents on your hard disk (or in the Excel Workbook folder on the workbook CD-ROM). This file contains a copy of the Employee list that you can use in practicing how to use comments in a spreadsheet:

1. Display the Reviewing toolbar by choosing View➪Toolbars➪Reviewing and then dock the floating toolbar on the right side of the worksheet (so that Comment-related buttons appear vertically, one on top of the other).

To dock a floating toolbar, drag it by its title bar to any of the four sides of the Excel worksheet and then, when the title disappears, drop it into place.

To undock a toolbar drag it by the dotted line that appears in front of the initial button and then when its title bar reappears, drop it onto the Excel program window.

2. Select cell J2 and then click the New Comment button on the Reviewing toolbar.

Excel responds by inserting a new text box with an arrow pointing to cell J2 containing your name.

3. Type **Verify this employee's status** as the text of this comment.

4. Resize the text box, making it wide enough for all the comment text to appear on a single line of the box and short enough that there's no longer lines of empty space below the text.

To resize a text box, position the mouse pointer over one of the eight sizing handles that appear as circles at the four corners and midpoints around the perimeter of the box. When the mouse pointer changes into a double-header arrow, drag the sides of the box until it is the size and shape you want (note that Excel automatically reflows the text in the box to accommodate these changes).

5. Select cell E6 and then add a comment to this cell reminding you to change Cindy's department from Accounting to Human Resources as of 01-01-07.

6. Move the text box for this comment you add to cell E6 so that the box no longer obscures cell entries in the Employee list by locating to the right somewhere in the blank columns of K, L, and M in the worksheet.

To move a text box, position the mouse pointer anywhere on the outline of the box outside of the eight sizing handles and then drag the outline of the box until it is positioned to the desired place in the worksheet.

7. Select cell F20 and then add a note to this cell reminding you to verify Miriam's salary and then resize to remove its unused space and reposition the comment's text box outside of the list in the empty columns K, L, and M.

8. Position the cell cursor in cell A1, and then position the mouse pointer over each of the three cells, J2, E6, and F20 that now contain comments.

Note that positioning the mouse pointer over a cell with a comment causes that comment's text box to be displayed. Also note that each of these three cells now contains a tiny red triangle in the upper-right corner, indicating that the cell has a comment attached to it.

9. Click the Show All Comments button on the Reviewing toolbar.

Note this button is a toggle switch that shows or hides all the comments in a worksheet.

10. Hide all three comments and then click the Next Comment button on the Reviewing toolbar to display each of the three comments in succession.

11. When you reach the last comment attached to cell F20, double-click the border of the text box to open the Format Comment dialog box.

12. Select the text of the comment and then change the comment text to 9-point Arial bold italic and the fill color of the text box to Gray-25%.

Normally, Excel only shows the comment indicator (that red triangle) except when you select a cell or engage the Show All Comments toggle button on the Reviewing toolbar. You can, however, change the comments display option so that the program always shows the comments added to the worksheet.

13. Select the Comment & Indicator option button on the View tab of the Options dialog box (Tools⇨Options) and then select OK.

As soon as you close the Options dialog box, all three comments are displayed in the worksheet. The only way to remove them from view (other than restoring the Comment Indicator Only default setting) is to click the Hide All Comments button on the Reviewing toolbar (which replaces the Show All Comments button).

Hide all the comments along with the Reviewing toolbar and then save this version of the Employee list with your notes with the filename *Solved4-10.xls* in your Chapter 4 folder in the My Practice Spreadsheets folder. Now close the workbook.

Using Find and Replace and Spell-Checking

Just like Microsoft Word, Excel is equipped with a Find, Find and Replace, and Spell-checking feature that you can use in editing your spreadsheets:

- **Find** (Ctrl+F) enables you to search for and locate text or values in the spreadsheet that potentially need changing.

- **Find and Replace** (Ctrl+H) enables you select whether or not Excel replaces one set of text or values it locates in the spreadsheet with another set that you specify.

- **Spelling** (F7) to catch and correct spelling errors using either the built-in dictionary or custom dictionary you build.

Keep in mind when using Find and Find and Replace to locate entries in the spreadsheet that you can change any of the following search options to refine the search. You can use the

- **Within** drop-down list box to choose between Sheet (the default) to look for the search text only in the cells of the current worksheet or Workbook to search the cells on all the sheets in the workbook.

- **Search** drop-down list box to choose between By Rows (the default) to conduct the search across the rows and then down the columns of the worksheet or By Columns to conduct the search down each column and then across each row.

- **Look In** drop-down list box to choose among Formulas (the default) to look for matches to the search text in the entries as they appear on the Formula bar, Values to look for matches in the entries as they appear in the cells of the worksheet, or Comments to look for matches in the comments added to the cells of the worksheet.

- **Match Case** check box to match the upper- and lowercase spelling in the cell entries with the search text.

- **Match Entire Contents** check box to match the entire contents of a cell with the search text.

- **Format** button to specify formatting that the cell or cell entries must match.

Try It

Exercise 4-11: Editing with Find and Replace and Spell Checking

Open the *Exercise4-11.xls* workbook file in the Chapter 4 folder inside your My Practice Spreadsheets folder in My Documents on the hard disk (or in the Excel Workbook folder on the workbook CD-ROM). This file contains a number of numeric (variations of 2500 and a variety of dates in 2006) and text (different Italian pastas, yum!) cell entries that you can use to practice using the Find, Find and Replace, and Spell-checking features in Excel:

1. Open the Find and Replace dialog box with the Find tab selected (Ctrl+F) and then enter **25?** in Find What text box. Continue to select the Find Next button to locate all the matches in the Find, Replace & Spell worksheet, and Excel returns the cell cursor to the cell with the first match.

You can use the wildcard characters, ? (question mark) or * (asterisk), to stand for missing characters in the search text. Note that Excel considers the 2500 entered in cells A2, D2, and D5 as matches but not the 2500 that's displayed in cell A7. This is because the 2500 in cell A7 is the calculated result of the formula =A5+A6 and not a static value entered on the Formula bar.

2. Click the Options button to display the search options and then select Values on the Look In drop-down list, and then select the Find All button to display the locations of all the cells with matching entries.

This time, Excel considers the 2500 calculated in A7 as well as those entered into cells A2 and D5 as matches. However, when Values is set as the Look In search option, the program no longer considers the $2,500.00 in D2 with its Currency Style number formatting as a match.

3. Select Comments in the Look In drop-down list and then select the Find Next button.

Excel jumps the cell cursor to cell C12 in the spreadsheet.

4. Position the mouse pointer over cell C12 and verify that the comment attached to this cell contains the value 25.

5. Modify the search text in the Find What text box slightly by adding a comma between the 2 and the 5 so that this text box now contains **2,5?**. Now select Values in the Look In drop-down list again before you select the Find All button.

Now, Excel considers only the $2,500.00 in D2 as a match, as none of the other 2500s have a comma between the 2 and 5 as these entries appear in the cells of the Find, Replace & Spell worksheet.

6. Modify the search text in the Find What text box again by prefacing 500 with a question mark wildcard character so that this text box now contains **?500**. Then, select the Find All button.

This time, Excel includes all the cells containing 2500 (including the $2,500.00 in cell D2) as matches as well as the 1500 entered into cell A6.

7. Select the Match Entire Cell Contents check box under Find search options before you select the Find All button.

When the Match Entire Cell Contents check box is selected, the $2,500.00 in cell D2 is no longer considered to be a match because of the decimal point and two zeros that trail the 500 (the question mark wildcard only pertains to characters that precede 500).

8. Select the Replace tab in the Find and Replace dialog box and then set up the following conditions:

- Position the cell cursor in cell A1 of the Find, Replace & Spell worksheet.
- Enter **25** in the Find What text box on the Replace tab.
- Enter **27** in the Replace With text box on the Replace tab.
- Deselect the Match Entire Contents check box on the Replace tab.

9. Use the Find and Replace feature to change the date May 25, 2005 in cell A17 to May 27, 2005.

Select the Find Next button until you locate the occurrence of the search text (25 in this case) that you want to replace and then (and only then) select the Replace button.

10. Select the 2005 Prod Sch worksheet and then use the Find and Replace feature to globally update the years in all the dates in the spreadsheet from 2005 to 2006.

Enter **2005** in the Find What text box and **2006** in the Replace With text box and then select the Replace All button — Excel then displays an alert dialog box indication the number of replacements.

Be extra careful with performing global replacements, as you can all too easily wreak havoc in the spreadsheet at the click of the Replace All button — should you make a major boo-boo with this feature, remember to hit the Undo button to with all due haste.

11. Rename the 2005 Prod Sch worksheet to 2006 Prod Sch by editing its sheet tab.

12. Close the Find and Replace dialog box and then select the Find, Replace & Spell worksheet and use Excel's Spelling Checker to check the spelling of the Italian pasta text entries (F7).

The unknown spelling occurs with Fetticine in cell E10. This is a misspelling, so you must change it.

13. Accept the Spelling Checker's suggestion of Fettuccine by clicking the Change button.

The second unknown spelling occurs with Maccaroni in cell E12. This is also a misspelling, so you must change it.

14. Accept the Spelling Checker's suggestion of Macaroni by selecting the Change button.

The third unknown spelling occurs with Capellini in cell C14. This is a correct spelling so you can either ignore it or add it to the dictionary.

15. Add the word to the dictionary by selecting the Add to Dictionary button.

16. Close the dialog box indicating that the spelling check is complete, and then select cell A1 and save this version of with the filename *Solved4-11.xls* in your Chapter 4 folder inside the My Practice Spreadsheets folder.

Group Editing

Group editing enables you to save time by making the same editing changes to multiple sheets in the workbook at the same time. To put Excel in Group Edit mode, all you have to do is select all the sheets in the current workbook that you want to edit together — Excel indicates that a workbook is in Group Edit mode by appending [Group] to its filename on the Excel program window's title bar.

Q. How do I select individual, nonadjacent worksheets to be included for group editing?

A. Ctrl+click the sheet tab of each worksheet you want to include in the group.

Q. How can I quickly select all the sheets in a workbook for group editing?

A. Right-click one of the sheet tabs and then select the Select All Sheets item on the shortcut menu.

Q. How can I easily take the workbook out of group-editing mode?

A. Click any single visible sheet tab on the status bar other than the one for the active worksheet (indicated by the sheet tab name in bold lettering).

Try It

Exercise 4-12: Editing Different Worksheets as a Group

Open the *Exercise4-12.xls* workbook file in the Chapter 4 folder inside your My Practice Spreadsheets folder or on the Excel Workbook CD-ROM. This version of the CG Media Sales workbook file contains three worksheets, 2004 Sales, 2005 Sales, and 2006 Sales, that you can use to practice group editing:

1. Quickly examine each of the three worksheets by clicking their sheet tabs in succession and then return to the first sheet, 2004 Sales.

2. Select all three worksheets for group editing.

To select a group of adjacent worksheets, hold down the Shift key as you click the tab of the last sheet in the group (2006 Sales in this case) — note the appearance of [Group] after the workbook's filename on the Excel program window's title bar.

3. Apply the Accounting 3 table AutoFormat to CG Media – 2004 Sales by Category and Date table without applying its font setting, and then the narrow column A to 22.14 characters (160 pixels).

Click the Options button in the AutoFormat dialog box and then deselect the check boxes for all the formats you don't want to change (Font, in this case) before clicking the preview of the AutoFormat (Accounting 3, in this instance) and then selecting OK.

4. Select the 2005 Sales worksheet and then the 2006 Sales worksheet to verify that they now share the same table formatting as the 2004 Sales sheet.

Note that the moment you click the sheet tab of the 2005 Sales worksheet, Excel automatically takes the workbook out of Group mode.

5. Regroup the three worksheets, 2004 Sales, 2005 Sales, and 2006 Sales, and then make the column headings in the cell range B2:R2 bold and the column headings in the range A3:A15 right-aligned and bold.

6. Take the workbook out of Group mode, and then select cell A1 on the 2004 Sales sheet. Next save the modified workbook under the filename *Solved4-12.xls* in your Chapter 4 folder inside the My Practice Spreadsheets folder and close the workbook.

Part II
Using Formulas and Functions

The 5th Wave   By Rich Tennant

Spreadsheet Creation .50¢ - Min.

In this part . . .

Formulas and spreadsheets go together like cake and ice cream, and the chapters that make up Part II are full of exercises that you give you a chance to create formulas of almost every flavor. Here, you get a taste of every kind of function that Excel has to offer. You also have an opportunity to practice building and copying the types of basic formulas that are a sure recipe for success in any spreadsheet you create.

Chapter 5

Building Formulas

*N*o one disputes that formulas are the center of almost every spreadsheet you create. Being able to build formulas (both those that perform simple arithmetic calculations as well as those that perform more sophisticated computations using Excel's built-in functions) is a critical skill. The exercises in this chapter give you a chance to practice building both types of formulas as well as modifying how and when the formulas in the spreadsheet are recalculated.

Building Formulas

All the formulas you build in an Excel spreadsheet regardless of their function and degree of complexity have one thing in common: They all begin with one simple character, = (the equal to sign). Typing an equal to sign activates the Insert Function, Enter, and Cancel buttons on the Formula bar. It also changes the nature of the Name Box drop-down box so that its list displays commonly used functions rather than the range names assigned to the workbook.

If you forget to type this as your initial character when creating formulas by hand (Excel is always sure to put one in for you when you build formulas with the Insert Function button), the program inserts the string of operands and operators you enter as a text reference.

If you build a legitimate formula, Excel either computes the answer and displays it in the current cell in the worksheet or, if unable to successfully calculate the answer, the program displays one of the following error values in the cell:

✔ **#NULL!** appears when your formula specifies an intersection of two ranges that do not, in fact, intersect.

✔ **#DIV/0!** appears when your formula attempts to divide by zero.

✔ **#VALUE!** appears when your formula contains some sort of improper argument type or operand (such as a text entry when the operator requires a value).

✔ **#REF!** appears when your formula contains an improper cell reference.

✔ **#NAME?** appears when your formula contains a text reference that Excel doesn't recognize (such as a reference to a range name that no longer exists in the workbook)

✔ **#NUM!** appears when your formula contains invalid numeric values (such as a text entry where a number is required)

✔ **#N/A** appears when your formula refers to a value that is not available to it

Building formulas by hand

To build a formula by hand, all you have to do is type an = (equal to) sign and then designate the string of operands and operators that the formula should use in making its calculation(s). Operands can be constants that you type into the formula (such as 5.5 or 100), or they can be cell references (such as B5 or A10:J17) that you point directly to in the worksheet or type.

Table 5-1 shows you a list of all the operators, including their type, character, and operation.

Table 5-1	The Different Types of Operators in Excel Formulas		
Type	*Character*	*Operation*	*Example*
Arithmetic			
	+ (plus sign)	Addition	=A2+B3
	- (minus sign)	Subtraction or negation	=A3-A2 or -C4
	* (asterisk)	Multiplication	=A2*B3
	/	Division	=B3/A2
	%	Percent (dividing by 100)	=B3%
	^	Exponentiation	=A2^3
Comparison			
	=	Equal to	=A2=B3
	>	Greater than	=B3>A2
	<	Less than	=A2<B3
	>=	Greater than or equal to	=B3>=A2
	<=	Less than or equal to	=A2<=B3
	<>	Not equal to	=A2<>B3
Text			
	&	Concatenates (connects) entries to produce one continuous entry	=A2&" "&B3
Reference			
	: (colon)	Range operator that includes all cells between the colon	=SUM(C4:D17)

Type	Character	Operation	Example
	, (comma)	Union operator that combines multiple references into one reference	=SUM(A2,C4:D17,B3)
	(space)	Intersection operator that produces one reference to cells in common with two references	=SUM(C3:C6C3:E6)

Try It

Exercise 5-1: Building Arithmetic Formulas

If Excel's not already running, launch the program. Use the first two blank worksheets of the Book1 workbook to create a practice spreadsheet that gives you experience in building various types of simple arithmetic formulas by hand:

1. Rename Sheet1 of the worksheet **Formulas** and Sheet2, **Ext Ref**.

2. Group the Formulas and Ext Ref sheets together and then increase the worksheet display magnification percentage for the two sheets to 175%.

3. Ungroup the two worksheets, enter **42** in cell A2, and then name this cell **source**.

4. Select cell A4, type = (equal to sign) to start a new formula, and click cell A2.

The formula you're in the process of entering into cell A4 now reads =*source*, both in the cell and on the Formula bar. A marquee showing the cell named *source* is displayed in cell A2.

5. Click the Enter button (the one with the check mark) on the Formula bar to complete the formula entry in cell A4.

The formula in cell A4 now returns 42 as its answer — this formula consists solely of an external reference to cell A2, the cell you named *source,* so whatever value you enter into the source cell is immediately brought forward and *dynamically* copied to cell A4.

6. Update the value in cell the source cell, A2, from 42 to **128**.

Because the link between cell A4 and A2 was created by your formula with the external reference, cell A4 of the worksheet now contains 128 as well.

7. Enter the following values into the designated cells of the Formulas worksheet:

- **34** in cell B4
- **47.5** in cell B5
- **2.2** in cell B6
- **10%** in cell B7
- **3** in cell B8

8. Create an addition formula in cell C4 that adds the value in cell A4 to that in cell B4 by pointing to these cells:

- Position the cell cursor in cell C4
- Type =
- Press ← twice to select cell A4 (the first operand)

- Type + (the addition operator)

- Press the ← one time to select B4 (the second operand)

- If the formula reads =A4+B4, click the Enter button on the Formula bar

9. Use this same pointing technique to create an addition formula in cell A5 that adds 5 to the value in cell A4 above.

The addition formula in cell A5 should read =A4+5 on the Formula bar and the answer should appear as 133 in the cell.

10. With the cell cursor in cell A5, drag the Fill handle down to the cell range A6:A8.

Excel copies the original formula you entered into cell A5 down to cells A6, A7, and A8, which now contain the calculated values, 138, 143, and 148, respectively.

11. Build the following arithmetic formulas in the designated cells:

- Subtraction formula in cell C5 that subtracts the value in cell B5 from that in cell A5 — remember that - (hyphen or dash) is the subtraction operator in Excel.

- Division formula in cell C6 that divides the value in cell A6 by that in B6 — remember that / (forward slash) is the division operator in Excel.

- Multiplication formula in cell C7 that multiplies the value in cell A7 by that in B7 — remember that * (asterisk) is the multiplication operator in Excel.

- Exponentiation formula in cell C8 that raises the value in cell A8 by that in cell B8 — remember that ^ (caret) is the exponentiation operator in Excel.

12. Save your workbook with the filename *Practice Formulas.xls* in the Chapter 5 folder inside the My Practice Spreadsheet folder, and then open *Solved5-1.xls* and compare your results before proceeding to Exercise 5-2.

Arithmetic formulas in the spreadsheet (when properly formed) always return numeric results. Excel supports another type of formula, known as a comparative formula, which returns only one of two possible results, TRUE or FALSE. Exercise 5-2 gives you some practice in creating these types of formulas.

Exercise 5-2: Building Comparative Formulas

Use the *Practice Formulas.xls* workbook that you created in Exercise 5-1 to get some experience with building comparative formulas:

1. Build a comparative formula in cell D4 that weighs the value in cell A4 against that in B4 and indicates whether they are equal to each other:

- Type = in cell D4 to begin the formula

- Press the ← key three times to select cell A4

- Type = again, this time as the comparative operator

- Press the ← key twice to select cell B4 so that the formula now reads, =A4=B4

- Click the Enter button on the Formula bar to complete the formula and compute the result (which is FALSE because the values in these two cells are not currently equal to one another)

2. Build the following comparative formulas in the designated cells:

- In cell D5, a formula that compares the values in cell A5 to that in cell B5 and indicates whether the one in A5 is larger than the one in B5 — use the > (greater than) symbol as the operator.

- In cell D6, a formula that compares the values in cell A6 to that in cell B6 and indicates whether the one in A6 is smaller than the one in B6 — use the < (less than) symbol as the operator.

- In cell D8, a formula that compares the values in cell A8 to that in cell B8 and indicates whether the one in A8 is unequal to the one in B8 — use the <> (less than and greater than back to back) symbols as the operator.

3. Change the value in the source cell, A2, from 128 to **34**.

Note how Excel immediately updates all the formulas in columns A, C, and D whose computations depend in some way on this value.

4. Save your changes to your *Practice Formulas.xls* workbook before proceeding on to Exercise 5-3.

Well-designed spreadsheets contain many dependent formulas like your *Practice Formulas.xls* workbook. The problem comes when any the formulas on which they depend return one of those dreaded error values covered earlier in this chapter. When that happens, the error values spread like wildfire to all the dependent formulas, making it very difficult, if not impossible, to identify the source of the problem.

Try It

Exercise 5-3: Working with Error Values in Formulas

Use your *Practice Formulas.xls* workbook to get some experience with the error values that formulas can return and how they infect all dependent formulas in a spreadsheet:

1. Open the Define Name dialog box (Insert⇨Name⇨Define) and then click Source in the list box before you select Delete and OK.

As soon as you click OK to close the Define Name dialog box, most of the cells in this spreadsheet contain the #NAME? error value because every formula you created in this worksheet is dependent in some way upon the *source* range name, inheriting this error value from the original formula in cell B4 with the external reference the moment you delete its name.

2. Use Undo to restore the *source* range name to the workbook and get rid of those awful #NAME? error values in the spreadsheet.

3. Now, delete the value (2.2) in cell B6 and see what effect this has on the division formula in cell C6.

As soon as you empty cell B6, a #DIV/0! error value is returned by the division formula in cell C6. This is because all empty cells in any Excel worksheet carry the value of zero, and this is why #DIV/0! is the most common type of error value to plague spreadsheets. Often, a template or new spreadsheet you create contains division formulas referring to empty cells for which you do not have or have not yet entered values. These all naturally return #DIV/0! error values (in Chapter 12, you find out how to create formulas using the IF function that prevent such formulas from returning this type of error value).

4. Use Undo to restore the original 2.2 value to cell B6 and remove the #DIV/0! error value from cell C6; in cell B7, enter the text **ten percent** to see what effect this has on the multiplication formula entered in cell C7.

Although it's possible to build formulas that deal with text, the one in cell C7 is not one of them. When you enter **ten percent** as a text entry in cell B7, its formula essentially chokes, returning the #VALUE! error value to the cell.

5. Use Undo to restore the original 10% value to cell and then press Ctrl+~ (tilde) to display the formulas in the cells of the worksheet.

Remember that you can always use the Ctrl+~ (tilde) key combination to display the formulas in your spreadsheet in their cells in the worksheet (very valuable for verifying its functioning). Check the contents of your formulas against those shown in Figure 5-1.

6. Press Ctrl+~ again to return the worksheet to its normal display wherein all formulas display their results in the worksheet and their contents on the Formula bar when the cell cursor is in their cells.

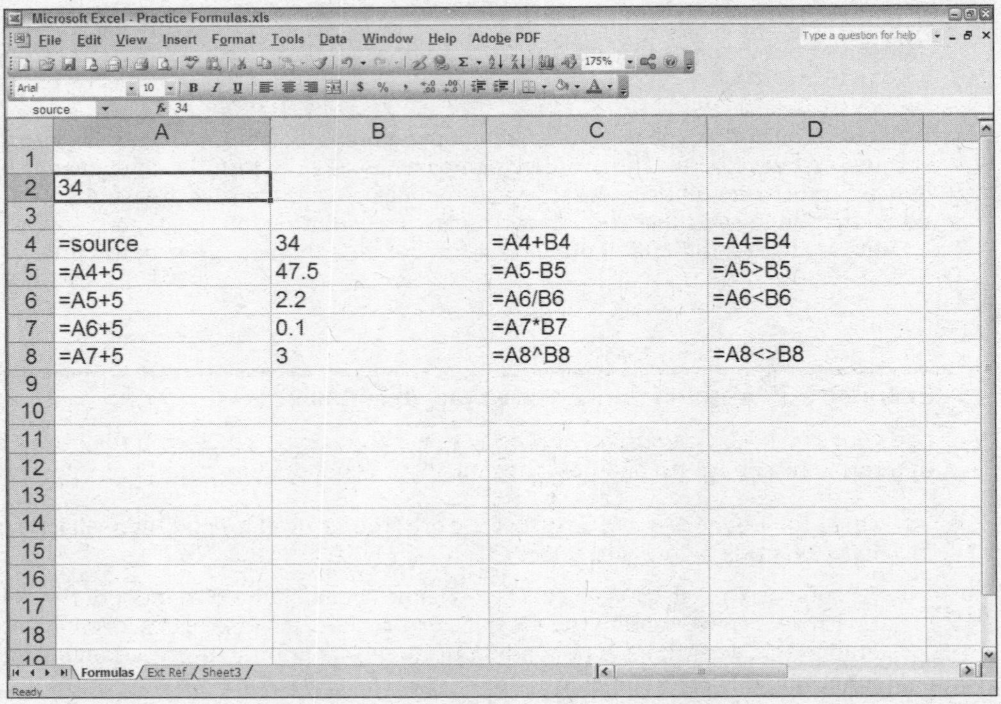

Figure 5-1:
Practice Formulas.xls with all its formulas displayed in their cells.

Building formulas with built-in functions

Excel offers you a wide assortment of built-in functions that can save valuable time in creating the formulas needed in your spreadsheet. In place of the operands and operators of your handmade formulas, built-in functions use function names and arguments. All the Excel functions follow the general syntax of the SUM function, the most widely used spreadsheet function:

```
=SUM(number1,number2, . . .)
```

Note the following about this syntax in this example:

✔ The function name is always shown in all caps because Excel automatically displays it that way on the Formula bar regardless of what case you use in entering its name. (This means that there are no case restrictions when typing in the function name — you just have to be careful to spell its name correctly.)

✔ The argument(s) used by the function immediately follow the function name and they are enclosed in a balanced pair of parentheses — this means that for every open parenthesis [(], you need a close parenthesis [)].

✔ The functions that require or can take more than a single argument separate the individual arguments within the parentheses with commas.

Even functions such as NOW that take no arguments require the use of a pair of parentheses to finish them off; for example, =NOW(). If you omit the empty pair of parentheses, Excel fails to recognize the function and returns the #NAME? error value to its cell.

Excel classifies each of its built-in functions into one of nine categories (with a tenth being custom functions that you define yourself), all of which are available from the Insert Function dialog box, which you open by clicking the Insert Function button on the Formula bar (the one with the *fx* marking).

Building a formula that uses a built-in function with the Insert Function dialog box carries many benefits. Besides starting your formula by automatically entering the requisite = (equal to) symbol on the Formula bar for you, this dialog box, shown in Figure 5-2, contains the following features that aid you in locating and using any function:

✔ **Search for a Function** enables you to look for a function by entering a brief description of the kind of calculation you want to do.

✔ **Or Select a Category** enables you to find a function by selecting a category (Financial, Date & Time, and so on) other than the default Most Recently Used that keeps a record of the most commonly used functions, including the ones you've used most recently.

✔ **Select a Function** enables you to display syntax information showing you the arguments plus a short description of any function you select in this list box.

✔ **Help on This Function** displays online help (that you can also print) about the usage and arguments required by the function currently selected in the Select a Function list box.

As soon as you select your function in the Insert Function dialog box by selecting it and clicking OK, Excel not only inserts the skeleton of the function on the Formula bar but also displays a Function Arguments dialog box for the function, which you can use in selecting the cell references and values to be used in the computation.

Figure 5-2:
The Insert Function dialog box directs you in correctly adding any Excel function to a formula in the spreadsheet.

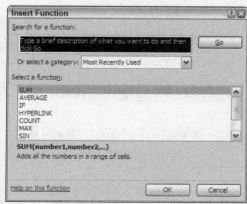

Q. Can I mix built-in functions with handmade formulas?

A. Yes, most definitely: Excel functions can serve as operand in any formula that you construct manually, as in =SUM(A5:J10)^2 to square the total of the range of values in the cell range A5:J10 of the worksheet returned by the SUM function.

`Try It`

Exercise 5-4: Building Formulas with AutoSum

Use your *Practice Formulas.xls* workbook to get some experience using the SUM, AVERAGE, and COUNT functions in the spreadsheet. These functions are so frequently used that Excel doesn't even require you to access them from the Insert Function dialog box, making them readily available from the AutoSum button on Standard toolbar:

1. Drag through the cell range A4:A8 to select all their values in the Formulas worksheet of your *Practice Formulas.xls* workbook.

Note that the AutoSum indicator on the Status bar immediately shows you that the total of the values in this range is 220 (Sum=220).

2. Right-click the AutoSum indicator and then select Average on its pop-up menu.

The AutoSum indicator on the Status bar changes to Average=44.

3. Return the AutoSum indicator to its default Sum setting and then click cell A9 to place the cell cursor in this cell and deselect the range A4:A8.

4. Click the AutoSum button on the Standard toolbar (the one with sigma _ on it).

Excel immediately responds by entering the SUM formula, =SUM(A4:A8) in cell A9. Note that the program also places a marquee bounding box around the cell range A4:A8 in the worksheet as well as selects the argument A4:A8 in the SUM function itself. This enables you to modify the range or ranges of cells to be totaled by the SUM function either by editing its argument in the function or dragging the boundaries of its marquee.

5. Click the Enter button on the Formula bar to complete this formula in cell A9.

Excel enters the formula, =SUM(A4:A8) in this cell as shown on the Formula bar and displays the total of the range, 220, in the cell.

6. Click the drop-down button attached to the AutoSum button on the Standard toolbar and then select Average on its drop-down list.

Excel now enters the formula =AVERAGE(A4:A8) for your editing or approval in cell A9.

7. Click the Enter button on the Formula bar to enter this formula in the cell.

Excel enters the formula =AVERAGE(A4:A8) in this cell as shown on the Formula bar, and displays the total of the range, 44, in the cell.

8. Use Undo to restore the SUM formula in cell A9 and then use the Count option on the AutoSum drop-down list to create a formula in cell B9 that returns the number of values in the range B4:B8.

The formula you construct in cell B9 should read =COUNT(B4:B9) and this formula should return 5 as its result.

9. Replace the value 10% in cell B7 with the text entry, **ten.**

Ignoring the reappearance of the #VALUE! error in cell C7 for the moment, note that the result returned to cell B9 changes from 5 to 4, indicating that the COUNT function counts *only* the numeric entries in the cells you include in its argument.

10. Restore 10% to cell B7 with Undo, position the cell cursor in cell C9, and click the Insert Function button on the Formula bar.

11. Move the Insert Function dialog box to the right out of the way of the values in your spreadsheet. Click SUM in the Select a Function list box before you select OK.

12. Drag through the cell range A4:A8 to replace the default Number1 argument of C4:C8 with this range.

Note how Excel automatically condenses the Function Arguments dialog box down to just the text box for the Number1 argument as you drag through the cell range and then immediately restores the dialog box the moment you release the mouse button.

13. Press Tab or click the Number2 argument text box and then drag through the cell range B4:B8 to select this range as the second to be included in the total.

Note that as soon as you select the Number2 argument text box, Excel adds a Number3 text box to the Function Arguments dialog box.

14. Designate the cell range C4:C8 as the third argument in the Number3 argument text box.

Note that the Function Arguments dialog box shows the subtotals of each of the three ranges you've selected immediately following their respective argument text boxes and that the Formula bar now contains the whole SUM formula ready for insertion into cell C9:

```
=SUM(A4:A8,B4:B8,C4:C8)
```

15. Select OK to close the Function Arguments dialog box and enter the SUM formula into cell C9.

16. Save your changes to the *Practice Formulas.xls* workbook file.

Editing formulas

Editing a formula, especially one that uses a function with multiple arguments, can take a little getting used to. Fortunately, Excel makes formula editing within the cells of the worksheet as easy as it can by isolating the ranges and displaying them in different color bounding boxes when you put the program in Edit mode.

The only problem comes when you're dealing with a formula so complex and long that its contents can't be displayed within the worksheet display. Fortunately, on the rare occasion when this occurs, you can still edit the formula on the Formula bar as it automatically expands its rows to accommodate the extra length.

Try It

Exercise 5-5: Editing Formulas in the Spreadsheet

Use your *Practice Formulas.xls* workbook to get some experience with formula editing. In this exercise, make changes to the SUM formula you previously constructed in cell C9 that totals the three ranges A4:A8, B4:B8, and C4:C8:

1. Position the cell cursor in cell C9 and then press F2 to put Excel into Edit mode.

Excel responds by displaying the contents of the SUM formula in cell C9 of the worksheet. The addresses of each of the cell ranges in the three arguments of this SUM function appear in a different color and each of these colors corresponds to that of the bounding box that encloses its cell range in the worksheet.

2. Use the ← to move the insertion point through the arguments in the SUM function until the insertion point is flashing between the 8 in the A8 and the comma that follows the first A4:A8 argument.

Note as you move the insertion point to the left through the SUM function how the syntax for the SUM function appears right below it and how Excel displays the Number3, Number2, and finally the Number1 argument in bold as the insertion point travels through the cell range in the equivalent argument in the function above.

3. Hold down the Shift key as press the ← key to select and highlight the range A4:A8 (from right to left).

4. Redefine the Number1 argument by dragging through the cell range A2:A8 in the worksheet.

A moving marquee appears in the cells you select as you redefine the cell range for the Number1 argument in the SUM function.

5. Check the formula on the Formula bar in cell C9 to make sure that cell range for the Number1 argument of the SUM function is now A2:A8. Next click the Enter button to complete the editing of the formula in cell C9.

6. Apply the Comma style format with two decimal places to cell C9 (widen column C to display the value in this new number formatting, if necessary).

7. Save your editing changes to the formula in cell C9 in the *Practice Formulas.xls* workbook file.

Altering the natural order of operations

When you build a formula that combines different operators, Excel follows the order of precedence shown in Table 5-2. When you use operators that share the same precedence level, the program performs the calculations designated computations on the operands in a strictly left-to-right order.

Table 5-2	Natural Order of Operator Precedence in Formulas	
Precedence	*Operator*	*Type/Function*
1	–	Negation
2	%	Percent
3	^	Exponentiation
4	* and /	Multiplication and Division
5	+and –	Addition and Subtraction
6	&	Concatenation
7	=, <, >, <=, >=, <>	All Comparative Operators

Sometimes, you need to override the natural order of precedence in order to get your formula to return the desired result. To override the natural order, you enclose the operand and operator of the operation you want performed first in parentheses.

For more complicated formulas, you may end up nesting sets of parentheses one within the other in order to obtain the desired computation order. When this is the case, Excel always performs the calculation within the inmost set of parentheses working its way out according the sequence shown in Table 5-2.

Exercise 5-6: Changing the Order in Which Formulas Are Calculated

Use your *Practice Formulas.xls* workbook to construct several new formulas and then experiment with adding parentheses to see what effect they have on the computed results:

1. Enter the following values in designated cells in the Formulas worksheet in your *Practice Formulas.xls* workbook:

- **100** in cell B11
- **50** in cell C11
- **2** in cell D11

2. Position the cell cursor in cell E11 and construct and enter the following formula:

```
=B11+C11/D11
```

Instead of an answer of 75, Excel returns one of 125 because it performs the division between cell C11 and D11 (50/2=25) with its higher level of precedence of 4 before doing the addition between cell B11 and C11 (100+25) with its lower precedence level of 5.

3. With the cell cursor in cell E11, press F2 to put Excel in Edit mode.

4. Press the ← key until the insertion point is located between the = and the B in B11, and then type (press the → key until the insertion point is between the second 1 in C11 and the / and then type).

The edited formula should appear as follows in cell C11:

```
=(B11+C11)/D11
```

5. Click the Enter button on the Formula bar to complete the edit of the formula in cell E11.

After the addition of the parentheses, the formula returns the result of 75, showing that it now performed the addition between cell B11 and C11 first (100+50) and then divided that result by the value in D11 (150/2).

6. Enter the following values in designated cells:

- **300** in cell A13
- **200** in cell B13
- **100** in cell C13
- **2** in cell D13

7. Position the cell cursor in cell E13 and construct and enter the following formula:

```
=A13+B13-C13/D13
```

Note that Excel returns a result of 450 when you enter this formula because, following the natural order of precedence, it performs the computations as follows:

- C13/D13 or 100/2 = 50 to cell C13
- A13+B13 or 300 + 200 = 500 to cell B13
- B13-C13 or 500 − 50 = 450 to cell E13

8. Use pairs of parentheses to alter the computation order in the formula in E13 so that Excel performs the subtraction between cells B13 and C13 first, adds this result to the value in cell A13, and then finally divides the result of that addition by the value in D13, giving you a final result of 200.

When editing this formula, begin by enclosing the first operation to be performed inside a pair of parentheses (B13-C13), and then enclose the second operation in second pair of parentheses, (A13+(B13-C13)) so that the edited formula appears as

```
=(A13+(B13-C13))/D13
```

9. With the cell cursor in cell E13, display all the formulas in the cells of the worksheet, reducing the display magnification percentage as needed so that you can see all the formulas on your screen. (Check your results against those shown in Figure 5-3.)

Note that in this display mode, when the cell cursor is in a cell that contains a formula, Excel employs the same type of color coding as it does when you edit a formula in its cell. The colors assigned to the cell references within the formula correspond to that of the bounding box surrounding the actual cell or cell range in the worksheet.

10. Use the arrow keys to move the cell cursor to other cells in this spreadsheet that contain formulas, including cell C9.

11. Turn off the display of the formulas in the worksheet and then save your changes to your *Practice Formulas.xls* workbook.

Using External Reference Links

External references in a formula are those that refer to cells outside of the current worksheet, either on other sheets of the same workbook file or in sheets in other workbook files. Because their cells reside outside of the current worksheet, it isn't sufficient to specify the cell reference only, as you do with purely local cell references.

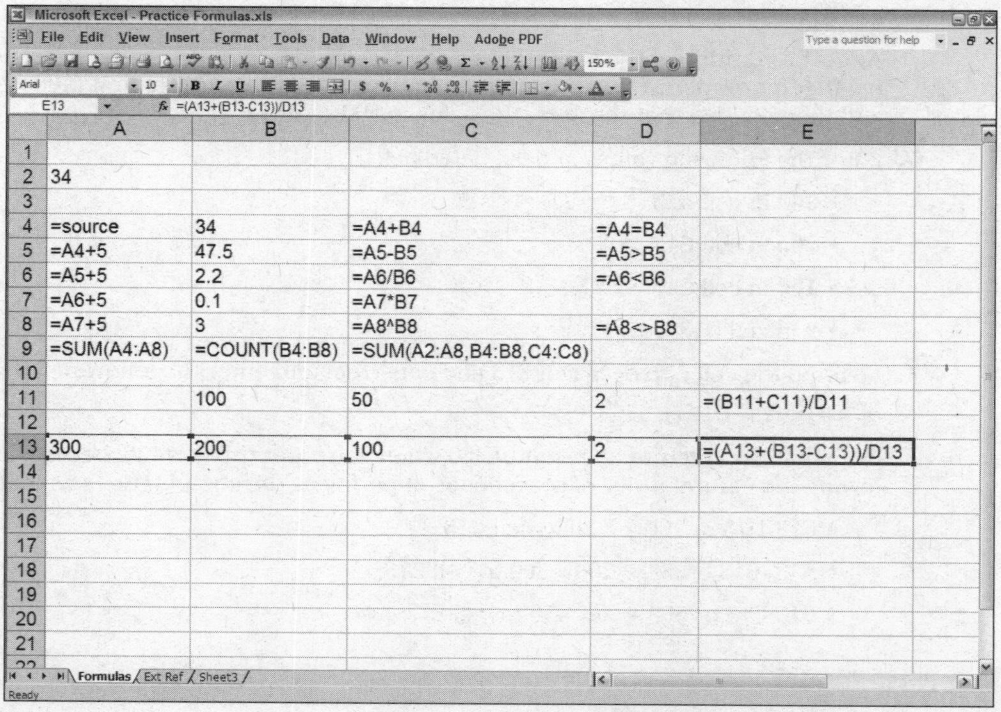

Figure 5-3:
The Formulas sheet of the *Practice Formulas.xls* workbook, with all its formulas displayed in the worksheet.

	A	B	C	D	E
1					
2	34				
3					
4	=source	34	=A4+B4	=A4=B4	
5	=A4+5	47.5	=A5-B5	=A5>B5	
6	=A5+5	2.2	=A6/B6	=A6<B6	
7	=A6+5	0.1	=A7*B7		
8	=A7+5	3	=A8^B8	=A8<>B8	
9	=SUM(A4:A8)	=COUNT(B4:B8)	=SUM(A2:A8,B4:B8,C4:C8)		
10					
11		100	50	2	=(B11+C11)/D11
12					
13	300	200	100	2	=(A13+(B13-C13))/D13
14					

Microsoft Excel - Practice Formulas.xls

File   Edit   View   Insert   Format   Tools   Data   Window   Help   Adobe PDF

E13   =(A13+(B13-C13))/D13

Formulas / Ext Ref / Sheet3 /

Ready

When you refer to a cell that resides in another worksheet of the same workbook, you preface the cell address with the sheet name separated by an exclamation point (!), following this syntax:

```
Sheet1!A1
```

When you refer to a cell that resides in a sheet in another workbook file, you need to include the filename (enclosed in square brackets) as well as the sheet name and cell reference, following this syntax:

```
'[file.xls]Sheet1'!A1
```

Many times, you use external references to create a link to values in another sheet that need to be brought forward to the new worksheet. When you set up a link rather than just pasting in a static value, any changes made to the value in the original cell is automatically updated in the linked cell.

The easiest way to create an external reference link is by copying the cell to the Clipboard (Ctrl+C) and then pasting it with the Paste Special command (Edit⇨Paste Special) using its Paste Link button.

Try It

Exercise 5-7: Building Formulas with External Links

Use your *Practice Formulas.xls* workbook to get experience with constructing links using external references:

1. Position the cell cursor in cell C9 of the Formulas worksheet that contains the SUM formula totaling the values in the cell ranges A2:A8, B4:B8, and C4:C8 and then copy the value in this to the Clipboard (Ctrl+C).

2. Switch to the Ext Ref worksheet in the workbook and then position the cell cursor in cell B3 of this sheet.

3. Choose Edit⇨Paste Special and then click its Paste Link button, and then use AutoFit to widen column B.

The value 157889.20 appears in cell B3 of the Ext Ref sheet and the following link formula with the external reference appears on the Formula bar:

```
=Formulas!$C$9
```

4. Enter the heading **Formulas Sheet Total** in cell A3 and, if necessary, widen column A of the Ext Ref sheet sufficiently to display the entire heading.

5. Switch back to the Formulas worksheet and then change the value in the source cell A2 of this sheet from 34 to **56**.

Note the effect that increasing this source value has on the total in cell C9 of this worksheet.

6. Switch to Ext Ref worksheet, position the cell cursor in cell B3, and verify that cell B3 in this worksheet now contains the same value as C9 in the Formulas worksheet, thanks to the linking formula you created there.

7. Open a new blank workbook and then enter the heading **Practice Formulas Workbook Total** in cell A2, widen column A to display the entire heading, and then increase the display magnification percentage to 200%.

8. Save the workbook file with the filename **External Link.xls** in your Chapter 5 folder in the My Practice Spreadsheets folder.

9. Switch to the *Practice Formulas.xls* workbook and then copy the value in cell B3 of the Ext Ref worksheet to the Clipboard (Ctrl+C).

10. Switch to the new *External Link.xls* workbook, select cell B2 of Sheet1, choose Edit⇨Paste Special, and then click its Paste Link button.

The value 439,589.40 appears in cell B2 of the Sheet1 worksheet and the following link formula with the external reference appears on the Formula bar:

```
='[Practice Formulas.xls]Ext Ref'!$B$3
```

11. Save your changes to the *External Link.xls* workbook and then close this file.

12. Select cell A2 in the Formulas sheet in the *Practice Formulas.xls* and then update the value in this cell from 56 to **72**.

13. Check that the contents in cell B3 of the Ext Ref sheet have been updated to 779,438.27 to reflect the change to the value in cell C9 of the Formulas sheet. Now save your changes to the *Practice Formulas.xls* workbook before you close it.

14. Open the *External Link.xls* workbook by selecting it from the File pull-down menu.

As soon as this file opens, Excel displays an alert dialog box, informing you that this workbook contains links to other sources.

15. Select the Update button in Excel alert dialog box to have the program update the value in cell B2 of Sheet1 to 779,438.27.

Note that the external reference displayed on the Formula bar now contains the entire pathname for the workbook file along with its sheet and cell reference.

16. Save your changes to the *External Link.xls* workbook and then close this file.

Controlling When Formulas Are Recalculated

As you've seen in the exercises in this chapter, Excel immediately and automatically recalculates all the formulas in a worksheet the moment you make a change to any cell that referred to in its formulas. This automatic recalculation mode is fine as long as your spreadsheet is relatively small and your edits to it are few.

Working in this mode can, however, be a real drag (both literally and figuratively) when the worksheet is large and contains lots and lots of formulas: You may be forced to wait quite a few seconds while Excel recalculates every loving formula before you can do anything more after each and every editing change you make.

To avoid this hassle, change the recalculation mode from automatic to manual on the Calculation tab of the Options dialog box (Tools⇨Options) so that Excel recalculates the formulas in the worksheet only when you specifically tell it to by selecting its Calc Now(F9) or Calc Sheet button or when you save changes to the worksheet.

Try It

Exercise 5-8: Controlling When Formulas Are Recalculated

Open your *Practice Formulas.xls* workbook in the Chapter 5 folder inside the My Practice Spreadsheets folder and use it to get some experience using Excel in both automatic and manual recalculation mode:

1. Update the value in cell A2 of the Formulas sheet from 72 to **102**.

Verify that Excel has automatically recalculated the formulas in both your Formulas and Ext Ref worksheets and that cell C9 on the Formulas sheet and B3 on the Ext Ref sheet now both contain the same value: 1,816,854.91.

2. Select the Manual option button on the Calculation tab of the Options dialog box (Tools⇨Options).

3. Update the value in cell A2 of the Formulas sheet from 102 to **144**.

Note that none of the calculated values in the Formulas sheet have been updated (C9 still contains 1,816,854.91) and that the Calculate indicator has now appeared on the Status bar.

4. Select the Calc Sheet button on the Calculation tab of the Options dialog box.

Note that Excel recalculates the formulas on the Formulas worksheet and that cell C9 now contains the value 4,412,310.20, but that the Calculate indicator has not disappeared from the Status bar. Then, switch to the Ext Ref sheet and note that the linked formula in cell B3 has not been updated and still contains the value 1,816,854.91.

5. Press F9 to have Excel recalculate all the formulas in the entire workbook.

Note that not only does cell B3 of the Ext Ref worksheet now contains the updated value 4,412,310.20, but that the Calculate indicator has now disappeared from the Status bar.

6. Switch back to the Formulas worksheet, and then update cell A2 to **165.88** before you press F9.

Check to make sure that all the formulas on both sheets of the workbook have now been updated by verifying that both cell C9 in the Formulas sheet and B3 in the Ext Ref sheet now contain 6,423,962.85.

7. Update cell A2 in the Formulas worksheet to 188 and then save this change to the *Practice Formulas.xls* workbook.

Note that Excel not only saves your change to cell A2 in *Practice Formulas.xls* workbook file, but also recalculates the formulas using this new value and then saves these updated values as well.

8. Save a copy of this workbook file under the filename **Solved5-8.xls** in your Chapter 5 folder inside the My Practice Spreadsheets folder.

Note that any changes you make to the recalculation mode are saved as part of the workbook file, so that they are in effect the next time anyone opens the file for editing.

Chapter 6

Copying and Correcting Formulas

. . . .

In This Chapter

▶ Copying formulas with relative cell references

▶ Copying formulas with absolute cell references

▶ Copying formulas with mixed cell references

▶ Using range names in formulas

▶ Creating array formulas

▶ Tracing and eliminating formula errors

▶ Dealing with circular references in a formula

. . . .

Copying an original formula to all the cells in the worksheet that perform the same type of computation is one of the more common tasks you perform as part of creating a new spreadsheet. Despite this fact, understanding just how Excel goes about adjusting the cell references when you copy a formula is not widespread among new users. The exercises in this chapter give you a chance to practice copying formulas using all the different types of cell references. In addition, you practice assigning range names to the cells that are referenced in spreadsheet formulas, creating array formulas that do away with the need for making formula copies, as well as tracing and eliminating the source of errors that have spread across the workbook.

Copying Formulas with Relative References

When your original formula uses cell references rather than constant values (as most should), Excel makes copying that formula to every place that requires the same type of computation a complete no-brainer. The program does this by automatically adjusting the cell references in the original formula to suit the position of the copies you make. It does this through a system known as *relative cell addresses*, whereby the column references in the cell address in the formula change to suit their new column position, and the row references change to suit their new row position.

Excel indicates that a cell reference is relative simply by stating its column letter and row number without preceding either part of the reference with a $ (dollar sign), the symbol denoting an absolute reference, as in A1 or BC457.

Exercise 6-1: Copying Formulas in the R1C1 Reference Style

If Excel isn't running, launch the program. Open the *Exercise6-1.xls* workbook file in your Chapter 6 folder in the My Practice Spreadsheets folder inside My Documents on your hard disk or on the Excel Workbook CD-ROM. This file contains a copy of the 2006 Production Schedule table without any formulas:

1. Position the cell cursor in cell K3 and use the AutoSum button to create a SUM formula that totals the Part 100s scheduled to be produced over the nine-month period from April to December in row 3.

AutoSum creates the following master formula in cell K3:

```
=SUM(B3:J3)
```

2. Use the Fill handle on the cell cursor to copy this formula down column K to the cell range K4:K7.

3. Position the white-cross mouse pointer on the Fill handle of the cell cursor and then, when the AutoFill Options drop-down button appears, click it. Select the Fill without Formatting item at the bottom of the drop-down list that appears (doing this restores the border along the top edge of cell K7 that Excel took out when copying the formatting from cell K3 to this range).

Now, take a moment to examine the copies you made of the original SUM formula in cell K3 by using the arrow keys to move the cell cursor through each cell K4, K5, K6, and K7. What do you note that is different in each copy of the formula and what is the same?

To help you understand what Excel is really doing when you make copies of a formula containing relative cell references down the rows of a column, turn on the R1C1 Reference system. In this system, both the rows and columns of the worksheet are given numbers so that the cell reference A1, for example, becomes R1C1 (because column A is the first column from the left edge of the worksheet) and cell D6 becomes R6C4 (because column D is the fourth column from the left edge of the worksheet).

4. Select the R1C1 Reference Style check box on the General tab of the Options dialog box.

You can tell you are "not in Kansas anymore" using the familiar row number, column letter reference type system — all the columns are now numbered from left to right just as the rows are from top down.

5. Position the cell cursor in cell K3 and examine the contents of the original SUM formula on the Formula bar.

In R1C1 notation, the formula entered in this cell now reads:

```
=SUM(RC[-9]:RC[-1])
```

The first thing to note about cell references in formulas in R1C1 notation is that they are completely egocentric; always referring to the cell that contains the formula (they could care less about the worksheet at large). This formula says, in essence, "Use the SUM function to total from the cell that is nine columns to the left of the current column through the cell that is one column to the left all in the same row." The minus sign in front of the number following the column reference denotes columns to the left of the current one just as the minus in front of a number following a row reference denotes rows above (positive integers in these references denote columns to the right and rows below the current one).

6. Press the ↓ key to move the cell pointer down column K through all the cells, K4, K5, and K6 that contain copies of the formula you constructed in cell K3, noting the contents of each copy on the Formula bar as you move the cursor down a row.

You will note that each and every cell in this column contains the exact same formula:

```
=SUM(RC[-9]:RC[-1])
```

Excel hasn't really adjusted anything in any of the formula copies you made! It's all a convenient fiction (that's fancy talk for a big lie) to say that Excel adjusts the relative row and column references in formula copies because that's the way it *appears* to work when the program is in its normal row number, column letter reference system. (Now that I've let you in on this little secret, just keep it under your hat.)

7. Position the cell cursor in cell R7C2 (erstwhile B7) and use AutoSum to construct a SUM formula that totals the part numbers scheduled to be produced in April, 2006.

This formula in R1C1 notation appears on the Formula bar as follows:

```
=SUM(R[-4]C:R[-1]C)
```

8. Use the Fill handle to copy this formula across the rest of the columns of the table to the range R7C3:R7C10 (C7:J7).

Verify that each of the copies in all these cells contains the identical formula in R1C1 notation as you constructed in cell B7, that is, R7C2.

9. Restore the old tried-and-true row number and column letter notation system by removing the check mark from the R1C1 Reference Style check box on the General tab of the Options dialog box.

10. Move the cell cursor across the cell range B7:J7, noting how Excel adjusts the column reference (in standard notation) and then up and down the cell range K3:K7, noting how the row reference changes.

11. Save this workbook under the filename **Solved6-1.xls** in your Chapter 6 folder inside the My Practice Spreadsheets folder on your hard disk and then close the workbook.

Copying Formulas with Absolute References

Absolute cell references, as their name implies do not change for nobody or nothing. A truly absolute reference firmly roots both the row and row reference (as opposed to a mixed reference that just plants either the row number or the column letter, but not both). This type of reference comes in handy when you need to refer to a cell that contains a value that acts like a constant that must remain unchanged in all formula copies.

Excel indicates that a cell reference is absolute by preceding both its column letter and row number with a $ (dollar sign), the symbol denoting an absolute reference, as in $A$1 or $BC$457. When building or editing a formula, you can convert a relative cell reference that contains the insertion point simply by pressing the F4 key.

Try It

Exercise 6-2: Copying a Formula with Absolute Cell References

Open the *Exercise6-2.xls* workbook file in your Chapter 6 folder in the My Practice Spreadsheets folder inside My Documents on your hard disk or on the Excel Workbook folder on the workbook CD-ROM. This file contains a copy of the 2006 Production Schedule table with all the formulas you created and copied in Exercise 6-1 for totaling the units to be produced by month across the columns and by part down the rows. In this exercise, you add a row of formulas that computes what percentage each monthly production quota represents of the projected nine-month total:

1. Enter the heading **% of Total** in cell A9 of the 2006 Prod worksheet. Now position the cell cursor in cell B9 and use AutoFit to widen column A so that this new heading is completely displayed in its cell.

2. Construct a formula in cell B9 that divides the April 2006 quota in cell B7 by the projected total in cell K7 and then format the cell with the Percent Style number format with two decimal places.

The formula in this cell should read:

```
=B7/K7
```

3. Use the Fill handle to copy the original formula you constructed in cell B9 to the cell range C9:J9.

Something is clearly wrong with the copies, as they all contain those dreaded #DIV/0! error values rather than the desired percentages.

4. Position the cell cursor in cell C7 to examine the formula that Excel copied there.

The formula in this cell reads:

```
=C7/L7
```

When Excel made the first copy, the program not only adjusted the column reference for the monthly quota (from B7 to C7) but for the projected total as well (J7 to L7), and because L7 is empty, the copy is, in essence, trying to divide by zero (all empty cells carry a zero value), thus the division error value.

To prevent this problem with the copies (and to correct it), in the original division formula, the divisor, K7, with the projected total must be an absolute cell reference (as in $K$7), so that it remains constant in all the copies in which Excel naturally adjusts the dividend (that is, the amount to be divided) containing the various monthly production quotas.

5. Position the cell cursor back in cell B9 with the original formula and then press F2 to put Excel in Edit mode.

6. Press F4 to convert the cell reference from the relative K7 to absolute $K$7 and then click the Enter button on the Formula bar.

7. Use the Fill handle to copy this edited version of the original formula in cell B9 to the cell range C9:J9.

That's more like it! This time all the formula copies return realistic percentages in place of those awful division errors.

8. Position the cell cursor in cell A1 of the 2006 Prod worksheet and then save the workbook with the filename **Solved6-2.xls** in your Chapter 6 folder inside the My Practice Worksheets folder before you close the workbook.

Copying Formulas with Mixed References

Just as you'd expect, mixed cell references are those that mix relative and absolute references in a cell. A mixed cell reference can either have the row reference absolute and column relative (as in A$3) or the column reference absolute and the row relative (as in $A3).

You can convert a cell reference you're entering or editing in a formula to either type of mixed reference by pressing F4 as follows:

✔ **First** time to convert the cell reference from completely relative to completely absolute (C5 to $C$5)

✔ **Second** time to convert from completely absolute to a mixed reference with the row absolute and the column relative ($C$5 to C$5)

✔ **Third** time to convert from a mixed reference with the row absolute and the column relative to one with the column absolute and row relative (C$5 to $C5)

✔ **Fourth** time to convert from a mixed reference with the column absolute and row relative back to a completely relative reference ($C5 to C5)

You only need to resort to mixed cell references in an original formula when you intend to copy this formula to empty cells in two directions; that is, both down the rows and then over the columns to the right or over to columns on the right and then down the rows, *and* need to prevent Excel from adjusting either the column letter or the row number reference in all the copies.

Exercise 6-3 gives you practice in constructing a loan payment table that requires just this kind of two-dimensional formula copying. To create this payment table, you need to copy an original formula using the PMT function, the arguments of which require all the different types of cell references (including both types of mixed cell references) in order for all the copies to refer to the correct cells.

Try It

Exercise 6-3: Creating a Loan Table with Mixed Cell References

Open a new workbook in Excel and use its blank Sheet1 worksheet to create this loan payment table. This table uses the PMT function to compute the monthly mortgage payments for a sequence of different loan amounts (principals) and interest rates. The PMT function is a Financial type function that requires three arguments: *Rate,* which is the interest rate per payment period, *Nper,* which is the number or payment periods for the loan, and *Pv,* which is the present value or loan amount (the function also accepts two other optional arguments that you won't need to use in this exercise).

You begin by entering the table headings and the three initial values (loan amount, term of the loan, and interest rate) to be used to generate the sequence of the different loan amounts and interest rates as well as in the construction of the original PMT formula that you then copy in two dimensions to the rest of table:

1. Enter the following headings in the designated cells and then widen column A to suit with AutoFit:

- **Loan Payment Table** in cell A1

- **Initial Principal** in cell A2

- **Starting Interest Rate** in cell A3

- **Loan Period** in cell A4

2. Enter the following values in the designated cells and format them as indicated:

- **400000** in cell B2 formatted with the Currency Style format with zero decimal places

- **3%** in cell B3 formatted with two decimal places

- **30** in cell B4 formatted with the Number format with zero decimal places

3. Create a formula in cell A7 that dynamically copies the initial principal value entered in cell B2 to this cell.

To create a dynamic link between the value in one cell and another cell in the same worksheet, type = to start the formula, followed by the reference of the cell with which you want the value linked.

4. Create a formula in cell A8 that adds 1000 to the value in cell A7 and then use the Fill handle to copy this formula down the rows to the cell range A9:A16.

5. Create a formula in cell B6 that dynamically copies the initial interest rate entered in cell B3 to this cell.

6. Create a formula in cell C6 that adds 0.25% to the value in cell B6, reduce the number of decimal places to two, and then use the Fill handle to copy this formula across the columns to the cell range D6:G6.

7. Position the cell cursor in cell B7 to build the original PMT formula and then click the Insert Function button on the Formula bar.

8. Type **loan payment** in the Search for Function text box in the Insert Function dialog box and then press Enter to search for the PMT function.

9. With the PMT function highlighted in the Select a Function list box, select OK to close the Insert Function dialog box and open the Function Arguments dialog box.

10. Move the Function Arguments dialog box to the right, out of the way.

The first argument to specify is the Rate argument, for which you will select cell B6 that is linked to the starting interest rate in cell B3. Note that you must consider what part of this cell reference, if any, should be adjusted when you copy this formula down the rows of this table (from 7 through 16) and then across the columns (from B through G) and adjust its reference accordingly.

Note that when you copy the PMT formula down the rows of the table, you definitely do *not* want Excel to adjust the row number because all of the interest rates are in row 6, meaning that this part of the cell reference must be absolute. When you then copy the PMT formula to columns on the right, you do, however, need the column letter to be adjusted in order to pick up the quarter percentage point entered into the succeeding columns in row 6, so you do need to keep this part of the cell reference relative. Therefore, for this argument, you need to convert B6 from its completely relative reference to the mixed cell reference, B$6 (column adjusted but not the row).

In addition, because the starting interest rate you enter into cell B3 and bring forward to cell B6 is a *yearly* rate and the PMT function calculates the *monthly* payment, you need to divide this yearly interest amount by 12 so that the Rate argument represents a monthly portion.

11. With the insertion point in the Rate text box, click cell B6 to select and enter its reference, and then press F4 twice to convert it to the mixed reference, B$6, before you type **/12** before you press Tab.

B$6/12 now appears in the Rate argument text box.

The Nper argument picks up the single loan period value entered in cell B4. Because this value acts a constant in the table, all the loan payments calculated by the PMT function refer to it. Therefore, this reference has to be completely absolute, $B$4, so that Excel adjusts neither its column letter nor its row number in any of the copies. In addition, because this period is in years (30 years to begin with), you need to multiple it by 12 so that the PMT function is dealing with the total number of months.

12. With the insertion point in the Nper text box, click cell B4, and then press F4 once to convert its reference to $B$4. Type ***12** before you press Tab.

$B$4*12 now appears in the Nper argument text box.

The last required argument is the present value or loan amount for which you will select cell A7 that is linked to the initial principal entered into cell B2. When you copy the PMT formula down the rows of column B, you want Excel to adjust the row number so that it picks and uses the increased principals (that increment by $1,000 in each subsequent row). You do not, however, want Excel to adjust the column letter in this argument when you copy the formula to the columns to the right because all the principals are entered in only one column. Therefore, for this last PMT argument, you need a mixed cell reference of $A7 (with column reference absolute and row reference relative).

13. With the insertion point in the Pv text box, click cell A7, and then press F4 three times to convert it to the mixed reference, $A7.

Check the arguments in your Function Arguments dialog box against those shown in Figure 6-1. When each argument checks out, including the Formula Result equal to ($1,686.42), proceed to Step 14. If you discover that you need to change the type of cell reference in any argument, position the insertion pointer in that reference and press F4 until the correct mixed or absolute reference appears.

14. Select the OK button to close the Function Arguments dialog box and to complete the formula with the PMT function in cell B7, and then use the Fill handle to copy this formula down the rows of column B to cell B16.

15. With the range B7:B16 still selected by the cell cursor, use its Fill handle to copy the original PMT formula across the columns of the table to and including column G (the entire cell range B7:G16 is selected when you finish copying the formulas in the second direction across the columns).

16. Use AutoFit to widen columns C:G sufficiently to display their contents.

The results in your loan table should match those shown in Figure 6-2.

17. Change the term from 30 to **15** in cell B4 and note the increase to the monthly payments in the table, and then use the Undo feature to return the loan term to its original 30 years.

18. Put Excel into manual recalculation mode and then experiment with changing the initial principal in cell B2 to **650000** and a starting interest rate in B3 of **2.50%**. Press F9 to recalculate the monthly payments in the table.

19. Use Undo to restore the original 400000 and 3% values in cells B2 and B3, respectively, and then save your Loan Payment Table with the filename **Solved6-3.xls** in your Chapter 6 folder inside the My Practice Spreadsheets folder. Close the workbook.

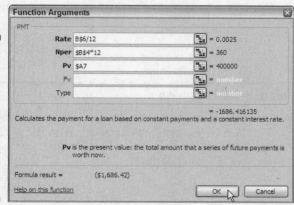

	A	B	C	D	E	F	G	H
1	Loan Payment Table							
2	Initial Principal	$ 400,000						
3	Starting Interest Rate	3.00%						
4	Loan Period	30						
5								
6		3.00%	3.25%	3.50%	3.75%	4.00%	4.25%	
7	$ 400,000	($1,686.42)	($1,740.83)	($1,796.18)	($1,852.46)	($1,909.66)	($1,967.76)	
8	$ 401,000	($1,690.63)	($1,745.18)	($1,800.67)	($1,857.09)	($1,914.44)	($1,972.68)	
9	$ 402,000	($1,694.85)	($1,749.53)	($1,805.16)	($1,861.72)	($1,919.21)	($1,977.60)	
10	$ 403,000	($1,699.06)	($1,753.88)	($1,809.65)	($1,866.36)	($1,923.98)	($1,982.52)	
11	$ 404,000	($1,703.28)	($1,758.23)	($1,814.14)	($1,870.99)	($1,928.76)	($1,987.44)	
12	$ 405,000	($1,707.50)	($1,762.59)	($1,818.63)	($1,875.62)	($1,933.53)	($1,992.36)	
13	$ 406,000	($1,711.71)	($1,766.94)	($1,823.12)	($1,880.25)	($1,938.31)	($1,997.28)	
14	$ 407,000	($1,715.93)	($1,771.29)	($1,827.61)	($1,884.88)	($1,943.08)	($2,002.20)	
15	$ 408,000	($1,720.14)	($1,775.64)	($1,832.10)	($1,889.51)	($1,947.85)	($2,007.11)	
16	$ 409,000	($1,724.36)	($1,779.99)	($1,836.59)	($1,894.14)	($1,952.63)	($2,012.03)	

B7 =PMT(B$6/12,$B$4*12,$A7)

Figure 6-2: The completed Loan Payment Table after copying the PMT function and widening the columns to suit.

Using Range Names in Formulas

In completing the exercises in Chapter 5, you got experience with assigning a range name to a cell that held a constant (named *source*) and then using that name in a linking formula. This linking formula then supplied the basic value used in most of the handmade formulas you then constructed on the worksheet.

Instead of assigning range names to constants that you actually enter into particular cells of the worksheet, you can create range names that store constant values not tied to entries in any cell. You can then paste the constant's range name into any formula that needs its value in order to successfully perform its calculations.

Another important use for range names is as identifiers of the cell references used in the operands and arguments of the formulas constructed for a typical data table. In this situation, you have Excel assign the table's row and column headings as the range names for data cells in the corresponding rows and columns. You then have Excel substitute these range names for the cell references in all the formulas in the table that refer to these data cells.

Try It

Exercise 6-4: Creating Range Names for Formulas

ON THE CD

Open the *Exercise6-4.xls* file in your Chapter 6 folder inside the My Practice Spreadsheets folder or on the Excel Workbook CD-ROM. This file contains a variation on the Spring Sale table that you can use to practice assigning a range name to a constant as well as create range names from a table's row and column headings:

1. Choose Insert⇨Name⇨Define to open the Define Name dialog box, and then type **discount_rate** (don't forget the underscore) as the range name. (This name replaces the title of the table that automatically appears as the suggested range name because its cell, A1, is selected in the worksheet.)

2. Press Tab twice to select ='2006 Spring Sale'!$A$1 in the Refers To text box, and then type **=15%** and select OK.

Excel now contains a range name called discount_rate that sets the discount percentage equal to a constant 15 percent. Note, however, that this range name does not refer to any particular cell in the worksheet.

3. Position the cell cursor in cell D3 and there construct a formula that multiplies the retail price of the table with the code number 12-305 in cell C3 by the 15% discount rate.

To insert a range name that you've defined in the workbook as an operand or function argument in a formula you're building, choose Insert⇨Name⇨Paste and then select the range name in the Paste Name list box and select OK.

4. Copy the formula that computes the amount of the discount for the table code numbered 12-305 in cell D3 down to the cell range D4:D7.

Note in each of the copies of the formula that although Excel adjusts the row number of each reference to the cell in the Retail Price column, it treats the range name, discount_rate, as an absolute reference.

5. Create a formula in cell E3 that computes the sale price of the table code numbered 12-305 by subtracting its discount amount from its retail price and then copy this formula down the cell range E4:E7.

Next, you're going to have Excel assign range names to the table cells in the range C3:E7 from the row and column headings in row 2 and column B of the Sale Table.

6. Select the cell range B2:E7 and then choose Insert⇨Name⇨Create to open the Create Names dialog box.

Note that the Top Row and Left Column check boxes are automatically selected in this dialog box, indicating that Excel will use the headings it finds in the top row (7) and the left column (B) of the current cell selection when assigning the ranges names.

7. Select OK in the Create Names dialog box to accept its default settings and close the box, and then make Sheet2 of the Exercise6-4.xls workbook active.

8. Rename Sheet2 to **Range Names,** enter the heading, **Range Name List,** in cell A1, and position the cell cursor in cell A2.

9. Choose Insert⇨Name⇨Paste and then select the Paste List button in the Paste Name dialog box.

Excel pastes an alphabetical list of range names in the cell range A2:B11. Note that this alphabetical listing the range names in the workbook is static so that you'd have to generate it again with the Paste List button were you to edit the names in this workbook and then want an up-to-date list.

10. Use AutoFit to widen column A of the Range Names sheet so that all the entries in the first column of this list are completely displayed in the worksheet.

Next, you create a new window in the *Exercise6-4.xls* workbook that enables you to compare the Sale Table in the 2006 Spring Sale and the Range Name Listing side by side on the screen.

11. Choose Window⇨New Window to create a new window in the workbook named Exercise6-4.xls:2, then choose Window⇨Exercise6-4.xls:1 to make the first window active. Finally, choose Window⇨Compare Side by Side with Exercise6-4.xls:2 to display both the Exercise6-4.xls:1 and the Exercise6-4.xls:2 window together on the screen, one on top of the other.

12. Click the 2006 Spring Sale sheet tab in the Exercise6-4.xls:1 window on the top to make the sheet with the Sale Table active in the top window and then change the magnification display percentage to 115% in the workbook.

Note that both the 2006 Spring Sale worksheet in the top window (Exercise6-4.xls:1) and the Range Names sheet in the lower window (Exercise6-4.xls:2) are affected equally by the zoom command. Also notice the appearance of the Compare Side by Side floating toolbar with its Close Side by Side button. (Your computer screen should now look like the one shown in Figure 6-3.)

Now, you're ready to apply the range names listed in the Range Name Listing on the Range Names sheet to the formulas you constructed and copied in the Sale Table in the 2006 Spring Sale worksheet.

13. Select the cell range with the formulas, D3:E7 in the Sale Table on the 2006 Spring Sale worksheet, and then choose Insert⇨Name⇨Apply to open the Apply Names dialog box.

This dialog box contains a list with all the range names you've defined in the workbook selected.

14. Select the Options button to expand the Apply Names dialog box, and then deselect the Omit Column Name If Same Column and the Omit Row Name If Same Name check boxes and select OK.

When these check boxes are selected, Excel does not bother to repeat row and column range names in the formulas. As a result, the formulas copied down the rows and across the columns of a table all end up with the same descriptions (which pretty much defeats the purpose of displaying them in the formulas in the first place).

15. Click the Close Side by Side button in the Compare Side by Side toolbar to close the second window and return to a full-screen view of 2006 Spring Sale worksheet.

16. Examine the use of the range names created from the row and column headings in all the formulas in the cell range D3:E7.

Note that the operand of each formula now includes both the row and the column range name (separated by a space that represents the Intersection operator) created from the cell's row and column heading. For example, the subtraction formula in cell E6 now reads:

```
=Buffet Retail_Price-Buffet Discount
```

This identifies the formula as subtracting the value in the cell at the intersection of the Buffet row and Discount column range names from the value in the cell at the intersection of the Buffet row and Retail_Price column range names.

17. Select cell A1 and then save your changes to this workbook with the filename **Solved6-4.xls** in your Chapter 6 folder inside the My Practice Spreadsheets folder, and then close both windows on the workbook.

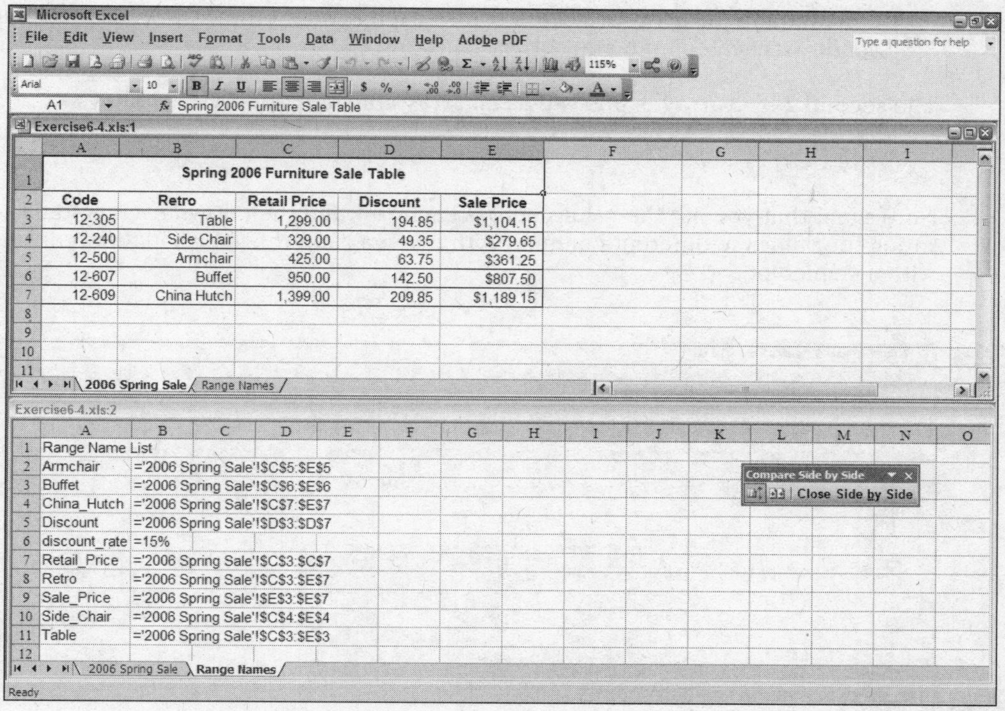

Figure 6-3: Exercise6-4. xls workbook with the 2006 Spring Sale sheet active in the top window and the Range Names sheet active in the bottom one.

Building Array Formulas

Instead of copying a formula to all the cells that perform the same type of calculation, you can build an *array formula* that performs the desired calculation not only in the active cell but in all the other cells to which you would normally copy the formula. An array formula is a special formula that operates on a range of values. If this range is supplied by a cell range (as is often the case), it is referred to as an *array range*. If this range is supplied by a list of numerical values, it is known as an *array constant*.

You are already quite familiar with arrays even though you may not realize it. This is because the Excel worksheet grid with its column-and-row structure naturally organizes your data ranges into one-dimensional and two-dimensional arrays (one-dimensional arrays take up a single row or column, whereas two-dimensional arrays take up multiple rows and columns).

Figure 6-4 illustrates a couple of two-dimensional arrays with numerical entries of two different sizes. The first array is a 3-by-2 array in the cell range B2:C4. This array is a 3-by-2 array because it occupies three rows and two columns. The second array 2-by-3 array in the cell range B6:D7. This array is a 2-by-3 array because it uses two rows in three columns. If you were to list the values in the first 3-by-2 array as an array constant in a formula, they would appear as follows:

```
{1,4;2,5;3,6}
```

Here are several things of note in this expression:

- The array constant is enclosed in a pair of braces ({}).
- Columns within each row are separated by commas (,) and rows within the array are separated by semicolons (;).

✔ Constants in the array are listed across each row and then down each column, *not* down each column and across each row.

The second 2-by-3 array expressed as an array constant appears as follows:

```
{7,8,9;10,11,12}
```

Note again that you list the values across each row and then down each column, separating the values in different columns with commas and the values in different rows with a semicolon.

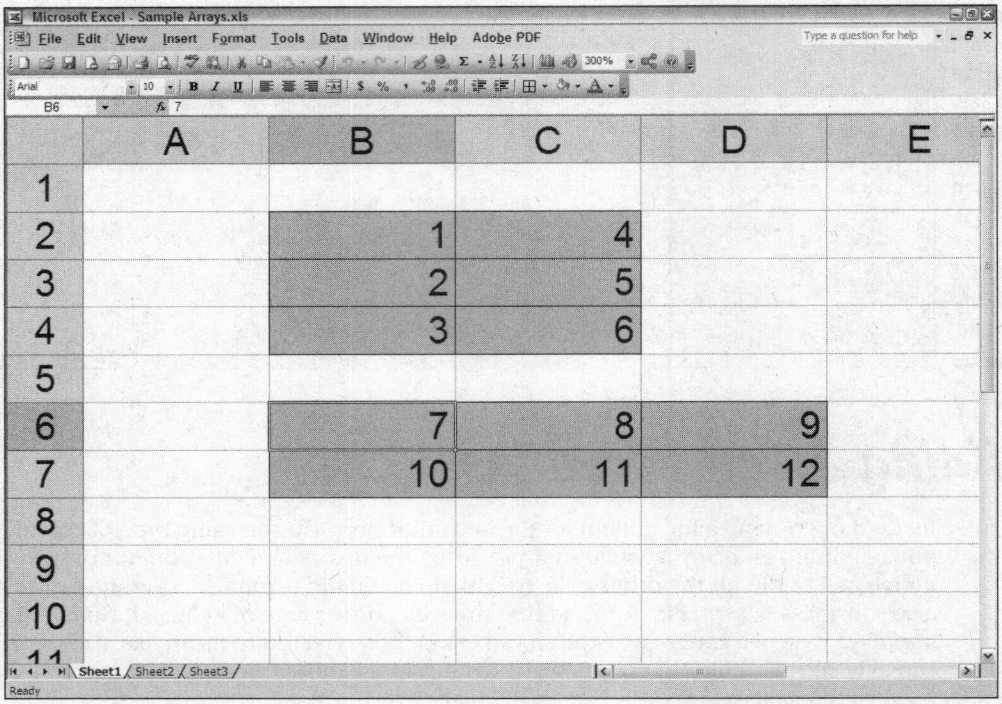

Figure 6-4:
Worksheet containing a 3-by-2 in the cell range B2:C4 and a 2-by-3 array in the cell range B6:D7.

The use of array formulas can significantly reduce the amount of formula copying that you have to do in a worksheet by producing multiple results throughout the array range in a single operation. In addition, array formulas use less computer memory than standard formulas copied in a range. This can be important when creating a large worksheet with many tables as it may mean the difference between fitting all of your calculations on one worksheet or having to split your model into several worksheet files.

Try It

Exercise 6-5: Constructing Array Formulas

Open the *Exercise6-5.xls* file in your Chapter 6 folder inside the My Practice Spreadsheets folder or on the Excel Workbook CD-ROM. This file contains a copy of the February 2006 Hourly Wage spreadsheet that you can use to practice constructing array formulas. This worksheet is designed to compute the biweekly wages for each employee by multiplying the hourly rate by the number of hours worked. Rather than create an original formula for each period that computes the wages for the first employee and then copying it down rows for all the others, do this with array formulas:

1. Position the cell cursor in cell R10 and then select the cell range R10:R13.

You are going to construct the following array formula that you then enter as a single entry into the cell range R10:R13 you just selected:

```
={A4:A7*R4:R7}
```

The range A4:A7 contains the hourly rates for all four employees, whereas the range R4:R7 contains the total hours each one worked in the first period.

2. Type = to start the array formula and then select the cell range A4:A7.

3. Type * (asterisk), the multiplication operator, and then select the cell range R4:R7.

To complete an array formula, you must press a very special key combination, Ctrl plus Shift plus Enter. This key combination lets Excel know you're constructing an array formula as well as informs it to enter this array formula into all the cells in the selected range.

4. Press Ctrl+Shift+Enter to complete the array formula and enter it into the selected range R10:R13.

Excel responds by entering the array formula in all the cells in the selected range R10:R13.

5. Construct an array formula in the cell range AI10:AI13 that multiplies the hourly rates in the cell range A4:A7 by the second-period hour totals in the cell range AI4:AI7.

The array formula you enter into the cell range AI10:AI13 appears on the Formula bar as follows:

```
={A4:A7*AI4:AI7}
```

6. Construct an array formula in the cell range AJ10:AJ13 that totals the two pay periods for each employee.

The array formula you enter into the cell range AJ10:AJ13 appears as follows on the Formula bar:

```
={R10:R13+AI10:AI13}
```

7. Select cell AJ10 to deselect the cell range and then press the Delete key to remove the addition formula from this cell.

Excel responds by displaying an alert dialog box informing you that you cannot change part of an array. When editing array formulas, you must work entirely with the ranges specified as the operands.

8. Select OK to close the alert dialog box and now select the range AJ10:AJ13 before you press Delete.

This time, Excel deletes the array formula from the entire range.

9. Select Undo to restore the deleted array formula to the range AJ10:AJ13, and then select cell A1 and save this workbook with the filename **Solved6-5.xls** in your Chapter 6 folder in the My Practice Spreadsheets folder before you close the workbook.

Tracing and Eliminating Formula Errors

As you found out firsthand when performing Exercise 5-3 in Chapter 5, an error value returned by a single faulty formula can spread like wildfire to all the cells that refer to its value throughout the entire spreadsheet, making it very difficult to determine its source. Fortunately, Excel offers some very effective tools on its Formula Auditing toolbar that you can use to track down the cell that's causing your error woes by tracing the relationships between the formulas in the cells of your worksheet.

By tracing the relationships, you can test formulas to see which cells, called *direct precedents* in spreadsheet jargon, directly feed the formulas and which cells, called *dependents* (nondeductible, of course), depend upon the results of the formulas. Excel even offers a way to visually backtrack the potential sources of an error value in the formula of a particular cell.

To display the precedents and dependents of a formula as well as for tracing the source of errors, you can either use the tools on the Formula Auditing toolbar (Tools⇨Formula Auditing⇨Show Formula Auditing Toolbar) shown in Figure 6-5, or select the equivalent items on the Tools⇨Formula Auditing submenu.

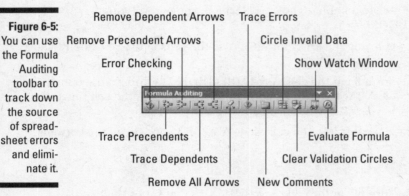

Figure 6-5: You can use the Formula Auditing toolbar to track down the source of spreadsheet errors and eliminate it.

Remove Dependent Arrows Trace Errors
Remove Precedent Arrows Circle Invalid Data
Error Checking Show Watch Window
Trace Precedents
Trace Dependents Evaluate Formula
Clear Validation Circles
Remove All Arrows New Comments

When you click the Trace Precedents and Trace Dependents buttons on the Formula Auditing toolbar (or choose the comparable commands on the Tools⇨Formula Auditing submenu), Excel shows the relationship between a formula and the cells that directly and indirectly feed it as well as those cells that directly and indirectly depend upon its calculation. The program establishes this relationship by drawing arrows from the precedent cells to the active cell and from the active cell to its dependent cells.

If these cells are on the same worksheet, Excel draws solid red or blue arrows (on a color monitor) extending from each of the precedent cells to the active cell and from the active cell to the dependent cells. If the cells are not located locally on the same worksheet (they may be on another sheet in the same workbook or even on a sheet in a different workbook), Excel draws a black dotted arrow. This arrow comes from or goes to an icon picturing a miniature worksheet that sits to one side, with the direction of the arrowheads indicating whether the cells on the other sheet feed the active formula or are fed by it.

Try It

Exercise 6-6: Finding the Source of Error Values in a Spreadsheet

ON THE CD

Open the *Exercis6-6.xls* workbook in your Chapter 6 folder inside the My Practice Spreadsheets folder or on the Excel Workbook CD-ROM. This workbook contains a copy of the Practice Formulas workbook you created as part of the exercises in Chapter 5. You can use its Formulas and Ext Ref worksheets to practice tracing and eliminating errors:

1. Display the floating Formula Auditing toolbar (Tools⇨Formula Auditing⇨Show Formula Auditing Toolbar).

2. Remove the range name, source, given to cell A2 in the Formulas worksheet by selecting source in the Define Name dialog box (Insert⇨Name⇨Define) and then clicking the Delete button before you select OK.

As soon as you remove the range name, the spreadsheet on the Formulas worksheet fills with #NAME? error values. Now use the Trace Error button to trace the source of this error value.

3. Position the cell cursor in cell C9 with the SUM function that sums the three cell ranges A2:A8, B4:B8, C4:C8.

4. Click the Error Checking button (the first one) on the Formula Editing toolbar.

Excel displays the Error Checking dialog box, which briefly explains that this error value is due to the fact that the formula now contains unrecognized text. This is not something that you can fix by editing the formula on the Formula bar, so, in this case, you need to trace the error.

5. Select the Trace Error button in the Error Checking dialog box.

Excel draws a diagonal arrow from cell A4 pointing to cell C9, indicating that this is the direct source of the error (if you select the Previous button in the Error Checking dialog box, Excel steps the cell cursor back through each of the cells with the #NAME? error value in the order in which they spread in this spreadsheet).

In this situation, you need to identify the cell or cells that feed the cells containing the #NAME? error values.

6. Click the Trace Precedents button on the Formula Auditing toolbar (the second from the left).

Excel adds three arrows pointing directly to cell C9, showing the precedents of its error value, the most telling of which is the one drawn from cell A2. If you didn't already know that cell A2 was the culprit causing all these error values (having removed its range name yourself), this precedents diagram would have tipped you off immediately.

7. Click the Trace Precedents button on the Formula Auditing toolbar a second time.

Clicking the Trace Precedents or Trace Dependents button a second time (or double-clicking it to begin with) displays all the indirect precedents and dependents of the formula in the current cell. In this case, Excel now shows the flow and direction of all the sum formulas both down the columns and across the rows that contribute both directly and indirectly to its computed value.

8. Click the Remove All Arrows button on the Formula Auditing toolbar (the one with the eraser) and then close the Error Checking dialog box.

9. Position the cell cursor in cell A4, the first one with a #NAME? error value, and then click the Trace Dependents button on the Formula Auditing toolbar (the one fourth from the left).

The program draws arrows showing the direct dependents of the formula in this cell, which include the formulas down the column that use its value to compute their own and the formulas across the row in C4 and D4 and, of course, the formula in cell C9.

10. Click the Trace Dependents button on the Formula Auditing toolbar a second time.

Excel draws arrows showing the indirect dependents of the formula in cell C9. Note that this includes a black dotted arrow line drawn from cell C9 to a graphic showing a tiny worksheet. This is Excel's way alerting you to the fact that there are cells dependent on this one on other worksheets of the workbook to which its error value has naturally spread.

11. Make the Ext Ref worksheet active and note that cell B3 that contains the linking formula also now contains a #NAME? error value.

12. Switch back to the Formulas worksheet and there, reassign the range name, **source**, to cell A2.

Note that the moment you rectify the source of the error (both literally and figuratively), all the nasty #NAME? error values in the spreadsheet immediately disappear along with all the arrows depicting the direct and indirect dependents.

13. Close the Formula Auditing toolbar and then close the *Exercise6-6.xls* workbook file without saving your changes.

Dealing with Circular References

A *circular reference* in a formula is one that depends, directly or indirectly, upon its own value. The most common type of circular reference occurs when you mistakenly refer in the formula to the cell in which you're building the formula itself. For example, suppose that cell B10 is active when you build the formula:

```
=A10+B10
```

As soon as you complete this formula entry in cell B10, Excel displays an alert box that says that it cannot calculate the formula due to the circular reference. As soon as you press Enter or select OK to close this alert box, the program displays the Circular Reference toolbar along with arrows tracing the formula's precedents and dependents and a help window on allowing or correcting a circular reference. The program also inserts 0 in the cell with the circular reference and the indicator Circular followed by the cell address with the circular reference appears on the Status bar.

Excel is not able to resolve this example of a circular reference in cell B10 because the formula's calculation depends directly upon the formula's result, creating an endless loop that continuously requires recalculating and can never be resolved.

Not all circular references are impossible for Excel to resolve. Some formulas contain a circular reference that can eventually be resolved after many recalculations of its formula (referred to as iterations) because, with each iteration of the formula, the results get closer and closer to a resolution point.

Try It

Exercise 6-7: Solving a Circular Reference in a Formula

Open the *Exercise6-7.xls* workbook in your Chapter 6 folder inside the My Practice Spreadsheets folder or on the Excel Workbook CD-ROM. This workbook contains an income statement spreadsheet with a circular reference in cell B15 that Excel catches the moment you open the file:

1. Read the text of the alert dialog box that appears the moment you open the *Exercise6-7.xls* workbook and then select OK to close it.

The moment you close this alert dialog box, the floating Circular Reference toolbar is displayed only to be overshadowed immediately by a Microsoft Help dialog box. This particular Help dialog box gives you information either on locating and removing a circular reference or on making a circular reference work by changing the number of times that the program evaluates it formula.

2. Click the Make a Circular Reference Work by Changing the Number of Times Microsoft Excel Iterates Formulas link to display its information in the Help dialog box. Look over this information or print it out before you close the Help dialog box.

Excel draws arrows that point to the cells involved in this circular reference, starting with cell B15 that computes the bonuses and then going to the formula in cell B17 that computes the total other income, and from there to cell B19 that computes total income (or loss) before taxes, and, finally, from there to cell B21 that computes the net income.

These computations constitute a circular reference because the formula in cell B15 computes the amount of the bonuses as a percentage of the net income in cell B21 (=B21*20%), which, in turn, is dependent upon the amount of the bonus as it is included in the other income calculation in cell B17 that is then fed to the total income (loss) calculation in cell B19, which is itself used in calculating the net income in cell B21.

3. Select the Iteration check box on the Calculation tab of the Options dialog box (Tools⇔Options).

The moment you select OK to close the Options dialog box and to put this new Calculation setting into effect, Excel resolves the circular reference in cell B15 that calculates the bonuses based on the net income and the Circular Reference toolbar. All the arrows showing all the cells involved in this circular reference disappear from the worksheet.

4. Save this version of the Income Statement with the filename **Solved6-7.xls** in your Chapter 6 folder inside the My Practice Spreadsheets folder on your hard disk and then close this file.

Chapter 7

Creating Date and Time Formulas

· ·

In This Chapter

▶ Building date and time formulas

▶ Using the Date functions

▶ Using the Time functions

· ·

*F*ormulas that perform calculations between elapsed dates and times are quite common in spreadsheets. The exercises in this chapter give you a chance to build formulas that calculate the difference between starting and ending dates and times as well as to use Excel Date and Time functions to perform a variety of tasks including returning the current date and time in a spreadsheet, converting text entries to valid date and time numbers, and more.

Constructing Date and Time Formulas

You already have some experience entering dates and times in a worksheet and then changing how they appear by assigning different date and time number formats. Remember that all you need to do when you need to enter a date or time number in a worksheet is to emulate one of these date or time number formats when making the entry.

The only thing the least little bit baffling about date and time entries in a worksheet is the actual way that Excel stores the date and time numbers into a cell when you make an entry following one of the standard number formats. Behind the scenes (that is, the date or time number formats) lies a serial number. In the case of dates, this serial number represents the number of days that have elapsed between the date you enter and the beginning of the twentieth century (making January 1, 1900 serial date number 1). In the case of time, the serial number is a fraction representing the number of hours, minutes, and seconds that have elapsed since midnight (which is serial number 0.00000000, so that 12 noon is 0.50000000).

To build a simple date formula that calculates the number of days that have elapsed between two dates entered in the worksheet, subtract the cell containing the starting date from the one containing the ending date. Excel then displays the calculated result in a date format, which you then you have to reformat with another number format (such as Number with no decimal points) to see the number of days that this "date" actually represents.

To build a simple time formula that calculates the fractional part of the day that has elapsed between two times entered in the worksheet, you subtract the cell containing the starting time from the one containing the ending time. Excel then displays the calculated result as a fraction that you can then convert into hours by multiplying by 24.

When entering times in a spreadsheet that you intend to use in formulas to compute elapsed times, be sure to enter all times after 12 noon either using a 24-hour clock (as in 13:05 for 1:05 PM) or with the PM signifier after the time number. Otherwise, Excel interprets all the times you enter as occurring in the AM.

Try It

Exercise 7-1: Building Formulas that Calculate Elapsed Dates and Times

Launch Excel, if the program is not currently running, and use a blank workbook to build some simple formulas that calculate elapsed times and dates:

1. Increase the display magnification percentage from 100% to 200% and then enter the following headings in the designated cells of Sheet1 in the new workbook:

- **Start** in cell A1
- **End** in cell B1
- **Elapsed** in cell C1

2. Enter the following dates in the designated cells:

- **11-6-05** in cell A2
- **2-15-06** in cell B2

3. Construct a formula in cell C2 that subtracts the ending date from the starting date.

Excel calculates the difference between the two dates and returns the result formatted as the date 4/10/1900 to cell C2.

4. Format cell C2 with the Number format and zero decimal places.

Excel now displays 101 as the answer in cell C2.

5. Enter the following dates in the designated cells:

- **4-26-04** in cell A3
- **7-21-06** in cell B3
- **11-30-03** in cell A4
- **5-19-06** in cell B4

6. Use the Fill handle to copy the formula in cell C2 down to the range C3:C4.

Because you formatted the calculated result in cell C2 before you copied its formula, the results returned to cells C3 and C4 automatically appear formatted as whole numbers rather than as dates.

7. Enter the following times in the designated cells:

- **8:12 AM** in cell A6
- **2:15 PM** in cell B6

8. Construct a formula in cell C6 that calculates the difference between the ending time and the starting time.

Excel calculates the difference between the two times and returns the result formatted as the date and time 1/0/1900 6:03, or simply 6:03 or 6:03 AM (depending upon your version of Excel), to cell C6.

9. Format cell C6 with the Number format with two decimal places.

Excel now displays 0.25 as the answer in cell C6.

10. Convert the fraction of the day into hours by editing the formula in cell C6 so that the program multiplies the difference between the two cells by 24.

When editing the formula, be sure to enclose the subtraction operation in parentheses so that Excel performs the subtraction first and then multiplies this difference by 24 as in

```
=(B6-A6)*24
```

11. Enter the following times in the designated cells:

- **7:35 AM** in cell A7
- **15:05** in cell B7
- **9:45** in cell A8
- **6 PM** in cell B8

12. Use the Fill handle to copy the formula in cell C6 down to the range C7:C8.

Because you edited the basic formula in cell C6 so that it returns the number of hours elapsed (rather than the fractional part of the day) and formatted the result with the Number format with two decimal places before you copied the formula, the copies in cells C7 and C8 automatically return the number of hours expressed with two decimal places.

13. Position the cell cursor in cell A1 and then save this new workbook with the filename **Solved7-1.xls** in your Chapter 7 folder in the My Practice Spreadsheets folder on your hard disk and then close the workbook.

Working with the Date Functions

Excel contains a number of Date functions that help you work with dates in your spreadsheets. These functions run the gamut from those that return the current date to those that convert text to date serial numbers (so you can use them in formulas that compute the number of days that have elapsed).

When you install and activate the Analysis ToolPak add-in program that comes with Excel, you have access to even more Date functions, many of which are specifically targeted to performing date computations involving the normal five-day, Monday through Friday, workweek.

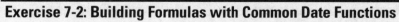

Try It

Exercise 7-2: Building Formulas with Common Date Functions

Open the *Exercise7-2.xls* workbook file in your Chapter 7 folder in the My Practice Spreadsheets folder on your hard disk or on the Excel Workbook folder on the workbook CD-ROM. This workbook contains several worksheets, the first two of which give you practice using the Date functions built into Excel and are available to you when you activate the Analysis ToolPak:

1. Insert the current date in cell B1 using Excel's TODAY function.

When working with a new function, use the Insert Function button on the Formula bar to enter the function. That way, you can learn the purpose of the function in the Insert Function dialog box and what arguments, if any, the function requires through the use of the Function Arguments dialog box.

2. Insert the current time in cell D1 using the NOW function and then format it with the Custom h:mm AM/PM time number format.

3. In cell D3, create a date entry using the DATE function with the three separate numeric entries in cells A3, B3, and C3 as its arguments in the following order:

- C3 as Year argument

- A3 as Month argument

- B3 as the Day argument

4. Format the date returned by the DATE function in cell D3 with the March 14, 2001, date format and then copy this DATE formula down to the cell range D4:D8.

Note that contents of the cell range D3:D8 is composed of DATE function formulas rather than date serial numbers. If you want to convert the formulas to their calculated values, you need to use the Values option in the Paste Special dialog box.

5. Select the cell range D3:D8 and then copy it to the Clipboard (Ctrl+C).

6. Position the cell pointer in E3 and then select the Values option button in the Paste Special dialog box.

Excel copies the date serial numbers into the range E3:E8. Note that the date serial numbers copied into this cell range are completely static: Unlike the DATE function formulas in the cell range D3:D8, revising the numeric entries made in the cells in the range A3:C8 would have no effect on them.

7. Use the DATEVALUE function in cell B10 to convert the text entry in cell A10 to the date serial number and then copy the formula down to the cell range C11:C14.

8. Position the cell cursor in cell B1 of the Date Formulas sheet and then save a copy of the workbook with the filename **Solved7-2-mine.xls** in your Chapter 7 folder in the My Practice Spreadsheets folder, but leave the workbook open for Exercise 7-3.

Add-in programs extend Excel's basic feature set, usually by giving you access to new, specialized functions. Excel ships with several add-in programs including the Analysis ToolPak with its extra Date functions. Before you can use the functions or features offered by an add-in program, you must activate it by selecting its check box in the Add-Ins dialog box (Tools⇨Add-Ins).

The Analysis ToolPak, which you activate in the next exercise, adds the following Date functions to Excel:

- **EDATE(*start_date,months*)** calculates the elapsed date so many months ahead (positive months argument) or behind (negative months argument) the start_date argument you specify.

- **EOMONTH(*start_date,months*)** calculates the last day of the month so many months ahead (positive months argument) or behind (negative months argument) the start_date argument you specify.

- **NEWORKDAYS(*start_date.end_date,[holidays]*)** calculates the number of work days between the start_date and end_date arguments — the optional holidays argument can specify a range of holiday dates to be excluded from the workday total.

- **WEEKNUM(*serial_number,[return_type]*)** calculates a number indicating where the week in the date specified by the serial_number argument falls within the year — the optional return_type argument can be the number 1 or 2, where 1 (or no return_type argument specified) starts the week on Sunday (1) and ends it on Saturday (7) and 2 starts the week on Monday (1) and ends it on Sunday (7).

- **WORKDAY(*start_date,days,*[*holidays*])** calculates the work date that is so many days ahead (positive days argument) or behind (negative days argument) the start_date argument you specify — the optional holidays argument can specify a range of holiday dates to be excluded from the calculation.

- **YEARFRAC(*start_date,end_date,*[*basis*])** calculates the fraction of the year between the start_date and end_date arguments you specify — the optional basis argument can be a number between 0 and 4 that signifies the following:

  - **0** (or no basis argument) bases the year fraction on the U.S. (NASD) method of 30/360 (whereby if the starting date is equal to the 31st of the month, it becomes equal to the 30th and if the ending date is equal to the 31st of the month, the ending date becomes the 1st of the following month).

  - **1** bases the year fraction on the actual days divided by the actual days.

  - **2** bases the year fraction on the actual days divided by 360.

  - **3** bases the year fraction on the actual day divided by 365.

  - **4** bases the year fraction on the European method of 30/360 (whereby starting and ending dates that fall on the 31st of the month are made equal to the 30th of the same month).

Try It

Exercise 7-3: Building Formulas with Date Functions in the Analysis ToolPak

Use the *Solved7-2-mine.xls* workbook file you created when doing the previous exercise. If you did not perform this exercise or no longer have access to this workbook, open the *Solved7-2.xls* file located in your Chapter 7 folder in the My Practice Spreadsheets folder on your hard disk or on the Excel Workbook CD-ROM. In this exercise, you activate the Analysis ToolPak add-in and then practice using its WEEKNUM and NETWORKDAYS functions:

1. Position the cell cursor in cell C10 and then select the Analysis ToolPak check box in the Add-Ins dialog box, if this check box is not already selected in your copy of Excel (Tools⇨Add-Ins).

   If you've not previously installed this add-in, Excel displays an alert dialog box asking you if you want to install this add-in.

2. Select Yes in the alert dialog box asking you to install this add-in if prompted to do so.

3. Select Date & Time as the category in the Or Select a Category drop-down list box in the Insert Function dialog box (Insert⇨Function) to display the list of Date and Time functions.

   Scroll through the list of Date & Time functions verifying that your activation of the Analysis ToolPak add-in has inserted the EDATE, EOMONTH, NETWORKDAYS, WEEKNUM, and YEARFRAC functions.

4. Select the WEEKNUM function in the Select a Function list box before you choose OK to close the Insert Function dialog box.

5. Select cell B10 for the Serial_number argument and choose OK to close the Function Arguments dialog box.

6. Copy the WEEKNUM formula in cell C10 down to the cell range C11:C14.

7. Switch to the 2006 Holidays worksheet and then use the individual calendar worksheets (Jan-06 through Dec-06) to enter the dates of the holidays missing in the cell range B3:B13.

   Martin Luther King Day is in January

   Presidents' Day is in February

   Memorial Day is in May

   Labor Day is in September

   Veteran's Day is in November as is Thanksgiving in the U.S.A.

8. Name the cell range B3:B13 **Holidays_06** and then position the cell cursor in cell D3.

9. Construct a formula in this cell using the NETWORKDAYS function that calculates the number of workdays between 12-31-05 and 12-31-06.

   Select cell B15 in Start_date text box and cell B16 in the End_date text box in the Function Arguments dialog box

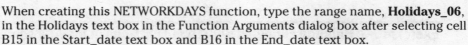

10. Construct a formula in cell D4 using the NETWORKDAYS function that calculates the number of workdays between 12-31-05 and 12-31-06 and that deducts the holidays that fall on workdays in the named range Holidays_06 in the 2006 Holidays worksheet.

    When creating this NETWORKDAYS function, type the range name, **Holidays_06**, in the Holidays text box in the Function Arguments dialog box after selecting cell B15 in the Start_date text box and B16 in the End_date text box.

11. Check your answers against those shown in the 2006 Holidays sheet in the *Solved7-3.xls* workbook file in your Chapter 7 folder inside the My Practice Spreadsheets folder or on your Excel Workbook CD-ROM. When everything checks out, save your workbook in the Chapter 7 folder with the filename **Solved7-3-mine.xls**.

Working with the Time Functions

Excel's Time functions are a smaller subset of the Date functions. They include the NOW function, which returns the current date and time; TIME, which creates a time fraction from values representing the hour, minutes, and seconds; and TIMEVALUE, which converts a time entered or imported into the worksheet as text so that you can use it in formulas that calculate elapsed times.

Try It

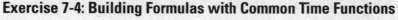

Exercise 7-4: Building Formulas with Common Time Functions

Open the *Exercise7-4.xls* file located in your Chapter 7 folder in the My Practice Spreadsheets folder on your hard disk or on the Excel Workbook CD-ROM. The file contains a Time Formulas worksheet that you can use to practice using some of the Time functions:

1. Display the current time in cell B1 using the NOW function — format the result with the 1:30 PM Time format.

2. In cell D3, use the TIME function to enter a time using the entry in cell A3 as its Hour argument, B3 as its Minute argument, and C3 as its Second argument.

3. Copy the formula down to the cell range D4:D7.

4. Copy the times calculated in the cell range D3:D4 and then paste their fractional values in the range E3:E7.

To copy only the values from a cell range, paste them into place using the Values option in the Paste Special dialog box (Edit⇨Paste Special).

5. In cell B10, use the TIMEVALUE function to convert the text entry in cell A10 to a bona fide time.

6. Format the result in this cell with the 13:30:55 time format and then copy this formula down to the cell range B11:B14.

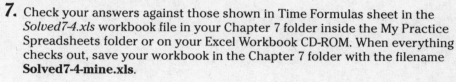

7. Check your answers against those shown in Time Formulas sheet in the *Solved7-4.xls* workbook file in your Chapter 7 folder inside the My Practice Spreadsheets folder or on your Excel Workbook CD-ROM. When everything checks out, save your workbook in the Chapter 7 folder with the filename **Solved7-4-mine.xls**.

Chapter 8

Financial Formulas and Functions

● ●

In This Chapter

▶ Understanding how the basic financial functions work

▶ Using the basic investment accumulation, discounting, and amortization functions

▶ Using the program's depreciation functions

● ●

As the old song says, "Money makes the world go 'round" and to that end, Excel supplies you with plenty of built-in functions for getting the latest spin on how much you're making and spending. In this chapter, you get the chance to practice using some of the basic investment, depreciation, and currency-conversion functions that make up a part of the program's financial group.

Working with Financial Functions

Excel offers a fair number of sophisticated financial functions for determining such things as the present, future, or net present value of an investment; the payment, number of periods, or the principal or interest part of a payment on an amortized loan; the rate of return on an investment; and the depreciation of your favorite assets.

By activating the Analysis ToolPak add-in, you add some 30-odd specialized financial functions that run the gamut from those that calculate the accrued interest for a security paying interest periodically and only at maturity all the way to those that calculate the internal rate of return and the net present value for a schedule of non-periodic cash flows.

The key to using many of Excel's financial functions is in understanding the terminology used by their arguments. Many of the most common financial functions such as PV (Present Value), NPV (Net Present Value), FV (Future Value), and PMT (Payment) take similar arguments:

✔ **Pv** is the present value that is the principal amount of the annuity

✔ **Fv** is the future value that represents the principal plus interest on the annuity

✔ **Pmt** is the payment made each period in the annuity. Normally, the payment is set over the life of the annuity and includes principal plus interest without any other fees.

✔ **Rate** is the interest rate per period. Normally, the rate is expressed as an annual percentage.

✔ **Nper** is the total number of payment periods in the life of the annuity. It is calculated by taking the Term (the amount of time that interest is paid) and multiplying it by the Period (the point in time when interest is paid or earned) so that a loan with a 3-year term with 12 monthly interest payments has 3 x 12, or 36, payment periods.

When using financial functions, keep in mind that the fv, pv, or pmt arguments can be positive or negative, depending on whether you're receiving the money (as in the case of an investment) or paying out the money (as in the case of a loan). Also keep in mind that you want to express the rate argument in the same units as the nper argument. For example, if you make monthly payments on a loan and you express the nper as the total number of monthly payments (as in 360 (30 x 12) for 30-year mortgage), you need to express the annual interest rate in monthly terms as well. So if, for example, you pay an annual interest rate of 7.5% on the loan, you express the rate argument as 0.075/12 so that it is monthly as well.

Using the Basic Investment Functions

The following six functions form the core Excel financial functions for determining whether a particular investment is worthwhile:

- ✓ **FV(*rate,nper,pmt,*[*pv*],[*type*])** — Future Value — calculates the future value of an investment, assuming a constant interest rate and constant payments on a periodic basis.

- ✓ **PV(*rate,nper,pmt,*[*fv*],[*type*])** — Present Value — calculates the present value of an investment; that is, the total amount that a series of future payments is worth now.

- ✓ **PMT(*rate,nper,pv,*[*fv*],[*type*])** — Payment — calculates the payment for a loan, assuming a constant interest rate and stream of payments.

- ✓ **RATE(*nper,pmt,pv,*[*fv*],[*type*])** calculates the interest rate for any type of annuity.

- ✓ **NPER(*rate,pmt,pv,*[*fv*],[*type*])** — Number of Periods — calculates the how many periods are required for an investment, assuming a constant interest rate and constant payments on a periodic basis.

- ✓ **NPV(*rate,value1,*[*value2*],[...])** — Net Present Value — calculates the present value of an investment by using a discount rate and a series of future payments (negative values) and income (positive values).

As you can see in this list, the syntax of these functions is similar, requiring, with the exception of NPV, its own particular combination of the standard rate, nper, pmt, and pv arguments discussed in the previous section. You will also note that the functions that use these combination take the following optional arguments (indicated in the square brackets):

- ✓ **[*Pv*]** optional argument in the FV function is the present value or lump-sum amount for which you wish to calculate the future value: If you omit the pv argument, Excel assumes a present value of zero (0).

- ✓ **[*Fv*]** optional argument in the PV, PMT, RATE, and NPER functions represents the future value or cash balance you want to have after making your last payment: If you omit the fv argument, Excel assumes a future value of zero (0).

- ✓ **[*Type*]** optional argument in the FV, PV, PMT, RATE, and NPER functions indicates whether the payment is made at the beginning or the end of the period — enter 0 (or omit the type argument) when the payment is made at the end of the period and use 1 when it is made at the beginning of the period.

In the following exercise, you get a chance to practice using the FV, PV, PMT, RATE, and NPER financial functions to solve a series of seven real-world problems found on the four worksheets (FV, PV, PMT, and NPER) in the *Exercise8-1.xls* workbook file.

Exercise 8-1: Building Formulas with the FV, PV, PMT, RATE, and NPER Functions

If Excel is not currently running, launch the program and then open the *Exercise8-1.xls* workbook file inside your Chapter 8 folder in the My Practice Spreadsheets folder on your hard disk or in the Excel Workbook folder on the workbook CD-ROM. Use the problems found on the FV, PV, PMT, and NPER worksheets in this workbook to practice creating financial formulas using the FV, PV, PMT, RATE, and NPER functions:

1. Position the cell cursor in cell C4 of the FV worksheet, the answer cell for Question 1, and construct a formula using the FV financial function (with the appropriate cells in the range B7:C11 as its arguments) that calculates the return on your investment.

When defining the arguments for your FV function in its Function Arguments dialog box, move the dialog box out of the way of the cell range B7:C11 and then click the appropriate cell in this range to define the three required (Rate, Nper, and Pmt) and two optional arguments (PV and Type) when the insertion point is located in its argument text box.

2. Position the cell cursor in cell C15 of the FV worksheet, the answer cell for Question 2, and construct a formula using the FV financial function (with the appropriate cells in the range B18:C22 as its arguments) that calculates the total amount of money that you pay on the loan.

3. Position the cell cursor in cell C4 of the PV worksheet, the answer cell for Question 3, and construct a formula using the PV financial function (with the appropriate cells in the range B7:C11 as its arguments) that calculates the amount of money you should pay for the property.

4. Position the cell cursor in cell C15 of the of the PV worksheet, the answer cell for Question 4, and construct a formula using the RATE financial function (with the appropriate cells in the range B7:C11 as its arguments) and your answer to Question 3 in cell C4 to check the interest rate.

The formula with the RATE function in cell C15 should compute the same 6.50% interest rate that is entered in cell C7.

5. Position the cell cursor in cell C4 of the of the PMT worksheet, the answer cell for Question 5, and there construct a formula using the PMT financial function (with the appropriate cells in the range B7:C11 as its arguments) that calculates your monthly loan payment.

Be sure that you convert the rate argument and the nper argument for the PMT function you construct to the equivalent months by entering the appropriate calculations to their cell references in the Rate and Nper argument text boxes of the Function Arguments dialog box for the PMT function.

6. Position the cell cursor in cell C15 of the PMT worksheet, the answer cell for Question 6, and construct a formula using the PV financial function with the appropriate cells in the range B7:C11 as its arguments to check the loan amount you used in Question 5.

The formula with the PV in cell C15 should compute the same $465,000 amount entered in cell C9 that you used as the PV argument of the PMT function in cell C4.

7. Position the cell cursor in cell C4 of the of the NPER worksheet, the answer cell for Question 7, and construct a formula using the NPER financial function (with the appropriate cells in the range B7:C11 as its arguments) that calculates how long it will take you to pay off your loan.

Be sure that you convert the answer returned by the NPER function in months to the equivalent years.

8. Check your answers against those in the equivalent worksheets in the *Solved8-1.xls* workbook located in your Chapter 8 folder in the My Practice Spreadsheets folder or on the Excel Workbook CD-ROM. If everything checks out with your financial formulas, proceed to step 9.

9. Position the cell cursor in cell A1 of the FV worksheet and then save your work in a new workbook file named **Solved8-1-mine.xls** in your Chapter 8 folder and then close both this new workbook and the *Solved8-1.xls* workbook file.

The NPV function returns the sum of any series of cash flows, discounted to the present day, using a particular discount rate. The cash flows tracked by the NPV function are either income (money you make) indicated by positive numbers in the function's values argument or payments (money you pay out) indicated by specifying negative numbers.

When using the NPV function to determine the wisdom of an investment, you keep in mind that this function assumes that the cash flows (be they income or payments) specified by the values argument(s) are all made at the end of the first period. As this assumption does not conform to the understanding of net present value in standard accounting, when using this function, you always need to include a Time 0 (even if its value is $0) in order for your answer to be in accord with the accepted definition of NPV.

In the next exercise, you get an opportunity to practice using both the NPV and IRR functions (Internal Rate of Return) to determine the advisability of making certain capital expenditures in the form of equipment purchases. The IRR function returns the interest rate received for an investment consisting of cash flows (income and payments) made at regular intervals. Note that unlike when using the RATE function, the cash flows do not have to be equal, although they must be made regularly on a periodic basis (monthly, quarterly, annually, and the like).

The IRR function computes its result using an iterative process (similar to that used to resolve certain circular references like the one you encountered in Chapter 6). For this reason, the function takes an optional guess argument, where you may specify your best guess or target percentage. If you don't specify a guess argument for an IRR function, Excel automatically uses 10% as its target.

To determine the prudence of making the proposed capital expenditures using the NPV and IRR functions in exercise ahead, you finish creating a partially constructed spreadsheet model on NPV & IRR worksheet in the workbook file *Exercise8-2.xls*.

Try It

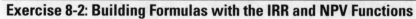

Exercise 8-2: Building Formulas with the IRR and NPV Functions

Open the *Exercise8-2.xls* workbook file inside your Chapter 8 folder in the My Practice Spreadsheets folder on your hard disk or in the Excel Workbook folder on the workbook CD-ROM. In this exercise, you finish the model constructed on its NPV & IRR worksheet. In doing so, you get practice using the NPV and IRR functions to determine the financial wisdom of making capital expenditures in the form of purchased equipment given the level of anticipated of income resulting from the asset acquisition, the anticipated taxes on that extra income, and the depreciation of those assets over their three year life:

1. Select the cell range B3:C7, and then choose Insert⇨Name⇨Create and make sure that only the Left Column check box is selected in Create Names dialog box before you select OK.

   You use the Create Names feature to assign the row headings in B3:B7 to the cells in C3:C7.

2. Make the following entries in the designated cells:

   - **38000** in cell C3
   - **1500** in cell C4
   - **15000** in cell C5
   - **6%** in cell C6
   - **27%** in cell C7

3. Position the cell cursor in cell H10 and type = - (an equal to sign followed by a minus sign with no spaces) and then click cell C3.

   In the cell and on the Formula bar, Excel inserts the equal to sign, a minus sign, and then cell's range name:

   ```
   =-Initial_Cost
   ```

4. Click the Enter button on the Formula bar to complete the cell entry and then position the cell cursor in cell C11.

5. Type an = (an equal to sign) and then click cell C5.

   In the cell and on the Formula bar, Excel inserts an equal to sign followed by the cell's range name:

   ```
   =Expected_Income
   ```

6. Click the Enter button on the Formula bar to complete the cell entry and then position the cell cursor in cell D11 to the right.

   In this cell, you insert the SLN (Straight Line depreciatioN) function that figures the depreciation on the $38,000 worth of equipment purchases.

7. Click the Insert Function button on the Formula bar and then, in the Insert Function dialog box, select the SLN function in the Financial Category before you select OK.

   The SLN function takes three arguments; cost, with the initial cost of your assets; salvage, with the value of the assets at the end of its useful life; and life, which indicates the number of years that the asset is expected to be in use.

8. While the insertion point is in the Cost argument text box, click cell C3 in the worksheet to insert the range name Initial_Cost in this box and then press Tab.

9. Click cell C4 in the worksheet to insert the range name Salvage_Value in the Salvage argument text box and then press Tab.

10. Type **3** in the Life argument text box and then select OK.

11. Position the cell cursor in cell E11 and construct a formula that subtracts the first-year depreciation amount in cell D11 from the pretaxable income in cell C11.

12. Position the cell cursor in cell F11 and construct a formula that deducts the estimated taxes using the tax rate percentage in cell C7 from the taxable income in cell E11.

The standard way to construct this type of formula is to multiply the taxable income by 1 minus the tax rate. In this particular case, this formula in F11 would appear as

```
=E11*(1-Tax_Rate)
```

13. Position the cell cursor in cell H11 and there construct a formula that adds the depreciation value in cell D11 to the after-tax income in cell F11 to salvage value in cell G11.

If you use the SUM function, this formula in G11 appears as

```
=SUM(D11,F11,G11)
```

14. Use the Fill handle to copy the entries in the cell range C11:H11 down to the range C12:H13.

15. Position the cell cursor in cell G13 and construct a formula with a reference to the Salvage_Value cell C4.

This formula in cell G13 appears as

```
=Salvage_Value
```

16. Position the cell cursor in cell F2 and type = (equal to sign), and then click the cell H10 in the worksheet to select it before you type + (plus sign).

The formula in the cell and on the Formula bar in F2 now reads

```
=H10+
```

17. Click the Insert Function button on the Formula bar and then, in the Insert Function dialog box, select the NPV function in the Financial Category before selecting OK.

18. Click cell C6 in the worksheet to insert the Interest_Rate range name in the Rate argument text box and then press Tab.

19. Select the cell range H11:H13 in the worksheet to insert this range address in the Value1 text box and then select OK.

Excel inserts the following formula in cell F2 that computes the net present value of the investment in cell F2 as $1,310:

```
=H10+NPV(Interest_Rate,H11:H13)
```

20. Position the cell cursor in cell H2 and then click the Insert Function button on the Formula bar. In the Insert Function dialog box, select the IRR function in the Financial Category before you select OK.

21. Select the cell range H10H13 in the worksheet to insert this range address in the Values argument text box and then select OK.

Excel computes an 8% internal rate of return on this investment, which is certainly acceptable.

22. Check your model against the one in the NPV & IRR worksheet in the *Solved8-2.xls* workbook in your Chapter 8 folder.

If everything checks out, proceed to step 24.

23. Change the following values in the designated cells:

- **1000** in the Salvage_Value cell C4
- **12000** in the Expected_Income cell C5

Note that at this salvage value and anticipated income amount, the net present value is a loss of $4,884 and the internal rate of return has now sunk to a dismal -1% — with these figures, the capital investment is decidedly not a wise one.

24. Click the Undo button on the Standard toolbar or press Ctrl+Z to restore the original salvage value and expected income figures to the spreadsheet.

25. Save your work in a workbook named **Solved8-2-mine.xls** in your Chapter 8 folder and then close both this new workbook and the *Solved8-2.xls* workbook file.

Figuring the Depreciation of an Asset

The moment you put an asset you purchase into service, it begins to depreciate (lose value). Excel lets you choose between four different Depreciation functions, each of which uses a slightly different method for depreciating an asset over time. These built-in Depreciation functions include

- ✔ **SLN** to calculate straight-line depreciation

- ✔ **SYD** to calculate sum-of-years-digits depreciation

- ✔ **DB** to calculate declining balance depreciation

- ✔ **DDB** to calculate double-declining balance depreciation

All four depreciation functions require the following cost, salvage, and life arguments, and in addition, all except the SLN function, require the period argument:

- ✔ Cost, indicating the initial cost of the asset that you're depreciating.

- ✔ Salvage, indicating the value of the asset at the end of the depreciation (also known as the salvage value of the asset).

- ✔ Life, indicating is the number of periods over which the asset is depreciated (also known as the useful life of the asset).

- ✔ Period, indicating the period over which the asset is being depreciated — note that the units you use in the period argument must be the same as those used in the life argument of the Depreciation function. For example, if you express the life argument in years, you must also express the period argument in years.

Note that the DB function accepts an optional month argument. This argument is the number of months the asset is in use in the first year. If you omit this optional argument from your DB function, Excel assumes the number of months of service to be 12. Also, when using the DDB function, you can add an optional factor argument. This argument is the rate at which the balance declines in the depreciation schedule. If you omit this optional argument, Excel assumes the rate to be 2 (thus, the name double-declining balance).

The following exercise gives you an opportunity to practice using all four types of depreciation in a partially completed Depreciation Table that then enables you to compare the amount you depreciate each year in the useful life of an asset.

Try It

Exercise 8-3: Building Formulas with the SLN, SYD, DB, and DDB Depreciation Functions

Open the *Exercise8-3.xls* workbook file inside your Chapter 8 folder in the My Practice Spreadsheets folder on your hard disk or in the Excel Workbook folder on the workbook CD-ROM. This workbook contains a Depreciation worksheet with a Depreciation Table comparing the four depreciation methods side by side that you will complete:

1. Select the cell range B3:C6 and then open the Create Names dialog box (Insert⇨ Names⇨Create) and select only the Left Column check box in this dialog box before you select OK.

2. Make the following entries in the designated cells:

    - **Office Furniture** in the Type_of_Asset cell, C3

    - **50000** in the Cost cell, C4

    - **10** in the Life_in_years cell, C5

    - **1000** in the Salvage cell, C6

3. Position the cell cursor in cell C9 and construct a formula that references the Cost cell, C4, and then use the Fill handle to copy this formula across the row to the cell range D9:F9.

4. Position the cell cursor in cell C10; there, type = (an equal sign) and then select cell C9 before you type – (minus sign).

    The formula in the cell and on the Formula bar now reads

    ```
    =C9–
    ```

5. Click the Insert Function button on the Formula bar and then in the Insert Function dialog box, select the SLN function in the Financial Category before you select OK.

6. Select the following cells to insert their names in the designated argument text boxes and then select OK:

    - Cost cell (C4) in the **Cost** text box

    - Salvage cell (C6) in the **Salvage** text box

    - Life_in_years cell (C5) in the **Life** text box

7. Copy the formula in cell C10 down to the cell range C11:C19.

8. Position the cell pointer in cell D10 and construct a formula that subtracts the cost amount in D9 from the first-year depreciation returned by the SYD function using the following arguments:

    - Cost cell in the **Cost** text box

    - Salvage cell in the **Salvage** text box

    - Life_in_years cell in the **Life** text box

    - Cell B10 in the **Per** text box

9. Copy the formula in cell D10 down the cell range D11:D19.

10. Position the cell pointer in cell E10 and construct a formula that subtracts the cost amount in E9 from the first-year depreciation returned by the DB function using the following arguments:

    - Cost cell in the **Cost** text box

    - Salvage cell in the **Salvage** text box

    - Life_in_years cell in the **Life** text box

    - Cell B10 in the **Per** text box

11. Copy the formula in cell E10 down the cell range E11:E19.

12. Position the cell pointer in cell F10 and construct a formula that subtracts the cost amount in F9 from the first-year depreciation returned by the DDB function using the following arguments:

    - Cost cell in the **Cost** text box

    - Salvage cell in the **Salvage** text box

- Life_in_years cell in the **Life** text box
- Cell B10 in the **Per** text box

13. Copy the formula in cell F10 down the cell range F11:F19.

14. Check the formulas in your Depreciation worksheet against those in the *Solved8-3.xls* workbook file in your Chapter 8 folder inside the My Practice Spreadsheets folder or on the Excel Workbook CD-ROM.

If everything checks out, proceed to step 14.

15. Make the following updates in the designated cells:

- **25000** in the Cost Cell (C4)
- **5** in the Life_in_years cell (C5)
- **500** in the Salvage cell (C6)

Note that when Excel finishes recalculating the Depreciation Table using your new inputs, the depreciation formulas in the Straight Line column (C) return negative values to all the rows below Year 5 and #NUM! error values to the SYD, Declining Balance, and Double-declining Balance columns.

16. Click the Undo button on the Standard toolbar or press Ctrl+Z until you have restored the original Cost, Life_in_years, and Salvage values to cells C4, C5, and C6 in the table. Next save your work in a workbook file named **Solved8-3-mine.xls** in your Chapter 8 folder inside the My Practice Spreadsheets folder before you close the file.

Chapter 9

Using Math Functions

In This Chapter

▶ Rounding off numbers in a spreadsheet

▶ Using functions for calculating products, powers, and square roots

▶ Summing the products in cell ranges or arrays

▶ Doing conditional summing

The Math & Trig group of functions includes a wide variety of mathematical functions for computing new values as well as for controlling the results of calculations. This group also includes a large assortment of trigonometric functions most often needed in engineering and scientific endeavors. In this chapter, you get a chance to practice using some of the math functions more commonly needed in spreadsheets for business applications.

Rounding Off Values

Rounding off the numbers that have fractions is one of the more frequent tasks you may undertake in Excel. Excel includes three functions in the Math & Trig category that you can use for rounding off the numbers in a worksheet:

✔ **ROUND(*number,num_digits*)** to round the value specified by the number argument to the number of digits specified by the num_digits argument

✔ **ROUNDUP(*number,num_digits*)** to round up the value away from 0 (zero) that is specified by the number argument to the number of digits specified by the num_digits argument

✔ **ROUNDDOWN(*number,num_digits*)** to round down the value toward 0 (zero) that is specified by the number argument to the number of digits specified by the num_digits argument

Q. What's the difference between using one of Excel's rounding functions to round off values to a particular decimal place and using a number format to control how many decimal places are displayed?

A. Formatting a number only changes the way the value appears in the cell, whereas rounding off a number with one of the Excel functions actually changes the number of digits in the value entered in that cell.

Try It

Exercise 9-1: Building Formulas the ROUND, ROUNDUP, and ROUNDDOWN Functions

If Excel isn't running, launch the program and then open the *Exercise9-1.xls* workbook file in your Chapter 9 folder in the My Practice Spreadsheets folder inside My Documents on your hard disk or in the Excel Workbook folder on the workbook

CD-ROM. This file contains a Rounding Formulas worksheet where you can practice using the ROUND, ROUNDUP, and ROUNDDOWN functions on the value of the mathematical constant pi, accurate to 15 placed returned by the PI function to cell A3:

1. Position the cell cursor in cell B3 and construct a formula using the ROUND function that rounds off the value of pi in cell A3 to no decimal places.

2. In cell B4, construct a formula with the ROUND function that rounds off the value of pi in cell A3 to one decimal place.

Because all the rounding formulas you're going to create for this exercise use the same value in cell A3, you can save time by making copies of the original ROUND formula and then editing the function name or the num_digits argument in the copies as needed. To do this, however, you must remember to convert the reference to cell A3 from relative to absolute when constructing the formula with the Insert Function feature.

3. In cell B5, construct a formula with the ROUND function that rounds off the value of pi in cell A3 to two decimal places.

4. In cell B6, construct a formula with the ROUND function that rounds off the value of pi in cell A3 to three decimal places.

5. In cell B7, construct a formula with the ROUNDUP function that rounds up the value of pi in cell A3 to two decimal places.

6. In cell B8, construct a formula with the ROUNDUP function that rounds up the value of pi in cell A3 to four decimal places.

7. In cell B9, construct a formula with the ROUNDDOWN function that rounds down the value of pi in cell A3 to two decimal places.

8. In cell B10, construct a formula with the ROUNDDOWN function that rounds down the value of pi in cell A3 to four decimal places.

Compare your spreadsheet to one shown in Figure 9-1. If everything checks out, proceed to Step 9.

9. Save your workbook file in the Chapter 9 folder with the filename **Solved9-1.xls**.

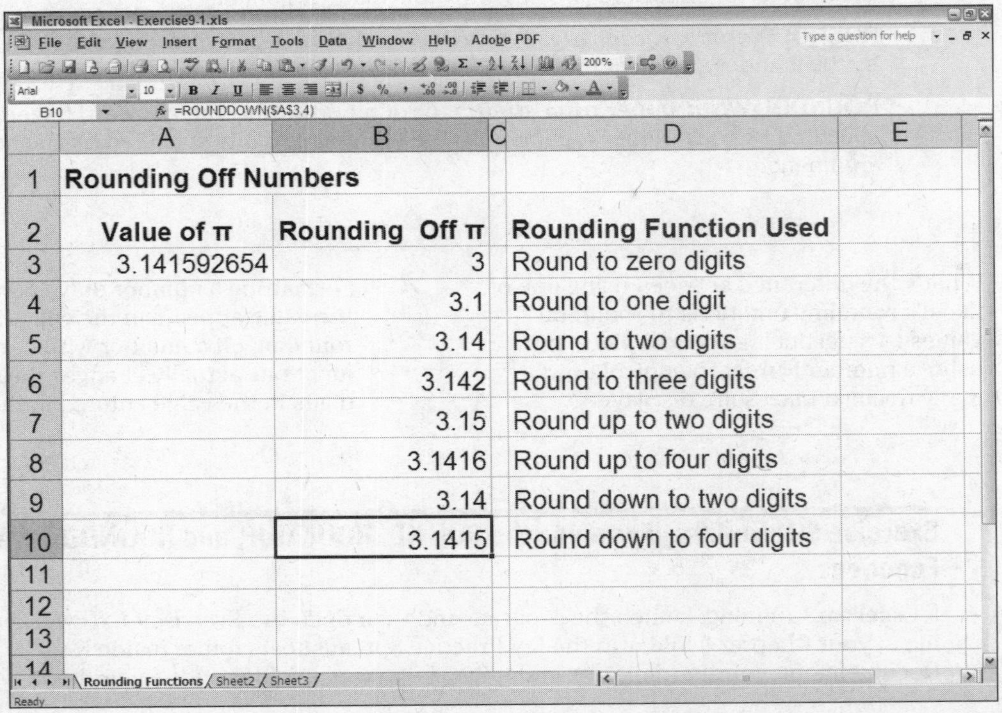

Figure 9-1:
The Exercise9-1.xls workbook with its ROUND, ROUNDUP, and ROUNDDOWN formulas.

	A	B	C	D	E
1	**Rounding Off Numbers**				
2	**Value of π**	**Rounding Off π**		**Rounding Function Used**	
3	3.141592654	3		Round to zero digits	
4		3.1		Round to one digit	
5		3.14		Round to two digits	
6		3.142		Round to three digits	
7		3.15		Round up to two digits	
8		3.1416		Round up to four digits	
9		3.14		Round down to two digits	
10		3.1415		Round down to four digits	
11					
12					
13					
14					

B10 =ROUNDDOWN($A$3,4)

Microsoft Excel - Exercise9-1.xls

Finding Products, Powers, and Square Roots

Although you can create formulas that multiply values using the asterisk (*) operator as well as those that raise a number to a particular power by using the caret (^), Excel also includes PRODUCT and POWER functions that perform these types of calculations for you. And for those times when you need to find the square root of a value, the program includes a SQRT function. These three Math functions work with the following arguments:

- **PRODUCT(*number1,number2, . . .*)** where the number1, number2 arguments are the values you want to multiply with one another

- **POWER(*number,power*)** where the number argument is the value you want to raise the power specified by the power argument

- **SQRT(*number*)** where the number argument is the value for which you want the square root

Try It

Exercise 9-2: Building Formulas with the PRODUCT, POWER, and SQRT Functions

Open the *Exercise9-2.xls* workbook file in your Chapter 9 folder in the My Practice Spreadsheets folder inside My Documents on your hard disk or in the Excel Workbook folder on the workbook CD-ROM. This file contains a Misc. Math Formulas worksheet where you can practice using the PRODUCT, POWER, and SQRT functions in a couple of tables:

1. Position the cell cursor in cell D3 and construct a formula using the PRODUCT function that multiplies the price in B3 by the quantity in cell C3.

2. Format the computed amount in cell D3 with the Currency Style format and then copy this formula down to the cell range D4:D5.

3. In cell B9, construct a formula that squares the value in cell A9 and then copy this POWER formula down to the cell range B10:B11.

4. In cell C9, construct a formula that cubes the value in cell A9 and then copy this POWER formula down to the cell range C10:C11.

5. In cell D9, construct a formula that finds the square root of the value in cell A9 and then copy this SQRT formula down to the cell range D10:D11.

Cell D11 returns a #NUM! error value in the cell because the SQRT function cannot compute square roots for negative numbers (multiplying one negative number by another always results in a positive product).

To avoid the #NUM! error in this formula, you can nest the ABS function that returns the absolute value of cell A11 (which is always positive) inside the SQRT function as follows:

```
=SQRT(ABS(A11))
```

6. Edit the original formula in cell D9 by positioning the insertion point between the T in SQRT and the open parenthesis. Type **(ABS** and then position the insertion point between 9 in A9 and the close parenthesis, and then type another close parenthesis before clicking the Enter button on the Formula bar.

The edited formula should appear on the Formula bar as follows:

```
=SQRT(ABS(A9))
```

7. Copy this edited version of the SQRT formula with the nested ABS function over the original formula copies in the cell range D10:D11.

Check your results against those shown in Figure 9-2. If everything checks out, proceed to Step 8.

8. Save your workbook file in the Chapter 9 folder with the filename **Solved9-2.xls**.

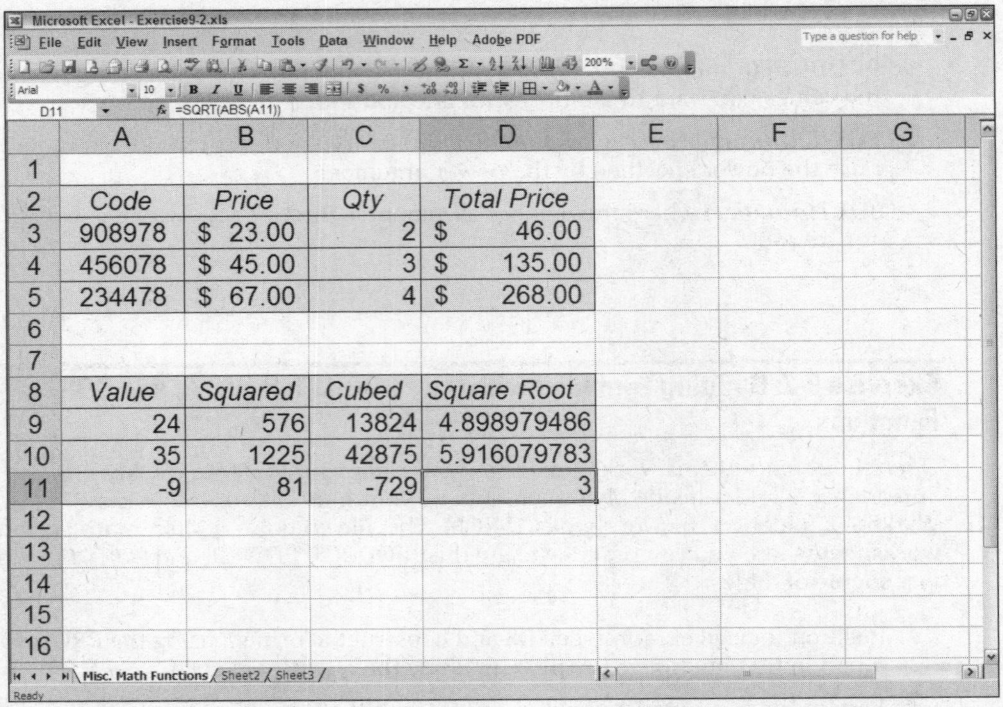

Figure 9-2:
The
Exercise9-2.
xls work-
book with its
PRODUCT,
POWER,
and SQRT
formulas.

Doing Fancier Sums

Without any doubt, SUM is the preeminent function in the Math & Trig category. This function is so central to spreadsheet formula-making that the Standard toolbar contains its own AutoSum button to facilitate the construction of all your SUM formulas.

The SUM function is not the only function in the Math & Trig category capable of computing totals. In addition, the program offers more specialized summing functions for use when you need to total the products or squares of the values in a range or total values only when a particular condition is met.

Summing products, squares, and their differences

You can use the SUMPRODUCT function to have Excel total the products returned by multiplying the values in corresponding arrays. For one array to correspond to another, each must consist of the same number of rows and columns.

For example, suppose you have a spreadsheet with a 2 x 1 array in the cell range B2:B3 that contains the values 4 and 5 (expressed as {4;5}), and another 2 x 1 array in the cell range D2:D3 that values 6 and 3 (expressed {6;3}) — see Chapter 6 for a quick refresher on arrays. Because both these arrays have the same number of rows (2) and columns (1), they correspond and can be used as arguments in the SUMPRODUCT function.

The SUMPRODUCT function uses the following syntax:

```
SUMPRODUCT(array1,array2, . . .)
```

Note that the SUMPRODUCT function accepts up to a maximum of 30 array arguments. The SUMPRODUCT function is not the only summing function to use these arguments. The following summing functions also follow the same syntax as SUMPRODUCT:

- ✔ **SUMX2MY2** (SUM X squared minus Y squared) to sum the difference between the squares of two corresponding arrays

- ✔ **SUMX2PY2** (SUM X squared plus Y squared) to return the grand total of the sums of the squares in two corresponding arrays

- ✔ **SUMXMY2** (SUM X minus Y squared) to sum the squares of the differences in two corresponding arrays

The SUMSQ function that totals the squares of the arguments is similar to these summing functions, except that you can use individual numbers as well as arrays for its arguments.

Try It

Exercise 9-3: Building Formulas with the SUMPRODUCT, SUMSQ, and SUMX2PY2 Functions

Open the *Exercise9-3.xls* workbook file in your Chapter 9 folder in the My Practice Spreadsheets folder inside My Documents on your hard disk or in the Excel Workbook folder on the workbook CD-ROM. This file contains a SUM Formulas worksheet with two 2 x 1 arrays, the first in light yellow in the cell range B2:B3 and the second in light green in the cell range D2:D3. You will use these arrays to practice using the SUMPRODUCT, SUMSQ, and SUMX2PY2 functions:

1. Position the cell cursor in cell F6 and construct a formula with the SUMPRODUCT function that totals the products of the first array in light yellow in the cell range B2:B3 and the second array in light green in the cell range D2:D3.

Excel returns a result of 39 in cell F9 as the sum of the products of the two arrays.

2. Verify the calculated result returned by the SUMPRODUCT formula in cell F6 by constructing the following simple formulas in the designated cells that replicate the computation made by the SUMPRODUCT function:

- • Formula in cell C6 that multiplies the value in B2 by that in D2

- • Formula in cell D6 that multiplies the value in B3 by that in D3

- • Formula in cell E6 that adds the value in C6 to that in D6

The calculated total returned to cell E6 should be 39, just like the one in cell F6 next door.

3. Position the cell cursor in cell G8 and construct a formula with the SUMSQ function that sums the squares of the value in cell B2 with that in cell D2.

Excel returns a total of 52 to cell G8.

4. Verify the calculated result returned by the SUMSQ formula in cell G8 by constructing the following simple formulas in the designated cells that replicate its computation:

- Formula in cell D8 that squares the value in B2
- Formula in cell E8 that squares the value in D2
- Formula in cell F8 that adds the value in D8 to that in E8

To square a value in a cell, insert the cell reference followed by the caret (^) operator and 2 (for example, =B2^2 to square the value in B2).

The calculated total returned to cell F8 should now match the one in cell G8 next door.

5. Position the cell cursor in cell G10 and construct a formula with the SUMSQ function that sums the squares of the first array in the cell range B2:B3 with that in the second array in the cell range D2:D3.

Excel returns a sum of 86 to cell G10.

6. Verify the calculated result returned by the SUMSQ formula in cell G10 by constructing the following simple formulas in the designated cells that replicate its computation:

- Formula in cell B10 that squares the value in B2
- Formula in cell C10 that squares the value in B3
- Formula in cell D10 that squares the value in D2
- Formula in cell E10 that squares the value in D3
- Formula in cell F10 that sums the values in cell range B10:E10

The calculated total returned to cell F10 should now match the one in cell G10.

7. Position the cell cursor in cell G12 and construct a formula with the SUMX2MY2 function that calculates the difference between the squares of the first array in the cell range B2:B3 and that in the second array in the cell range D2:D3.

Excel returns a sum of -4 to cell G12.

8. Verify the calculated result returned by the SUMX2MY2 formula in cell G10 by constructing the following simple formulas in the designated cells that replicate its computation:

- Formula in cell B12 that squares the value in B2
- Formula in cell C12 that squares the value in B3
- Formula in cell D12 that squares the value in D2
- Formula in cell E12 that squares the value in D3
- Formula in cell F12 that subtracts the sum of B12 plus C12 from the sum of D12 plus E12

When constructing the formula in cell F12 that subtracts the sum of B12 and C12 from the sum of D12 plus E12, be sure to enclose the values to be summed (B12+C12) and (D12+E12) in parentheses.

The calculated total returned to cell F12 should now match the one in cell G12.

9. Open the *Solved9-3.xls* workbook in the Chapter 9 folder and check the results in your SUM formulas sheet against its formulas. If everything checks out, save your workbook in the Chapter 9 folder with the filename **Solved9-3-mine.xls** and then close both workbooks.

Conditional totals

All the variations of the SUM function you've used up to now calculate their totals come rain or shine. The SUMIF function, however, is a little different: It only sums its designated values when a particular condition is true. The SUMIF function, although located in the Math & Trig category, could have just as easily been classified as one of the Logical functions (see Chapter 12) because it basically works only when its comparative condition returns the logical value TRUE (refer to Chapter 12 for a refresher on creating comparative formulas that return TRUE or FALSE as their answers).

The syntax of the SUMIF function includes the following arguments:

```
SUMIF(range,criteria,[sum_range])
```

The range argument specifies the cells that you want Excel to evaluate using the condition or conditions specified by the criteria argument. The optional sum_range argument specifies the cells you want Excel to sum when the condition in the criteria argument is found TRUE. You only need to specify a sum_range argument when the cell range to be summed is not the same as the one whose values are evaluated as to whether they meet the condition set up in the criteria argument.

To get some practice using the SUMIF function, you will work with the Jan-06 Sales worksheet in the workbook containing the data list of the January 2006 sales for the fictitious company, Chris's Cookies. This data list tracks the sales by store location, the type of baked item sold (lemon tarts, blueberry muffins, Lots of Chips cookies, and strawberry pie), the date of sale, the number of dozens sold, the price per dozen, and the daily sales total. Most of these fields tracked in the data list have range names assigned to their data (Store_name to the data in the Store field, Date_sold to the data in the Date field, Item_sold to data in the Item field, and Daily_sales to the data in the Daily Sales field) that you can refer in place of cell ranges in the formulas you construct using the SUMIF function.

Try It

Exercise 9-4: Using the SUMIF Function

Open the *Exercise9-4.xls* workbook file in your Chapter 9 folder in the My Practice Spreadsheets folder inside My Documents on your hard disk or in the Excel Workbook folder on the workbook CD-ROM. Use its Jan-06 Sales worksheet to practice using the SUMIF function.

1. Position the cell cursor in cell I3 and construct a formula using the SUMIF function that totals the daily sales for all lemon tarts sold in the month of January 2006.

This SUMIF function uses the Item_sold range as its range argument and the Daily_sales range as its sum_range argument. The condition for the criteria argument is where the item sold is equal to lemon tarts, which is expressed as follows:

```
"=lemon tarts"
```

Note that because you are evaluating a text string in this comparative expression that contains a space, you must enclose the entire criteria argument inside double quotation marks.

2. Select the SUMIF function in the Math & Trig category in the Insert Function dialog box and then select OK to open the Function Arguments dialog box for this function.

3. With the insertion point in the Range text box, choose Insert⇨Name⇨Paste and then select Item_sold in the Paste Name dialog box before you select OK.

Use the Paste Name dialog box to insert range names already defined in the workbook that you want to use as the operands or functional arguments of the formulas you're building.

4. Press Tab to select the Criteria text box and then type **"=lemon tarts"** here.

5. Press Tab to select the Sum_range text box and then select Daily_sales in the Paste Name dialog box.

Check the values in your argument text boxes against those shown in the one in Figure 9-3. If everything checks out, proceed to Step 6.

6. Select OK to insert the SUMIF function in cell I3.

Excel returns a total of $815.00 for the lemon tarts sold in January 2006.

7. Construct a SUMIF function in cell I4 that totals the daily sales for just blueberry muffins.

Be sure the criteria argument for this SUMIF function includes the quotation marks:

```
"=blueberry muffins"
```

8. Construct a SUMIF function in cell I5 that totals the daily sales for just Lots of Chips cookies.

9. Construct a SUMIF function in cell I6 that totals the daily sales for just strawberry pie.

10. Construct a SUMIF function in cell I8 that totals the daily sales for all items except for strawberry pie.

Use the <> operator with strawberry pie to have Excel exclude it from the total, while at the same time summing the daily sales for all the other baked items:

```
"<>Strawberry pie"
```

11. Save your work under the filename **Solved9-4.xls** and leave this workbook open to use in completing Exercise 9-5 on using the Conditional Sum Wizard.

Figure 9-3: The Function Arguments dialog box for the SUMIF function that totals the daily sales for lemon tarts.

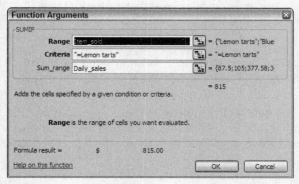

The SUMIF function works great when you only have only one criterion that you want to apply in doing the summing. It does not, however, work when you have multiple criteria that you need to use in determining which numbers get added to the total and which don't. For those situations, you have to turn to the Conditional Sum Wizard, a nifty little Excel add-in tool that walks you through the steps of building more complex SUM formulas that utilize IF conditions that can include multiple criteria.

In the next exercise, you use the Conditional Sum Wizard to construct a formula using the Chris's Cookies monthly sales list in the Jan-06 Sales worksheet that sums the daily sales made at the Anderson Road store location for all baked items except for strawberry pie after the date of January 1, 2006.

Try It

Exercise 9-5: Using the Conditional Sum Wizard

Use the _Solved9-4.xls_ workbook that you created in Exercise 9-4 to complete this exercise using the Conditional Sum Wizard:

1. Select the Conditional Sum Wizard check box in the Add-Ins dialog box (Tools➪ Add-Ins) and then select Yes if prompted by an alert dialog box to install the add-in.

2. Position the cell cursor in cell I10 to use the Conditional Sum Wizard to construct the formula that sums all baked goods except for strawberry pie sold after January 1 at the Anderson Road store location.

3. Open the Step 1 of 4 Conditional Sum Wizard dialog box by choosing Tools➪ Conditional Sum.

In this dialog box, you indicate the entire range of the data list, including its column labels (field names). In this case, you need to select the cell range of the entire data list A2:G62

4. Drag the cell cursor through the cell range A2:G62.

The text box in the Step 1 of 4 dialog box now contains the range 'Jan-06 Sales'!$A$2:$G$62.

5. Select the Next button to proceed to the Step 2 of 4 Conditional Sum Wizard dialog box.

In the Step 2 of 4 dialog box, you indicate the column to sum as well as the column(s) to evaluate and the condition(s) to be used.

6. Leave Daily Sales in the Column to Sum text box, select Date in the Column drop-down list box below, > (greater than) in the Is drop-down list box, and leave 1/1/2006 selected in This Value drop-down list box before you select the Add Condition button.

7. Using these drop-down list boxes and the Add Condition button, add a second condition where the Item is not equal to (<>) strawberry pie.

8. Add a third and final condition with these controls where the store is equal to (=) Anderson Road.

9. Check your Step 2 of 4 Conditional Sum Wizard dialog box against the one shown in Figure 9-4: If everything checks out, click the Next button.

10. In the Step 3 of 4 Conditional Sum Wizard dialog box, leave the Copy Just the Formula to a Single Cell option button selected and then click the Next button.

If you were to select the Copy Formula and Conditional Values, the Wizard would then prompt you for cell references for each column used in a condition and its associated SUMIF formula.

11. In the Step 4 of 4 Conditional Sum Wizard dialog box, click cell I10 in the worksheet to insert the reference 'Jan-06 Sales'!$I$10 in its text box and then select the Finish button.

Excel then inserts a long SUM function containing several nested IF conditions in cell I10.

12. Open the *Solved9-5.xls* workbook in your Chapter 9 folder inside the My Practice Spreadsheets folder and then check the SUMIF formulas and SUM formula with nested IF functions in your workbook against those found in this workbook file. If everything checks out OK, save your workbook under the name **Solved9-5-mine.xls** and then close both the workbook files as you exit Excel.

Figure 9-4:
The Step 2 of 4 Conditional Sum Wizard dialog box after specifying the column to sum and the conditions to use.

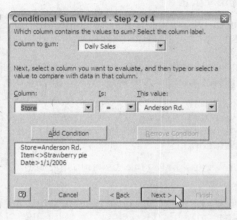

Chapter 10

Using Statistical Functions

*E*xcel includes one of the most complete sets of statistical functions available outside of a dedicated statistics software program. These functions run the gamut from the more mundane AVERAGE, MAX, and MIN functions to the more exotic and much more specialized CHITEST, POISSON, and PERCENTILE statistical functions. In addition, the program offers an assortment of counting functions that enable you to count the number of cells that contain values, are nonblank (and thus contain entries of any kind), or count only the cells in a cell range that meet the criteria you specify. In this chapter, you get a chance to practice working with the most commonly used statistical functions, AVERAGE, MAX, and MIN, as well as the different counting functions.

Computing Averages

The average is the arithmetic mean computed by summing all the values to be averaged and then dividing this total by the number of values. Excel's AVERAGE function, which calculates the average of a range or series of values, uses the following syntax:

```
AVERAGE(number1,[number2],[. . .])
```

One way to understand the workings of the AVERAGE function is to display the corresponding SUM and COUNT formulas that return the exact same result. For example, suppose you want to find the average of the values in the cell range D4:D8 in your spreadsheet by entering the following formula in a cell:

```
=AVERAGE(D4:D8)
```

In place of this AVERAGE function, you could obtain the same result by entering the following formula:

```
=SUM(D4:D8)/COUNT(D4:D8)
```

Note that the COUNT function shown as the divisor in this equivalent formula returns the number of cells in the specified range that contain numeric entries (see Exercise 10-3 later in this chapter for practice on using COUNT).

Note that if the values in the number arguments of the AVERAGE function contain cells with text entries, logical values (TRUE or FALSE), or that are blank, Excel ignores them in the counting calculation (they are naturally ignored in the summing). However, if the cells in the number arguments contain 0 (zero) values, they are used in the counting calculation (even though they add nothing to the sum).

In addition to the AVERAGE function used to calculate the arithmetic mean in range or series of values, Excel also includes a MEDIAN function, which takes the same kind of arguments. Instead of the arithmetic mean, the MEDIAN function returns the value that lies precisely in the middle of those in the range or series specified as its arguments, with half greater and half less.

Exercise 10-1: Building Formulas with the AVERAGE and MEDIAN Functions

If Excel is not currently running, launch the program. Then, open the *Exercise10-1.xls* workbook file in your Chapter 10 folder inside the My Practice Spreadsheets folder or in the Excel Workbook folder on the workbook CD-ROM. This workbook contains a Home Sales-06 worksheet with a concise data table showing the recent house sales during April and May in a small subdivision. You can use the sampling in this sales table to practice using the AVERAGE and MEDIAN functions:

1. Select the cell range D4:D8 in the *Home Sales-06* worksheet and then assign to this selected cell range, the range name, **Selling_price**.

2. Position the cell cursor in cell D10 and then enter a formula there using the AVERAGE function (in the Statistical function category in the Insert Function dialog box) with the range Selling_price as its argument.

Use the Insert⇨Name⇨Paste command to insert the range name in the Number1 text box in the Function Arguments dialog box for the AVERAGE function.

3. Enter the following formula in cell E10:

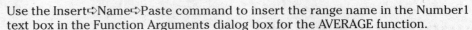

```
=SUM(Selling_price)/COUNT(Selling_price)
```

As you can see, this division formula using the SUM and COUNT functions in cell E10 returns the same value as the AVERAGE function in D10.

4. Enter a formula in cell D12 using the MEDIAN function that uses the Selling_price range name as its sole argument.

Note the difference between the average and the median sales price as computed by Excel in cells D10 and D12. The average selling price for a home in the sample shown in this table is nearly $100,000 more than the median.

5. Save your work in a new workbook file named **Solved10-1.xls** in the Chapter 10 folder inside the My Practice Spreadsheets folder and leave this file open in Excel for the next exercise.

Finding the Highest and Lowest Values

The MAX and MIN functions compute the highest and lowest values in a cell range or series, respectively. They take the same type of arguments as the AVERAGE and MEDIAN statistical functions. Although they may not seem very powerful when using them on very small samples (such as the selling prices in the Home Sales-06 worksheet you used in Exercise 10-1), where you can visually pick out the highest and lowest selling prices in an instant, they come in quite handy when dealing with large data sets, where it would take a long time to locate these key values.

Try It

Exercise 10-2: Building Formulas with the MAX and MIN Functions

Use the *Solved10-1.xls* workbook you created at the end of Exercise 10-1 to practice adding MAX and MIN functions to the spreadsheet table located on the *Home Sales-06* worksheet:

1. Locate the cell cursor in cell D14 in the *Home Sales-06* worksheet and construct a formula using the MAX function with the range name Selling_price (assigned in Exercise 10-1) as its argument to find the largest selling price in the range.

No surprise here: Excel returns $1,085,000 as the highest selling price in this range.

2. Construct a formula in cell D16 using the MIN function with Selling_price as its argument to find the lowest selling price in the range.

Again no surprise here: Excel returns $550,000 as the lowest selling price in the range.

3. Insert two new rows into the sales table immediately above the row containing the sales data for 566 Elm Street in the cell range B7:D7.

To insert two rows of blank cells in this table, select the cell range B7:D8 and then choose Insert⇨Cells and select OK when the Shift Cells Down option button is selected.

4. Update the sales table by making the following data entries into the newly inserted blank rows of cells:

  • **211 River Road** in cell B7, **5/15/06** in cell C7, and **495000** in cell D7

  • **8989 King Place** in cell B8, **5/23/06** in cell C8, and **1,500,000** in cell D8

Note the effect that your table edits have on the average price, high price, and low price cells in the spreadsheet as calculated by the AVERAGE, MAX, and MIN functions, respectively.

5. Save your work in a new workbook named **Solved10-2.xls** in the Chapter 10 folder inside the My Practice Spreadsheets folder and then close this workbook file.

Counting Cells

Excel includes three counting functions, COUNTA, COUNT, and COUNTBLANK. You can use these functions to build formulas that compute the number of cells in a particular region or worksheet that are occupied, contain numeric entries, or are blank. The syntax of these functions is as follows:

✔ **COUNTA(*number1*, [*number2l*], [. . .])** to return the number of nonblank cells in the number argument(s)

✔ **COUNT(*number1*, [*number2*],[. . .])** to return the number of cells containing numeric entries in the number argument(s)

✔ **COUNTBLANK(*range*)** to return the number of blank cells in the range argument

In addition to these standard counting functions, the program includes a COUNTIF function that works much like the SUMIF function you encountered in Chapter 9. You can use this function to return the count in a cell range of only those cells whose entries meet the condition you set up in its criteria argument. This function uses the following syntax:

```
COUNTIF(range, criteria)
```

When specifying a number for the criteria argument of the COUNTIF function, you simply enter the number or the reference to the cell that contains the number. When specifying a comparative expression or text for the criteria argument, you must remember to enclose the argument in a set of double quotation marks. For example, to use COUNTIF to find the number of cells in the range E15:E45 that contain the number 50, you would enter the following formula:

```
=COUNTIF(E15:E45,50)
```

If, however, you want to know the number of cells in this range that contain values greater than or equal to 50, you would enter this formula:

```
=COUNTIF(E15:E45,">=50")
```

Further, suppose that cell D10 contains the numeric entry 50 and you want to construct the COUNTIF formula using this cell reference in the criteria argument rather than the number itself. You would have to enter this version of the formula as

```
=COUNTIF(E15:E45,">="&D10)
```

Remember from Table 5-1 that the & (ampersand) acts as the concatenation text operator that connects text to another entry (in this case, it connects the text ">=" to the cell reference, D10) to produce one continuous entry.

If you enclose a cell reference (such as D10 in the previous example) inside quotation marks in the COUNTIF criteria argument, Excel interprets the cell address as a text string to locate in the entries in the function's range argument.

Try It

Exercise 10-3: Building Formulas with the COUNT, COUNTBLANK, COUNTA, and COUNTIF Functions

Open the *Exercise10-3.xls* workbook file in your Chapter 10 folder inside the My Practice Spreadsheets folder or in the Excel Workbook folder on the workbook CD-ROM. This workbook contains a version of the *Home Sales-06* worksheet that you can use to practice using the counting functions:

1. Select the cell range B1:D8 in the *Home Sales-06* worksheet and assign the range name **Sales_table** to it.

2. Position the cell cursor in D12 and construct a formula using the COUNTA statistical function with Sales_table as its argument that returns the number of cells with entries of any kind in this range.

3. Position the cell cursor in D14 and construct a formula using the COUNT function with Sales_table as its argument that returns the number of cells with numeric entries in this range.

4. Position the cell cursor in D16 and construct a formula using the COUNTBLANK function with Sales_table as its argument that returns the number of empty cells in this range.

5. Position the cell cursor in cell D10 and construct a formula that computes the total number of cells in the Sales_table range.

The total number of cells in the Sales_table range is equal to the number of occupied cells returned by the COUNTA function in cell D12 plus the number of empty cells returned by the COUNTBLANK function is cell D16.

6. Position the cell cursor in cell D18 and create a formula with the COUNTIF function that returns the number of addresses in the cell range B4:B8 of the Sales table that have the word *Street* in them.

When specifying text in the *criteria* argument of the COUNTIF function, you can use the * (asterisk) as the wildcard character to stand in for multiple, unnamed characters or the ? (question mark) to stand in for individual characters, as in "*Street" to find the addresses of any length that end with the word *Street*.

7. Position the cell cursor in cell D20 and create a formula with the COUNTIF function that returns the number of selling prices in the cell range D4:D8 of the Sales table that are above $600,000.

Don't forget to enclose the criteria argument with the > (greater than) operator in a set of double quotation marks.

8. Enter the value 400000 in cell F3 and then format it with Currency style with no decimal places.

9. Edit the formula in cell D20 so that the criteria argument immediately following the ">" (greater than) operator refers to contents in cell F3 rather than the static value of 600000.

When referring to a cell reference in the criteria argument of the COUNTIF function, don't omit the & (ampersand) text operator immediately following the ">" (greater than) operator and immediately preceding the reference to cell F3.

10. Replace the $400,000 entered into cell F3 with **$700,000**.

Note that COUNTIF function immediately updates the result in cell D20 from 5 to 2 (only two entries in the range D4:D8, cells D4 and D8, have selling prices over $700,000).

11. Save your workbook in a new file named **Solved10-3.xls** in your Chapter 10 folder inside the My Practice Spreadsheets folder on your hard disk and then close the file.

Using the Statistical Functions in the Analysis ToolPak Add-in

For you serious statisticians out there, the Analysis ToolPak add-in — which you first encountered in Chapter 7 if you completed its exercises — contains a whole bunch of extra statistical functions that may come in handy in your work. Before you can access these supplementary statistical functions, you must install and activate the Analysis ToolPak by selecting its check box in the Add-Ins dialog box (Tools⇨ Add-Ins).

After that, you access their functions from the Data Analysis dialog box (Tools➪Data Analysis) shown in Figure 10-1. To use a particular function, select its name in the Analysis Tools list box and then select OK. To get online information about the purpose of these statistical functions, select the Help button in this dialog box.

After selecting OK, Excel opens another dialog box specific to the function you selected in the Data Analysis dialog box. This new dialog box contains all the controls and text boxes needed to select and fill in the function's arguments (for help on the arguments, select its Help button). After filling in the necessary arguments, select OK to have Excel compute the statistical result and return it to the current cell.

Figure 10-1:
The Data
Analysis
dialog box
enables you
to access
the extra
statistical
functions
included in
the Analysis
ToolPak
add-in.

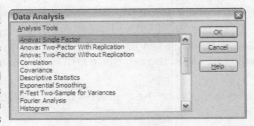

Chapter 11

Using the Lookup Functions

The Lookup functions in the Lookup & Reference category of Excel functions are designed to automate the process of matching values in two separate lists or tables in a work-book and then returning a related value. For example, you can set up a price lookup table in a worksheet where you store and update the prices for all the items your company sells. After that, you construct formulas in a sales table using the appropriate lookup function that match an item number entered into a field in the sales table with an item number entered into the price lookup table. When the function finds a match between these item numbers, Excel then copies the price associated with that item number in the price lookup table and pastes it into the appropriate field in the sales table.

The Reference functions are primarily designed to return specific types of information about particular cells or regions of a worksheet. This part of the Lookup & Reference cate-gory also includes functions that create hyperlinks to different worksheets and documents and that transpose the data in a table so that data that originally ran across the rows now runs down the columns, and vice versa.

In this chapter, you get a chance to practice creating formulas that automate table lookup, including looking up a single value, either across a row of a lookup data table or down one of its columns, as well as using the Lookup Wizard to perform a lookup that uses two values to find the matching data in a lookup data table.

Returning Single Values from a Lookup Table

The most popular of the Lookup & Reference functions are the HLOOKUP (for Horizontal Lookup) and VLOOKUP (for Vertical Lookup) functions. The VLOOKUP function searches vertically (top to bottom) the leftmost column of a lookup table until the program locates a value that matches or exceeds the one you are looking up. The HLOOKUP function searches horizontally (left to right) the topmost row of a lookup table until it locates a value that matches or exceeds the one you're looking up.

The VLOOKUP function uses the following syntax:

```
VLOOKUP(lookup_value, table_array, col_index_num, [range_lookup])
```

The HLOOKUP follows the nearly identical syntax:

HLOOKUP (*lookup_value*, *table_array*, *row_index_num*, [*range_lookup*])

The arguments of these two Lookup functions can be explained as follows:

- ✔ The lookup_value argument designates the range that contains the values or text to be looked up in the table.

- ✔ The table_array argument designates the range with the data table you want looked up in the lookup table as well as the data you want returned from the lookup table.

- ✔ The col_index_num argument in the VLOOKUP function designates the number of the column in the lookup table (starting with 1 for the leftmost column and increasing one each column to the right) that contains the data you want returned to the data table.

- ✔ The row_index_num argument in the HLOOKUP function designates the number of the row in the lookup table (starting with 1 for the topmost row and increasing one down each row) that contains the data you want returned to the data table.

- ✔ The optional range_lookup argument is a TRUE or FALSE value that indicates whether you want Excel to find an approximate (TRUE or argument omitted) or exact match (FALSE) to numerical entries in the range designated by the function's lookup_value argument.

When using the VLOOKUP and HLOOKUP functions, the text or numeric entries in the lookup column or row (that is, the leftmost column of a vertical lookup table or the top row of a horizontal lookup table) must all be unique (no duplicates allowed). These entries must also be arranged or sorted in ascending order; that is, alphabetical order for text entries, lowest-to-highest order for numeric entries. (See Chapter 16 for exercises on sorting data in a list or table.)

Performing a horizontal lookup

You use the HLOOKUP function when you're dealing with a lookup table where the data to look up is entered in the first (top) row, arranged sequentially (that is, alphabetically for text entries and from smallest to largest in the case of numeric entries) by columns from left to right. Figure 11-1 shows just such a lookup table at the top of the *Jan-06 Sales* worksheet — the Price Lookup Table in the cell range C3:F4.

First off, note that bakery items listed in the top, lookup row of this Price Lookup Table are text values arranged in alphabetical order from left to right as follows:

- ✔ Blueberry muffins in cell C3

- ✔ Lemon tarts in cell D3

- ✔ Lots of Chips cookies in cell E3

- ✔ Strawberry pie in cell F3

Second, note that the price per dozen for each bakery item is listed in a corresponding column immediately below in the second row of the table (cell range, C4:F4). The order of the values in the cells in this row is dictated entirely by the order of their associated bakery items in the row above.

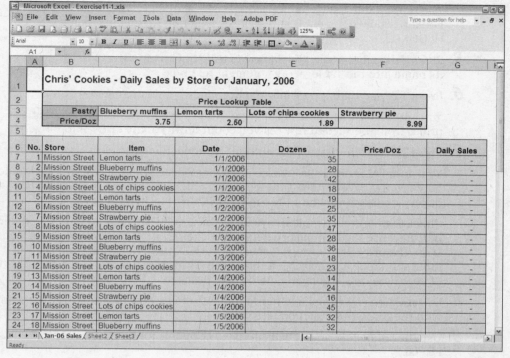

Chris' Cookies - Daily Sales by Store for January, 2006

		Price Lookup Table			
Pastry	**Blueberry muffins**	**Lemon tarts**	**Lots of chips cookies**	**Strawberry pie**	
Price/Doz	3.75	2.50	1.89	8.99	

No.	Store	Item	Date	Dozens	Price/Doz	Daily Sales
1	Mission Street	Lemon tarts	1/1/2006	35		-
2	Mission Street	Blueberry muffins	1/1/2006	28		-
3	Mission Street	Strawberry pie	1/1/2006	42		-
4	Mission Street	Lots of chips cookies	1/1/2006	18		-
5	Mission Street	Lemon tarts	1/2/2006	19		-
6	Mission Street	Blueberry muffins	1/2/2006	25		-
7	Mission Street	Strawberry pie	1/2/2006	35		-
8	Mission Street	Lots of chips cookies	1/2/2006	47		-
9	Mission Street	Lemon tarts	1/3/2006	28		-
10	Mission Street	Blueberry muffins	1/3/2006	36		-
11	Mission Street	Strawberry pie	1/3/2006	18		-
12	Mission Street	Lots of chips cookies	1/3/2006	23		-
13	Mission Street	Lemon tarts	1/4/2006	14		-
14	Mission Street	Blueberry muffins	1/4/2006	24		-
15	Mission Street	Strawberry pie	1/4/2006	16		-
16	Mission Street	Lots of chips cookies	1/4/2006	45		-
17	Mission Street	Lemon tarts	1/5/2006	32		-
18	Mission Street	Blueberry muffins	1/5/2006	32		-

Figure 11-1:
The Jan-06 Sales worksheet showing a Price Lookup Table immediately above the Daily Sales spreadsheet.

In the following exercise, you use the information kept in this Price Lookup Table to supply the missing information to the Price/Doz column in the Daily Sales data list below it. To do this, you construct a formula using the HLOOKUP function that matches the bakery item listed as sold in the Item column of the data list (C7:C66) against the items shown in the top row of the Price Lookup Table. It then returns the price per dozen for the matched item to the appropriate cell in the Price/Doz column in the data list (F7:F66).

Try It

Exercise 11-1: Building Formulas that Perform Horizontal Lookups in a Table

ON THE CD

If Excel is not currently running, launch the program. Then, open the *Exercise11-1.xls* workbook file in your Chapter 11 folder inside the My Practice Spreadsheets folder or in the Excel Workbook folder on the workbook CD-ROM. This workbook contains the Jan-06 Sales worksheet with the Price Lookup Table and the Daily Sales data list you need to practice using the HLOOKUP function:

1. Assign the following range names to the designated cell ranges:

- **Item_match** to cell range C7:C66

- **Price_info** to cell range C3:F4

2. Position the cell cursor in cell F7 and then click the Insert Function button on the Formula bar.

3. Select Lookup & Reference in the Select a Category drop-down list box, and then click HLOOKUP in the list and select OK.

4. Choose Insert⇨Name⇨Paste and then click Item_match and select OK in the Paste Name dialog box.

The range name Item_match encompassing C7:C66 is now listed in the Lookup_value argument text box of the Function Arguments dialog box for HLOOKUP.

5. Press Tab and then use the Paste Name dialog box to select Price_info and insert its name into the Table_array argument text box.

6. Press Tab and then type **2** into the Row_index_num argument text box.

You enter 2 for this value because you want Excel to return the appropriate prices from the second row (as you count down) of the Price_info range.

7. Press Tab and then type **false** into the optional Range_lookup argument text box.

You enter FALSE into this argument text box because you only want exact matches between the bakery items entered into the Item_match range (C7:C66) and the bakery items entered into the top row of the Price_info range.

Check the Formula Result shown at the bottom of the Function Arguments dialog box. Because the first bakery item sold in cell C7 of the Daily Sales list is lemon tarts, the price per dozen returned by the HLOOKUP function from the Price_info table should be listed as 2.5. If this is the Formula result displayed at the bottom of your Function Arguments dialog box, proceed to Step 8.

8. Select OK to close the Function Arguments dialog box and insert the formula with the HLOOKUP function into cell F7.

9. Use the Fill handle on the cell cursor to copy this formula down to the cell range F8:F66.

Check the prices returned by the copies of the original HLOOKUP formula in the top rows of the Daily Sales data list against those shown for the various bakery items in the Price Lookup Table. The price per dozen for the blueberry muffins should be returned as 3.75, strawberry pie as 8.99, and Lots of Chips cookies as 1.89.

10. Increase the price per dozen for Lots of chips cookies in cell E4 of the Price Lookup Table from 1.89 to 3.89.

Note that this change to the basic price is immediately updated in all the sales of Lots of Chips cookies in the Daily Sales data list. By using a lookup table to supply the basic price per dozen data to this list, you only need make a single change to a price in the Price Lookup Table in order to update every single sale of that item in the entire data list.

11. Save your work in a new workbook named **Solved11-1.xls** in your Chapter 11 folder inside the My Practice Spreadsheets folder and then close this workbook file.

Performing a vertical lookup

You use the VLOOKUP function when the data to look up is entered in the first (leftmost) column, arranged sequentially (that is, alphabetically for text entries and from smallest to largest in the case of numeric entries) by rows from top to bottom. Figure 11-2 shows you just such a vertical lookup table in the form of its Tip Schedule in the cell range B4:C103 (of which only the first 21 rows are visible in the figure).

The Tip Schedule in the Tip Lookup worksheet is arranged in two columns: Pretax Total and Tip Amount. Because the Pretax Total column is the first or leftmost column in this table, it contains the data to look up and match against the Food Total entered in cell F2 of this spreadsheet. As the lookup column, you note that its values are arranged in numerical order from smallest to largest.

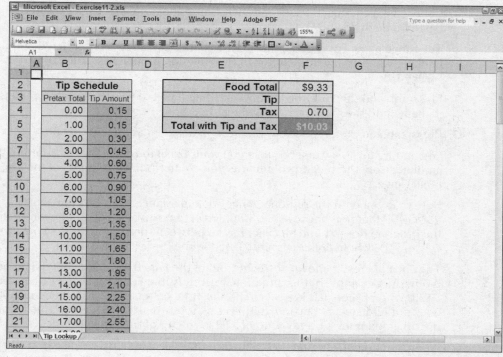

Figure 11-2:
The Tip
Lookup
worksheet
with Tip
Schedule
for looking
up the tip
amount
based on
the pretax
food total.

In the following exercise, you construct a formula using the VLOOKUP function that returns the tip amount to cell F3 from the Tip Amount column of the Tip Schedule table based on the Food Total entered into cell F2 and matched against the amounts listed in the Pretax Total column. Note that this represents a situation where you do *not* want Excel to use exact matching because the amount entered into the Food Total cell can often fall between the whole dollar amounts listed in the Pretax Total column of the Tip Schedule. When this happens (and you don't specify FALSE as the optional range_lookup argument in the VLOOKUP function), Excel returns the amount from the row above.

Try It

Exercise 11-2: Building Formulas that Perform Vertical Lookups in a Table

Open the *Exercise11-2.xls* workbook file in your Chapter 11 folder inside the My Practice Spreadsheets folder or in the Excel Workbook folder on the workbook CD-ROM. This workbook contains the Tip Lookup worksheet with the Tip Schedule that you need to practice using the VLOOKUP function:

1. Assign the following range names to the designated cells and cell ranges:

- **Food_total** to cell F2

- **Tip_table** to the cell range B4:C103

When naming the Tip_table range, try using the AutoSelect feature to select the cell range B4:C103 in a couple of clicks.

2. Position the cell cursor in cell F3 and then click the Insert Function button on the Formula bar.

3. Select Lookup & Reference in the Select a Category drop-down list box, and then click VLOOKUP in the list and select OK.

4. Choose Insert➪Name➪Paste and then click Food_total and select OK in the Paste Name dialog box.

The range name Food_total, the name assigned to cell F2, is now listed in the Lookup_value argument text box of the Function Arguments dialog box for VLOOKUP.

5. Press Tab and then use the Paste Name dialog box to select Tip_table and insert its name into the Table_array argument text box.

6. Press Tab and then type **2** into the Row_index_num argument text box.

You enter 2 for this value because you want Excel to return the appropriate tip amounts from the second column (as you count from left to right) of the Tip_table range.

Note that you omit the optional *range_lookup* argument for this particular VLOOKUP function because you want Excel to return a tip amount even when the program doesn't find an exact match between the amount in the Food_total cell and the whole dollar amounts listed in the Pretax Total column.

The Formula result shown at the bottom of the Function Arguments dialog box is a perfect example of this situation. Currently, the Food_total cell F2 contains $9.33. When Excel matches this in Pretax Total column of the Tip Schedule, it does not find an exact match. In this case, it returns 1.35 as the formula result, the tip amount for a pretax total of 9.00 in row 13 of the Tip Schedule.

When you don't use exact matching for numerical values, Excel always selects the value from the row in the table_array argument in a VLOOKUP function or the column in an HLOOKUP function whose value is closest but doesn't exceed the value specified by the lookup_value argument.

7. Select OK to close the Function Arguments dialog box and insert the formula with the VLOOKUP function into cell F3.

8. Change the Food Total value in cell F2 from $9.33 to **$87.20**.

The moment you complete the edit in this cell, Excel returns a new tip amount of $13.05 to cell F2 (this tip amount is 15% of 87.00, the nearest value in the Tip Schedule that does not exceed the Food Total value).

9. Save your changes to the Tip Lookup worksheet in a new workbook named **Solved11-2.xls** in your Chapter 11 folder in the My Practice Spreadsheets folder and then close the workbook file.

Using the Lookup Wizard

The HLOOKUP and VLOOKUP functions are just fine when you only need Excel to look up a single value in a horizontal or vertical lookup table and then return the nearest or exact match based on that single value. Sometimes, however, you need Excel to perform a two-way lookup, whereby the program returns a value from a data table based on both a lookup value in its top row as well as a lookup value in its leftmost column.

When such a need arises, it's time to call upon the Lookup Wizard. This nifty add-in enables you to perform two-way lookups in a table without having to worry about constructing the final complex formula with its required INDEX and MATCH Reference functions.

Figure 11-3 shows you a situation where you need to look up two values, the Part Number and the Date, in order to return the Quota from the 2006 Production Schedule table. You will use the Lookup Wizard add-in in the following exercise to return the production quota from this table based on these two lookups.

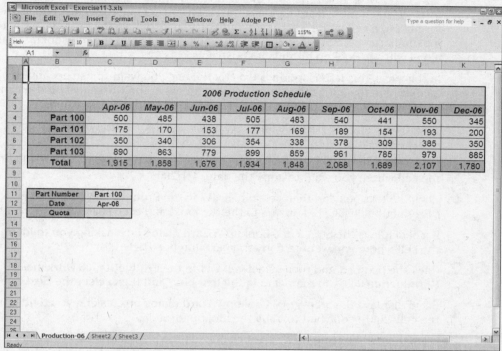

Figure 11-3: Performing a two-way lookup in the Production Schedule table.

2006 Production Schedule

	Apr-06	May-06	Jun-06	Jul-06	Aug-06	Sep-06	Oct-06	Nov-06	Dec-06
Part 100	500	485	438	505	483	540	441	550	345
Part 101	175	170	153	177	169	189	154	193	200
Part 102	350	340	306	354	338	378	309	385	350
Part 103	890	863	779	899	859	961	785	979	885
Total	1,915	1,858	1,676	1,934	1,848	2,068	1,689	2,107	1,780

Part Number	Part 100
Date	Apr-06
Quota	

Try It

Exercise 11-3: Using the Lookup Wizard to Build Formulas that Perform Two-Way Lookups in a Table

Open the *Exercise11-3.xls* workbook file in your Chapter 11 folder inside the My Practice Spreadsheets folder or in the Excel Workbook folder on the workbook CD-ROM. This workbook contains the Production-06 worksheet with the 2006 Production Schedule you need to practice performing a two-way lookup using the Lookup Wizard add-in:

1. Select the Lookup Wizard check box in the Add-Ins dialog box (Tools⇨Add-Ins) and then select OK.

Select the Yes button in the alert dialog box if you are prompted to install this add-in.

2. Choose Tools⇨Lookup on the Excel menu bar.

Excel opens the Step 1 of 4 Lookup Wizard dialog box that prompts you to indicate the cell range to search including its row and column labels. In this case, you must select the range B3:K7.

3. Select the cell range B3:K7 in the Production-06 worksheet ('Production-06'!$B$3:$K$7 appears in the text box) and then select the Next button.

The Step 2 of 4 Lookup Wizard dialog box now appears, asking you to identify by its heading the column and the row that contain the data to look up.

4. Leave Apr-06 selected in the Column Label drop-down list box and Part 100 selected in the Row Label drop-down list box and then select the Next button.

The Step 3 of 4 Lookup Wizard dialog box now appears, asking you to select the form in which the Wizard displays the result. By default, Excel just copies the formula to a cell in the worksheet, but you can also have the program copy the lookup parameters; that is, the column lookup value and the row lookup value along with the lookup formula it constructs.

In this case, this latter option is exactly the one you want to use because it enables you to change these lookup parameters in the worksheet later on and have the lookup formula find a new result based on these new values.

5. Select the Copy the Formula and Lookup Parameters option button selected and then select the Next button.

Excel displays the Step 4 of 6 Lookup Wizard dialog box, asking you to identify the cell where you want to copy the date, 4/1/2006.

6. Click the text box and then select cell C12 in the Production-06 worksheet ('Production-06'!$C$12 appears in the text box) and then select the Next button.

Excel displays the Step 5 of 6 Lookup Wizard dialog box, asking you to identify the cell where you want to copy the part number, Part 100.

7. Click the text box and then select cell C11 in the Production-06 worksheet ('Production-06'!$C$11 appears in the text box) and then select the Next button.

Excel displays the Step 6 of 6 Lookup Wizard dialog box, asking you to identify the cell where you want to copy the lookup formula.

8. Click the text box and then select cell C13 in the Production-06 worksheet ('Production-06'!$C$13 appears in the text box) and then select the Finish button.

Excel returns the result 500 to the Quota cell, C13.

9. Position the cell cursor in cell C13 and then examine the formula Excel entered there on the Formula bar.

Note that Excel has constructed a formula using an INDEX function with two nested MATCH functions as its arguments. Both of these Reference functions are needed in order to perform a two-way lookup in a table.

10. Change the Part Number in cell C11 to **Part 102**.

As soon as you change the Part Number to Part 102, Excel recalculates its lookup formula and returns 350 to the Quota cell, C13 (you can check that this is the correct value in the 2006 Production Schedule table above).

11. Change the Date in cell C12 by entering **Sep-2006** in this cell.

As soon as you change the Date Number to Sep-06 in this cell, Excel recalculates its lookup formula and returns 378 to the Quota cell, C13.

12. Save your changes to the Production-06 worksheet in a new workbook named **Solved11-3.xls** in your Chapter 11 folder in the My Practice Spreadsheets folder and then close this workbook file and exit Excel.

Chapter 12

Using the Logical Functions

The Logical function category is a small but powerful group of six functions (TRUE, FALSE, IF, AND, OR, and NOT) that you can use in decision-making formulas. (A decision-making formula is one where one set of values should be used or action taken when a particular condition is met and another when it is not.) You can also combine them with certain Information functions (such as ISBLANK, ISNUMBER, ISTEXT, and ISERROR) to create error-trapping formulas that prevent Excel error values (especially #DIV/0!, #NUM!, and #VALUE! errors) from spreading to other dependent formulas in the spreadsheet.

In this chapter, you get a chance to practice using the Logical functions in spreadsheets to create both decision-making and error-trapping formulas.

Working with the Logical Functions

The Logical functions, as their name implies, deal exclusively with the Logical values of TRUE and FALSE. With the exception of the TRUE, FALSE, and NOT functions (whose only purpose is to enter the Logical values, TRUE, FALSE, and its opposite into a cell of the worksheet), the other three Logical functions, IF, AND, and OR, evaluate expressions entered as their arguments as either TRUE or FALSE.

The granddaddy of all the Logical functions is the IF function, which follows this syntax:

```
IF(logical_test,value_if_true,value_if_false)
```

The IF function works by evaluating a comparative expression that you enter as its logical_test argument as being either TRUE or FALSE. If the expression is found to be TRUE, Excel then uses the value or text or executes the expression you enter as the value_if_true argument of the function. If the expression is found to be FALSE, the program uses the value or text or executes the expression you enter as the value_if_false argument.

When entering a number or reference to a cell that contains a number or formula that returns a number for the value_if_true and value_if_false arguments, you simply enter the value or cell address. When entering text for these arguments, you need to enclose the text in a set of double quotation marks. And when entering an expression, you enter the operands and operator or function name and arguments as you would in any formula.

Constructing Decision-Making Formulas

The biggest use for the IF function is performing conditional operations in a formula, one set of operations when the IF condition expressed by its *logical_test* argument is found to be TRUE and another when it is not. These decision-making formulas can be one of two types: formulas that perform their computations using alternate values depending upon the outcome of the condition or those that perform alternate calculations based on the outcome.

Selecting between alternate values

Figure 12-1 shows an example of the first type of decision-making formula, where alternate values can be put to good use. The spreadsheet shown in this figure contains a variation of the Tip Lookup worksheet you encountered in Chapter 11. In this version, the Tip Schedule contains tip amounts for alternate tip percentages (15% in column C and 20% in column D), and the input section of the spreadsheet contains a Tip Percentage cell (G2), where the user can specify either a tip percentage of 15 or 20 percent.

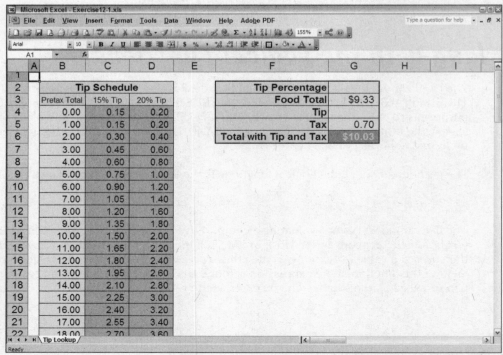

Figure 12-1: The Tip with alternate 15% and 20% tip percentages.

To take advantage of the alternate percentages in this revised Tip Schedule in the following exercise, you need to nest an IF function inside the VLOOKUP function as its col_index_num argument. This IF function then selects the appropriate column of the Tip Schedule to use (2 for the 15% Tip amount in column C or 3 for the 20% Tip amount in column D), depending upon whether the Tip Percentage cell, G2, contains 15% or 20% as its data entry.

Try It

Exercise 12-1: Using the IF Function to Build Formulas that Select Alternate Values

If Excel is not currently running, launch the program and open the *Exercise12-1.xls* workbook file in your Chapter 12 folder in the My Practice Spreadsheets folder on your hard disk or in the Excel Workbook folder on the workbook CD-ROM. You will use this expanded version of the Tip Lookup worksheet to practice adding the IF function to a VLOOKUP function that selects between the 15% or 20% column of the Tip Schedule, depending upon which percentage is entered into the Tip Percentage cell, G2:

1. Position the cell cursor in cell G2.

This Tip Percentage cell can contain only one of two entries: 15% or 20%. You will use Excel's Data Validation feature in this cell to ensure that it can contain no other data entry.

2. Choose Data⇨Validation to open the Data Validation dialog box.

3. Select the List option in the Allow drop-down button and then enter 15% and 20% in the Source text box separated by a comma (with no spaces, as in 15%,20%) before you select OK.

When you select the List as the Data Validation option, you can either select the cell range that contains the allowable data entries in the Source text box or type in the allowable entries.

4. Click the drop-down button that now appears on the right side of the Tip Percentage cell, G2, and then select 20% on its drop-down menu.

5. Assign the following range names to the designated cells or cell ranges:

- **Tip_percent** to cell G2
- **Food_total** to cell G3
- **Tip_table** to the cell range B4:D103

6. Position the cell cursor in cell G4.

This is the cell where you will construct your lookup formula using the VLOOKUP function with an IF function, as its col_index_num argument.

As you may remember from Exercise 11-2, the VLOOKUP function takes the following arguments:

- *Lookup_value* argument that specifies the cell containing the value you want looked up in the first column of the vertical lookup table (the cell named Food_total, in this case)

- *Table_array* argument that specifies the cell range containing the values in the lookup table (the cell range named Tip_table, in this case)

- *Col_index_num* that specifies the number of the column, counting from left to right, that contains the values you want returned from the lookup table (in this case, that number is 2 when the Tip Percentage is 15% or 3 when the Tip Percentage is 20%)

7. Click the Insert Function button on the Formula bar, select VLOOKUP in the Lookup & Reference category, and select OK.

8. Use the Paste Name dialog box (Insert⇨Name⇨Paste) to paste the range name Food_total in the Lookup_value argument text box and Tip_table in the Table_array argument text box in the Function Arguments dialog box.

   Now all you need is to construct a formula using the IF function in the Col_index_num text box. The IF function inserts 2 as the column index number when the cell named Tip_percent contains 15% as its entry; otherwise, it inserts 3. This is how this function should appear in the Col_index_num argument text box:

   ```
   IF(Tip_percent=15%,2,3)
   ```

9. Click the Col_index_num argument text box to put the insertion point inside it, and then do the following:

   - Type **IF(** — don't forget the open parenthesis and make sure you don't put a space between it and IF.

   - Open the Paste Name dialog box and then use it to insert the range name Tip_percent immediately following the open parenthesis.

   - Type **=15%,2,3)** — don't forget the commas or the close parenthesis and make sure that there are no spaces between any of the values.

   The Formula result shown at the bottom of the Function Arguments dialog box for the VLOOKUP function should now read $1.80 (the tip amount for a food total of $9.33 at 20%). If this checks out, proceed to step 10.

10. Select OK in the Function Arguments dialog box to close it and to enter the lookup formula in the Tip cell, G4.

11. Change the Tip Percentage from 20% to 15% by positioning the cell cursor in this cell and then selecting 15% on its drop-down list.

    Excel immediately decreases the tip amount in cell G4 from $1.80 to $1.35.

12. Increase the food total in cell G3 to 75.50.

    Excel increases the tip amount in cell G4 from $1.35 to $11.25.

13. Type **17** in the Tip Percentage cell and then click the Enter button on the Formula bar.

    Excel beeps at you and displays an error dialog box with the message, "The value you entered is not valid."

14. Select the Cancel button and then open the Data Validation dialog box again (Data⇨Validation).

    Data Validation enables you to enter an input message that the user sees whenever he selects the cell, as well as an error message that is displayed whenever he tries to enter a value that is no longer allowed.

15. Click the Input Message tab and then, in the Input Message text box, type **Click this drop-down button and then select 15% or 20% on its drop-down menu**.

16. Click the Error Alert tab and then, in the Error Message text box, type **The entry in this cell is limited to 15% or 20% only! Click Cancel and then select 15% or 20% on the cell's drop-down list** before you select OK.

    A text box with your input message now appears next to the lower-right of cell G2.

17. Click the text box with your input message and drag it up until the top of the message box is even with the top of the Tip Percentage cell, G2, and position its left edge so that it's now touching the cell's drop-down button without obscuring any part of it.

18. Type **12** in the Tip Percentage cell, G2, and then press Enter.

This time, Excel displays your custom error message in its error alert dialog box.

19. Select the Cancel button in the error alert dialog box to close it and restore the current 15% entry to the cell.

20. Save your work in a new workbook called **Solved12-1.xls** in your Chapter 12 folder inside the My Practice Spreadsheets folder on your hard disk and then close the workbook file.

Selecting between alternate calculations

In addition to selecting alternate values, you can use IF functions to perform alternate calculations depending upon the outcome of the condition stated by its logical_test argument. A common situation is to have Excel perform the calculation only when the IF condition is TRUE and perform no computation when it is FALSE.

Figure 12-2 shows you an example of this situation. Here, you see a slightly different version of the Spring Sale worksheet that you used in earlier exercises. This table contains a Discounted column, which determines whether a furniture item is to be discounted based on its suggested retail price listed in the Retail Price column. It also contains a Discount Amount column, which computes the amount of the discount only if the Discounted column indicates that the furniture item is eligible for a discount.

Code	Description	Retail Price	Discounted	Discount Amount	Sales Price
02-305	36-inch round table	1,250.00			$ 1,250.00
02-240	72-inch dining table	1,400.00			$ 1,400.00
04-356	Hutch	2,500.00			$ 2,500.00
01-234	Side chair	350.00			$ 350.00
03-003	Arm chair	500.00			$ 500.00
01-240	Armoire	1,750.00			$ 1,750.00

Figure 12-2: The Spring Sale worksheet with Discounted and Discount Amount columns.

In Exercise 12-2, you will construct the necessary formulas with IF functions for this version of the Spring Sale worksheet — one set to determine whether or not the furniture item should be discounted and another set to compute the discount amount only when the item is eligible for the discount.

Try It

Exercise 12-2: Using the IF Function to Build Formulas that Perform Alternate Calculations

Open the *Exercise 12-2.xls* workbook file in your Chapter 12 folder in the My Practice Spreadsheets folder on your hard disk or in the Excel Workbook folder on the workbook CD-ROM. You will use this expanded version of the Spring Sale worksheet to practice constructing the formulas with IF functions needed to determine whether a furniture item is eligible for a discount. If it is, you create formulas to compute the discount amount and sale price:

1. Position the cell cursor in cell D4 where you build the formula that determines whether the 36-inch round table is to be discounted.

2. Click the Insert Function button on the Formula bar. Next, double-click IF in the Select a Function list box after selecting Logical in Select a Category drop-down list box to open the Function Arguments dialog box for the IF function.

The determinant for eligibility for a discount is whether the suggested retail price is greater than or equal to $1,000. In terms of the Logical_text argument text box, you need to create this type of comparative expression using cell C4, as in

```
C4>=1000
```

3. Select cell C4 in the worksheet and then type **>=1000** before pressing Tab.

4. Type **"Yes"** (and be sure to enclose Yes in the pair of double quotation marks) in Value_if_true argument text box before you press Tab.

5. Type **"No"** (and be sure to enclose No in the pair of double quotation marks) in Value_if_false argument text box.

The Formula result at the bottom of the Function Arguments dialog box should be equal to Yes as the value currently entered into cell C4 is indeed greater than 1000. If this checks out, proceed to step 6.

6. Select OK to close the Function Arguments dialog box and enter the formula with the IF function into cell D4.

7. Use the Fill handle to copy this formula in D4 down to the cell range D5:D9.

Now, you need to create a formula using the IF function that checks whether the cell in the Discounted column contains Yes or No and then calculates the discounted amount accordingly.

8. Position the cell pointer in cell E4.

9. Construct a formula in this cell using the IF function that multiplies the value in the Retail Price column by 20% if the Discounted column contains Yes; otherwise, the formula enters 0 (zero) into the cell.

The argument text boxes in the Function Arguments dialog box for the IF function you create for this formula should contain the following values:

- D4="Yes" in the Logical_text argument text box
- C4*20% in the Value_if_true argument text box
- 0 in the Value_if_false argument text box

10. Use the Fill handle to copy this formula in cell E4 down to the cell range E5:E9.

In the final table, all the furniture items except for the Side chair and Arm chair should be discounted and have discounted amounts computed in column E. Check your final results against those shown in the *Solved12-2.xls* workbook file in your Chapter 12 folder. If everything checks out, proceed to step 11.

11. Save your changes to a new workbook named **Solved12-2-mine.xls** in your Chapter 12 folder inside the My Practice Spreadsheets folder and leave this file open for Exercise 12-3.

Nesting IF functions

IF functions in decision-making formulas are great when you're dealing with situations that only require two alternatives — one that comes into play when a certain condition exists and the other that comes into play when it does not. But what about a situation where you have more than two alternatives?

For example, in the Spring Sale worksheet you used in the previous IF function exercise, suppose you still only want to discount furniture that retails over $1,000 but want to use two different discount amounts as well: 15% for suggested retail prices that are lower than $1,500 and 20% for suggested retail prices that are above $1,500.

To accommodate such a case, you would have to nest a second IF function within the original one, making the second nested IF function either the value_if_true or value_if_false argument of the original. Specifically, in for the Spring Sale worksheet example, you would nest the second IF function as the value_if_true argument of the original IF function. The first IF condition then tests if the furniture item is to be discounted (indicated by a Yes in the Discounted column, meaning that the item's retail is above $1,000). If this item is found to be eligible for a discount, the second value_if_true argument IF function determines whether it receives a 20- or 15-percent discount.

Try It

Exercise 12-3: Building Formulas with Nested IF Functions

Use the *Solved12-2-mine.xls* workbook file you created in Exercise12-2 (if you don't have access to this file, open the *Solved12-2.xls* workbook in your Chapter 12 folder in the My Practice Spreadsheets folder on your hard disk or in the Excel Workbook folder on the workbook CD-ROM). You will use this version of the Spring Sale worksheet with the completed formulas in the Discounted and Discount Amounts columns to practice using one IF function as an argument of another:

1. Position the cell cursor in cell E4 that contains the formula with the IF function that currently computes a 20% discount when the Discounted column contains Yes.

2. On the Formula bar, click the insertion point in immediately in front of the C in C4 in the value_if_true argument of the IF function in this cell.

3. Type **IF(** — open parenthesis — and then click cell C4 in the worksheet.

The edited formula on the Formula bar should now read:

```
=IF(D4="Yes",IF(C4C4*20%,0)
```

4. Type **>1500,** — a greater than sign, 1500, and a comma — to complete the value_if_true argument for the new nested IF function.

The edited formula on the Formula bar should now read

```
=IF(D4="Yes",IF(C4>1500,C4*20%,0)
```

5. Click the I-beam mouse pointer to position the insertion point between the % (percent sign) and the , (comma) immediately preceding 0 in this formula — be sure not to press the → key.

6. Type , (comma) and then click cell C4 in the worksheet.

The edited formula on the Formula bar should now read

```
=IF(D4="Yes",IF(C4>1500,C4*20%,C4,0)
```

7. Type ***15%)** — that is an asterisk, 15% and a close parenthesis — to complete the value_if_false argument for the nested IF function.

The final edited formula on the Formula bar should now read

```
=IF(D4="Yes",IF(C4>1500,C4*20%,C4*15%),0)
```

In essence, this edited form of the formula with nested IF function in the value_if_true argument of the original IF function is saying

- Evaluate the contents of cell D4 and, if Excel finds that this cell contains Yes as its entry, the program evaluates the contents of cell C4; otherwise, it just enters 0 (zero) in the current cell.

- If Excel does end up evaluating the contents of cell C4, the program checks to see if this cell contains a value greater than 1,500. If the cell does, it then multiplies this value by 20 percent; otherwise, the program multiplies the value in C4 by 15 percent.

8. Click the Enter button on the Formula bar and then copy this edited formula down to the cell range E5:E9.

In this version of the Spring Sale table, the Hutch and Armoire are now discounted 20 percent, the 36-inch round table and 72-inch dining table are both discounted 15 percent, and the Side and Arm chairs still receive no discount at all. Check your final results against those shown in the *Solved12-3.xls* workbook file in your Chapter 12 folder. If everything checks out, proceed to step 9.

9. Save your changes to a new workbook named **Solved12-3-mine.xls** in your Chapter 12 folder inside the My Practice Spreadsheets folder and then close this file.

Constructing Error-Trapping Formulas

Sometimes, you know ahead of time that certain error values are unavoidable in a worksheet as long as certain data entries are missing. The most common error value that gets you into this kind of trouble is the #DIV/0! error value. This error value appears not only when the divisor in a division formula is actually 0 (zero) but also when the divisor refers to an empty cell (which carries the numerical equivalent) in which you haven't yet had an opportunity to make any data entry (as when generating a new workbook from an Excel template file).

Fortunately, you can use the IF function to suppress the appearance of such error values in formulas. When you do this, you not only get the benefit of not having to look at them (there is, after all, nothing subtle about them), but you also ensure that they don't spread to any other parts of the spreadsheet containing dependent formulas. This means that in suppressing the display of error values in their original formulas, you also end up trapping them in their original cells.

When using IF functions in the construction of error-trapping formulas, you often use them in combination with some of the functions in the Information category, the most versatile of which is the ISERROR function. This nifty little function evaluates the cell reference you specify as its value argument and returns TRUE if the cell contains any of those pesky error values #N/A, #VALUE!, #REF!, #REF!, #DIV/0!, #NUM!, #NAME?, and #NULL) and FALSE if it contains any other kind of entry. You can use its little brother function, ISERR, to test for all error values in a cell, excluding #NA, for Not Available, which some users do not consider an error value per se.

Figure 12-3 shows you a situation where you need to construct an error-trapping formula. Here, you see an empty version of the Production Schedule worksheet that is on its way to being saved as an Excel template file. Before that can happen, however, you would need to suppress all those #DIV/0! error values in the cell range B9:J9 until you begin entering the production quota figures for the particular months. (The error values appear because cell K7 with the grand total that it used as the divisor in their formulas contains 0 (zero).) The way to do that, as you will see in Exercise 12-4, is by constructing a formula that traps this error in the original formula and all its copies.

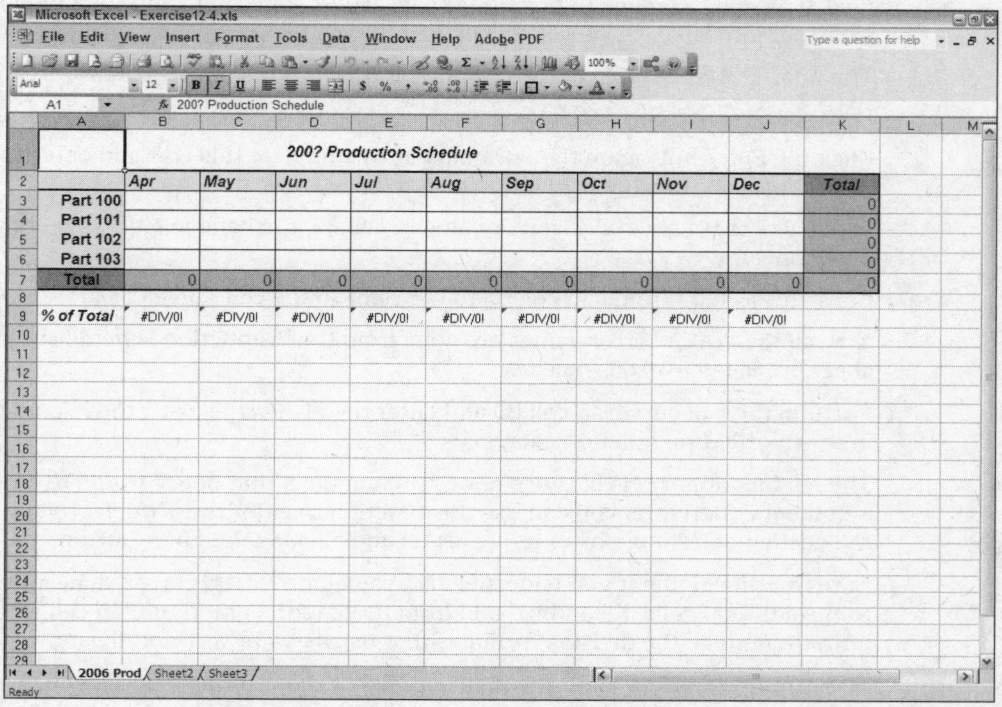

Figure 12-3:
Empty
Production
Schedule
worksheet
containing
#DIV/0!
error values
due to the 0
(zero) in the
grand total
in cell K7.

Try It

Exercise 12-4: Building Formulas that Trap Error Values

Open the *Exercise12-4.xls* workbook in your Chapter 12 folder in the My Practice Spreadsheets folder on your hard disk or in the Excel Workbook folder on the workbook CD-ROM. You will use this empty version of the Production Schedule worksheet to practice constructing error-trapping formulas using the IF function:

1. Position the cell pointer in cell B9 that contains the original division formula.

You need to edit this formula by adding an IF function that inserts 0 (zero) rather than the #DIV/0! error value in the cell if cell K7 is empty or contains 0 (zero) as is currently the case.

2. Press F2 to place Excel in Edit mode and then press the ← key to position the insertion point between = (equal to sign) and the B in B7.

3. Type **IF(** — open parenthesis — and then select cell K7.

The edited formula in the cell and on the Formula bar should now read:

```
=IF(K7B7/$K$7
```

4. Press F4 one time to convert the relative cell reference, K7, to the absolute reference, $K$7.

5. Type **=0,0,** (that is, the equal to sign followed by zero, a comma, and then another zero and comma).

The edited formula in the cell and on the Formula bar should now read

```
=IF($K$7=0,0,B7/$K$7
```

6. Click the I-beam mouse pointer at the very end of the formula, after the 7 in the final $K$7 cell reference to position the insertion point there and then type **)** — close parenthesis.

The final, edited formula in the cell and on the Formula bar should now read

```
=IF($K$7=0,0,B7/$K$7)
```

7. Click the Enter button on the Formula bar to complete this edit and enter the edited formula with the IF function into cell B9.

In place of that ugly #DIV/0! error value in cell B9, the benevolent 0.00% should now appear.

8. Copy the edited formula in cell B9 to the right to the cell range C9:J9.

Now all the #DIV/0! error values are gone from the Production Schedule worksheet, replaced by 0.00% entries.

9. Position the cell cursor in cell B3 and enter the #NA value using the NA function in the Information function category.

The NA function is one of those few Excel functions that doesn't require any arguments; therefore, you can use this function to enter the #NA error value into the current cell simply by entering =NA() and clicking the Enter button.

Note that the moment you enter the #NA value into B3, this error value spreads to the subtotal cells, K3 and B7, and from there to the grand total in cell K7 and from there to all the division formulas that use its value as their divisor.

To trap this in cell K7 and prevent its spread to the cell range B9:J9, you need to edit the original formula in cell B9 by adding the ISERROR function and then copy this version across the columns of this row.

10. Position the cell cursor in cell B9.

11. Edit the IF function in this cell's formula by replacing the logical_test argument, $K$7=0, with **ISERROR($K$7)**.

Don't forget to enclose the $K$7 as the value argument of the ISERROR function in its own pair of open and close parentheses nested within the IF function's pair of open and close parentheses.

The final, edited formula in the cell and on the Formula bar should now read

```
=IF(ISERROR($K$7),0,B7/$K$7)
```

12. Copy this new version of the error-trapping formula to the cell range C9:J9.

As soon as you finish copying this revised error-trapping formula, Excel replaces all the #NA values in this cell range with 0.00%.

13. Position the cell cursor in the Home cell, A1, and then save your work in a new workbook file named **Solved12-4.xls** in your Chapter 12 folder inside the My Practice Spreadsheets folder and then close this file.

Chapter 13

Text Formulas and Functions

At first, thinking about text formulas and functions in spreadsheets may seem strange, accustomed as we all are to thinking of them as number crunchers. Nevertheless, not only can you construct formulas that use text as operands with the special concatenation or linking operator, but you can also build formulas using any number of Text functions that require text exclusively in their arguments.

In this chapter, you get a chance to practice building text formulas that link together separate text cell entries whose text should be entered together in the same cell. You also get a chance to use Text functions to convert text entries to the proper upper- and lowercase letters.

Constructing Text Formulas

Simple text formulas (that is, those that don't rely on any Text functions) merely join pieces of text together using the & (ampersand) operator. It's the so-called *concatenation* operator, which means to join or string together in a series. Here are a couple of caveats to text formulas:

- ✔ The text operands must be enclosed in sets of quotation marks.

- ✔ Spaces must be included in the operands (and within the quotes) if you don't want the text to glom altogether as a single illegible clump of letters.

For example, if you want to create a text formula in cell B2 that joins the word *Summary* to the text entry *Order,* entered in cell A2, and you enter the following formula in this cell:

```
=A2&Summary
```

Excel returns the #NAME? error value because you didn't enclose the text *Summary* in quotation marks. Note that this is necessary even when the text you're entering is just a single word with no spaces.

Also, suppose you have the first name *Keith* entered in cell A3, and the last name *Smith* entered next door in cell B3, and you enter the following text formula in cell C3:

```
=A3&B3
```

Excel returns to cell C3 the following glommed-together text:

```
KeithSmith
```

To have the text formula return the first and last name separated by the customary space, you need to enter this version of the text formula in cell C3:

```
=A3&" "&B3
```

Note that in this version, the invisible-to-the-eye space (entered by pressing the spacebar) is enclosed in quotation marks, although there are no spaces between these quotation marks and the & (ampersand) concatenation operators.

Q. When would I typically need to create text formulas in a spreadsheet?

A. Often you work with data lists where pieces of information such as the first, middle, and last name as well as the person's title along with his street, city, state, and ZIP code are all stored in separate cells (for purposes of sorting). Text formulas that join these separate pieces of information can save hours of retyping when you need to reassemble this disparate information in mailing lists.

Try It

Exercise 13-1: Building Simple Text Formulas that Join Data Entries

If Excel is not currently running, launch the program and then open the *Exercise 13-1.xls* workbook file in your Chapter 13 folder in the My Practice Spreadsheets folder on your hard disk or in the Excel Workbook folder on the workbook CD-ROM. You use the entries in the Client Address list in its Text Formulas worksheet to practice creating simple text formulas:

1. Position the cell cursor in cell G1 and construct a text formula that joins the text entry *Client* in cell B1 with the text entry *Addresses* in cell C1.

Remember that you must add a space enclosed inside quotation marks and sandwiched between & (ampersand) operators in the middle of the cell references to prevent the two text entries from being joined into ClientAddresses in the cell.

2. Copy the formula in cell G1 to the Clipboard (Ctrl+C) and then position the cell cursor in cell B1. Use the Values option in the Paste Special dialog box (Edit⇨Paste Special) to paste the text and not the formula on top of the Client entry in cell B1.

Note the repetition of Addresses in G1, which still contains the formula that combines the text in B1 (Cell Addresses) with the text entry in C1 (Addresses) so that it now reads Cell Addresses Addresses.

3. Delete the Addresses entry in cell C1.

Note that both B1 and G1 now show Client Addresses. In cell B1, this is the result of a text entry created from a copy of the original text formula; whereas in G1, it is the result of the original text formula you constructed.

4. Position the cell cursor in cell G3 and construct a new text formula that joins the house number in cell A3 with the street name in B3.

The text formula you enter in cell G3 should appear on the Formula bar as

```
=A3&" "&B3
```

Note that the entry in cell A3 is the number *123* (not entered as a text with a preceding quotation mark nor formatted with the Text format), yet Excel has no problem joining this value to the obvious text entry in cell B3 using the concatenation operator.

5. Copy the text formula in cell G3 down to the cell range G4:G17 and then use AutoFit to widen column G as needed to display all the conjoined street addresses.

6. Position the cell cursor in cell H3 and construct a text formula that combines the city name in cell C3 with the state abbreviation in cell D3 and the ZIP code in cell E3, making sure that there is a comma and a space immediately following the city and spaces between the state and ZIP code.

The result in H3 should appear as

```
Centerville, IL 60789
```

Don't forget to enclose the comma and the trailing space after the reference to cell C3 with the city in quotation marks, as in

```
=C3&", "&
```

7. Copy the text formula in cell H3 down to the cell range H4:H17 and then use AutoFit to widen columns as needed to display all the conjoined city, state, and ZIP code information.

8. Position the cell cursor in cell I3 and construct a formula that joins the text in cell G3 with that in cell H3. Make sure that this formula inserts a comma and a trailing space between the street address in cell G3 and the city, state, and ZIP in cell H3.

9. Copy the text formula in cell I3 down to the cell range I4:I17 and then use AutoFit to widen column I to suit (you may also have to scroll the screen to the right to display all the data).

10. While the cell range I3:I17 still selected, click the Sort Ascending button on the Standard toolbar (the one with the A over Z and the arrow pointing downward). If a Sort Warning dialog box appears, select the Continue with the Current Selection option button before you select its Sort button. (Excel is concerned that you forgot to include data that needs sorting in the cell range G3:H17.)

Note that nothing changes in the order of the addresses in the selected range when you finish the Sort operation. This is because the cells contain text formulas rather than the actual text entries you see displayed. If you want to be able to find and sort text entries that you create in a spreadsheet with text formulas, you need to replace the formulas with their values. In this particular case, you copy the value on top of the formulas, thereby replacing them.

11. While the cell range I3:I17 still selected, click the Copy button on the Standard toolbar or press Ctrl+C and then (without doing a thing to the cell selection) open the Paste Special dialog box (Edit⇨Paste Special). Select the Values option button in the Paste section before you select OK.

Excel replaces the formulas with their calculated values in the same range (you can verify this because the contents of the Formula bar now reads 123 Niles Avenue, Centerville, IL 60789 instead of =G3&", "&H3).

12. Click the Sort Ascending button on the Standard toolbar again and then, if a Sort Warning dialog box appears, select the Continue with the Current Selection option button before you click its Sort button.

Note how, at the time you use the Sort Ascending button, Excel rearranges the text in the cell selection.

13. Click the Sort Descending button on the Standard toolbar (the one with the Z over the A followed by a downward pointing arrow). Select the Continue with the Current Selection option button before you select the Sort button if a Sort Warning dialog box appears.

This time, Excel arranges the addresses in descending order (following the street number — for more on how Excel sorts values, see Chapter 16).

14. Position the cell cursor in cell A1 and then save your work with the filename *Solved13-1.xls* in your Chapter 13 folder in the My Practice Spreadsheets folder and leave the workbook open as you will need it to complete Exercise 13-2.

Using Text Functions

Excel's Text functions offer a wide variety of methods for searching and manipulating text entries in a spreadsheet. These functions include the CONCATENATE function for joining together strings of text (specified as its *text* arguments) — just like the & (ampersand) operator in the handmade formulas you constructed in Exercise 13-1 — and, perhaps even more useful to most, the UPPER, LOWER, and PROPER functions for changing the capitalization of text entries in the spreadsheet. (Most of the other Text functions are seldom required outside of macros and specialized VBA programming applications.)

Figure 13-1 shows you an example of a spreadsheet that is in desperate need of the PROPER function, which changes the case of the text specified as its sole argument to Title case, where only the first letter in each word is uppercase.

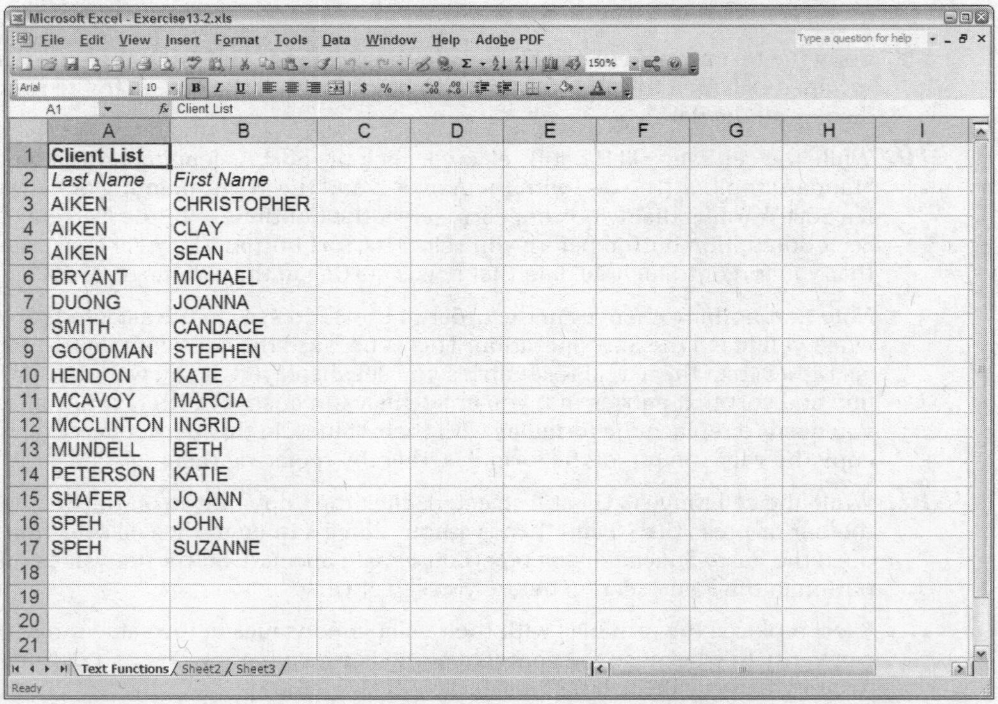

Figure 13-1:
Client List spreadsheet with the names in all capital letters.

As you can see in this figure, both the first and last names of each of the clients in the list are all uppercase letters and need to be converted to the Title case. This is a situation that you sometimes encounter when using data lists stored in text files that you import with the Text Import Wizard into an Excel worksheet. (This wizard opens automatically when you try to open a text file with File⇨Open.)

Exercise 13-2 shows you how easy it is to take of this type of problem using the PROPER function. Knowing how to convert text entries to the desired case in a spreadsheet is very important because it can literally save you from hours of text editing, not to mention retyping, both of which are a colossal waste of your time.

Try It

Exercise 13-2: Building Formulas with Text Functions that Join Data Entries and Change Their Case

Open the *Exercise13-2.xls* workbook file in your Chapter 13 folder in the My Practice Spreadsheets folder on your hard disk or in the Excel Workbook folder on the workbook CD-ROM. You will use the uppercase first and last name text entries in the Client List in its Text Functions worksheet to practice using a couple of Excel's Text functions:

1. Position the cell cursor in cell C3 and then click the Insert Function button on the Formula bar to open the Insert Function dialog box.

2. After selecting Text in the Select a Category drop-down list box, click PROPER in the Select a Function list box before selecting OK.

3. Click cell A3 in the worksheet to enter its cell reference into the Text Argument text box in the Function Arguments dialog box and then select OK.

   The PROPER function returns *Aiken* to cell C3.

4. Use the Fill handle to copy this formula with the PROPER function down to the cell C4:C17 and then over to the cell range D3:D17.

   Note that all the first and last name entries are now correct with the exception of the *Mcavoy* (which should be *McAvoy*) in cell C11 and *Mcclinton* in cell C12 (which should be *McClinton*). You will have to manually edit these entries later on as the PROPER function is only able to deal with the first letters in words.

5. Position the cell cursor in cell E3 and then select the CONCATENATE function in the Insert Function dialog box and select OK.

   You will now use the CONCATENATE function to enter the first and last names in columns C and D as one piece of information in column E.

6. Click cell D3 in the worksheet to enter its cell reference in the Text1 Argument text box and then press Tab.

   In the Text2 Function Argument text box, you must add a blank space; otherwise, the first and last names are glommed onto each other as a single unit.

7. In the Text2 Argument text box, type " (a double quotation mark), then press the spacebar, and then type " (a double quotation mark) again before you press Tab.

8. Click cell C3 in the worksheet to enter its cell reference in the Text3 Argument text box.

   Check the Formula Result area at the bottom of the Function Arguments dialog box for the CONCATENATE function. This should now read *Christopher Aiken*.

9. Select OK to close the Function Arguments dialog box and enter the formula with the CONCATENATE function in cell E3.

10. Copy the formula in cell E3 down to the cell range E4:E17 and then use AutoFit to widen column E.

11. Replace the CONCATENATE formulas in the selected cell range E3:E17 by copying their values on top of their formulas using the Edit⇨Paste Special command.

12. Edit the entries in E11 and E12, changing *Mcavoy* in cell E11 to *McAvoy* and *Mcclinton* in cell E12 to *McClinton*.

13. Choose Window⇨Arrange and then select the Vertical option button before you select OK.

    Excel now displays windows with parts of the *Exercise13-2.xls* workbook and *Solved13-1.xls* workbook side by side.

14. Scroll the Text Function worksheet in the *Exercise13-2.xls* workbook so that column F is visible in the window.

15. Click a cell in the *Solved13-1.xls* workbook to make it active and then scroll column I into view and select the cell range I3:I17 (containing the joined addresses).

16. Hold down the Ctrl key and position the mouse pointer somewhere along the bottom of edge of the cell selection. Drag the outline of the selection from the Text Formulas worksheet in the *Solved13-1.xls* workbook to the cell range F3:F17 in the Text Functions worksheet in the *Exercise13-2.xls* workbook. When the outline fills the cell range F3:F17 in this worksheet, release the mouse button.

17. Click a cell in Text Formulas worksheet in the *Solved13-1.xls* workbook to activate it and then close the workbook by clicking its Close button in the upper-right corner of the program window without saving your changes.

18. Click the Maximize button in the upper-right corner of the *Exercise13-2.xls* workbook.

19. Use the AutoFit feature to widen column F in the Text Functions worksheet.

20. In cell G3, use the CONCATENATE function to join the first and last name in cell E3 with the address information in cell F3, making sure to add a comma and trailing space after the last name.

21. Copy the formula in cell G3 down to the cell range G4:G17 and then widen column G and scroll the worksheet as needed to completely display the names and addresses in this range on your screen.

22. Replace the formulas in the cell range G3:G17 with their text values and then sort the selection with the Sort Ascending button on the Standard toolbar.

23. Check your results against those shown in Figure 13-2. If they match, proceed to the final step.

24. Select cell A1 and then save your work in a new workbook named **Solved13-2.xls** in your Chapter 13 folder inside the My Practice Spreadsheets folder. Close the workbook file and exit Excel.

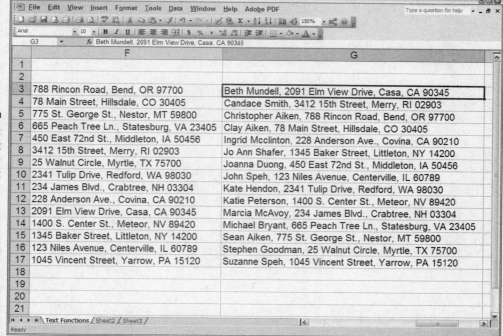

Figure 13-2:
The Text Functions worksheet after sorting the names and addresses in the cell range G3:G17 alphabetically by first name.

Part III
Working with Graphics

The 5th Wave   By Rich Tennant

"No, it's not a pie chart, it's just a corn chip that got scanned into the document."

In this part . . .

Part III is living proof that there is indeed life beyond number-crunching in the Excel spreadsheet. Here, you have an opportunity to tap into your more "artistic" side as you get practice in creating and gussying up charts of various types as well as experience in adding and using graphics in your spreadsheets.

Chapter 14

Charting
Spreadsheet Data

· ·

In This Chapter

▶ Understanding how Excel charts spreadsheet data

▶ Using the Chart Wizard to create a new chart

▶ Creating a chart on a separate chart Sheet

▶ Formatting the basic chart

▶ Editing a chart

· ·

Outside of the actual data entry and the building of the formulas for a spreadsheet, charting that data may well be one of the most essential tasks you perform in Excel. By presenting spreadsheet data in a visual form, relationships between the data that were not apparent in numerical form often become quite obvious. Fortunately, Excel offers you a wealth of different types of charts with which to depict these relationships. Half the fun of charting is selecting the most appropriate chart type and customizing it to your needs.

In this chapter, you get a chance to practice charting spreadsheet data, both in the worksheet and on separate chart sheets. You also get practice with customizing the various parts of the basic chart so that they present the data in the clearest possible way.

Understanding Excel Charts

Excel charts are directly tied to the spreadsheet data they represent in the worksheet. As a result, the editing changes you make to the underlying data have a direct and immediate effect on their contents (somewhat analogous to the way that changes you make to data entries referred to in a formula immediately affect the calculated result when Automatic Recalculation is in effect).

Figure 14-1 shows you a typical Clustered Column chart created as part of a worksheet from the data in a spreadsheet table (not currently visible). As you see in this figure, a typical Excel chart contains a variety of distinct elements (explained in Table 14-1). It's important that you become familiar with these elements, as each is an editable part of the chart that you're often required to modify after construction of the basic chart.

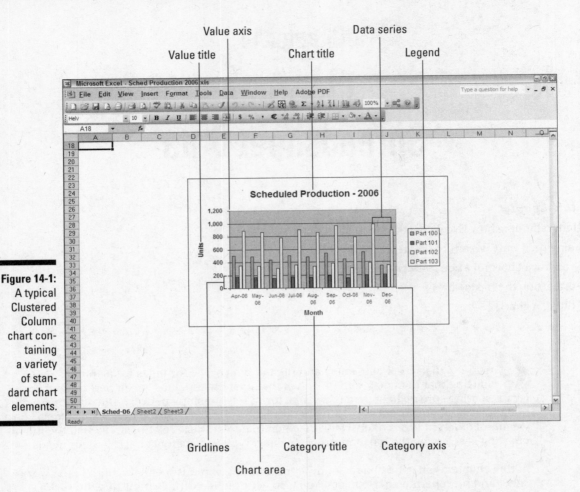

Value title

Value axis

Chart title

Data series

Legend

Gridlines

Chart area

Category title

Category axis

Figure 14-1:
A typical
Clustered
Column
chart con-
taining
a variety
of stan-
dard chart
elements.

Table 14-1	**Typical Chart Elements**
Element	**Description**
Chart	Everything inside the chart window including all parts of the chart (label axes, data markers, tick marks, and other elements in this table).
Chart toolbar	The toolbar that appears when you first create a chart that enables you to modify different parts of the current chart.
Data marker	A symbol on the chart, such as a bar in a bar chart, a pie in a pie chart, or a line on a line chart that represents a single value in the spreadsheet. Data markers with the same shape or pattern represent a single data series in the chart.
Chart data series	A group of related values, such as all the values in a single row in the chart — all the production numbers for Part 100 in the sample chart, for example. A chart can have just one data series (shown in a single bar or line), but it usually has several.
Series formula	A formula describing a given data series. The formula includes a reference to the cell that contains the data series name (such as the name Jan-92), references to worksheet cells containing the categories and values plotted in the chart, and the plot order of the series. The series formula can also have the actual data used to plot the chart. You can edit a series formula and control the plot order.

Element	Description
Axis	A line that serves as a major reference for plotting data in a chart. In two-dimensional charts, there are two axes — the x (horizontal) axis and the y (vertical) axis. In most two-dimensional charts (except, notably, column charts), Excel plots categories (labels) along the x-axis and values (numbers) along the y-axis. Bar charts reverse the scheme, plotting values along the y-axis. Pie charts have no axes. Three-dimensional charts have an x-axis, a y-axis, and a z-axis. The x- and y-axes delineate the horizontal surface of the chart. The z axis is the vertical axis, showing the depth of the third dimension in the chart.
Tick mark	A small line intersecting an axis. A tick mark indicates a category, scale, or chart data series. A tick mark can have a label attached.
Plot area	Area where Excel plots your data, including the axes and all markers that represent data points.
Gridlines	Optional lines extending from the tick marks across the plot area, making it easier to view the data values represented by the tick marks.
Chart text	Label or title that you add to the chart. *Attached text* is a title or label linked to an axis, data marker, or other chart object. If you move the object, you move the attached text as well. You cannot move the attached text independently. *Unattached text* is text you add with the Text Box button on the Drawing toolbar.
Legend	A key that identifies patterns, colors, or symbols associated with the markers of a chart data series. The legend shows the data series name corresponding to each data marker (such as the name of the red columns in a column chart).

Excel not only offers you a wide array of basic chart types from which to choose, but it also enables you to decide where you want to place the chart — either in the worksheet along with the data it represents graphically or on a separate chart sheet in the workbook.

A chart like the one shown in Figure 14-1 that is placed on the worksheet is referred to as an *embedded chart* (although it's not so embedded that you can't still move and resize it on the worksheet as needed). Figure 14-2, on the other hand, shows you this same Clustered Column chart now on its own chart sheet.

You select and manipulate a chart sheet in the Excel workbook via its sheet tab, just the same as you do with a regular worksheet.

Q. What benefits do I accrue by placing a chart on its own chart sheet rather than embedding it in the worksheet?

A. Charts that you place on their own chart sheets generally print larger and are easier to print — all you have to do is select the chart sheet before you open the Print dialog box (File➪Print). In addition, you may find it somewhat easier to edit a chart that you place in its own sheet as you don't have to worry about inadvertently selecting the Chart Area when you intend to select Chart Title or Legend for editing.

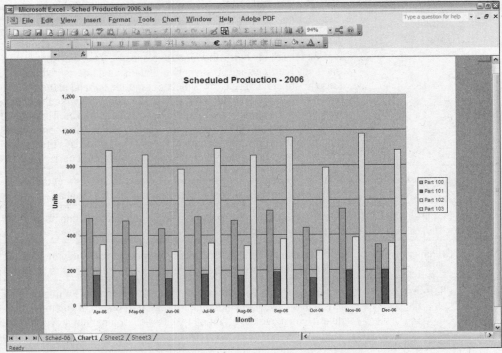

Try It

Exercise 14-1: Changing the Location of Existing Charts

If Excel is not currently running, launch the program and then open the *Exercise14-1.xls* workbook file in your Chapter 14 folder in the My Practice Spreadsheets folder on your hard disk or in the Excel Workbook folder on the workbook CD-ROM. You will use the embedded Clustered Column chart in the Sched-06 worksheet to practice selecting different parts of the chart and switching the chart placement between embedding in the worksheet and placing it on a separate chart sheet:

1. Click anywhere on the embedded Clustered Column chart right below the 2006 Production Schedule table to select this chart.

Eight sizing handles (those black squares) appear around the perimeter of the embedded Clustered Column chart indicating that it is now selected. In addition, the floating Chart toolbar appears and the spreadsheet data used in creating the chart is indicated by different-colored bounding boxes surrounding the row and column heads as well as the data entries.

2. Position the mouse pointer on the sizing handle that's located in the middle on the right edge. When the pointer changes to a double-headed arrow, drag the dotted outline of the Chart Area until its right edge is flush with the right edge of column J in the worksheet. Release the mouse button.

Note that Excel redraws the Clustered Column chart to fit in the new width. Now the titles along the Category Axis (the ones that show the month and year under each cluster of columns in the chart) are all displayed on a single row.

3. Click somewhere in the area of the Chart Title, *Scheduled Production – 2006*.

Eight sizing handles appear on the perimeter of a box drawn around the text in the Chart Title, indicating that you can now move or resize the title in the Chart Area. Also note that Chart Title now appears as the current selection in the Chart Objects drop-down list box at the very beginning of the Chart toolbar.

4. Position the I-beam mouse pointer after the dash in the title and then click the mouse to place the insertion point. Press the Backspace key to delete the dash and then type **for** so that the Chart Title reads, *Scheduled Production for 2006.*

5. Click Legend on the Chart Objects drop-down list to select the Legend in the chart.

Note that not only does Excel select the Legend (indicated by the appearance of sizing handles around its perimeter), but at the same time deselects the Chart Title and completes your edit to its text.

6. Position the mouse pointer somewhere inside the selected Legend and then drag it upward until its top edge and the top edge of the Plot Area in the chart are flush with one another.

7. Click Value Axis Title on the Chart Objects drop-down list to select the Units text going up the left side of the chart and then click the Italic button on the Excel Formatting toolbar.

8. Repeat this general procedure to italicize the Category Axis Title *Month* as well.

9. Make the following editing changes to entries in the designated cells noting the change in the column of the chart representing the data point you're changing:

- **353** in cell D4 containing the scheduled production of Part 101 for June 2006

- **560** in cell E4 containing the scheduled production of Part 101 for July 2006

- **675** in cell E6 containing the scheduled production of Part 103 for July 2006

10. Click anywhere on the embedded Clustered Column chart to select it and then choose Chart⇨Location on the pull-down menu to open the Chart Location dialog box.

Note that the Chart menu only appears between the Tools and Window menus on the Excel menu bar when you select the Chart Area of the embedded chart or one of its other elements.

11. Select the As New Sheet option button and then replace the generic Chart1 name in the associate text box with Sched-06 Chart before you select OK.

Excel inserts a new chart sheet named Sched-06 Chart as the first sheet in your *Exercise14-1.xls* workbook containing the erstwhile embedded Clustered Column chart.

12. Reposition the Sched-06 Chart sheet so that it is located immediately after the Sched-06 worksheet in the workbook by dragging its sheet tab.

13. While the Sched-06 Chart sheet is still selected, click the Print Preview button on the Standard toolbar.

Note that Excel automatically selects the landscape orientation for the chart and prints it full size on the page.

14. Click the Close button on the Print Preview window's toolbar to return to the normal view of the Sched-06 Chart sheet.

15. Change the placement of the Clustered Column chart back to embedded and then move the chart so that the top edge of the Chart Area is flush with the top edge of row 9 and the left edge is flush with the left edge of column B.

16. Resize the embedded chart by dragging the sizing handle in its lower-right corner so that the bottom edge of the Chart Area is flush with the bottom edge of row 27 and the right edge is flush with the right edge of column J.

17. Position the cell cursor in cell A1 and then save your work in a workbook named **Solved14-1.xls** in your Chapter 14 folder in the My Practice Spreadsheets folder on your hard disk and then close the workbook file.

Creating Charts

Excel's Chart Wizard — opened by clicking the Chart Wizard button on the Standard toolbar (the one with the tiny column chart on it) — is the key to generating a new chart from your spreadsheet data. The Chart Wizard consists of the following four dialog boxes that walk you through all the steps necessary to build a new embedded chart or one on its own chart sheet:

- ✔ **Chart Type** (Step 1 of 4), where you select the type of chart you want to create from the different types and subtypes of charts

- ✔ **Chart Source Data** (Step 2 of 4), where you verify the range of data to be charted

- ✔ **Chart Options** (Step 3 of 4), where you select any options you want to add to your chart such as titles, gridlines, data labels, and so on

- ✔ **Chart Location** (Step 4 of 4), where you decide between embedding the chart in the current worksheet or placing it on a separate chart sheet

Q. Do I have to select the data I want to graph before I open the Chart Wizard?

A. No, as long as the cell cursor is located in one of the cells of the table of data you want to chart, you can have Excel make a guess as to the data range to be graphed (which you can refine, if the program leaves out necessary data or includes extraneous data).

Try It

Exercise 14-2: Creating a New Embedded Chart

Open the *Exercise14-2.xls* workbook file in your Chapter 14 folder in the My Practice Spreadsheets folder on your hard disk or in the Excel Workbook folder on the work-book CD-ROM. You use the CG Media - 2006 Quarterly Sales Totals table (note that this worksheet contains many hidden columns) on its Sales-06 worksheet to practice creating a new chart with the Chart Wizard:

1. While the cell cursor is still located in cell A1, click the Chart Wizard button on the Standard toolbar.

Excel opens the Chart Wizard –Step 1 of 4 – Chart Type dialog box. Note in Figure 14-3 that this dialog box contains a Chart Type list box with a tiny thumbnail and the name of each chart type on the left. The dialog box also contains a larger thumbnail with a name and description of each chart subtype in the Chart Sub-Type list box on the right.

2. Click the Bar thumbnail in the Chart Type list box on the left and then click and hold down the Press and Hold to View Sample button at the bottom of the Chart Sub-Type list box while the Clustered Bar thumbnail is selected in the Chart Sub-Type list box on the right. After previewing the data in this kind of chart, release the Press and Hold to View Sample button.

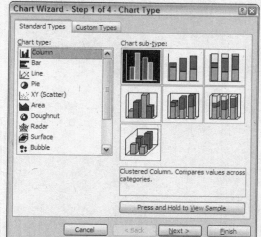

Excel previews the data in the 2006 Quarterly Sales Totals as a Clustered Bar chart in the Sample area as long as you continue to click the Press and Hold to View Sample button.

3. Click the Line thumbnail in the Chart Type list box. Next click and hold down the Press and Hold to View Sample button to view the Production Schedule data as a Line chart with markers displayed at each data value and then release the button.

4. Click Area in the Chart Type list box. Next click and hold down the Press and Hold to View Sample button to view the Production Schedule data as a Stacked Area chart with markers displayed at each data value and then release the button.

5. Click the Bar thumbnail in the Chart Type list box on the left again and, while the Clustered Bar thumbnail is selected in the Chart Sub-Type list box on the right, select the Next button.

The Chart Wizard – Step 2 of 4 – Chart Source Data dialog box as shown in Figure 14-4 appears, along with a marquee around the entire data table (A1:R15). Note that this cell range is displayed in absolute form along with the sheet name in the Data Range text box (='Sales-06'! $A$1:$R$15). Also note that the Series in Rows option button is selected so that the data series occur in the row of the table and subsequently the row titles are used in the Legend.

You can adjust the data to be charted by selecting its range directly in the worksheet while the Data Range text box is selected or by adding or removing data series on Series tab of the Chart Source Data dialog box.

6. Click the Series in Columns option button on the Data Range tab to preview the Clustered Bar chart when the columns are used as the data series and the schedule dates appear in the Legend.

Note that in this view the parts produced rather than the production dates are prominent but that the Legend is so crowded as to almost be illegible.

7. Select the Series in Rows option button once again and then click the Series tab.

Note in the Series list box on the Series tab that the row with the total sales is included in the Clustered Bar chart.

8. Click the Compact Discs, Cassettes, and Total Sales in Series list box in succession followed by the Remove button so that chart includes only Total CD Sales (the total quarterly sales for CDs) and Total Cassette Sales (the total quarterly sales for cassettes). Select the Next button.

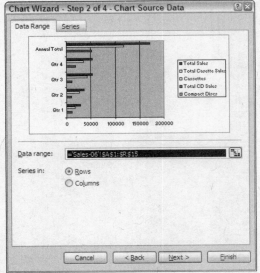

Figure 14-4:
The Chart
Wizard –
Step 2 of
4 – Chart
Source Data
dialog box.

The Chart Wizard –Step 3 of 4 – Chart Options dialog box with the Titles tab selected as shown in Figure 14-5 appears. This dialog box contains a variety of options for enhancing the legibility of the chart arranged on six tabs.

9. Type **Quarterly Sales Totals for 2006** in the Chart Title text box and then press Tab to select the Category (X) Axis text box.

10. Select the Value (Y) Axis text box and then type **Sales (in thousands)** as the title that appears below the Y-axis at the bottom of the Clustered Bar chart.

Note that as you type the titles for the chart in these text boxes, their text appears in the preview of the chart on the right side of the Chart Options dialog box.

11. Click the Gridlines tab and then Minor Gridlines check box in the Value (Y) Axis area.

Excel draws extra vertical lines between the major tick marks on the Value (Y) Axis.

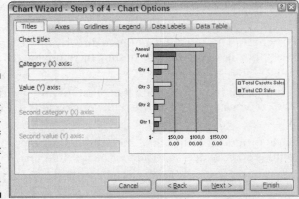

Figure 14-5:
The Chart
Wizard –
Step 3 of
4 – Chart
Options
dialog box.

12. Click the Data Labels tab in the Chart Options dialog box and then experiment with selecting and deselecting the Series Name, Category Name, and Value check boxes in succession.

Note that data labels identify the various data series in a chart either with the data series names (the part numbers in this case), category names (the dates), or values.

13. Click the Data Table tab and then select the Show Data Table check box.

Excel draws a data table in the preview right below the preview of the Clustered Bar chart. This table shows all the values that are graphed in the chart. Adding a data table to chart that you place on a separate chart sheet is sometimes an effective way to include the underlying data in chart's printout.

14. Remove the check mark from the Show Data Table check box and then select the Next button.

The Chart Wizard –Step 4 of 4 – Chart Locations dialog box, where you can choose between embedding the new chart in the worksheet as a graphic object (the default) or on a new sheet, appears.

15. Leave the As Object In option button with the Sales-06 worksheet selected as you select the Finish button.

16. Move the chart so that its top edge is flush with the top edge of row 17 and its left edge is flush with the left edge of column E before you resize the chart so that its bottom edge is flush with the bottom edge of row 35 and its right edge flush with the right edge of column R.

Check your embedded Clustered Bar chart against the one shown in Figure 14-6. If everything checks out, proceed to step 18.

17. Save your work with the filename **Solved14-2.xls** in your Chapter 14 folder in the My Practice Spreadsheets folder on your hard disk and then leave the workbook file open for Exercise 14-3.

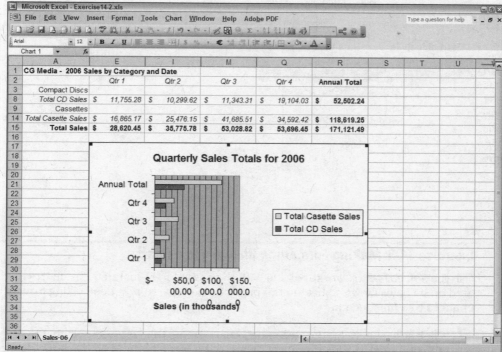

Figure 14-6: The embedded Clustered Bar chart after moving and resizing it.

Formatting Charts

Many times you find that you have to finesse the formatting of elements in the particular chart that the Chart Wizard produces for you. This is especially true in the case of embedded charts, where the overall size of the Chart Area may make the fonts uses in the titles, legend, and data labels too big in relation to the data markers in the plot area.

You can change the formatting of a particular element in your chart in one of two ways:

✔ Click the element in the chart to select it and then press Ctrl+1. Alternatively, click the Format button on the Chart toolbar (the second one from the left) to open the Format dialog box associated with that element.

✔ Select the element to format with the Chart Objects drop-down list box in the Chart toolbar and then click its Format button. Alternatively, press Ctrl+1 to open the Format dialog box associated with that element.

In addition to enabling you to select a particular chart element (Chart Objects button) and then open its associated Format dialog box (Format button), as you can see in Figure 14-7, the Chart toolbar gives you access to many different charting tools. For example, you can choose a new type of chart (Chart Type button), add or remove the chart legend (Legend button) and data table (Data Table button), and select between the rows (By Rows button) and columns (By Columns button) of the spreadsheet data as the chart's data series. Note that you can use the Angle Clockwise and Angle Counterclockwise buttons on the Chart toolbar to save space by displaying the Category (X) Axis labels or Value (Y) Axis labels diagonally at a 45-degree angle.

Figure 14-7: You can use the buttons on the Chart toolbar to further format any chart you create.

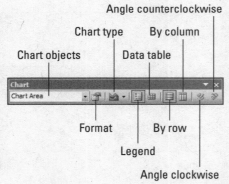

Try It

Exercise 14-3: Making Formatting Changes to a Chart

Use the *Solved14-2.xls* workbook file with the embedded Clustered Bar chart you created on its Sales-06 worksheet in the previous exercise to practice making formatting changes to a finished chart:

1. Click somewhere on the embedded chart. Doing this not only selects the graphic object, but also adds the Chart menu to the Menu bar and displays the floating Chart toolbar onscreen.

2. Click the Chart Objects drop-down list button and then click Legend on its drop-down menu. While the Legend is selected in the chart, click the Format Legend button on the Chart toolbar to open the Format Legend dialog box.

Note that the Format button on the Chart toolbar is renamed with whatever object is selected in the chart so that its ToolTip currently identifies it as the Format Chart button.

3. Select the Shadow check box on the Patterns tab of the Format Legend dialog box and then click the light yellow color square in the Area section on the right side of this tab.

4. Click the Font tab, click 8 in the Size list box, and then select OK.

5. Select Chart Area on the Chart Objects drop-down list and then click the Format Chart Area button to open the Format Chart Area dialog box.

6. Select the Shadow and Round Corners check boxes in the Border section and then click the light green color square in the Area section.

7. Click the Properties tab and then select the Don't Move or Size with Cells option button before you select OK.

You need to select the Don't Move or Size with Cells option to prevent Excel from stretching and radically distorting the embedded Clustered Bar chart whenever you redisplay the hidden columns in the worksheet.

To see how this works, take a moment to redisplay the hidden columns that contain the underlying monthly sales totals and see how this affects the display of the embedded chart in the worksheet. In this case, the columns were hidden by using Excel's Auto Outline feature (Data⇨Group and Outline⇨Auto Outline) and then the outline buttons that you can use to control what level of detail is displayed both in terms of hidden columns and rows.

8. Click cell A1 to deselect the chart and then press Ctrl+8 to redisplay the outline buttons to the left of the row headings and above the column headings.

9. Click the 3 button in the stack of vertical buttons immediately above the row 1 heading to redisplay the hidden columns with the monthly sales for each of the four quarters.

Note that although the Clustered Bar chart does not move and is not resized, it does change: Excel adds data points and bars for the newly displayed monthly sales to the Clustered Bar chart.

10. Click the 2 button in the vertical stack and then Press Ctrl+8 again to hide the monthly sales as well as the outline buttons; click the embedded Clustered Bar chart to reselect it.

11. Using the Chart Objects drop-down button and associated Format buttons on the Chart toolbar, make the following formatting changes:

- Chart Title — 10-point Arial bold type, enclosed in a light-yellow colored text box with a drop shadow

- Value Axis Title — 9-point Arial bold

- Category Axis — 8-point Arial bold

12. Position the mouse pointer along the value axis along the bottom of Clustered Bar chart. When the Value Axis ToolTip appears, click the axis to select it and press Ctrl+1 to open the Format Axis dialog box.

13. On the Font tab of the Format Axis dialog box, select Bold in the Font Style list box and 8 in the Size box.

14. On the Number tab, enter **0** in the Decimal Places.

15. On the Scale tab, make the following changes:

- **125000** in Maximum text box

- **25000** in Major Unit text box

- **5000** in Minor Unit text box

16. Select OK in the Format Axis dialog box and then click the Angle Counterclockwise button at the end of the Chart toolbar.

17. Select the Plot Area on the Chart Objects drop-down list, click the Format Plot Area button and then click the white color square in the Area section of the Patterns tab before you select OK.

18. Check your formatted Clustered Bar chart against the one shown in *Solved14-3. xls* in the Chapter 14 folder and then, if everything checks out, save your work under the filename **Solved14-3-mine.xls** in the same folder. Close the *Solved14-3. xls* workbook and leave the *Solved14-3-mine.xls* open for Exercise 14-4.

Editing Charts

Excel makes it easy to edit any chart you create. All you have to do is select the chart before you click the Chart Wizard button on the Standard toolbar. If you're editing an embedded chart, you select it by clicking somewhere on the graphic object in the worksheet. If you're editing a chart on a separate chart sheet, you select it by clicking its sheet tab.

After clicking the Chart Wizard button, Excel then opens the Chart Wizard – Step 1 of 4 – Chart Type dialog box. You can then use any of the options on the tabs of any of the four Chart Wizard dialog box to make all necessary changes to the selected chart, from selecting a new chart type and subtype all the way to changing its location from worksheet to chart sheet and vice versa.

Try It

Exercise 14-4: Editing the Structure, Contents, and Location of a Chart

Use the *Solved14-3-mine.xls* workbook file with the embedded Clustered Bar chart you formatted on its Sales-06 worksheet in the previous exercise to practice making editing changes to a finished chart:

1. Click your Clustered Bar chart to select it and then click the Copy button on the Standard toolbar or press Ctrl+C to copy the graphic object to the Windows Clipboard.

2. Scroll down to cell E38 in the Sales-06 worksheet and then click this cell to put the cell cursor in it before you click the Paste button on the Standard toolbar or press Ctrl+V.

Excel inserts a copy of the embedded Clustered Bar chart that covers roughly the cell range A38:S60.

3. While the copy of the Clustered Bar chart is still selected, click the Chart Wizard on the Standard toolbar to open the Chart Wizard – Step 1 of 4 – Chart Type dialog box.

4. Click the Column thumbnail in the Chart Type list box and then click the 3-D Column thumbnail at the bottom of the Sub-Type list box.

5. Click the Press and Hold to View Sample button to preview the data as a 3-D Column chart. After releasing this button, select the Next button to open the Chart Wizard – Step 2 of 4 – Chart Source Data dialog box.

6. While the Data Range text box is selected, drag through the cell range A2:Q15 so that the range ='Sales-06'! $A$2:$Q$15 appears in this text box.

7. Click the Series tab and then remove the Compact Discs and Cassettes from the Series list box so that it contains only Total CD Sales, Total Cassette Sales, and Total Sales.

8. Select the Next button to open the Chart Wizard – Step 3 of 4 – Chart Options dialog box and then click the Data Table tab. Select the Show Data Table check box and deselect the Show Legend Keys check box.

9. Select the Next button and then in the Chart Wizard – Step 4 of 4 – Chart Locations dialog box, select the As a New Sheet option button and enter the name **3-D Column Chart** in its text box before you select the Finish button.

Excel creates a new 3-D Column Chart sheet that contains the copy of the original Clustered Bar chart changed into a 3-D Column chart.

10. Reposition the Chart1 sheet so that it follows the Sales-06 worksheet in the workbook by dragging its sheet tab.

11. Increase the font in the Legend text box to 10 points and then resize its text box so that it is large enough to accommodate the larger text size.

12. Click the Value Axis with the dollar amounts to select it and then click the Angle Counterclockwise button at the end of the Chart toolbar to straighten its titles.

13. Click the Series Axis (the one with Total CD Sales, Total Cassette Sales, and Total Sales titles) and then make its font 9-point Arial bold.

14. Click the corner in the front of the floor of the 3-D Column chart where the Category Axis (the one with the Qtr 1, Qtr 2, Qtr 3, and Qtr 4 titles) meets the Series Axis and then drag the outline of the 3-D chart box down slightly so that the angle that Category Axis makes with the straight line on the top of the Data Table is not so steep.

15. Check your 3-D Column chart against the one shown in *Solved14-4.xls* in the Chapter 14 folder and then, if you're satisfied with your chart, select cell A1 in the Sales-06 worksheet and save your work under the filename **Solved 14-4-mine.xls** in the same folder. Close both the *Solved14-4.xls* workbook and *Solved14-4-mine.xls* as you exit Excel.

Chapter 15

Adding Graphics to the Spreadsheet

· ·

In This Chapter

▶ Understanding what graphic objects are and how Excel treats them

▶ Adding clip art to the spreadsheet

▶ Importing graphics files into the spreadsheet

▶ Using the tools on the Drawing toolbar to add and draw shapes

▶ Adding text boxes to the spreadsheet

▶ Constructing WordArt, organizational charts, and other diagrams

· ·

As you discovered in Chapter 14, the embedded charts you add to a spreadsheet are actually graphic objects that you can move and resize as needed. Embedded charts are by no means the only graphic objects you can have in your worksheet. Excel also enables you to add graphic objects you create yourself as well as those you import from Clip Art and other kinds of graphics files.

In this chapter, you get a chance to practice using all these different types of graphic objects to improve the overall look of your spreadsheets and make their data and charts even more interesting and legible to the user.

Understanding Graphic Objects

The most important thing to remember about graphic objects is that they are distinct objects separate from the cells of the worksheet that float above on their own layers. Because they are distinct objects, you can select them for moving and resizing as you did your embedded chart in Exercise 14-1 in Chapter 14. Because graphic objects remain on separate layers, you can move them one on top of the other, with the object on the topmost layer obscuring parts of the objects on layers below.

To select a graphic object, you must click some part of it (which can sometimes be a bit tricky when different objects overlap each other). As Figure 15-1 demonstrates, when you select a graphic object, Excel displays the name of the object in the Name box on the Formula bar (AutoShape 1, in this case) while at the same time displaying white circular sizing handles around the perimeter of its shape and a green circular rotation handle at the top. (You can use the Rotation handle to change the orientation of the object by rotating it to any desired angle.) Some graphic objects, such as the block arrow shown selected in Figure 15-1, also display a shaping handle that you can use to modify the basic shape (in this case, the thickness of the body of the arrow in relation to its arrowhead).

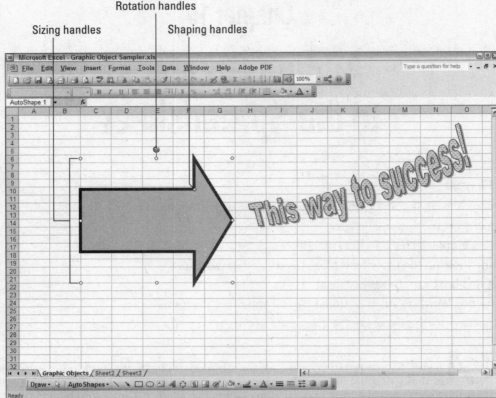

Figure 15-1:
When you
select a
graphic
object,
its name
appears in
the Name
box on the
Formula bar
along with
various
handles for
manipulat-
ing it.

To move the selected graphic object, position the mouse pointer somewhere inside the object's perimeter. Then, when the pointer becomes an arrowhead with a double-cross at its point, drag the object to its new position within the worksheet. To copy the selected object, hold down the Ctrl key as you drag the graphic (when you press the Ctrl key, a plus sign, indicating that the object is being copied, appears above the arrowhead pointer).

You can "nudge" a selected graphic object into its desired position by pressing the arrow keys (or, if the Drawing toolbar is displayed, by clicking the Draw button and then choosing Nudge⇨Up, ⇨Down, ⇨Left, or ⇨Right). When you press an arrow or choose one of the Nudge commands, Excel moves the object just a very little bit in that direction. Nudging is very useful when you have an object that's almost in place and requires very little handling to get it into just the right position.

When graphic objects overlay each other, you can move an object that is on higher levels to lower levels by right-clicking the object to select it and, at the same time, open its shortcut menu, where you select Order⇨Send Backward. To move up an object that's on a lower level up toward the top, you repeat this procedure, this time selecting Order⇨Bring Forward on its shortcut menu.

Excel also makes it possible to group different graphic objects together to create a single composite graphic object by selecting the individual objects (by Ctrl+clicking them) and then selecting Grouping⇨Group on their shortcut menu. Excel indicates that the selected graphics are now grouped (and for all intents and purposes, a single graphic object) by placing a single set of sizing handles around the perimeter formed by all the former separate graphics. You can then manipulate the grouped graphic as a single entity, moving, sizing, rotating, and so on as you would any other object.

The great thing about grouping a bunch of different objects is that Excel never forgets that they were once separate objects that you could independently manipulate. That means that you can always turn them back into separate graphics by ungrouping them. To do this, right-click the composite graphic object and then choose Grouping⇨Ungroup on its shortcut menu.

Try It

Exercise 15-1: Resizing and Grouping Graphic Objects

If Excel is not currently running, launch the program and then open the *Exercise15-1.xls* workbook file in your Chapter 15 folder in the My Practice Spreadsheets folder on your hard disk or in the Excel Workbook folder on the workbook CD-ROM. The Graphic Objects worksheet in this workbook contains the block arrow and "This way to success!" WordArt graphic object that you see in Figure 15-1. You use these two graphics to practice manipulating graphic objects, including moving and resizing them, sending them to different layers, and finally grouping them together as one composite graphic:

1. Click the block arrow to select it.

2. Drag the block arrow's shape handle downward to narrow the body of the arrowhead until it's just slightly wider than the widest part of the text, "This way to success!," in the WordArt graphic object.

3. Drag the block arrow's rotation handle downward to the left to increase up the angle of the block arrow until it's approximately at a 45 degree angle.

4. Click somewhere on the WordArt graphic object to select it.

Note that selecting this object causes Excel to display the WordArt toolbar (with which you will become familiar when you perform Exercise 15-3).

5. Drag the WordArt graphic object until it overlays the block arrow.

6. Adjust the angle of the WordArt object to match that of the block arrow using its rotation handle.

7. Right-click somewhere on the arrowhead of the block arrow to select this object and then select Order⇨Bring Forward on its shortcut menu.

Excel positions the block arrow on top of the WordArt graphic object obscuring most of its text.

8. Right-click the block arrow and then select Order⇨Send Backward on its shortcut menu.

9. Using only the cursor arrow keys on your keyboard, nudge the block arrow until none of the WordArt text extends beyond the blunt end of the arrow.

10. Select the WordArt graphic object and rotate it as needed so that the words, "This way to" all fit within the body of the block arrow.

Use the graphics shown in Figure 15-2 as a guide, but don't worry if yours are not exactly the same.

11. Right-click the WordArt graphic object and then select Format WordArt to open the Format WordArt dialog box.

12. Click the Color drop-down list button and then click the Yellow color square in the pop-up palette before you close the Format WordArt dialog box.

13. Hold down the Ctrl key as you click somewhere on the block arrow (make sure that you see two green rotation handles) to select both graphic objects.

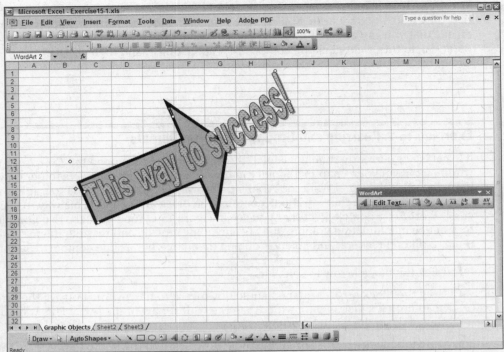

Figure 15-2:
The block arrow and WordArt graphic objects after overlaying and rotating.

14. Right-click on one of the letters in the WordArt graphic object and then select Grouping⇨Group on its shortcut menu.

15. Test out that you're dealing with a single graphic object by using the → and ← keys to move the block arrow with WordArt graphic object.

16. Widen column D to 17.27 (128 pixels).

Note the effect that widening column D has on the block arrow and the WordArt graphic object.

17. Click the Undo button on the Standard toolbar or press Ctrl+Z to restore the column to its original width and accordingly the composite graphic object to its original size.

18. Open the Format Object dialog box for the composite graphic and then click the Properties tab.

The Properties tab contains three positioning options: Move and Size with Cells (selected by default), Move but Don't Size with Cells, and Don't Move or Size with Cells. Select the Move but Don't Size with Cells option when you want the graphic size to remain stationary while still allowing it move with cells that it overlays. Choose the Don't Move or Size with Cells option when you want its size and position to remain unaffected by changes in the cells it overlays.

19. Select the Don't Move or Size with Cells option button before you select OK.

20. Widen column C to 26.43 (190 pixels).

This time, widening a column that the graphic object overlays has no effect on it.

21. Right-click the block arrow with WordArt graphic object and select Grouping⇨Ungroup on its shortcut menu.

22. Click one of the cells outside the block arrow or WordArt graphic object to deselect both objects.

23. Click the WordArt graphic and then try nudging it with one of the arrow keys.

24. Use the Regroup option on the Grouping shortcut menu to re-create the composite block arrow with WordArt graphic object.

25. Save your work as a new workbook with the filename **Solved15-1.xls** in your Chapter 15 folder in the My Practice Spreadsheets folder and then close the workbook.

Using the Drawing Toolbar

Excel's Drawing toolbar is packed with great tools for creating and adding all types of graphic objects. About the only graphic that you can't bring in from this toolbar is one that you create on a scanner or import from a digital camera attached to your computer (to do that, you have to rely on the Insert⇨Picture⇨From Scanner or Camera menu command). For all the rest of your graphic needs, the Drawing toolbar is your ticket.

Figure 15-3 shows the Drawing toolbar and identifies the buttons that use only icons without text. When you first open the Drawing toolbar (by choosing View⇨Toolbar⇨ Drawing), Excel automatically docks this toolbar at the bottom of the Excel window right above the Status bar. You can then move the Drawing toolbar to another side of the Excel window or even float it if you wish.

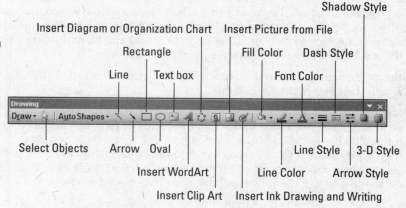

Figure 15-3: You can use the tools on the Drawing toolbar for almost all your graphic needs.

Note that drop-down menus from which you can select drawing commands and predefined shapes to draw are attached to the Draw and AutoShapes buttons. Pop-up palettes, from which you can select new fill, line, and font color, shading, and 3-D effect for selected graphic objects, are attached to the Fill Color, Line Color, Font Color, Shadow Style, and 3-D Style buttons.

Inserting clip art

Microsoft includes a wide variety of ready-to-use images called Clip Art that you can easily insert in your worksheets. To make it easy to do this, later versions of Excel include an Insert Clip Art Task pane from which you can conduct word searches for the types of images you want to use.

To choose a clip to paste into a worksheet, click the Insert Clip Art button on the Drawing toolbar. Doing this opens the Insert Clip Art Task bar, where you can search for the type of clips you want to use. The first time that you use the Clip Art button, Excel opens the Add Clips to Gallery dialog box that prompts you to collect and catalog all the media files on your computer system (including sound, pictures, digital movies, and Clip Art). Click the Now button to have Excel catalog your media files. When you do so, the program opens an Auto Import Settings dialog box, where you can indicate which folders to search for the media files on your computer. Once you finish indicating which folders to search, click the Catalog button to have the Microsoft Media Gallery catalog the media clips on your system.

Try It

Exercise 15-2: Adding Clip Art to a Spreadsheet

Open the *Exercise15-2.xls* workbook file in your Chapter 15 folder in the My Practice Spreadsheets folder on your hard disk or in the Excel Workbook folder on the workbook CD-ROM. This workbook contains the ITB Invoice worksheet with a copy of an invoice template for a store called Into the Blue that sells kites and accessories. In this exercise, you get to practice finding and adding clip art by sprucing up the otherwise dull invoice heading with an image of a kite:

1. Display the Drawing toolbar by choosing View➪Toolbars➪Drawing.

Excel docks the Drawing toolbar at the bottom of the Excel program window.

2. Click the Insert Clip Art button on the Drawing toolbar.

Excel displays the Clip Art task pane. If this is the first time you opened this task pane, the program displays the Add Clips to Gallery dialog box, which prompts you to collect and catalog all the media files on your computer system (including sound, pictures, digital movies, and Clip Art). Go ahead and have the program catalog the media files on your computer by clicking the Now button.

3. Enter **kites** as the search text in the Search For text box at the top of the Clip Art task pane and then select the Go button.

Depending upon your version of Excel, the program may locate several kite images including a single clip art image of a pink kite (which does not go very well with the blue background of the invoice header). If you have access to the Internet, go ahead and follow steps 4 to 9 to find and download other, better-suited kite images from Microsoft's Clip Art Web site. If you don't have Internet access, go ahead and use the pink kite image and skip ahead to step 10.

4. Click the Clip Art on Office Online hyperlink near the bottom of the Clip Art task pane.

Excel launches your Web browser, which goes online and opens the Microsoft Office Clip Art and Media Home Page.

5. At the top of Microsoft Office Clip Art and Media Home Page, select Clip Art on the Search drop-down list and then type **kite** in the Search text box before selecting its Go button.

The first of eight Web pages of kite images appears.

6. Search through the first few pages of kite images, selecting the check boxes for a few clip art images whose colors and kite drawing seem best suited to the background color and type **style** in the Into the Blue invoice header.

Note that the Download link in the pane on the left of the Web page keeps tabs on the number of images you select.

7. Click the Download link to open the Download page and then click the Download Now button (also, if a File Download security alert dialog box appears, click its Open button to proceed with the image downloading).

After all your selected images are downloaded, the Microsoft Clip Organizer dialog box automatically opens.

8. Verify that your kite images are successfully downloaded by clicking the Downloaded Clips folder in the left pane of the Microsoft Clip Organizer dialog box.

Excel displays all the clip art images you downloaded from the Microsoft Office Clip Art and Media Home Page on the right side of the dialog box. You can then move these images into appropriate folders (such as Leisure or Sports) if you so desire.

9. Close the Microsoft Office Clip Art and Media Home Page and your browser. In Excel close the Microsoft Clip Organizer dialog box and select the Go button again to rerun the search for kite clip art images.

This time, Excel finds all the kite images you downloaded from the Microsoft Office Clip Art and Media Home Page along with the sole local image.

10. In Clip Art task pane, click the thumbnail of the kite image you want to add to the invoice header.

Excel immediately inserts a copy of the image into the worksheet.

11. Drag the kite image to the right side of the invoice header and then use its sizing handles to resize the graphic so that it fits entirely within the blue background.

Note that selected clip art images have only sizing handles — these images do not offer a rotation handle for changing the orientation or a shaping handle for manipulating the shape.

12. Use the Increase Indent button on the Formatting toolbar to indent the Into the Blue heading in cell B2 and the Kites & Accessories for All Ages heading in cell B3 until this text and the kite clip art image appear as a unit (use my invoice header shown in Figure 15-4 as a guide).

13. Close the Clip Art task pane and select cell A1. Save your work as a new workbook with the filename **Solved15-2.xls** in your Chapter 15 folder in the My Practice Spreadsheets folder and then close the workbook.

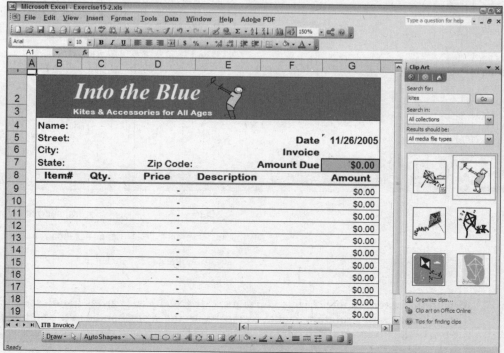

Figure 15-4:
The header I created for the Into the Blue invoice template uses a boy-flying-a-kite clip art image downloaded from Microsoft's Clip Art and Media Web page.

Importing graphics files

In addition to the clip art images stored on your computer system, you can also insert graphic files that you keep in any folder containing your artwork and digital photographs such as My Pictures in My Documents on your hard disk.

To insert a picture into the worksheet, click the Insert Picture from File button on the Drawing toolbar. Doing this opens the Insert Picture dialog box. This dialog box works just like the Open dialog box except that it's set to display only the graphics files that Excel can import, and it automatically looks in the My Pictures folder on your hard disk (which you can change by selecting another folder in the Look In drop-down list box).

After you locate the graphics file with the image you want to insert in the worksheet, click its thumbnail in the Insert Picture dialog box and then click the Insert button to import it into the current worksheet. Excel then displays the image from the file you selected along with the Picture toolbar (see Figure 15-5) in the current worksheet.

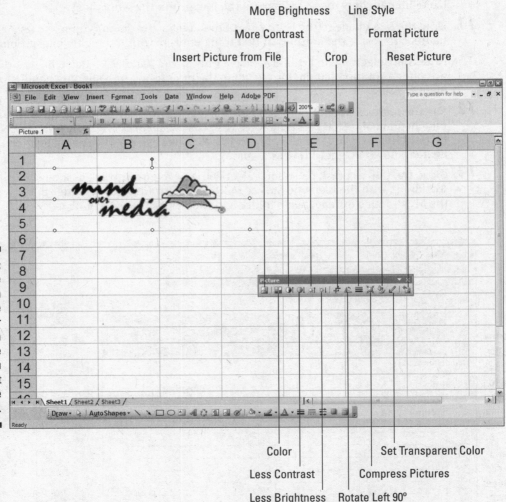

Figure 15-5:
You can use the tools on the Picture toolbar to edit a graphic file that you import into the worksheet.

As with the other graphic objects you work with, Excel places sizing handles around the perimeter with a rotation handle connected to the sizing handle in the middle at the top of the image. You can then reposition, resize, or rotate the image as needed.

You can also use the tools on the Picture toolbar to edit the photo. Among other things, these tools make it possible to heighten or lessen the brightness or contrast of the image, crop out unwanted areas around the edges, and compress the image so that it doesn't bulk up the size of your workbook (as only high resolution images can).

If you have a scanner or digital camera connected to your computer, you can use Excel's Insert⇨Picture⇨From Scanner or Camera command to bring a scanned image or digital photo that you've taken directly into your Excel worksheet.

Try It

Exercise 15-3: Importing Images from Graphics Files into a Spreadsheet

Open the *Exercise15-3.xls* workbook file in your Chapter 15 folder in the My Practice Spreadsheets folder on your hard disk or in the Excel Workbook folder on the workbook CD-ROM. This workbook contains a copy of the Home Sales 2006 worksheet that you worked with earlier. You will add a new worksheet to use this copy of the workbook for the 905 Hudson Lane listing in which you will add a couple of digital photos:

1. Insert a new worksheet into the *Exercise15-3.xls* workbook that you name **905 Hudson Ln** and which you place after the Home Sales 2006 worksheet.

2. Copy the street address in cell A8 of the Home Sales 2006 worksheet to cell A1 of the 905 Hudson Ln worksheet and then make its font bold and increase its font size to 14 points and then use AutoFit to resize column A.

3. Make the following entries in the designated cells:

   • **Sold** in cell in cell A2

   • **Sales Price** in cell A3

4. Format the entries in cells A2 and A3 so that they are bold and right-aligned in their cells.

5. Copy cell B8 in the Home Sales 2006 worksheet to cell B2 in the 905 Hudson Ln worksheet.

6. Create a formula in cell B3 in the 905 Hudson Ln worksheet with an external reference to cell C8 in the Home Sales 2006 worksheet that copies and links to its value.

   The easiest way to do this is to position the cell cursor in cell B3 in the 905 Hudson Ln worksheet, type = (equal to), and then click the Home Sales 2006 sheet tab followed by cell C8 before you press Enter.

7. Position the cell cursor in cell A5 of the 905 Hudson Ln worksheet and then click the Insert Picture from File button on the Drawing toolbar.

   Excel opens the Insert Picture dialog box in the My Pictures folder on your computer. The photos you want to insert are located in the Graphics folder inside of your Chapter 15 folder in My Practice Spreadsheets.

8. Click the My Documents button in the left pane, and then double-click My Practice Spreadsheets folder icon, followed by the Chapter 15 folder icon, followed by the Graphics folder icon.

   This folder contains three graphics files: two digital photos saved in the JPEG graphics format and one company logo graphic saved in the GIF graphics format. Note that the Files of Type drop-down list box is automatically set to display all the graphic file formats that Excel supports. Also note that Excel automatically displays thumbnails of each of these graphics files along with their filenames.

9. Click the *Hudson Lane Exterior.jpg* thumbnail to select it and then select the Insert button to bring it into the 905 Hudson Ln worksheet.

Excel inserts the selected photo complete with sizing and rotation handles, while at the same time displaying the Picture toolbar.

10. Move the photo so that its left edge is flush with the left edge of column B and its top edge is flush with the top of row 5; resize the graphic so that its right edge is flush with the right edge of column F and its bottom edge is flush with the bottom of row 19.

11. Use the More Contrast button to increase the contrast in this photo.

12. Click the Line Style button and then select 2¼ pt on its drop-down menu to put a border around the picture.

13. Click the Format Picture button on the Picture toolbar to open the Format Picture dialog box and then select the Don't Move or Size with Cells option button on the Properties tab before you select OK.

14. Click cell H5 to position the cell cursor in this cell, and then import the *Hudson Lane Interior.jpg* file into the worksheet, sizing it so that it covers the cell range H5:L19, and formatting it to match the photo of the house exterior to its left.

15. Click cell A1 in the 905 Hudson Ln worksheet and then click the Print Preview button to open this sheet in the Print Preview window.

16. Click the Setup button and then select the Landscape and Fit to 1 Page(s) Wide by 1 Tall option buttons on the Page tab.

17. Click the Header/Footer tab and then select the Custom Header button.

18. Click the Right Section and then click the Insert Picture button (the one second-to-the-last on the right).

19. Double-click the thumbnail of the *momtrdmk.gif* file with the Mind Over Media, Inc. logo.

Excel inserts an &[Picture] code in the Right section.

20. Click the Format Picture button (the very last one) and enter 75% in the Height text box in the Scale section of the Size tab in the Format Picture dialog box before you select OK.

21. Select 905 Hudson Ln, Page 1 in the Footer drop-down list box.

22. Select OK to close the Header dialog box and OK again to close the Page Setup dialog box.

The Print Preview window now displays Page 1 of the report in landscape mode with both the entire exterior and interior photos together on the page, the Mind Over Media, Inc. logo in the upper-right top margin, and the sheet name centered and the page number right-aligned in the bottom margin.

23. Check your 905 Hudson Ln worksheet against the one shown in *Solved15-3.xls* in your Chapter 15 folder. When everything checks out, proceed to step 24.

24. Click the Close button to exit Print Preview and then select cell A1 of the Home Sales 2006 worksheet and save the workbook in a new file named **Solved15-3-mine.xls** in your Chapter 15 folder in the My Practice Spreadsheets folder before you close the file.

Drawing and adding graphic shapes

The Drawing toolbar enables you to manually draw straight lines, lines with arrowheads (simply referred to as arrows), rectangular and square shapes, and oval and circular shapes. To draw any of these shapes, click the appropriate button and drag the thin, black cross pointer to draw its outline. When drawing a line or arrow, Excel draws the line from the place where you originally click the mouse button to the place where you release it.

When drawing a rectangle or an oval, you can constrain the tool to draw a square or circle by holding down the Shift key as you drag the mouse. Note that when drawing a two-dimensional shape such as a rectangle, square, oval, or circle, Excel automatically draws the shape with a white fill that obscures any data or graphic objects that are beneath the shape on layers below.

After you've drawn the basic shape, you can then use the Fill Color, Line Color, Line Style, Dash Style, Shadow Style, and 3-D Style buttons on the Drawing toolbar to enhance the basic shape. In addition to drawing your own shapes, you can insert any number of ready-made shapes (including lines, arrows, flow chart symbols, banners, and callouts) by selecting them from the AutoShapes pop-up menu and then sizing them in the worksheet.

After selecting a shape from one of the AutoShapes menus, you position and size it in the worksheet by dragging the thin, black cross mouse pointer. To constrain the shape so that you can't possibly mess up its proportions when dragging the outline to size the AutoShape, hold down the Shift key as you drag.

Note that when you insert one of the callouts on the Callouts cascading palette, Excel positions the insertion point within the callout AutoShape, enabling you to then enter the text of the callout. (Callouts are the only AutoShapes that combine text and graphics.) After you finish entering the text, click somewhere outside of the shape to deselect the callout.

Try It

Exercise 15-4: Creating and Adding Graphics with the Drawing Toolbar

Open the *Exercise15-4.xls* workbook file in your Chapter 15 folder in the My Practice Spreadsheets folder on your hard disk or in the Excel Workbook folder on the workbook CD-ROM. This workbook contains a copy of the 3D Column chart from Exercise 14-4 in the previous chapter on its own chart sheet (that in this workbook precedes the Sale-06 worksheet). You will use this 3-D Column chart to practice drawing and adding graphic shapes:

1. Click the Oval button on the Drawing toolbar and then draw an oval shape around only the purple column representing the third quarter total cassette sales in the 3-D Column chart.

   As soon as you release the mouse button, Excel draws a white oval shape that obscures the columns representing third and fourth quarter cassette sales.

2. Press Ctrl+1 to open the Format AutoShape dialog box (you can also open it by clicking the Format Selected Object button on the Chart toolbar).

3. Select No Fill on Color drop-down list in the Fill section on the Color and Lines tab of the Format AutoShape dialog box.

4. Click the yellow color square on the drop-down palette attached to the Color drop-down list button in the Line section of the Color and Lines tab and then increase the line weight to 2 pt in the Weight text box before you select OK.

   As soon as the Format AutoShape dialog box closes, you see only the outline of the oval (with no fill) in yellow.

5. Adjust the position, shape, and size of the oval so that it encircles and highlights primarily just the 3-D column representing third quarter total cassette sales in the chart (use Figure 15-6 as a guide).

6. Select Callouts on the AutoShape pop-up menu and then click the thumbnail of Line Callout 3 on the Callouts pop-up palette (the one third from the left in the second row).

7. Click the thin black-cross mouse pointer on the top edge of the oval and then drag upward diagonally to draw the callout box in the upper-right corner of the Chart Area of the 3-D Column chart.

8. Type **Summer Blow-out Sale** in the callout text box and then adjust the size and shape of the callout text box so that all the text is visible.

9. Click the outline of the callout text box, press Ctrl+1, and then make the following formatting changes using options in the Format AutoShape dialog box:

- On the Colors and Lines tab, change the Color in the Fill section to light yellow

- Increase the weight in the Line section to 1.75 pt

- Select the first arrowhead shape on the second row of the End Style drop-down list box in the Arrows section

- Select the last arrowhead size on the third row of the End Size drop-down list box in the Arrows section

- On the Font tab, select Arial 10-point bold as the font

- On the Alignment tab, select Center as the setting for both the Vertical and Horizontal Text Alignment

10. Adjust the size of the text box so that the formatted text all fits on a single line in the text box and then click somewhere off the callout text box in the Chart Area to deselect the callout.

11. Select Stars and Banners on the AutoShape pop-up menu and then click the thumbnail of Horizontal Scroll on the Stars and Banners pop-up palette (the second one from the left in the fourth row).

12. Draw a scroll to fill the blank area in the upper-left corner of the chart (see Figure 15-6).

Check your chart against the one shown in Figure 15-6 before you proceed to step 13.

13. Deselect the horizontal scroll AutoShape by clicking somewhere in the area outside the 3-D Column chart and then save your work in a new workbook called **Solved15-4.xls** in your Chapter 15 folder in the My Practice Spreadsheets folder. Leave this workbook file open for Exercise 15-5.

Adding text boxes

Text boxes are a special type of graphic object that combines text with a rectangular graphic object (the only other objects that do this are the callouts that you insert from AutoShapes Callout pop-up menu). They're great for calling attention to significant trends or special features in the charts that you create. To create a text box, click the Text Box button on the Drawing toolbar and then drag the mouse pointer to draw the outline of the box. As soon as you release the mouse button, Excel places the insertion point in the upper-left corner of the box.

You can then start typing the text you want displayed in the text box. When the text you type reaches the right edge of the text box, Excel automatically starts a new line. If you reach the end of the text box and keep typing, Excel then scrolls the text up and you then have to resize the text box to display all the text you've entered. If you want to break the line before it reaches the right edge of the text box, you press the Enter key. When you finish entering the text, click anywhere on the screen outside of the text box to deselect.

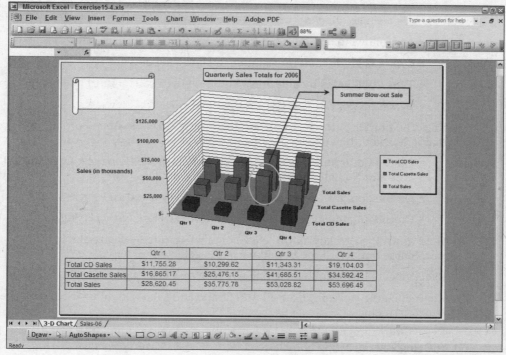

Figure 15-6:
3-D Column chart after adding an oval shape along with the line call-out and horizontal scroll banner AutoShapes.

Unlike other graphic objects in Excel, when you select text boxes, they only display sizing handles without any rotation handle (because Excel can't display text at just any angle you might select). Also, unlike other graphic objects, text boxes display two different border patterns when you select them:

- Single cross-hatched pattern when you click inside the text box, enabling you to format and edit the text (including deleting individual text characters)

- Double cross-hatched pattern when you click the border of the text box or start dragging the box to reposition it, indicating that you can format and edit the box itself (including deleting the text box along with all its text characters)

Keep in mind that text boxes are similar to the comments you created in Exercise 4-10 in Chapter 4 in the sense that they also display the text that you enter in a rectangular box. Text boxes differ from comments, however, in that they are *not* attached to particular cells and *are* always displayed in the worksheet.

Try It

Exercise 15-5: Adding Text Boxes to a Spreadsheet

Use the 3-D Column chart saved in the workbook file *Solved15-4.xls* with the Line Callout 3 and Horizontal Scroll AutoShapes you added in Exercise 15-4 to practice creating a text box:

1. Click the Text Box button on the Drawing toolbar and then click the cross-hair part of the mouse pointer in the upper-left corner of the Horizontal Scroll banner you added to the 3-D Column chart; draw the outline of the text inside this AutoShape.

When you release the mouse button, the outline of the selected text box appears on top of the Horizontal Scroll AutoShape. You can tell that the text box is ready to accept text because it contains the insertion point and the outline of the text box uses a single, diagonal cross-hatched pattern.

2. Enter the following text on three lines inside the selected text box:

   • Type **CG Media** and press Enter to start a second line

   • Type **2006 Sales by** and press Enter again to start a third line

   • Type **Category & Quarter** on the third line

3. Click the border of the text box and then press Ctrl+1 to open Format Text Box dialog box and then use its options to make the following changes:

   • On the Color and Lines tab, select No Fill for the Color setting in the Fill area and No Line for the Color setting in the Line area

   • On the Font tab, select Bold for the Font Style and 10 for the Size

   • On the Alignment tab, select Center for the Horizontal setting

4. Hold down the Ctrl key as you click somewhere on the Horizontal Scroll AutoShape outside of the boundary of the selected text box.

   Excel selects the AutoShape along with the text box.

5. Right-click the Horizontal Scroll AutoShape and then Grouping⇨Group on the shortcut menu.

   Excel groups the text box and scroll banner as one graphic object (indicated by the single set of sizing handles).

6. Click the I-beam mouse pointer in the text on the banner after the *a* in *Media* in the first line and then type a , (comma) followed by **Inc.** (period).

   Even though the text box is now combined with the banner, you can still edit and format its text. Remember that you can also separate the text box from the banner AutoShape by ungrouping the joined graphic objects, if need be.

7. Click somewhere in background area outside of the chart to deselect it.

   Check your text-box-plus-banner graphic object against the one shown on the 3-D Chart sheet in the *Solved15-5.xls* workbook in your Chapter 15 folder. When everything checks out, proceed to step 8.

8. Save your work in a new workbook called **Solved15-5-mine.xls** in your Chapter 15 folder in the My Practice Spreadsheets folder and then close this workbook file.

Constructing WordArt

The WordArt button on the Drawing toolbar enables you to insert super-fancy text in your worksheets. However, because WordArt text characters are all essentially graphics, you can't edit them directly as you can the characters you enter in a text box. Also, WordArt styles are only intended for large font sizes (36 points being the default) and many styles don't really work well with regular text font sizes (say those below about 24 points in size).

To insert a WordArt graphic object in your worksheet, you first click the WordArt button on the Drawing toolbar to open the WordArt Gallery dialog box. The WordArt Gallery contains a wide variety of different styles at different angles with some styles that even run the text down in a vertical line.

After selecting a WordArt style by clicking its thumbnail in the WordArt Gallery dialog box and then selecting OK, Excel opens the Edit WordArt Text dialog box, where you replace the dummy text *Your Text Here* with the words or phrase that you want presented in the WordArt style you just selected in the Gallery dialog box.

The Edit WordArt Text dialog box contains a Font drop-down list box and Size combo box that you can use to change the font and font size of the text you enter. It also contains a Bold and Italic button that you can click to enhance the text you enter by making it bold and/or italic.

After you finish entering and enhancing your text in the Edit WordArt Text dialog box, click its OK button. Excel inserts your WordArt graphic object in the worksheet, while at the same time displaying the WordArt toolbar that you can use to further format or make changes to the new graphic object.

Try It

Exercise 15-6: Constructing WordArt in a Spreadsheet

Open the *Exercise15-6.xls* workbook file in your Chapter 15 folder in the My Practice Spreadsheets folder on your hard disk or in the Excel Workbook folder on the workbook CD-ROM. This workbook contains a copy of the 3-D Column chart without the Horizontal Scroll AutoShape and text box that you added in Exercise 15-5. You will use this earlier version of the 3-D Column chart to practice heading from a WordArt graphic object:

1. Click the Insert WordArt button on the Drawing toolbar to open the WordArt Gallery dialog box.

2. Click the second style in the first row (with the black text on a diagonal pointing upward) and then select OK to open the Edit WordArt Text dialog box.

3. Replace the Your Text Here by typing **CG Media** and then select OK.

   Excel inserts a WordArt graphic object containing the text *CG Media* in the middle of the 3-D Column chart, while at the same time displaying the floating WordArt toolbar (see Figure 15-7).

4. Drag the WordArt graphic from the center of the chart to the upper-left corner of the 3-D Column chart.

5. Click the Format WordArt button on the WordArt toolbar to open the Format WordArt dialog box.

6. On the Color and Lines tab, click the Turquoise color square on the Color drop-down palette in the Fill section before you select OK.

   The company name now appears in turquoise rather than black letters.

7. Click the WordArt Shape button on the WordArt toolbar to open the pop-up palettes of shapes and then click the Triangle Down shape on the palette (the fourth one from the left in the top row).

   Excel redraws the WordArt graphic as a 3-D shape that fits into a downward-pointing triangle.

8. Click the WordArt Gallery button on the WordArt toolbar to reopen the WordArt Gallery dialog box and then click the thumbnail of the style that is located second from the left in the third row (with purple text on a diagonal pointing upward) before you select OK.

   Excel redraws the WordArt graphic object using the new diagonal style with gradient-purple shaded letters.

9. Resize the WordArt graphic and reposition it as needed (use Figure 15-8 as your guide).

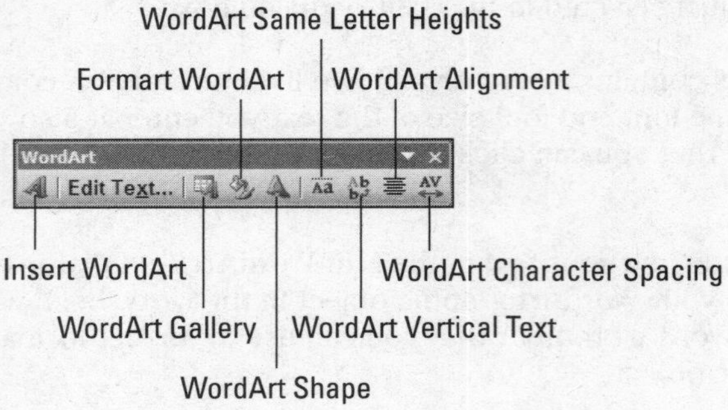

Figure 15-7:
You can use
the tools on
the WordArt
toolbar
to further
edit and
format your
WordArt
graphic.

WordArt Same Letter Heights

Formart WordArt   WordArt Alignment

Insert WordArt

WordArt Gallery   WordArt Vertical Text

WordArt Shape

WordArt Character Spacing

10. Click the background outside of the 3-D Column chart to deselect the WordArt graphic object and then save your work in a new workbook called **Solved15-6.xls** in your Chapter 15 folder in the My Practice Spreadsheets folder and close the workbook file by exiting Excel.

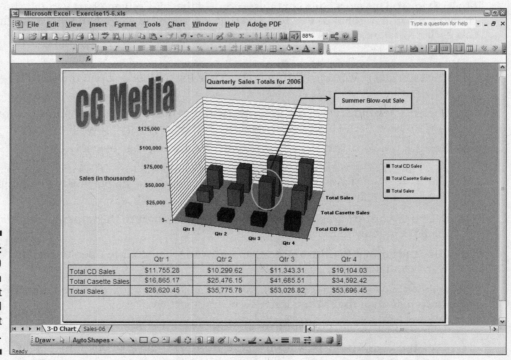

Figure 15-8:
A 3-D
Column
chart
with final
WordArt
graphic.

Part IV
Managing and Securing Data

The 5th Wave   By Rich Tennant

"My girlfriend ran a spreadsheet of my life, and generated this chart. My best hope is that she'll change her major from 'Computer Sciences' to 'Rehabilitative Services'."

In this part . . .

Part IV offers what you'd call a mixed bag of tricks. Here, you not only get a chance to work with all the basic aspects of creating, maintaining, and querying data lists (also known as database tables) but you also practice the various techniques for securing just that kind of data from any unwanted and unintended changes.

Chapter 16

Building and Maintaining Data Lists

*I*n addition to its considerable computational abilities, Excel is also very accomplished at maintaining vast collections of related data in what are referred to as *data lists or database tables*. This chapter gives you a chance to practice all the basic aspects of creating and maintaining data lists in Excel including building the list, adding and editing its data, filtering the list to temporarily remove unwanted data, subtotaling values in a data list, and creating lists from data external to the worksheet.

Creating a Data List

In Excel, a data list or database table is a table of worksheet data with a special structure. Unlike the other types of data tables that you might create in an Excel, a data list uses *only* column headings (technically known as *field names*) to identify the different kinds of items the data list tracks. Each column in the data list contains information for each item you track in the database, such as the client's company name or telephone number (technically known as a *field* of the data list). Each row in the data list contains complete information about each entity that you track in the data list, such as ABC Corporation or National Industries (technically known as a *record* of the data list).

All you have to do start a new data list in a worksheet is to enter the names of the fields that you want to track in the top row of the worksheet and then enter the first record of data beneath. When entering the field names (as column headings), be sure each field name in the data list is unique and, whenever possible, keep the field name short. When naming fields, you can align the field name in the cell so that its text wraps to a new line (by pressing Alt+Enter). Also, you should *not* use numbers or formulas that return values as field names. (You can, however use formulas that return text such as a formula that concatenates labels entered in different cells.)

When deciding on what fields to create, you need to think of how you'll be using the data that you store in your data list. For example, in a client data list, you split the client's name into separate first name, middle initial, and last name fields if you intend to use this information in generating form letters and mailing labels with your word processor. That way, you are able to address the person by his or her first name (as in *Dear John*) in the opening of the form letter you create, as well as by his or her full name and title (as in *Dr. John Smith*) in the mailing label you generate.

Likewise, you split up the client's address into separate street address, city, state, and ZIP code fields when you intend to use the client data list in generating form letters and you want to be able to sort the records in descending order by ZIP code or send letters only to clients located in certain states. By keeping discrete pieces of information in separate fields, you are assured that you can use that field in finding particular records and retrieving information from the data list such as finding all the records where the state is California, or the ZIP code is between 94105 and 95101.

When entering the row with the first data record, be sure to format all the cells the way you want the entries in that field to appear in all the subsequent data records in the data list. For example, if you have a salary field in the data list, and you want the salaries formatted with the Currency style number format without any decimal places, be sure to format the salary entry in the first record in this manner. That way, all subsequent records pick up that same formatting for the salary field when you enter them with Excel's data form.

After entering the top row with the field names and the next row with the first data record, you can then use the data form that Excel generates when you choose the Data⇨Form command to add the rest of the records.

Try It

Exercise 16-1: Constructing a New Data List and Adding Records with the Data Form

If Excel is not currently running, launch the program and then use the Sheet1 worksheet of the new Book1 workbook to practice creating a new data list and then adding and editing its data with the data form:

1. Enter the following field names for your new Employee Data List in the designated cells in row 1 of Sheet1. Next select these names, center them, and make them bold:

- **ID No** in cell A1
- **First Name** in cell B1
- **Last Name** in cell C1
- **Gender** in cell D1
- **Dept** in cell E1
- **Salary** in cell F1
- **Location** in cell G1
- **Date Hired** in cell H1
- **Years of Service** in cell I1
- **Profit Sharing** in cell J1

2. Make the following data entries in the designated cells in row 2 as the first record in your new data list:

- **'000928** in cell A2
- **Joy** in cell B2

- **Adamson** in cell C2

- **F** in cell D2

- **Accounting** in cell E2

- **$35,000** in cell F2

- **Boston** in cell G2

- **10-21-87** in cell H2

- **Yes** in cell J2

3. Construct the following formula in cell I2 and format the cell with Number format using no decimal places:

```
=YEAR(TODAY())-YEAR(H2)
```

4. Turn on the Wrap Text option for the field names in row 1 and then adjust the width of the columns of the data list to suit both the field names and the data entries you made in the first record in the second row.

5. Give Sheet1 the name **Employee Data List** and then choose the Data⇨Form command to open the data form for the Employee Data List.

6. Click the New button to start a new record and then enter the following entries into the designated fields (press Tab to move the insertion point to the next field and Shift+Tab to move it back to the previous field):

- **'000634** in the ID No field

- **Gene** in the First Name field

- **Poole** in the Last Name field

- **M** in the Gender field

- **Engineering** in Dept field

- **75000** in the Salary field

- **Chicago** in the Location field

- **9-15-2000** in the Date Hired field

- **No** in the Profit Sharing field

7. Press the Enter key after you finish entering the last part of the second record in the Profit Sharing field.

Excel responds by clearing the fields in the data form so you can enter the next (third) record, while at the same time entering the data entries you made in the Data Form into the appropriate columns in the second row of the data list itself.

Note that you don't have to use the data form to enter records for your data list. If you prefer, you can make entries in the appropriate cells in the data list itself. Adding records via the Data Form does, however, offer the advantage of automatically formatting the new entries to match the others in that field (column) as well as copying any formulas needed to produce the correct results in calculated fields (as in the Years of Service field in the Employee Data List).

8. Select the Close button in Employee Data List data form, position the cell cursor in cell A1, and then save your new data list in a new workbook named **Employee Data List.xls** in your Chapter 16 folder in the My Practice Spreadsheets folder on your hard disk before you close the workbook file.

The data form is not only useful for appending new records to a data list but also for editing field entries in existing records or even deleting entire records from the data list. You can use the Criteria button in the data form to quickly find the records that need editing (this is especially helpful in longer data lists where it is no longer practical to search the records manually). When you click the Criteria button in the data form, Excel clears all the field text boxes so that you can enter the criteria to search for in the record that needs editing.

When entering the criteria for locating matching records in the data form, you can use the question mark (?) and the asterisk (*) wildcard characters just as you do when using Excel Find feature to locate cells with particular entries (see Chapter 4).

When using the Criteria button in the data form to find records, you can use the following comparative operators when entering search criteria in fields that use numbers or dates:

- Equal to (=) for finding records the same the text, value, or date you enter
- Greater than (>) for finding records after the text characters (in the alphabet) or the date, or larger than the value you enter
- Greater than or equal to (>=) for finding records the same as the text characters, date, or value you enter or after the characters (in the alphabet), after the date, or larger than the value
- Less than (<) for finding records before the text characters (in the alphabet) or date or smaller than the value you enter
- Less than or equal to (<=) for finding records the same as the text characters, date, or value you enter or before the characters (in the alphabet) or the date, or larger than the value
- Unequal to (<>) to find records not the same as the text, value, or date you enter

For example, to find all the records where the employee's annual salary is $50,000, you can enter =50000 or simply 50000 in the Salary field text box. However, to find all the records for employees whose annual salaries are less than or equal to $35,000, you enter <=35000 in the Salary field text box. To find all the records for employees with salaries greater than $45,000, you would enter >45000 in the Salary field text box instead. If you wanted to find all of the records where the employees are female *and* make more than $35,000, you would enter F in the Gender field text box and >35000 in the Salary field text box in the same Criteria data form.

Try It

Exercise 16-2: Finding and Editing Records with the Data Form

Open the *Exercise16-2.xls* file in your Chapter 16 folder in the My Practice Spreadsheets folder on your hard disk or in the Excel Workbook folder on the workbook CD-ROM. This workbook contains a much more complete version of the Employee Data List you created in the previous exercise. You use this version of the Employee Data List worksheet to practice using the data form to find records that need editing:

1. Open the data form for the Employee Data List and then select the Criteria button.

Excel displays a blank data form where you can enter the search criteria in the appropriate fields.

You need to find Sherry Caufield's record in the data list to edit it. Unfortunately, you don't remember how she spells her last name, only that it begins with a C (and not a K) and that she works in the Boston office.

2. Enter **C*** the Last Name field and **Boston** in the Location field.

The wildcard character, the asterisk (*), you entered after the C stands for all other the missing letters in her name.

3. Select the Find Next button in the data form.

   The first record that Excel finds where the last name begins with the letter C and the office location is Boston is that of William Cobb.

4. Click the Find Next button a second time.

   This time, Excel locates Sherry Caufield's record, the 25th record of the 32 total.

5. Change Sherry's profit sharing status from no to yes by replacing No with **Yes** in the Profit Sharing field in the data form. Click the Criteria button.

   Next, find Charles Smith's record in the Employee Data List, an employee in the Administration department.

6. Select the Clear button to clear the previous search criteria and then enter **Smith** in the Last Name field and **Administration** in the Dept field. Click the Find Next button.

   Excel finds the record for Steven Smith in Administration.

7. Select the Find Next button a second time.

   This time, Excel locates Charles Smith's record, the 29th record of the 32 total.

8. Change Charles Smith's location from San Francisco to **Chicago**. Click the Close button to make the change and, at the same time, close the data form.

9. Save your changes to the Employee Data List worksheet in a new workbook named **Solved16-2.xls** in your Chapter 16 folder in the My Practice Spreadsheets folder on your hard disk and then leave the workbook file open for the next exercise.

Sorting Lists

Excel's Sorting feature makes it easy to rearrange the records or even the fields in your data list. You sort the records in your data list by sorting by rows, whereas you sort the fields in the data list by sorting by columns.

In sorting, you can specify either ascending or descending sort order for your data. When you specify ascending order (which is the default), Excel arranges text in A-to-Z order and values from smallest to largest. When you specify descending order, Excel reverses this order and arranges text in Z-to-A order and values range from largest to smallest. When sorting on a date field, keep in mind that ascending order puts the records in least-recent-to-most-recent date order, whereas descending order gives you the records in most-recent-to-least-recent date order.

When you choose the ascending sort order for a field that contains many different kinds of entries, Excel places numbers (from smallest to largest) before text (in alphabetical order) followed by Logical values (TRUE and FALSE), Error values, and, finally, blank cells. When using the descending sort order, the program uses the same general arrangement for the different types of entries but numbers go from largest to smallest, text runs from Z to A, and the FALSE logical value precedes the TRUE logical value.

Using sorting keys

To sort your data, Excel uses *sorting keys* to determine how the records or fields should be reordered in the data list. When sorting records, you indicate by cell address which field (that is, column) contains the first or *primary* sorting key. When sorting fields, you indicate which record (row) contains the primary sorting key.

Excel then applies the selected sort (ascending or descending) to the data in the key field or row to determine how the records or fields will be reordered during sorting.

When a key field contains duplicates entries, Excel simply lists these records in the order in which they were entered in the data list. To indicate how Excel should order records with duplicates in the primary key, you define a secondary key. For example, if, when organizing the data list in alphabetical order by the Last Name field, you have several records where the last name is Smith, you can have Excel order the Smiths' records in alphabetical order by first name by defining the First Name field as the secondary key. If the secondary key contains duplicates (say you have two John Smiths in your company), you can define a third key field (the Middle Name field, if your data list has one) that determines how the duplicate John Smith records are arranged when the data list is sorted.

Keep in mind that although sorting is most often applied to rearranging and maintaining data list records and fields, you can use the Data⇨Sort command to reorder data in any worksheet table, whether or not the table follows the strict data list structure.

Try It

Exercise 16-3: Sorting the Records in a Data List

Use the Employee Data List in the *Solved16-2.xls* file that you edited in the previous exercise to practice sorting records in a data list:

1. Choose Data⇨Sort to open the Sort dialog box.

The Sort dialog box appears and Excel selects all of the records in your data list (omitting the field names in the first row because the Header Row option button in the My Data Range Has section is selected).

The Sort dialog box contains three text boxes, the first of which indicates the field (column) to use as the primary sorting key, the second of which indicates the field to use as the secondary sorting key, and the third of which indicates the field to use as the tertiary sorting key.

Begin by sorting the records in the data list so that they are in alphabetical order by department and then by descending order by salary.

2. Select the Dept field in the Sort By drop-down list box and leave its Ascending option button selected. Next select the Salary field in the first Then By drop-down list box and select its Descending option button before you select OK.

Excel reorders the records in the Employee Data List so that first they are in alphabetical order by department (Accounting, Administration, Engineering, and so on) and then within each department in order from highest to lowest salary ($38,000, $34,400, $29,000 and so on).

Next sort the records in the data list alphabetically by department, location, and then last name. To perform this sort operation, you need to define three keys all using the Ascending option.

3. Open the Sort dialog box and then define the Dept field as the Sort By key, the Location field as the first Then By key, and the Last Name field as the second Then By key, each with its Ascending option button selected, before you select OK.

Excel reorders the records in the Employee Data List so that that first they are in alphabetical order by department (Accounting, Administration, Engineering, and so on), and then within each department in order by location (Boston, Detroit, San Francisco, and so on), and finally in order by Last Name (Edwards, Percival, Savage, and so on).

4. Sort the records in the Employee Data List in order from the most recent date of hire to the least recent.

Be sure to clear all but the Sort By key in the Sort dialog box.

Be sure to select its Descending option button after selecting Date Hired as the Sort By key.

5. Sort the Employee Data List so that its records are in order from the highest to the lowest salary.

6. Close the *Solved16-2.xls* workbook file without saving your changes.

Sorting on more than three keys

Sometimes, you may need to sort on more three fields (the maximum you can define in one sorting operation). For example, suppose you are working with a personnel data list and you want to organize the records in alphabetical order by first by department, and then by supervisor, and finally by last name, first name, and middle name. To sort the records in this data list by these five fields, you have to perform two sorting operations:

- ✔ For the first sort, define the Last Name field as the primary key, the First Name field as the secondary key, and the Middle Name field as the third key

- ✔ For the second sort, define the Department field as the primary key and the Supervisor field as the secondary key

Try It

Exercise 16-4: Sorting the Records in a Data List on More Than Three Keys

Open the *Exercise16-4.xls* file in your Chapter 16 folder in the My Practice Spreadsheets folder on your hard disk or in the Excel Workbook folder on the workbook CD-ROM. This workbook contains a copy of the Personnel Data List that you will sort in alphabetical order by first by the department name, and then by the supervisor's name, and finally by the employee's last, first, and middle name:

1. Choose Data➪Sort to open the Sort dialog box and then select the Sort By and Then By keys to sort the Personnel Data List in alphabetical order by last, first, and middle name before you select OK.

Check the Last Name, First Name, and Middle Name fields in the sorted data list and verify that they are now all in alphabetical order by last, first, and middle name.

2. Sort the Personnel Data List a second time, this time in alphabetical order by department and then by supervisor.

Check the Department and Supervisor fields in the re-sorted data list and verify that they are now in alphabetical order first by department name and then by supervisor name. Note in the case of supervisor Jones in the Sales department that the name of her employees are in order by last name and then first name.

3. Save your sorted Personnel Data List worksheet in a new workbook file named **Solved16-4.xls** in your Chapter 16 folder in the My Practice Spreadsheets folder and leave the workbook file open for the next exercise.

Sorting the fields (columns) in a data list

You can use Excel's column sorting capability to change the order of the fields in a data list without having to resort to cutting and pasting various columns. To sort the fields in a data list, add a row at the top of the list containing numbers from 1 to the number of the last field in the data list (these numbers indicate the desired order of the fields). You then sort the list by column using this row as the sole sorting key.

When sorting the columns in a data list, you must remember to click the Options button and select the Sort Left to Right radio button in the Orientation section of the Sort Options dialog box. Otherwise, Excel sorts your records instead of your columns and, in the process, the row of field names becomes sorted in with the other data records in your list!

To see how to go about sorting the columns of a list, sort the columns of the Personnel Data List you worked with in the previous exercise so that the fields appear in the following order: SSN, Department, Supervisor, First Name, Middle Name, Last Name, Title, Salary.

Try It

Exercise 16-5: Sorting the Fields in a Data List

Use the Personnel Data List in the *Solved16-4.xls* workbook file whose records you sorted in the previous exercise to practice sorting the fields of a data list:

1. Select row 1 in the Personnel Data List worksheet and then insert a blank row (Insert➪Rows).

2. Make the following numerical entries in the designated cells of the new, blank row 1:

- **1** in cell A1
- **6** in cell B1
- **4** in cell C1
- **5** in cell D1
- **2** in cell E1
- **3** in cell F1
- **7** in cell G1
- **8** in cell H1

3. Make sure that the cell cursor is positioned in one of the cells in the range of the Personnel Data List (A1:H20) and then choose Data➪Sort to open the Sort dialog box.

Note that Excel does not select the top row with the field ordering numbers.

4. Select the No Header Row option button beneath the second Then By drop-down list box.

Excel now selects the entire data list cell range, A1:H20, including the top row. Note that Column A is now automatically selected as the primary sorting key in the Sort By drop-down list box. However, you don't want to sort the records of the list using the entries in column A. Rather, you want to sort the columns of the list using the entries in row 1. In order to do this, you must now change the sort orientation from its default of top to bottom to left to right.

5. Select the Options button to open the Sort Options dialog box and there select the Sort Left to Right option button in the Orientation section before you select OK.

As soon as the Sort Options dialog box closes, you see that the Sort By drop-down list box in the Sort dialog box now contains Row 1 as its setting.

6. Select the OK button in the Sort dialog box to reorder the fields using the values in row 1.

The fields of the Personnel Data List are now arranged in this order: SSN, Department, Supervisor, First Name, Middle Name, Last Name, Title, and Salary.

7. Delete the top row of the Personnel Data List (Edit⇨Delete and select Entire Row option button).

8. Widen column B with the Department field so that all of its entries are displayed in the worksheet.

9. Save the Personnel Data List with the sorted fields and records in a new workbook named **Solved16-5.xls** in your Chapter 16 folder in the My Practice Spreadsheets folder and then close the workbook file.

Subtotaling a List

You can use Excel's Subtotals feature to subtotal data in a sorted data list. To subtotal a data list, you first sort the records in the list on the field you want subtotaled and then designate the field that contains the values you want totaled. (These don't necessarily have to be the same fields in the data list.)

When you use the Subtotals feature, you aren't restricted to having the values in the designated field added together with the SUM function. You can instead have Excel return the number of entries with the COUNT function, the average of the entries with the AVERAGE function, the highest entry with the MAXIMUM function, the lowest entry with the MINIMUM function, or even the product of the entries with the PRODUCT function.

Try It

Exercise 16-6: Subtotaling the Records in a Data List

Open the *Exercise16-6.xls* file in your Chapter 16 folder in the My Practice Spreadsheets folder on your hard disk or in the Excel Workbook folder on the workbook CD-ROM. This workbook contains a copy of the Employee Data List that you can use to practice using Excel's Subtotal feature:

1. Sort the Employee Data List first alphabetically by department and then numerically, from highest-to-lowest order by salary.

Be sure to select the Descending option button after selecting Salary as the first Then By key.

You sort the records in the data list by the Dept field and then the Salary field because you want Excel to subtotal the salaries in each department. The Dept field provides what is referred to as the *break* in the subtotals report because each time the department entry changes, Excel computes a subtotal (in this case, a subtotal of the values entered in the Salary field).

2. Choose Data⇨Subtotals to select the data in the Employee Data List while at the same time opening the Subtotal dialog box.

You must supply at least three pieces of information in the Subtotal dialog box:

- Field at which the subtotals break in the At Each Change In drop-down list box

- Function to use in computing the subtotals (SUM is the default, but you can also select COUNT, AVERAGE, MAX, MIN, or PRODUCT) in the Use Function drop-down list box

- Field(s) whose values are to be subtotaled by selecting the check box in front of the field name in the Add Subtotals To list box

3. Select Dept in the At Each Change In drop-down list box.

4. Select Sum in the Use Function drop-down list box.

5. Select only the Salary check box in the Add Subtotals To list box and then select OK.

Excel subtotals the salaries in Employee Data List by department, while at the same time adding outline buttons to the rows (Figure 16-1 shows how the first part of this data list should now appear your Employee Data List in Excel).

You can use these outline buttons to collapse and expand the subtotals in the data list.

6. Click the number 1 button at the top of the row header to collapse the subtotals down to the grand total of all the salaries for all departments in row 39 and then widen column F to display its grand total.

The first level of the outlined rows shows only the grand total. Next, display the subtotals for each of the departments in the data list.

7. Click the number 2 button at the top of the row header.

Excel now displays the rows with the salary totals for the Accounting in row 7, Administration in row 13, Engineering in row 26, Human Resources in row 33, and Information Services in row 38, along with the grand total of all salaries in row 39.

8. Click the number 3 button at the top of the row header to redisplay the rows with all the records in the data list along with the salaries department subtotals and salary grand total. Press Ctrl+8 to hide the outline buttons.

Ctrl+8 is a shortcut key combination that you can use to hide and then redisplay the buttons and other controls in any spreadsheet you've outlined.

9. Save the Employee Data List with the subtotals in a new workbook file named **Solved16-6.xls** in your Chapter 16 folder in the My Practice Spreadsheets folder and then close the workbook file.

Figure 16-1:
The first part of the Employee Data List after subtotaling its salaries by department.

	ID No	First Name	Last Name	Gender	Dept	Salary	Location	Date Hired	Years of Service	Profit Sharing		
2	000222	Mary	King	F	Accounting	$38,000	Detroit	03/10/97	8.0	No		
3	000928	Joy	Adamson	F	Accounting	$34,400	Boston	10/21/87	18.0	Yes		
4	000226	Adam	Rosenzweig	M	Accounting	$29,000	Detroit	03/01/01	4.0	No		
5	000159	Sherry	Caulfield	F	Accounting	$24,100	Boston	03/19/94	11.0	No		
6	000174	Cindy	Edwards	F	Accounting	$21,500	San Francisco	08/15/85	20.0	No		
7					Accounting Total	$147,000						
8	000199	Steven	Smith	M	Administration	$100,000	Seattle	10/11/00	5.0	Yes		
9	000339	Charles	Smith	M	Administration	$87,800	San Francisco	07/09/98	7.0	No		
10	000146	Edward	Krauss	M	Administration	$86,200	Chicago	07/13/99	6.0	Yes		
11	000101	Michael	Bryant	M	Administration	$30,440	Santa Rosa	02/01/91	14.0	Yes		
12	000192	Deborah	Mosley	F	Administration	$20,800	Detroit	08/23/01	4.0	No		
13					Administration Tota	$325,240						
14	000634	Gene	Poole	M	Engineering	$75,000	Chicago	09/15/00	5.0	No		
15	000211	Stuart	Johnson	M	Engineering	$62,000	Seattle	12/29/00	5.0	No		
16	000210	Victoria	Morin	F	Engineering	$40,700	Seattle	12/20/96	9.0	No		
17	000247	Elaine	Savage	F	Engineering	$38,900	Atlanta	05/27/99	6.0	No		
18	000366	Richard	Zucker	M	Engineering	$37,500	San Francisco	12/26/00	5.0	No		
19	000361	Linda	Robinson	F	Engineering	$37,000	Detroit	11/11/98	7.0	No		
20	000118	Janet	Kaplan	F	Engineering	$34,000	Boston	06/22/91	14.0	Yes		
21	000220	Jack	Edwards	M	Engineering	$32,200	Atlanta	02/14/97	8.0	Yes		
22	000284	Miriam	Morse	F	Engineering	$29,600	Chicago	11/02/97	8.0	No		
23	000297	James	Percival	M	Engineering	$29,200	Atlanta	12/18/97	8.0	Yes		
24	000307	Robert	Bjorkman	M	Engineering	$25,000	Chicago	02/24/98	7.0	Yes		
25	000141	Angela	Dickinson	F	Engineering	$23,900	Detroit	11/13/96	9.0	No		
26					Engineering Total	$465,000						
27	000185	Rebecca	Johnson	F	Human Resources	$50,200	Boston	02/04/96	9.0	No		
28	000162	Kimberly	Lerner	F	Human Resources	$34,900	Chicago	06/28/99	6.0	No		
29	000324	George	Tallan	M	Human Resources	$29,700	Chicago	05/20/99	6.0	No		
30	000139	William	Cobb	M	Human Resources	$27,500	Boston	05/28/01	4.0	Yes		
31	000367	Amanda	Fletcher	F	Human Resources	$26,500	Boston	01/03/99	6.0	No		
32	000262	Lance	Bird	M	Human Resources	$21,100	Boston	08/13/97	8.0	Yes		

Filtering a List

It is one thing to set up a data list and load it with tons of data, and it's quite another to get just the information you need out of the list. The procedure for specifying what data you want displayed in an Excel data list is called *filtering* the data list or database. The procedure for extracting only the data you want from the database table or data list is called *querying* the database.

At the most basic level, Excel enables you to filter out all but the information that you want to work with. Its AutoFilter feature temporarily hides the display of unwanted records, leaving behind only the ones you wanted to see.

To use AutoFilter, you choose the Data➪Filter➪AutoFilter Excel command while the cell cursor is positioned in any cell within the data list. The program then adds drop-down buttons to each of the field names in the top row of the list (as shown in Figure 16-2).

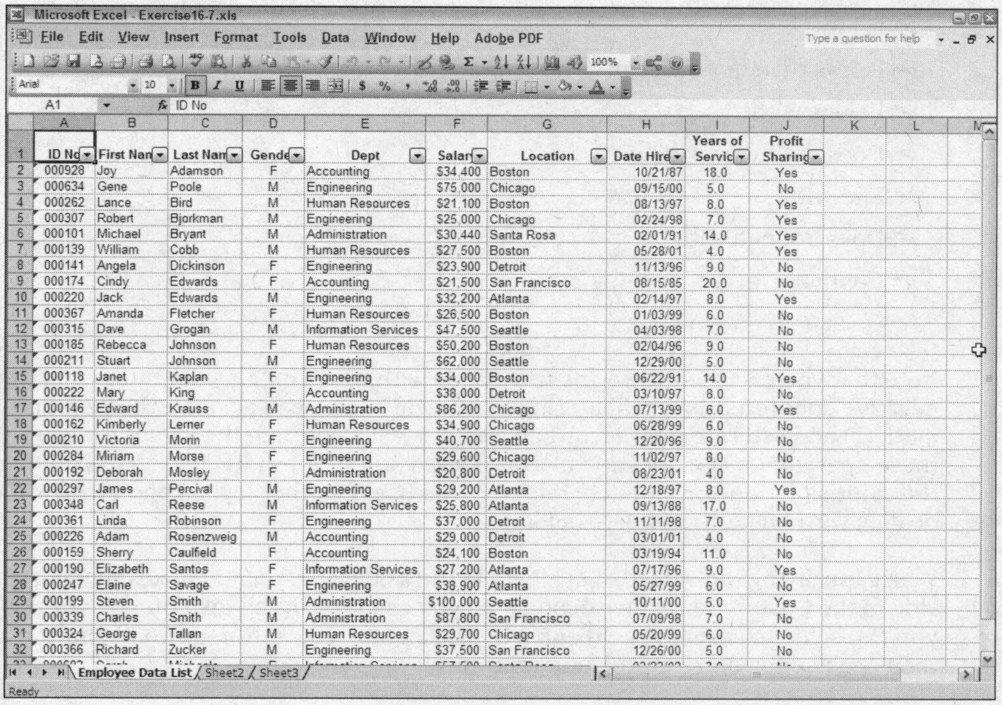

Figure 16-2: The Employee Data List with the AutoFilter drop-down buttons displayed after each field name.

When you click a drop-down button next to a field, Excel displays a menu that contains the following three items near the top of the menu:

- ✔ **(All)** to display all records with an entry in that field.
- ✔ **(Top 10)** to display only the records with the top 10 values or in the top 10 percent.
- ✔ **(Custom)** to open the Custom AutoFilter dialog box. In the Custom AutoFilter dialog box, you can specify multiple criteria for filtering the list using either an AND or OR condition, as well as criteria using logical operators such as "is greater than," "is less than," "begins with," "end with," and so on.

You can use the (Custom) item on a field's pop-up menu to open the Custom AutoFilter dialog box, where you can specify more complex filtering criteria using

AND and OR conditions. When you click the (Custom) item on a field's pop-up menu, Excel opens the Custom AutoFilter dialog box, where you select the type of operator to use in evaluating the first and the second condition in the top and bottom drop-down list boxes and the values to be evaluated in the first and second condition in the associated combo boxes. You also specify the type of relationship between the two conditions with the AND or OR radio buttons (the AND radio button is selected by default).

When selecting the operator for the first and second condition in the leftmost drop-down list boxes at the top and bottom of the Custom AutoFilter dialog box, you have the following choices:

- ✔ Equals
- ✔ Does not equal
- ✔ Is greater than
- ✔ Is greater than or equal to
- ✔ Is less than
- ✔ Is less than or equal to
- ✔ Begins with
- ✔ Does not begin with
- ✔ End with
- ✔ Does not end with
- ✔ Contains
- ✔ Does not contain

Note that you can use the Begins with, Ends with, and Contains operators and their negative counterparts when filtering a text field — you can also use the question mark (?) and asterisk (*) wildcard characters when entering the values for use with these operators. (The question mark wildcard stands for individual characters and the asterisk for one or more characters.) You use the other logical operators when dealing with numeric and date fields.

When specifying the values to evaluate in the associated combo boxes on the right side of the Custom AutoFilter dialog box, you can type in the text, number, or date, or you can select an existing field entry by clicking the box's drop-down list button and then clicking the entry on the pop-up menu.

Try It

Exercise 16-7: Filtering the Records in a Data List

Open the *Exercise16-7.xls* file in your Chapter 16 folder in the My Practice Spreadsheets folder on your hard disk or in the Excel Workbook folder on the workbook CD-ROM. This workbook contains a copy of the Employee Data List that you can use to practice querying a data list by filtering out all records except for those that contain the data with which you want to work:

1. Choose the Excel Data⇨Filter⇨AutoFilter command.

Excel responds by adding drop-down list boxes to each of the field names in row 1 of the Employee Data List.

Start by filtering the data list to just the records where the employee is part of the profit sharing plan.

2. Click the drop-down list box in the Profit Sharing field name and then select Yes on the drop-down list.

Excel hides all the records where the Profit Sharing is No, leaving displayed only those where the Profit Sharing entry is Yes.

3. Click (All) near the top of the Profit Sharing field's drop-down list to restore the display of all the records in the data list.

When you filter the records in a data list, Excel simply temporarily hides the records.

4. Click (Top 10...) on the Years of Service drop-down list to open the Top 10 AutoFilter dialog box and select OK.

The Top 10 AutoFilter dialog box enables you to display only the records with the top or bottom 10 (more or less) values (by selecting Items in the rightmost drop-down list box) or percentage (by selecting Percent in this drop-down list box) in the selected field.

5. Click the Sort Descending item near the top of the Years of Service drop-down list to sort the filtered records so that they are displayed in order from the longest to shortest top ten years of service.

6. Redisplay all the records in the data list and then click the (Custom) item on the Salary drop-down list to open the Custom AutoFilter dialog box.

Use the Custom AutoFilter dialog box to filter out all the records except for those where the annual salary is between $40,000 and $75,000.

7. Select Is Greater Than or Equal To in the first drop-down list box and then click the second combo box to its immediate right and type **40000**. Select Is Less Than or Equal To in the second drop-down list box below the AND and OR option buttons (of which the AND should be selected) and then type **75000** in the combo box to its immediate right. Click OK.

8. Sort the filtered records so that they are displayed in descending order by salary.

Because the AutoFilter only temporarily hides the display of the records in a data list, you need to copy the filtered records to a new part of the worksheet or to a new worksheet when you want to retain the subset for future reference and use.

9. Copy the filtered and sorted records currently displayed in the cell range A1:J33 (including the field names in row 1) on the Employee Data List worksheet to the same range on the Sheet2 worksheet. Rename the Sheet2 worksheet to **Salary Subset** and then click the Employee Data List worksheet to reselect it.

10. Redisplay all the records in the data list on the Employee Data List worksheet and then filter the list so that only the records where the department is either Engineering or Information Services are displayed and the records are sorted in ascending order by department name.

Be sure to select the OR option button in the Custom AutoFilter dialog box. Note that you can select the department names, Engineering and Information Services, from the two Combo boxes after selecting the Equals or Contains operator in the associated drop-down list boxes in this dialog box.

11. Copy the filtered and sorted records (including the field names to the equivalent cell range in Sheet3) and then rename Sheet3 to **Department Subset**.

12. Redisplay all the records in the data list on the Employee Data List worksheet, position the cell cursor in cell A1, and then save your work in a new workbook called **Solved16-7.xls** in your Chapter 16 folder in the My Practice Spreadsheets folder and close the workbook file.

Querying External Database Tables

Excel makes it possible to query other external databases to which you have access and then extract the data that you're interested in into your worksheet for further manipulation and analysis. The external databases that you can query can be as simple as those you maintain with a dedicated database-management program such as Microsoft Access all the way up and including the corporate database itself.

To create a query that acquires data from an external database, you must complete two procedures:

- Define the data source; that is, the external database that contains the data you want to query
- Specify the query itself, including all the columns of data that you want extracted along with the criteria for selecting them

Try It

Exercise 16-8: Querying an External Data Table

Create a blank worksheet in a new workbook. In your Chapter 16 folder is a copy of the sample Northwind database that accompanies Microsoft Access. Use the blank workbook to practice querying records in Northwind:

1. Choose the Data⇨Import External Data⇨New Database Query menu command. If an alert dialog box appears informing you that the Microsoft Query feature is not currently installed and asking you if you want to install it, click Yes.

After Microsoft Query is installed, the Microsoft Query Choose Data Source dialog box appears with the <New Data Source> item selected on its Databases tab.

2. Select OK in the Choose Data Source dialog box to create a new data source.

The Create New Data Source dialog box appears with the What Name Do You Want to Give Your Data Source? text box selected. By naming your data source definition, you can reuse it to perform the same query on the external database whenever the need arises.

3. Type **Product Query** as the name for the data source.

As soon as you begin typing the data source name, the Select a Driver for the Type of Database You Want to Access drop-down list box becomes active. Here, you select a driver for the type of database program used to create the database tables you want to query.

4. Select Microsoft Access Driver (*.mdb) on the Select a Driver for the Type of Database You Want to Access drop-down list and then select the Connect button.

Because you selected the Microsoft Access Driver, Excel now opens the ODBC Microsoft Access Setup dialog box (you see a slightly different dialog box when you select a different driver). Here you select the name of the Access database to query.

5. Select the Select button to open the Select Database dialog box and then use its folder hierarchy in the Directories list box on the right to find the *Northwind.mdb* file. First, find the My Practice Spreadsheets folder and double-click its folder icon to open it. Next, find the Chapter 16 folder and then double-click its folder icon to open it. Finally, click the *Northwind.mdb* filename in the Database Name text box before you select OK.

As soon as the Select Database dialog box closes, you are returned to the ODBC Microsoft Access Setup dialog box, where the path to the *Northwind.mdb* database file now appears.

6. Select the OK button to close the ODBC Microsoft Access Setup dialog box to close it and return to the Create New Data Source dialog box.

Here, you could select the name of a data table in the Northwind database to use by default in the query. Also, you would select the Save My User ID and Password in the Data Source Definition check box if the particular database (such as the corporate database) you're querying requires you to use a login and password in order to access its data.

7. Select the OK button to complete the Product Query data source definition by closing the Create New Data Source dialog box and returning to the Choose Data Source dialog box.

The name of the data source definition, Product Query, which you just defined, now appears selected at the bottom of the Databases list box in the Choose Data Source dialog box.

8. Verify that the Product Query data source is selected in the Databases list box as well as the Use the Query to Create/Edit Query check box at the bottom of the Choose Data Source dialog box before you select OK.

As soon as you select OK, the Query Wizard — Choose Columns dialog box appears, where you specify the fields whose data you want to extract into the Excel worksheet during the database query.

9. Click the expand button (with the plus sign) in front of the tables named Products and Categories in the Available Tables and Columns list box on the left.

As soon as you click its expand buttons, all the fields in the Categories and Products data tables are displayed in Available Tables and Columns list box in the order in which they appear in the table.

10. Move the following fields in the designated table from the Available Tables and Columns list box over to the Columns in Your Query list box in the following order by clicking each of the field names followed by the > button:

- ProductID in Products

- ProductName in Products

- UnitPrice in Products

- UnitsInStock in Products

- UnitsOnOrder in Products

- CategoryName in Categories

- Description in Categories

The list of fields in the Columns in Your Query list box from which to extract data during the external query should now match the one shown in Figure 16-3.

11. Click the ProductName field in the Columns in Your Query and then select the Preview Now button to sample the data entered in that field in the Preview Data in Selected Column list box.

The Preview Now button enables you to preview the data in any field that you add to the Columns in Your Query list box. If you discover that you've selected a field whose data you don't need, you can move the field back to the Available Tables and Columns list box by clicking the < button (click the << button to move all the fields you added to the Columns in Your Query list box back).

The order in which the fields appear in the Columns in Your Query list box determines the order in which they appear in the worksheet. You can use the triangle buttons on the right side of this list box to promote and demote the fields in the Columns in Your Query list. The triangle button pointing upward promotes the selected field by moving it up one in the list, whereas the triangle button pointing downward demotes the field by moving it down one in the list.

Figure 16-3:
The Query Wizard –
Choose
Columns
dialog
box after
selecting
the fields
to extract
from the
Products
and
Categories
data tables.

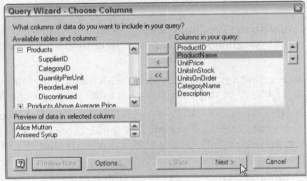

12. Select the Next button to open the Query Wizard – Filter Data dialog box to open the Query Wizard – Filter Data dialog box.

The Query Wizard – Filter Data dialog box enables you to set up any filtering criteria that specifies which records are to be extracted from the designated fields during the data query to the external database. In this case, you want to include records only where the Unit Price of the item is greater than or equal to $7.45.

13. Click the UnitPrice field in Column to Filter list box and then select Is Greater Than or Equal To in first drop-down list box under Unit Price in the Only Include Rows Where section and type **7.45** in the associated combo box to its immediate right.

The filter criteria for the UnitPrice field in your Query Wizard — Filter Data dialog box should now match the one shown in Figure 16-4.

14. Select the Next button to open the Query Wizard — Sort Order dialog box.

The Sort Order dialog box enables you to specify the order in which you want the records extracted from the tables in the external database to be sorted in the Excel worksheet. In this case, you want the records in the worksheet to be sorted alphabetically by product name.

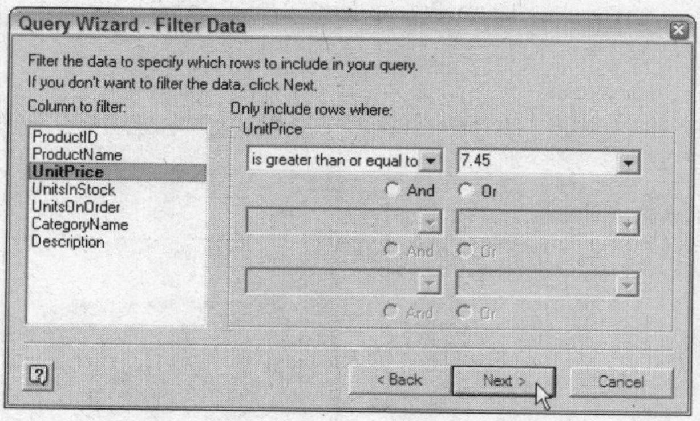

Figure 16-4:
The Query Wizard — Filter Data dialog box after specifying the criteria by which to filter the extracted data.

```
Query Wizard - Filter Data                                    [x]

Filter the data to specify which rows to include in your query.
If you don't want to filter the data, click Next.
Column to filter:              Only include rows where:
                               ┌─ UnitPrice ──────────────────────┐
 ProductID                     │                                  │
 ProductName                   │ is greater than or equal to ▼  7.45    ▼ │
 UnitPrice                     │          ○ And    ○ Or           │
 UnitsInStock                  │                          ▼            ▼ │
 UnitsOnOrder                  │                                  │
 CategoryName                  │          ○ And    ○ Or           │
 Description                   │                          ▼            ▼ │
                               │          ○ And    ○ Or           │
                               └──────────────────────────────────┘
 [?]              < Back      Next >       Cancel
```

15. Select the ProductName field in the Sort By drop-down list box and with the Ascending option button selected, select the Next button to open Query Wizard – Finish dialog box.

    The Query Wizard — Finish dialog box enables you to save the Query as well as to designate where to view the records extracted during the query to the external database (either in a Microsoft Query window or the Excel worksheet).

    When you save the query, Excel saves it in a separate query file (indicated by the .dqy file extension) that you can then later rerun in any workbook file simply by selecting its query filename in the Select Data Source dialog box (Data➪Import External Data➪ Import Data).

    Note that Excel automatically saves the data source definition as file (indicated by the .dsn) when you next save the current workbook but not the query itself.

16. Select the Save Query button to open the Save As dialog box. In the Save As dialog box, edit the suggested filename, *Query from Product Query.dgy* to **Product Query.dqy** before you click the Save button to save the query in the Queries folder.

    Excel closes the Save As dialog box and returns you to the Query Wizard — Finish dialog box, where the Return Data to Microsoft Excel option button is selected by default.

17. Click the Finish button to close the Query Wizard and open the Import Data dialog box.

    This dialog box enables you to select the cell range within the current worksheet where the extracted data records are to appear (starting at cell A1 by default) or to select a new worksheet in which to extract the records.

18. Click OK in the Import Data dialog box to extract the records from the Northwind Access database into the current worksheet starting at cell A1.

    Excel performs the query, extracting the fields you designated from the records where the unit price is greater than or equal to $7.45 into Sheet1 beginning at cell A1, as shown in Figure 16-5. At the same time, the program displays the External Data toolbar with tools that enable you to edit the query (at which time you can include different fields or vary the filtering criteria) as well as to refresh the extracted data by rerunning the query itself.

19. Save the data extracted by the external data query under the filename **Solved 16-8.xls** in your Chapter 16 folder in the My Practice Spreadsheets folder and then close the workbook file by exiting Excel.

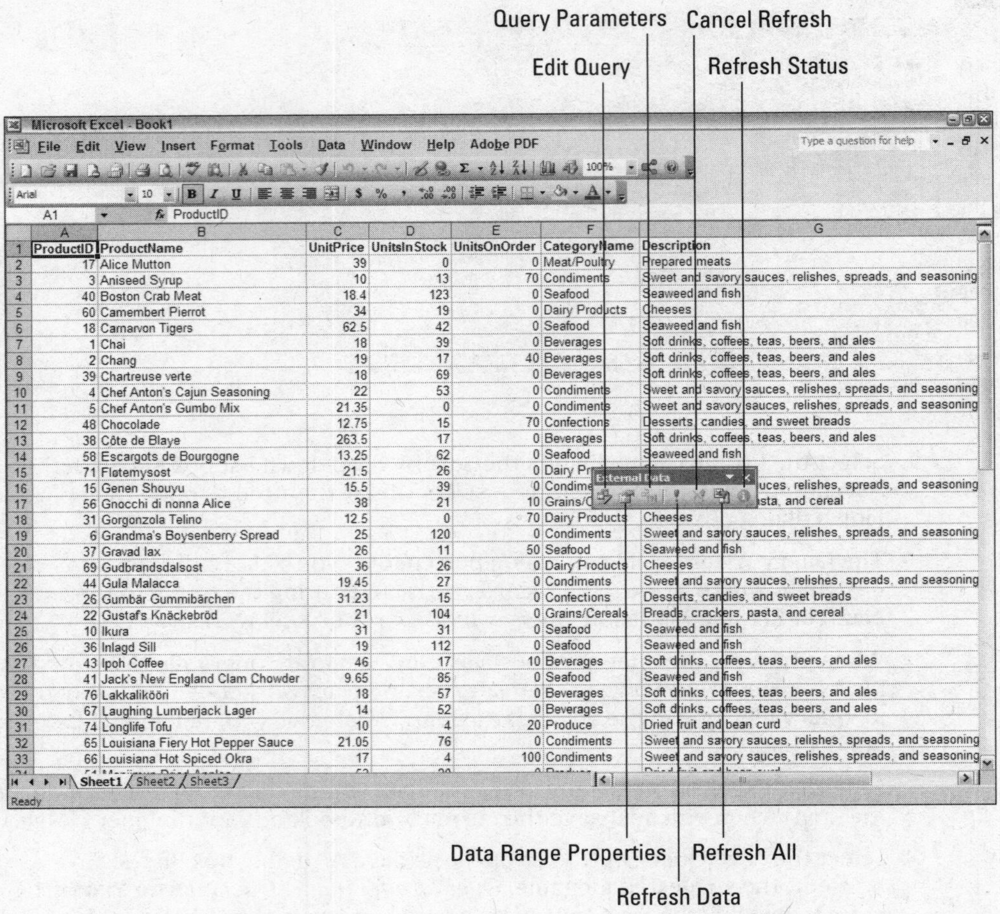

Query Parameters   Cancel Refresh

Edit Query   Refresh Status

Figure 16-5:
The Excel
worksheet
with the
External
Data toolbar
after
extracting
the data
from
Northwind
Access
database
using the
external
database
query.

Data Range Properties   Refresh All

Refresh Data

Chapter 17

Protecting the Spreadsheet

- -

- -

Excel enables you to secure your work on two levels: protecting the workbook file so that only the people you entrust with the password can open the file to view, print, or edit the data, and protecting the worksheets in a workbook from unwarranted changes so that only people with that password can modify the contents and design of the spreadsheet.

In this chapter, you get the chance to practice securing your Excel workbooks and worksheets on both these levels. In addition, you get the opportunity to experience doing data entry in a protected spreadsheet in which all your movements and edits are automatically restricted to the unlocked cells where such changes are allowed.

Password-Protecting the Workbook

By password-protecting the workbook, you can prevent unauthorized users from opening the workbook and editing it. You set a password for opening the workbook file when it contains spreadsheets whose data are of a sufficiently sensitive nature that only a certain group of people in the company should have access to them (such as spreadsheets dealing with personnel information and salaries). Of course, after you set a password for opening a workbook, you must supply this password to those people who need access to it in order for them to be able to open the file.

You set a password for modifying the workbook when you're dealing with spreadsheets whose data needs to be viewed and printed by different users, none of whom are authorized to make changes to any of the entries. For example, after a workbook has been through a complete editing and review cycle and all of the suggested changes have been merged, you might assign a password for modifying it to those who have the authority to do so before distributing it company-wide.

When you're dealing with a spreadsheet whose data is of a sensitive nature and should not be modified by *any* of those authorized to open it, you need to set both a password for opening and a password for modifying the workbook file. You assign either one or both of these types of passwords to a workbook file at the time you save it with the File⇨Save As command on the Excel menu bar.

A password-protected workbook file for which you can't reproduce the correct password is the ultimate nightmare (especially if you're talking about a really important spreadsheet with loads and loads of vital data), so, for heaven's sake, don't forget your password or you'll be stuck. Excel does not provide any sort of command for overriding the password and opening a protected workbook, nor does Microsoft offer any such utility. If you think that you might forget the workbook's password, be sure to write it down somewhere and keep that piece of paper in a secure place (preferably under lock and key). It's always better to be safe than sorry when it comes to passwords for opening files.

Try It

Exercise 17-1: Assigning a Password for Opening and Editing a Workbook

If Excel is not currently running, launch the program and then open *Exercise17-1.xls* in your Chapter 17 folder in the My Practice Spreadsheets folder on your hard disk or in the Excel Workbook folder on the workbook CD-ROM. This workbook contains a copy of the Employee Data List, Salary Subset, and Department Subset worksheets you created when completing Exercise 16-7 in the previous chapter. You will use this file to practice assigning a password for opening the workbook and another for editing its worksheets:

1. Choose the Excel File⇨Save As command to open the Save As dialog box.

2. Replace Exercise in the filename *Exercise17-1.xls* with **Solved** so that you save the password-protected workbook with new filename *Solved17-1.xls* in your Chapter 17 folder.

   Microsoft has cleverly hidden the password-protecting settings in the Save Options dialog box that you can only access by selecting the General Options item on the Tools drop-down list on the Save As dialog box's toolbar.

3. Click the Tools drop-down button on the toolbar at the top of the Save As dialog box and then select General Options on its drop-down list to open the Save Options dialog box.

   The Save Options dialog box contains a Password to Open and a Password to Modify text box where you can enter these passwords. In addition, this dialog box contains a Always Create Backup check box that, when checked, tells Excel to automatically make a backup copy of the workbook you're saving to disk (that you can use in the event that the original file is corrupted and becomes inoperable). The Read-Only Recommended check box, when checked, assigns read-only status to the workbook you're saving (preventing you from saving changes to the file without either changing its filename or the folder in which it is located).

4. Type **opensesame** (all lowercase letters) as the password in the Password to Open text box and then select the Password to Modify text box.

   Note that Excel automatically masks each character as you type it by replacing it with a dot. Keep in mind that all passwords are case-sensitive; for example, the passwords *opensesame*, *Opensesame*, and *OpenSesame* are three different passwords.

5. Type **abracadabra** in the Password to Modify text box and then select OK.

Excel displays the Confirm Password dialog box, where you must reenter the *opensesame* password for opening the *Solved17-1.xls* workbook file.

6. Type **opensesame** in the Reenter Password to Proceed text box and then select OK.

A second Confirm Password dialog box appears, where you must reenter the *abracadabra* password for modifying the *Solved17-1.xls* workbook file.

7. Type **abracadabra** in the Reenter Password to Proceed text box and then select OK.

Assuming that you were able to faithfully and exactly reproduce the *opensesame* password to open and *abracadabra* password to modify, Excel displays no more Confirm Password dialog boxes, returning you to the Save As dialog box.

8. Select the Save button to save *Solved17-1.xls* with the password to open and password to modify the workbook.

9. Close the *Solved17-1.xls* workbook file (Ctrl+W) and then reopen the file by opening the File pull-down menu and typing its number (**1**).

Excel displays a Password dialog box, informing you that the file is protected.

10. Type the password to open the file, **opensesame**, in the Password text box and then select OK.

As soon as you select OK to close the first Password dialog box where you entered the password to open the workbook file, a second one appears prompting you to enter the password for write access to the file. Note that if you are unable to provide this password, Excel opens the workbook file in read-only mode (so that changes to the file can only be saved in a copy of the file).

11. Type the password to modify, **abracadabra**, in the second Password text box and then select OK.

As soon as you correctly enter the second password, Excel opens the *Solved17-1.xls* workbook for editing or printing just as it would a nonprotected workbook.

Go ahead and remove the password to modify the workbook as this kind of protection amounts to little more than saving the workbook file as a read-only file.

12. Choose File⇨Save As and then open the Save Options dialog box by clicking the Tools drop-down button and selecting General Options on its drop-down list.

To remove a password from a file, all you have to do is delete it from the Password to Open or Password to Modify text box in the Save Options dialog box.

13. Select all the masked characters in the Password to Modify text box and then press the Delete key to remove them before you select OK.

14. Click the Save button in the Save As dialog box, and then click Yes to save the *Solved17-1.xls* workbook without a write-access password.

15. Close the *Solved17-1.xls* workbook and then try reopening it again.

This time, you only need to reproduce the *opensesame* password to open the workbook file.

16. Close the *Solved17-1.xls* workbook a last time without saving any further changes to it.

Protecting the Worksheet

After you've got your spreadsheet the way you want it, you are wise to use Excel's Protection feature to keep it that way: Nothing is quite as bad as having an inexperienced data entry operator doing major damage to the formulas and functions that you've worked so hard to construct and validate. To keep the formulas and standard text in a spreadsheet safe from all unwarranted changes, you need to protect its worksheet.

All cells in the workbook can have one of two different protection formats: locked or unlocked and hidden or unhidden. Whenever you begin a new spreadsheet, all of the cells in the workbook have the locked and unhidden status. However, this status in and of itself means nothing until you turn on protection in the worksheet. At that time, you are then prevented from making any editing changes to all locked cells and from viewing the contents of all hidden cells on the Formula bar when they contain the cell cursor.

What this means in practice is that prior to turning on worksheet protection, you go through the spreadsheet removing the Locked protection format from all the cell ranges where you or your users still need to be able to do data entry and editing even when the worksheet is protected. You also assign the Hidden protection format to all cell ranges in the spreadsheet where you don't want the contents of the cell to be displayed when protection is turned on in the worksheet. Then, after activating protection, the user can make changes only to the unlocked cells and display on the Formula bar the contents of the unhidden cells in the sheet.

When setting up your own spreadsheet templates, you will want to unlock all the cells where users need to input new data and keep locked all the cells that contain headings and formulas that never change. You may also want to hide cells with formulas if you're concerned that their display might tempt the users to waste time trying to fiddle with or finesse them. Then, turn on worksheet protection prior to saving the file in the template file format. You are then assured that all spreadsheets generated from that template automatically inherit the same level and type of protection as you assigned in the original spreadsheet.

When you open the Protect Sheet dialog box (Tools⇨Protection⇨Protect Sheet) to turn on protection, Excel gives you an opportunity to assign a password to remove the protection from the sheet (a wise move in most cases). This dialog box also contains the following list of check box options that enable you to specify what particular editing actions users of the worksheet are still allowed to perform:

✔ **Select Locked Cells** to enable the user to still be able to move the cell cursor into the locked cells of the worksheet even when he can't change their contents — note that this check box is selected by default but you can deselect it when you want to restrict movement to just the cells containing the unlocked protection format that allow data entry.

✔ **Select Unlocked Cells** to enable the user to be able to move the cell cursor into the unlocked cells of the worksheet so that he can make changes to them — note that deselecting this check box automatically deselects the Select Locked Cells check box as well, making it impossible to move the cell cursor to any cells in the worksheet and subsequently make any type of editing changes in the worksheet, which is very rarely your intention.

✔ **Format Cells** to enable the formatting of cells (with the exception of changing the locked and hidden status on the Protection tab of the Format Cells dialog box).

- ✔ **Format Columns** to enable formatting so that users can modify the column widths and hide and unhide columns.

- ✔ **Format Rows** to enable formatting so that users can modify the row heights and hide and unhide rows.

- ✔ **Insert Columns** to enable the insertion of new columns in the worksheet.

- ✔ **Insert Rows** to enable the insertion of new rows in the worksheet.

- ✔ **Insert Hyperlinks** to enable the insertion of new hyperlinks to other documents, both local and on the Web (see Chapter 21).

- ✔ **Delete Columns** to enable the deletion of columns in the worksheet.

- ✔ **Delete Rows** to enable the deletion of rows in the worksheet.

- ✔ **Sort** to enable the sorting of data in unlocked cells in the worksheet (see Chapter 16).

- ✔ **Use AutoFilter** to enable the filtering of data in the worksheet (see Chapter 16).

- ✔ **Use Pivot Table Reports** to enable the manipulation of pivot tables in the worksheet (see Chapter 19).

- ✔ **Edit Objects** to enable the editing of graphic objects such as text boxes, embedded images, and the like, in the worksheet (see Chapter 15).

- ✔ **Edit Scenarios** to enable the editing of what-if scenarios, including modifying and deleting them (see Chapter 18).

Try It

Exercise 17-2: Protecting a Worksheet

Open *Exercise17-2.xls* in your Chapter 17 folder in the My Practice Spreadsheets folder on your hard disk or in the Excel Workbook folder on the workbook CD-ROM. This workbook contains a copy of the Depreciation worksheet that you worked with in Chapter 8. You will use the Depreciation Table on this worksheet to practice unlocking cells before turning on protection in the worksheet:

1. Select the cell range C3:C6 in the Depreciation worksheet and then open the Format Cells dialog box (Ctrl+1), click the Protection tab, and deselect the Locked check box before you select OK.

These four cells constitute the input cells for the Depreciation Table where you need to still be able to enter new values even after turning on worksheet protection. By leaving the protection status of the other cells set to locked in the spreadsheet, you ensure that no one can make any changes to the formulas in the table itself, either intentional or otherwise.

2. Choose Tools⇨Protection⇨Protect Sheet to open the Protect Sheet dialog box.

When the Protect Sheet dialog box first opens, only the Protect Worksheet and Contents of Locked Cells check box located above the Password to Unprotect Sheet text box and the Select Locked Cells and Select Unlocked Cells in the Allow Users of This Worksheet To list box located below it are selected.

3. Type **stet** (the Latin command meaning "Let it stand") in all lowercase letters in the Password to Unprotect Sheet text box and then select OK without bothering to deselect any of the three check boxes that are automatically selected.

4. Retype **stet** in the Reenter Password to Proceed text box in the Confirm Password dialog box before selecting OK.

5. Make the following changes to the designated cells in the Depreciation worksheet:

- **35000** in the Cost cell, C4
- **7** in the Life_in_years cell, C5
- **5000** in the Salvage cell, C6

Excel enables you to make these changes because you assigned the unlocked protection formatting to these cells before turning on worksheet protection. Because the worksheet still uses the default automatic recalculation setting, the program recalculates the depreciation values in the Depreciation Table (C9:F19) each time you update an input value.

6. Position the cell cursor in cell D17 containing the first of the #NUM! error values in the table and then press F2 to put Excel in Edit mode.

Excel beeps at you and displays a warning dialog box indicating that the cell or chart you're trying to change is protected.

7. Position the cell cursor in the merged cell B2 and then press the Delete key to remove its contents.

Again, Excel beeps at you and displays the warning dialog box indicating that the cell or chart you're trying to change is protected.

8. Open the Insert and Format pull-down menus and notice how many of the commands are grayed out, indicating that they are currently unavailable.

9. Choose Excel's Tools⇨Protection⇨Unprotect Sheet menu command.

Excel displays the Unprotect Sheet dialog box where you need to enter the password.

10. Type **stet** in the Password text box of the Unprotect Sheet dialog box and then select OK.

11. Reopen the Protect Sheet dialog box (Tools⇨Protection⇨Protect Sheet) and then select the Format Cells check box (in addition to the Select Locked Cells and Select Unlocked Cells check boxes) before selecting OK (don't bother to assign a password to unprotect this time).

By selecting the Format Cells check box in the Allow Users of This Worksheet To list box before turning on the worksheet protection another time, you enable formatting changes to locked cells in the worksheet, while at the same time denying the ability to make changes to their contents or delete them.

12. While the cell cursor is still located in cell B2, click the Italic button on the Standard toolbar to format the Depreciation Table heading in this cell with italics.

13. Click the I-beam mouse pointer on the Formula bar to attempt to edit this heading in cell B2.

This time, Excel reverts back to beeping at you and displaying the warning dialog box indicating that the cell or chart you're trying to change is protected.

14. Press the Delete key to attempt to remove the heading from cell B2.

Again, Excel refuses to follow your command, instead beeping at you and displaying the same old tired warning dialog box indicating that the cell or chart you're trying to change is protected.

15. Position the cell cursor in cell A1 and then save the protected version of the Depreciation worksheet in a new file named **Solved17-2.xls** in your Chapter 17 folder in the My Practice Spreadsheets folder. Close the workbook.

Doing Data Entry in a Protected Worksheet

When protecting a worksheet, you can easily set it up so that you and your users can jump right to the unlocked cells and avoid ever having to deal with the locked ones (that you can't change anyway) by using the Tab and Shift+Tab keys to navigate the worksheet. All you have to do is format the cells that need changing as unlocked and then remove the check mark from the Select Locked Cells check box in the Protect Sheet dialog box when you turn on the worksheet protection.

When you press the Tab key in such a protected worksheet, Excel jumps the cell pointer to the next unlocked cell to the right of the current one in that same row. When you reach the last unlocked cell in that row, the program then jumps to the first unlocked cell in the rows below. To move back to a previous unlocked cell, press Shift+Tab. When Excel reaches the last unlocked cell in the spreadsheet, it automatically jumps back to the very first unlocked cell on the sheet.

Of course, provided that you haven't changed the behavior of the Enter key on the Edit tab of the Options dialog box (Tools⇨Options), you can also use the Enter key to move down the columns instead of across the rows. Keep in mind, however, that pressing the Enter key to progress down a column selects locked cells in that column as well as the unlocked ones, whereas Tab skips all those with the Locked protection format.

Try It

Exercise 17-3: Doing Data Entry in a Protected Worksheet

Open *Exercise17-3.xls* in your Chapter 17 folder in the My Practice Spreadsheets folder on your hard disk or in the Excel Workbook folder on the workbook CD-ROM. This workbook contains a copy of the Spring Sale worksheet that is missing the furniture description and retail price information (all the other data is entered along with the formulas that determine the sale price). Use the sales table in this worksheet to practice doing data entry in a protected worksheet where your movements are restrained to just the unlocked cells in the sheet:

1. Select the cell range C4:D9 in the Spring Sale worksheet and then open the Format Cells dialog box (Ctrl+1), click the Protection tab, and deselect the Locked check box before you select OK.

   You unlock these cells because you still need to be able to make data entries in them after you turn on the worksheet protection.

2. Open the Protect Sheet dialog box (Tools⇨Protection⇨Protect Sheet) and here deselect the Select Locked Cells check box before you select OK (don't bother to assign a password to unprotect the worksheet).

   After turning on worksheet protection with this check box unselected, Excel constrains the movement of the cell cursor to just the unlocked cell range C4:C9 in the worksheet.

3. Press the Tab key repeatedly until you've moved the cell cursor through each of the cells in the unlocked cell range, C4:C9.

4. Click cell A1 to attempt to locate the cell cursor in the Home cell of the Spring Sale worksheet.

   Note that clicking any cell outside of the unlocked cell range C4:C9 is no longer allowed as long as worksheet protection is in effect.

5. Position the cell cursor in cell C4 and then make the following data entries across the rows of the unlocked cell range in the designated cells by pressing Tab to complete each entry and, at the same time, move the cell cursor to the next cell in the same or next row:

- **36-inch round table** in cell C4
- **1250** in cell D4
- **72-inch dining table** in cell C5
- **1400** in cell D5
- **Hutch** in cell C6
- **2500** in cell D6

6. While the cell cursor is positioned in cell C7, make the following data entries down the columns of the unlocked cell range in the designated cells by pressing the Enter key to complete each entry and, at the same time, move the cell cursor to the next cell in the same or next column:

- **Side chair** in cell C7
- **Arm Chair** in cell C8
- **Armoire** in cell C9
- **350** in cell D7 (press Enter three times to position the cell cursor here)
- **500** in cell D8
- **1750** in cell D9

7. Save the protected worksheet version with the completed Spring Sale Furniture Prices table in a new workbook named **Solved17-3.xls** in your in your Chapter 17 folder in the My Practice Spreadsheets folder and then close the workbook.

Protecting the Entire Workbook

You can apply one last level of protection to your spreadsheet files and that is to protect the entire workbook. When you protect the workbook, you ensure that its users can't change the structure of the file by adding, deleting, or even moving and renaming any of its worksheets.

To protect your workbook, you open the Protect Workbook dialog box (Tools⇨ Protection⇨Protect Workbook). The Protect Workbook dialog box contains two check boxes: Structure (which is automatically checked) and Windows (which is not selected). This dialog box also contains a Password (Optional) text box, where you can enter a password that must be supplied before you can unprotect the workbook.

When you protect a workbook with the Structure check box selected, Excel prevents you or your users from doing any of the following tasks to the file:

✔ Insert new worksheets

✔ Delete existing worksheets

✔ Rename worksheets

✔ Hide or view hidden worksheets

✔ Move or copy worksheets to another workbook

✔ Display the source data for a cell in a pivot table or display a table's page fields on separate worksheets (see Chapter 19)

✔ Create a summary report with the Scenario Manager (see Chapter 18)

When you turn on protection for a workbook after checking the Windows check box in the Protect Workbook dialog box, Excel prevents you from opening new windows on the same workbook (so that you can compare different sections in one screen) as well as freezing columns and rows in the worksheet.

After you've enabled protection in a workbook, you can then turn it off by choosing the Tools⇨Protection⇨Unprotect Workbook on the Excel menus. If you've assigned a password to unprotect the workbook, you must accurately reproduce it in the Password text box in the Unprotect Workbook dialog box that then appears.

Try It

Exercise 17-4: Protecting the Entire Workbook

Open *Exercise17-4.xls* in your Chapter 17 folder in the My Practice Spreadsheets folder on your hard disk or in the Excel Workbook folder on the workbook CD-ROM. This workbook contains a copy of the Employee Data List, Salary Subset, and Department Subset worksheets you created when completing Exercise 16-7 in the previous chapter. You will use this file to practice protecting the workbook from further changes:

1. Choose Excel's Tools⇨Protection⇨Protect Workbook menu command to open the Protect Workbook dialog box.

2. Select the Windows check box to prevent changes to the size and position of the workbook window as well as to its structure (as the Structure check box is automatically selected).

3. Enter **stet** as the protect workbook password in the Password (Optional) text box and then select OK.

4. Retype **stet** in the Reenter Password to Proceed text box in the Confirm Password dialog box that appears and then click its OK button.

5. Double-click the sheet tab for the Employee Data List worksheet in an attempt to rename it.

Excel beeps at you and displays an alert box declaring, "The Workbook is protected and cannot be changed."

6. Select OK in the alert dialog box and this time attempt to drag the sheet tab for the Employee Data List worksheet in an attempt to reposition it as the last worksheet in the workbook.

Excel now resists all attempts at reordering the sheets in a workbook: Any attempt to drag any sheet to a new position in the workbook only results in the displaying of the International No symbol (a circle with a backslash in it).

7. Open the Window pull-down menu and note that the New Window, Compare Side by Side With, Split, and Freeze Panes menu items are all currently grayed out and unavailable. Then, select Hide on the Window pull-down menu.

Excel displays an Exercise17-4.xls is Protected dialog box that prompts you to enter the password.

8. Type **stet** in the Password text box and then select OK to hide the *Exercise17-4.xls* workbook.

When workbook protection is turned on and a password has been assigned, you must enter that password in order to both hide and to unhide the workbook.

9. Choose Excel's Window⇨Unhide command to open the Unhide dialog box and, with *Exercise17-4.xls* highlighted in the Unhide Workbook list box, click its OK button.

10. Type **stet** again in the new Password text box and then select OK to bring back the screen display of the *Exercise17-4.xls* workbook.

11. Save the protected workbook in a new file named **Solved17-4.xls** in your Chapter 17 folder in the My Practice Spreadsheets folder and then close the workbook as you exit Excel.

Part V
Doing Data Analysis

The 5th Wave   By Rich Tennant

Well, obviously one of the cells in the navigational spreadsheet is corrupt!

In this part . . .

In being able to perform data analysis in your spread-sheets, you begin to tap into the real power of Excel. Part V introduces you to data analysis in two forms: what-if analysis, which enables you to test out different possible outcomes based on different assumptions, and pivot tables, which enable you to summarize large groups of data based on varied criteria that you manipulate on the fly as you will.

Chapter 18

Performing What-If Analysis

· ·

In This Chapter

▶ Doing what-if analysis with one- and two-variable data tables

▶ Creating and playing with different scenarios

▶ Performing goal seeking

▶ Creating models with the Solver add-in

· ·

*U*sing what-if analysis in the spreadsheet to project possible future outcomes based on different variables is, to put it mildly, one of Excel's fortes. The program offers you what-if analysis in the form of its one- and two-variable data tables, goal seeking, and Scenario Manager. And if this is not enough, it also includes the Solver add-in utility, which enables you to model more complex problems. In this chapter, you get a chance to practice performing what-if analysis using all of these tools.

Using Data Tables

In the normal Excel spreadsheet, you see the effect of changing an input value on the result returned by a formula as soon as you enter that new input: Each time you change this input value, Excel automatically recalculates the formula and shows you the new result based on the new value. This method is of limited use, however, when you are performing what-if or sensitivity analysis and need to be able to see the range of results produced by using a series of different input values in the same worksheet so that you can compare them to each other.

To perform this type of what-if analysis, you can use Excel's Data Table command. When creating a data table, you enter a series of input values in the worksheet, and Excel then uses each of them in the formula you specify. When Excel finishes computing the data table, you see the results produced by each change in the input values in a single range of the worksheet. You can then save the data table as part of the worksheet if you need to keep a record of the results of a series of input values.

Creating single-variable data tables

In a one-variable data table, Excel substitutes a series of different values for a single input value in a formula. To create a one-variable data table, you need to set up the master formula in your worksheet and then, in a different range of the worksheet, enter the series of different values that you want substituted for a single input value in that formula.

Exercise 18-1: Constructing a One-Variable Data Table in a Spreadsheet

If Excel is not currently running, launch the program and then use Sheet1 of the new blank workbook to practice creating a single-variable data table that computes projected sales growth for 2007 based on various growth rate percentages:

1. Enter the title, **2007 Sales Projections**, in cell A1, make it bold italic, and then widen column A to display this entire title.

2. Make the following data entries in the designated cells:

- **Sales 2006** in cell A2

- **Growth Rate** in cell A3

- **Projected Sales** in cell A4

- **$875,000** in cell B2

- **2.75%** in cell B3

3. Name the cells in the cell range B2:B4 with the headings you entered in the cell range A2:A4.

Select the entire range A2:B4, open the Create Names dialog box (Insert⇨Name⇨Create), and then be sure that the only the Left Column check box is selected before you select OK.

4. Position the cell cursor in the Projected_Sales cell, B4, and construct the following formula:

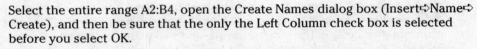

```
=Sales_2006+(Sales_2006*Growth_Rate)
```

5. Format the cell with the Currency number format with zero (0) decimal places.

6. In cell C6, create a formula with an external reference to the Projected_Sales cell, B4, that brings its value forward to the cell and then format the result with the Currency number format with zero (0) decimal places.

7. Enter the following potential growth rate percentages in the designated cells:

- **1.0%** in cell B7

- **1.5%** in cell B8

8. Use the Fill handle to copy this series of half-percentage point increases down column B to the cell range B7:B17 so that the series ends with a 6.00% growth rate.

Be sure to select cell B7 and B8 as a range with the cell cursor before you drag the Fill handle down to cell B17.

9. Select the cell range B6:C17 and then choose Data⇨Table to open the Table dialog box.

This Table dialog box contains two text boxes: Row Input Cell, where you indicate the variable from the top row of the data table that is to be substituted in the master formula, and Column Input Cell, where you indicate the variable that is to be substituted from its first column.

Because this one-variable input table contains the substitute values in a single column of the data table (cell range B7:B17), you only need to use the Column Input Cell text box in this case. And because the Growth_Rate cell, B3, contains the original value you want substituted in the master formula in cell B4, you need to enter this cell reference in this text box.

10. Position the cell pointer in the Column Input Cell text box in the Table dialog box, and then select the Growth_Rate cell, B3, in the worksheet before you select OK.

Excel then fills in the data table, substituting in succession the growth rate percentage entered in the cell range C7:C17 for the Growth_Rate cell in the master formula. Check your results against those shown in Figure 18-1.

11. Use the Format Painter on the Standard toolbar to copy the formatting in cell C6 to the range C7:C17.

12. Position the cell cursor in cell C7 and examine the contents of the formula on the Formula bar.

Excel inserts the following array formula (see Chapter 6) using the TABLE function in the cell range C7:C17 of the data table:

```
={TABLE(,B3)}
```

The TABLE function can take two arguments, row_ref and column_ref, which represent the row input cell and column input cell for the data table, respectively. In this example, the data table uses only a column input cell, so B3 is the second and only argument of the TABLE function. Because Excel enters the results in a Data table using an array formula, Excel won't allow you to clear individual result cells in its output range. If you try to delete a single result in the data table, Excel displays an alert dialog box telling you that you cannot change part of a table.

13. Name the worksheet, **Data Table**, and the save your one-variable data table with the filename **Solved18-1.xls** in your Chapter 18 folder in the My Practice Spreadsheets folder and then leave the workbook open for the next exercise with a two-variable data table.

Figure 18-1: The completed one-variable data table.

	A	B	C
1	*2007 Sales Projections*		
2	Sales 2006	$875,000	
3	Growth Rate	2.75%	
4	Projected Sales	$ 899,063	
5			
6			$ 899,063
7		1.00%	$ 883,750
8		1.50%	$ 888,125
9		2.00%	$ 892,500
10		2.50%	$ 896,875
11		3.00%	$ 901,250
12		3.50%	$ 905,625
13		4.00%	$ 910,000
14		4.50%	$ 914,375
15		5.00%	$ 918,750
16		5.50%	$ 923,125
17		6.00%	$ 927,500

Creating two-variable data tables

In a two-variable data table, Excel substitutes a series of different values for two input values in a formula. When you create a two-variable data table, you enter two ranges of input values to be substituted in the master formula: a single-row range in the first row of the table and a single-column range in the first column of the data table. When you create a two-variable data table, you place a copy of the master formula in the cell at the intersection of this row and column of input values.

Try It

Exercise 18-2: Constructing a Two-Variable Data Table in a Spreadsheet

Use the *Solved18-1.xls* workbook containing the one-variable data table on the Data Table worksheet that you created in the last exercise to convert it into a two-variable data table that not only uses a series of growth rate percentages but also a series of projected expenses to sales percentages in calculating possible projected incomes:

1. Delete the range C7:C17 on the Data Table worksheet.

Because this range contains the array formula with the TABLE function, you must select the entire range, C7:C17, in order to be able to make any deletions.

2. Insert two new blank cells in the range A4:B4, shifting down the existing entries (Projected Sales and the formula =Sales_2006+(Sales_2006*Growth_Rate) with the calculated result $899,063) to the range A5:B5.

Be sure to select the Shift Cells Down option button in the Insert dialog box.

3. Make the following data entries in the designated cells:

- **Expenses/Sales** in cell A4
- **3%** in cell B4

4. Assign the range name **Expense_Rate** to cell B4 containing the 3.00% rate of expenses to sales.

5. Edit the formula in cell B5 as follows:

```
=Sales_2006+(Sales_2006*Growth_Rate)-(Sales_2006*
        Expense_Rate)
```

6. Move the formula with the external reference to the Projected_Sales cell, B5, that is currently in cell C6 to cell B7 of the Data Table worksheet.

When creating a two-variable data table, you place the formula at the intersection of the row and column in the table that contains the series of input values.

7. Make the following data entries in the designated cells:

- **2%** in cell C7
- **2.5%** in cell D7

8. Format cell C7 with Percent Style number format with two decimal places and then use the Fill handle to copy this series of half-percentage point increases across row 7 to the cell range E7:G7 so that the series ends with a 4.00% expense/sales growth rate.

HINT

Be sure to select cell C7 and D7 as a range with the cell cursor before you drag the Fill handle across the row to cell G7.

9. Select the data table's cell range B7:G18 and then choose the Data➪Table command.

10. Select the Expense_Rate cell, B4, as the Row Input Cell and the Growth_Rate cell, B3, as the Column Input Cell in the Table dialog box. Select OK.

Excel then fills in the data table, substituting in succession the growth rate percentage entered in the cell range C8:C18 for the Growth_Rate cell in the master formula and the expense rate percentage entered in the cell range C7:G7 for the Expense_Rate cell. Check your results in your data table against those shown in Figure 18-2.

11. Use the Format Painter on the Standard toolbar to copy the formatting in cell C8 to the range C8:G18 and then widen columns D through G sufficient to display all the entries in the range D8:G18.

12. Position the cell cursor in cell C8 and examine the contents of the formula on the Formula bar.

Excel inserts the following array formula in the cell range C8:G18 of the data table (note that the TABLE function in this formula uses both the row_ref and column_ref arguments):

```
={TABLE(B4,B3)}
```

13. Save the Data Table worksheet with your two-variable data table in a new workbook with the filename **Solved18-2.xls** in your Chapter 18 folder in the My Practice Spreadsheets folder. Close the workbook.

Figure 18-2:
The completed two-variable data table.

Microsoft Excel - Solved18-2.xls

File Edit View Insert Format Tools Data Window Help Adobe PDF

C8   fx {=TABLE(B4,B3)}

	A	B	C	D	E	F	G
1	**2007 Sales Projections**						
2	Sales 2006	$875,000					
3	Growth Rate	2.75%					
4	Expenses/Sales	3.00%					
5	Projected Sales	$ 872,813					
6							
7		$ 872,813	2.00%	2.50%	3.00%	3.50%	4.00%
8		1.00%	$ 866,250	$861,875	$857,500	$853,125	$848,750
9		1.50%	$ 870,625	$866,250	$861,875	$857,500	$853,125
10		2.00%	$ 875,000	$870,625	$866,250	$861,875	$857,500
11		2.50%	$ 879,375	$875,000	$870,625	$866,250	$861,875
12		3.00%	$ 883,750	$879,375	$875,000	$870,625	$866,250
13		3.50%	$ 888,125	$883,750	$879,375	$875,000	$870,625
14		4.00%	$ 892,500	$888,125	$883,750	$879,375	$875,000
15		4.50%	$ 896,875	$892,500	$888,125	$883,750	$879,375
16		5.00%	$ 901,250	$896,875	$892,500	$888,125	$883,750
17		5.50%	$ 905,625	$901,250	$896,875	$892,500	$888,125
18		6.00%	$ 910,000	$905,625	$901,250	$896,875	$892,500
19							
20							
21							

Data Table / Sheet2 / Sheet3 /

Ready

Exploring Various Scenarios

Excel enables you to create and save sets of input values that produce different results as *scenarios* using its Tools⇨Scenario command. A scenario consists of a group of input values in a worksheet to which you assign a name such as *Best Case, Worst Case, Most Likely Case,* and so on.

Then, to reuse the input data and view the results they produce in the worksheet, you simply select the name of the scenario you want to use and Excel applies the input values stored in that scenario to the appropriate cells in the worksheet. After creating your different scenarios for a worksheet, you can also use the Scenario Manager to create a summary report showing you both the input values stored in each scenario as well as key results produced by each.

Try It

Exercise 18-3: Constructing Various Scenarios for the Spreadsheet

Open the *Exercise18-3.xls* workbook file in your Chapter 18 folder in the My Practice Spreadsheets folder on your hard disk or in the Excel Workbook folder on the workbook CD-ROM. The Sales Forecast worksheet in this workbook contains a Sales Forecast for 2007 table that you will use to practice creating and using different growth scenarios using different rate of sales growth, COGS (cost of goods sold), and expenses:

1. Select the following changing cells for your scenarios as one cell selection (by holding down the Ctrl key as you click them):

    • Sales_Growth cell, H4

    • COGS cell, H5

    • Expenses cell, H7

2. While cells H4, H5, and H7 are selected, choose Tools⇨Scenarios to open the Scenario Manager dialog box.

3. Select the Add button in this dialog box to open the Add Scenario dialog box and then enter **Most Likely** in its Scenario Name text box before you select OK.

    As soon as you select OK, the Add Scenario dialog box closes and the Scenario Values dialog box opens. Here, you indicate the values to be used by the changing cells in the particular scenario you're building. In this case, Excel picks up the values 0.05, 0.2, and 0.28 for the Sales_Growth, COGS, and Expenses changing cells from the entries made in cells H4, H5, and H7, respectively.

4. Select OK to accept the values in the Scenario Values dialog box picked up from the Sales_Growth, COGS, and Expenses cells in the Sales Forecast table.

    As soon as you select OK, the Scenario Values dialog box closes and the Scenario Manager dialog box reappears.

5. Click the Add button and then enter **Worst Case** as the name for a second scenario in the Add Scenario dialog box and then select OK.

6. Change the values in the designated changing cells as follows:

    • **0.02** in Sales_Growth

    • **0.3** in COGS

    • **0.3** in Expenses

7. Select OK to return to the Scenario Manager dialog box that now contains both a Most Likely and a Worst Case scenario.

8. Add a third scenario named Best Case with the following changing values:

- **0.1** in Sales_Growth

- **0.05** in COGS

- **0.1** in Expenses

9. With Best Case selected in the Scenario Manager dialog box, select the Show button.

As soon as you select Show, Excel plugs the Best Case scenario's values into the changing cells in the Sales Forecast for 2007 table.

10. Take a look at the Worst Case scenario in the Sales Forecast table by double-clicking Worst Case in the Scenarios list box of the Scenario Manager dialog box.

11. Display the Most Likely scenario in the Sales Forecast table and then close the Scenario Manager dialog box.

12. Enter the following values in the designated changing cells in the Sales Forecast for 2007 table:

- **17%** in the Sales_Growth cell, H4

- **25%** in the COGS cell, H5

- **18%** in the Expenses cell, H7

13. Reopen the Scenario Manager dialog box and then click the Summary button near the bottom of the Scenario Manager dialog box to open the Scenario Summary dialog box.

14. Select the cell range B8:G8 in the worksheet table to insert the cell range =$B$8:$G$8 in the Results Cells text box before you select OK.

As soon as you select OK, Excel inserts a Scenario Summary worksheet in front of the Sales Forecast worksheet in the *Exercise18-3.xls* workbook. This worksheet contains an outlined summary table that displays the total projected income for all four quarters along with the values of the Most Likely, Worst Case, and Best Case scenarios used to calculate these totals (as shown in Figure 18-3).

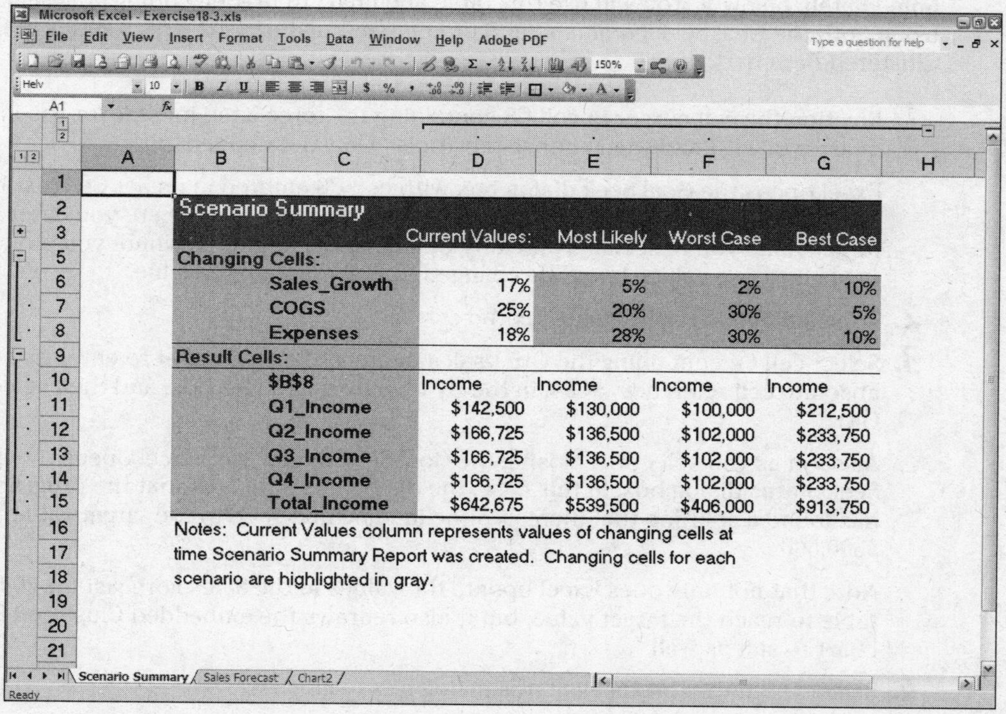

Figure 18-3: Scenario Summary worksheet with summary table showing projected income using current changing cells plus those in all defined scenarios.

15. Move the Scenario Summary worksheet so that it follows the Sales Forecast worksheet, and then click cell A1 in the Sales Forecast worksheet. Save your work in a new workbook file named **Solved18-3.xls** in your Chapter 18 folder in the My Practice Spreadsheets folder and then close the workbook file.

Performing Goal Seeking

Sometimes, you know the outcome that you want to realize in a spreadsheet and you need Excel to help you find the input values necessary to achieve those results. This procedure, which is just the opposite of the what-if analysis you've been doing so far, is referred to as *goal seeking*.

When you only need to find the value for a single variable that will give the desired result in a particular formula, you can perform this simple type of goal seeking with Excel's Goal Seek command. If you have charted the data and created a two-dimensional column, bar, or line chart, you can also perform the goal seeking by directly manipulating the appropriate marker on the chart.

To use the Goal Seek command, you simply select the cell containing the formula that will return the result you are seeking (referred to as the *set cell*), indicate what value you want this formula to return, and then indicate the location of the input value that Excel can change to return the desired result.

`Try It`

Exercise 18-4: Doing Goal Seeking in a Spreadsheet

Open the *Exercise18-4.xls* workbook file in your Chapter 18 folder in the My Practice Spreadsheets folder on your hard disk or in the Excel Workbook folder on the workbook CD-ROM. The workbook contains a version of the Sales Forecast for 2007 table that you worked with in the previous exercise with an embedded Clustered Bar chart immediately below it. You will use this table and chart to practice doing goal seeking using both the Goal Seek command and direct manipulation of the data series in the Clustered Bar chart:

1. Position the cell cursor in cell C8 containing the forecasted income for the first quarter of 2007 and then choose the Tools⇨Goal Seek command.

Excel opens the Goal Seek dialog box with cell C8 entered in its Set Cell text box. The Goal Seek dialog box also contains a To Value text box, where you enter the target value you're seeking, and a By Changing Cell text box, where you indicate the cell whose value should be changed to reach the target value.

2. Type **300000** in the To Value text box.

3. Select cell C4 containing the Qtr 1 sales figure in the worksheet to enter its absolute cell reference, $C$4, in the By Changing Cell text box, and then select OK.

As soon as you select OK closing the Goal Seek dialog box, Excel opens the Goal Seek Status dialog box. In this case, the dialog box indicates that the program has found a solution that increases the income in cell C8 to the target value, $300,000.

Note that not only does Excel update the values in the Sales Forecast for 2007 table to reach the target value, but it also redraws the embedded Clustered Bar chart to suit as well.

4. Select OK in the Goal Seek Status dialog box to close it.

5. Click the Undo button on the Standard toolbar or press Ctrl+Z to restore the original values to the Sales Forecast table and Clustered Bar chart.

6. Click the Redo button on the Standard toolbar or press Ctrl+Y to return to the values entered as the result of your goal seeking.

7. Click somewhere on the embedded Clustered Bar chart in the Sales Forecast worksheet to select it and display the Chart toolbar in the Excel window.

8. Select Series "Income" on the Chart Objects drop-down list box on the Chart toolbar.

Excel selects the bars representing the projected income for the four quarters in the Clustered Bar chart.

9. Hold down the Ctrl key as you click income bar for Qtr 1 at the bottom of the embedded chart.

Holding down the Ctrl key as you click ensures that you select only the Qtr 1 income bar in the chart (and not all the bars representing the Income data series).

10. Release the Ctrl key and then position the mouse pointer at the end of the Qtr 1 income bar. When the pointer changes to a double-headed arrow, drag this bar until it reaches the $350,000 tick mark in the chart (indicated by a reading of 350000 from the ToolTip).

The moment you release the mouse button after dragging the Qtr 1 income bar to $350,000 tick mark in the Chart, the Goal Seek dialog box appears, this time with values in both the Set Cell and To Value text boxes.

11. Click cell C4 with the Qtr 1 Sales in the worksheet to enter its absolute cell reference in the By Changing To text box and then select OK.

The Goal Seek Status dialog box replaces the Goal Seek dialog box, indicating that a solution has been found in cell C8.

12. Select OK to close the Goal Seek Status dialog box, and then select cell A1. Save your work in a new workbook file named **Solved18-4.xls** in your Chapter 18 folder in the My Practice Spreadsheets folder and then close the workbook file.

Creating Complex Models with Solver

Although the Data Table and Goal Seek commands work just fine for simple problems that require determining the direct relationship between the inputs and results in a formula, you need to use the Solver add-in when dealing with more complex problems. For example, you would use the Solver to find the best solution when you need to change multiple input values in your model and you need to impose constraints on these values or the output value.

The Solver works by applying iterative methods to find the "best" solution given the inputs, desired solution, and the constraints that you impose. During each iteration, the program applies a trial-and-error method (based on the use of linear or nonlinear equations and inequalities) that attempts to get closer to the optimum solution.

When using the Solver, you need to keep in mind that for many problems, especially the more complicated ones, there are many solutions. Although the Solver returns the optimum solution, given the starting values, the variables that can change, and the constraints you define, this solution is often not the only one possible and, in fact, may not be the best solution for you. To be sure that you are finding the best solution, you may want to run the Solver more than once, adjusting the initial values each time you solve the problem.

When setting up the problem in your worksheet model to be solved by the Solver, you define the following items:

- ✔ **Target cell**, which is the cell in your worksheet whose value is to be maximized, minimized, or made to reach a particular value

- ✔ **Changing cells**, which are the cells in your worksheet whose values are to be adjusted until the answer is found

- ✔ **Constraints**, which are the limits you impose on the changing values or the target cell

After you finish defining the problem with these parameters and you have the Solver solve the problem, the program returns the optimum solution by modifying the values in your worksheet. At that point, you can choose to retain the changes in the worksheet or restore the original values to the worksheet. You can also save the solution as a scenario to view later before you restore the original values.

You can use the Solver with the Scenario Manager to help set up a problem to solve or to save a solution so that you can view it at a later date. The changing cells that you define for the Scenario Manager are automatically picked up and used by the Solver when you select this command, and vice versa. Also, you can save the Solver's solution to a problem as a scenario (by clicking the Save Scenario button in the Solver dialog box) that you can then view with the Scenario Manager.

Try It

Exercise 18-5: Using Solver to Modify Multiple Input Values in a Spreadsheet

Open the *Exercise 18-5.xls* workbook file in your Chapter 18 folder in the My Practice Spreadsheets folder on your hard disk or in the Excel Workbook folder on the workbook CD-ROM. The workbook contains a copy of the Sales Forecast worksheet with the Sales Forecast for 2007 table that you will use to practice using the Solver add-in to reach a target income based on changes to multiple parameters:

1. Choose Tools➪Add-Ins and then select the Solver Add-In check box in the Add-Ins dialog box before you select OK.

    If the Solver add-in is not currently installed as part of Excel, the program displays an alert dialog box indicating that the feature is not currently installed and prompting you to install it. Go ahead and install Solver by selecting the Yes button in this alert dialog box. After Excel finishes installing the Solver add-in, proceed to step 2.

2. Position the cell pointer in the Total_Income cell, G8, and then choose Tools➪Solver to open the Solver Parameters dialog box.

    This dialog box displays Target_Income in the Set Target Cell text box. Next, you need to set the target equal to a new value and then indicate the changing cells.

3. Select the Value Of option button to the right of Equal To and then type **650000** in the text box to its immediate right.

4. Select the By Changing Cells text box and then click the COGS cell, H5, in the worksheet and Ctrl+click the Expenses cell, H7.

    The By Changing Cells text box now contains references to COGS and Expenses separated by a comma.

5. Select the Solve button in the Solver Parameters dialog box.

As soon as you select the Solve button, Excel closes the Solver Parameters and then beeps before opening the Solver Results dialog box. In this case, Solver was able to find a solution to the problem by balancing changes to the COGS and Expenses that would result in the desired target net income of $650,000.

The Solver Results dialog box gives you a choice between retaining the adjusted values in the Sales Forecast for 2007 table (Keep Solver Solution) and restoring its original values (Restore Original Values). You can also save the solution as a scenario.

6. Select the Save Scenario button to open the Save Scenario dialog box and then type **Optimal** as the name in Scenario Name text box before you select OK.

As soon as Excel closes the Save Scenario button, you are returned to the Solver Results dialog box.

7. Select the Restore Original Values option button in the Solver Results dialog box and then select OK.

Because you saved the Solver's solution with the scenario name, Optimal, you can restore these values to the Sales Forecast table simply by opening the Scenario Manager dialog box and then selecting its name before you select the Show button.

8. Open the Solver Parameters dialog box again.

Note that the Solver Parameters dialog box retains your earlier settings for the target cell, value, and changing cells in their respective used in obtaining the first solution.

9. Select the Add button to the right of the Subject to the Constraints list box to open the Add Constraint dialog box and then click the COGS cell, H5, in the worksheet to insert $H$5 in the Cell Reference text box. Accept the default <= comparative operator. Click the insertion point in the Constraint text box and type 15% before you select its Add button.

Excel clears the Cell Reference and Constraint text boxes so that you can define a new constraint.

10. This time, click the Expenses cell, H7, in the worksheet to insert $H$7 in the Cell Reference text box, and then click the insertion point in the Constraint text box and type 12% before you select the OK button.

As soon as you select OK, Excel closes the Add Constraint dialog box and returns you to the Solver Parameters dialog box, where the following comparative expressions now appear in the Subject to Constraints list box:

- COGS<=15%
- Expenses<=12%

11. Select the Solve button.

This time, when the Solver Results dialog box appears, it indicates that the Solver could not find a feasible solution. When the cost of goods sold and the expenses are kept down to these lower percentages, the projected net income must necessarily exceed the target of $650,000 (note that the Solver has actually returned $757,375 to the Total_Income cell, G8, using these percentages).

12. Select the Restore Original Values option button in the Solver Results dialog box and then select OK.

13. Position the cell cursor in cell A1 and then save your work in a new workbook named **Solved18-5.xls** in your Chapter 18 folder in the My Practice Spreadsheets folder. Close the workbook file as you exit Excel.

Chapter 19

Generating Pivot Tables

In This Chapter

▶ Understanding how pivot tables summarize data and enable you to analyze data lists

▶ Creating a pivot table with the PivotTable Wizard

▶ Pivoting the elements in a pivot table

▶ Changing the summary function used in the pivot table

▶ Formatting a pivot table and changing pivot table options

▶ Creating a pivot chart with your pivot table

Excel's pivot tables and charts enable you to quickly and extemporaneously summarize vast amounts of spreadsheet data. As such, they're often considered to be the most versatile of the program's many data-analysis features, if not its coolest and most powerful. In this chapter, you get the chance to practice creating and using pivot tables and charts to see how they can help reveal complex relationships in the data that might otherwise go completely unnoticed.

Understanding Pivot Tables

Pivot tables are great for summarizing particular values in a data list or database table because they do their magic without requiring you create formulas to perform their calculations. Unlike the Subtotals feature, another summarizing feature you encountered in Chapter 16, pivot tables let you play around with the arrangement of the summarized data, even after you generate the table. (The Subtotals feature only lets you hide and display different levels of totals in the list.) It's this capability to change the arrangement of the summarized data by rotating row and column headings that gives the pivot table its name.

Pivot tables are also flexible in their capability to summarize data using a variety of summary functions (although totals created with the SUM function will probably remain your old standby). When setting up the original pivot table — made really simple with the help of the PivotTable and PivotChart Wizard — you make several decisions: what summary function to use, which columns (fields) the summary function is applied to, and which columns (fields) these computations are tabulated with. You can also use pivot tables to cross-tabulate one set of data in your data list with another. For example, you can use this feature to create a pivot table from an employee database that totals the salaries for each job category cross-tabulated (arranged) by department or job site.

Try It

ON THE CD

Exercise 19-1: Modifying an Existing Pivot Table

If Excel is not currently running, launch the program and then open the workbook *Exercise19-1.xls* in your Chapter 19 folder in the My Practice Spreadsheets folder on your hard disk or in the Excel Workbook folder on the workbook CD-ROM. This workbook contains a Employee Data List worksheet with a copy of the Employee data list you worked with in Chapter 16, followed by a Data List Pivot Table worksheet containing a pivot table generated from the this data list. You will use this pivot table to practice modifying what data from the Employee Data List are displayed in the table as well as the manner in which they are displayed:

1. **Click the Data List Pivot Table sheet tab to display the pivot table generated with data from the Employee Data List along with the PivotTable toolbar.**

   The Employee List pivot table that appears on this worksheet uses the following field from the Employee Data List:

   • Profit Sharing and Gender fields as the two page fields (in cells B1 and B2, respectively)

   • Location field as the sole row field (in cell A5)

   • Dept field as the sole column field (in cell B4)

   • Salary field for the data items in the body of the pivot table (in the cell range B6:G13) using the SUM function (A4)

   Note that the PivotTable toolbar appears automatically whenever you position the cell cursor in any cell of the pivot table and disappears just as automatically when you move the cursor to a cell outside the pivot table.

2. **Click the Show Field List button at the very end of the PivotTable toolbar.**

   Excel displays the PivotTable Field List dialog box indicating which fields from the data list are used in the table in boldfaced type.

3. **Click the drop-down button attached to the Profit Sharing page field in cell B1 and then select Yes on its drop-down list to display the sum of the salaries in the various departments and locations where the employees participate in the profit-sharing plan.**

   You use the drop-down buttons attached to the page, row, and column fields to select the various filtering criteria for the data displayed in the body of the pivot table.

4. **Click the drop-down button attached to the Gender page field in cell B2 and then select M on its drop-down list.**

   Now the body of the pivot table displays the sum of the salaries in the various departments and locations only where the male employees participate in the profit-sharing plan.

5. **Restore the (All) settings to both the Profit Sharing and Gender page fields by selecting (All) on their respective drop-down lists and then double-click Sum of Salary in cell A4 to open the PivotTable Field dialog box.**

6. **Click Average in the Summarize By list box so that the Name text box contains Average of Salary before you select OK.**

   The pivot table now displays the averages of the salaries for all the departments and locations in the company regardless of whether the employees are part of profit sharing or are male or female.

7. **Click the Format Report button on the PivotTable toolbar (the one immediately to the right of the first PivotTable drop-down button) and then select the thumbnail for the Table 10 style in the AutoFormat dialog box before you select OK.**

   This table format makes the cells in the pivot table with the department names and departmental salary totals really stand out with their black background and gold lettering.

8. Use the Format Report button on the PivotTable toolbar to reopen the AutoFormat dialog box and there select the thumbnail for the Report 4 style before you select OK.

Excel now redraws the pivot table so that its summary data now appears in a more vertical report-type format (with the Location row field now appearing side by side the Dept column field at the top of the report followed by the Average of Salary column).

9. Restore the sum of the salaries to the pivot table by double-clicking the Average of Salary cell, C4, to open the PivotTable Field dialog box and then selecting Sum in the Summarize By list box before selecting OK.

10. Select Table 1 as the format for the pivot table.

Click the Format Report button on the PivotTable toolbar to open the AutoFormat dialog box and then select the thumbnail for the Table 1 style before you select OK.

11. Click the Location field's drop-down list button in cell A5 and then click the (Show All) check box to deselect all the check boxes for all the cities. Click the check boxes for just Boston, Chicago, San Francisco, and Seattle before you select OK.

The pivot table now just shows the sum of the salaries for all the departments in just the Boston, Chicago, San Francisco, and Seattle locations.

12. Click the (Show All) item at the top of the Location field's drop-down list to reselect the check boxes for all the company locations on its list before you select OK.

13. Select cell A1 on the Employee Data List worksheet and then save your changes in a new workbook named **Solved19-1.xls** in your Chapter 19 folder in the My Practice Spreadsheets folder. Close the workbook file.

Creating Pivot Tables

You use the PivotTable and PivotChart Wizard opened by choosing the Excel Data⇨ PivotTable and PivotChart Report menu command. This wizard consists of the following three dialog boxes:

✔ **Step 1 of 3,** where you indicate the source of the data you want to summarize and choose between creating a simple pivot table or a pivot chart, which represents the summary data graphically with a supporting pivot table. The data source can be a Microsoft Excel List or Database, an External Data Source (Chapter 16), Multiple Consolidation Ranges, or Another PivotTable, or PivotChart Report.

✔ **Step 2 of 3,** where you indicate what data you want to use in the Excel worksheet (when specifying a Microsoft Excel List or Database, Multiple Consolidation Ranges, or Another PivotTable or PivotChart Report as the data source), or execute an external data query that gets the data (when specifying an External Data Source).

✔ **Step 3 of 3,** where you indicate whether the pivot table should be placed in a new worksheet or in a cell range somewhere in the current worksheet — when generating a pivot chart, Excel places the chart on its own chart sheet and places the support pivot table on the sheet you specify in this dialog box.

When you finish going through the options offered in the three dialog boxes of the PivotTable and PivotChart Wizard, you end up with a new (and somewhat blank) pivot table similar to the one shown in Figure 19-1.

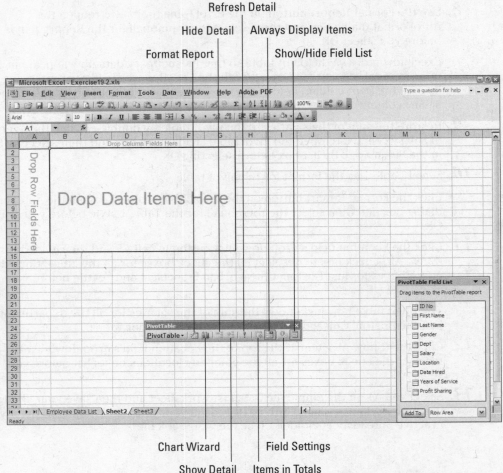

Figure 19-1:
Worksheet
with a blank
pivot table
showing the
PivotTable
Field list
and toolbar.

This new pivot table contains a blank framework with the various areas of the pivot table identified. To the right of the blank table, Excel places a floating PivotTable Field List task pane (which you can dock on the right side of the worksheet window). This task pane contains a complete list of the names of the fields in your data source. You use these field names to bring the blank pivot table to life. In addition to the PivotTable Field List task pane, Excel also displays the PivotTable toolbar in the Excel window.

The key to completing the new pivot table is to assign the fields in the Field List task pane to the various parts of the table. You can do this either by dragging a field name from the task pane and then dropping it on a particular part of the pivot table or by clicking the field name in the Field List task pane, selecting the part of the table to which to attach the field in its drop-down list box, and then clicking the Add To button at the bottom of the pane. However, before you start doing this, you need to understand the use and significance of the various areas of a pivot table:

✔ **Drop Page Fields Here:** This area contains the fields that enable you to page through the data summaries shown in the actual pivot table by filtering out sets of data. For example, if you designate the Year field from a data list as a Page field, you can display data summaries in the pivot table for individual years or for all years represented in the data list.

✔ **Drop Column Fields Here:** This area contains the fields that determine the arrangement of data shown in the columns of the pivot table.

✔ **Drop Row Fields Here:** This area contains the fields that determine the arrangement of data shown in the rows of the pivot table.

✔ **Drop Data Items Here:** This area contains the fields that determine which data are presented in the cells of the pivot table and then summarized in its last column (totaled by default).

Try It

Exercise 19-2: Creating a New Pivot Table

Open the workbook *Exercise19-2.xls* in your Chapter 19 folder in the My Practice Spreadsheets folder on your hard disk or in the Excel Workbook folder on the workbook CD-ROM. This workbook contains a copy of the Employee Data List worksheet with the data list you will use in creating your first pivot table:

1. Click cell A1 on Sheet2 of the *Exercise19-2.xls* workbook and then choose the Data⇨PivotTable and PivotTable Chart Report menu command.

   Excel opens the PivotTable and PivotTable Chart - Step 1 of 3 dialog box, where the Microsoft Office Excel List or Database option button is selected in the Where Is the Data You Want to Analyze? section at the top. The PivotTable option button is selected in the What Kind of Report Do You Want to Create? section at the bottom.

2. Leave the default options selected and then click the Next button.

   Excel opens the PivotTable and PivotTable Chart - Step 2 of 3 dialog box, where you indicate the cell range of the data to use (in this case, the data list in the cell range A1:J33 of the Employee Data List worksheet).

3. Click the Employee Data List sheet tab and then drag through the cell range A1:J33 in the worksheet so that the range address 'Employee Data List'!$A$1:$J$33 appears in the Range text box, before you click the Next button.

   Excel opens the PivotTable and PivotTable Chart - Step 3 of 3 dialog box, where you indicate where you want to locate the new pivot table in the workbook. In this case, you accept the default setting of Existing Worksheet and the cell address $A$3.

4. Accept the default settings in this dialog box by selecting the Finish button.

   Excel opens the PivotTable toolbar and PivotTable Field List dialog box in the worksheet while at the same time drawing the blank framework for the new pivot table indicating where to drop the page, row, and column fields along with the fields to be used as the data items.

5. In the PivotTable Field List dialog box, click the Location field and then select the Add To button.

   Because Row Area was selected at the time you selected the Add To button, Excel adds the company sites from the Location field in the Employee Data List to the first column of the pivot table as the row field.

6. Drag the Dept field from the PivotTable Field List dialog box and drop it on the Drop Column Fields Here section of the pivot table in the cells of the worksheet.

   You can also add fields to a new pivot table by dragging them to the desired position.

7. Click Data Area on the drop-down list at the bottom of the PivotTable Field List dialog box, and then click the Salary field before you select the Add To button.

   Excel adds the Salary field for the data items in the pivot table and Sum of Salary appears in cell A3, indicating the SUM function is being used.

8. Make the Gender and Profit Sharing fields the two page fields for this pivot table.

   You can do this either by dragging the Gender and Profit Sharing fields from the PivotTable Field List dialog box and dropping them on the Drop Page Fields Here cells in the worksheet, or by selecting Page Area in the drop-down list at the bottom of this dialog box and then selecting these fields in succession followed by the Add To button.

9. Apply the Table 3 style to your completed pivot table.

   Click the Format Report button on the PivotTable toolbar to open the AutoFormat dialog box and then select the thumbnail of the Table 3 style before you select OK.

10. Rename the Sheet2 worksheet to Pivot Table, select cell A1 in this sheet, and then save your changes in a new workbook named **Solved19-2.xls** in your Chapter 19 folder in the My Practice Spreadsheets folder. Leave the workbook file open for Exercise 19-3.

Modifying the Pivot Table

The fun just begins with the creation of the basic pivot table. After that, you refine its look by formatting the table with the AutoFormat styles as you did in the previous exercise, or by selecting different portions of the table and individually formatting them. You can also show and hide new levels of detail in the table. Perhaps most important, you can modify the structure of the table by pivoting its row, column, and paging fields. Finally, you can change the table's basic summary function as well as add your own calculated fields to the pivot table.

Modifying the table formatting

The one thing that stands out like a sore thumb in the pivot tables you create is their lack of basic formatting. When Excel creates a new pivot table, it does not pick any formatting from the original data source. This means that you have to manually apply whatever number formats and other kinds of table formatting you want to apply.

Fortunately, as you've seen, Excel makes it easy to format the overall table itself with the AutoFormat styles available by clicking the Format Report button on the PivotTable toolbar. In addition, you can format individual parts of the pivot table by selecting them and then applying particular formatting to them.

Try It

Exercise 19-3: Modifying the Formatting in a Pivot Table

Use the *Solved19-2.xls* workbook you created in the previous exercise to practice formatting individual parts of the basic pivot table as well as hiding and showing different levels of detail:

1. Click the Format Report button on the PivotTable toolbar to open the AutoFormat dialog box and then select the thumbnail of the PivotTable Classic style before you select OK.

2. On the PivotTable toolbar, choose Select⇨Entire Table on the PivotTable's drop-down button's list to select all the cells in the pivot table (including the page fields).

3. Choose Select⇨Label on the PivotTable's drop-down button's list to select all the cells with labels in the pivot table.

4. Click the Bold button on the Formatting toolbar to display the titles in the pivot table in boldface type.

5. On the Formatting toolbar, click the Light Green color square on the Fill Color button's drop-down list to display the cells containing the pivot table titles with a light-green colored background.

6. Choose Select⇨Data on the PivotTable's drop-down button's list to select only the cells with data items in the pivot table.

7. Click the Currency Style button on the Formatting toolbar and then the Decrease Decimal button twice. The salary totals in the pivot table now appear in the Currency number format with no decimal places.

8. On the Formatting toolbar, click the Light Yellow color square on the Fill Color button's drop-down list to display the cells containing the pivot table data items with a light-yellow colored background.

9. Click cell A1 in the Pivot Table worksheet and then save your changes in a new workbook named **Solved19-3.xls** in your Chapter 19 folder in the My Practice Spreadsheets folder. Leave the workbook file open for Exercise 19-4.

Pivoting the table's fields

As the name "pivot" implies, the fun of pivot tables is being able to rotate the data fields used as the rows and columns of tables as well as to change what fields are used on the fly. For example, suppose in the Employee Data List pivot table that, after making the Dept field the pivot table's sole column field and the Location field the sole row field, you now want to see what the table looks like with the Location field as the column field and the Dept field as row field.

No problem: All you have to do is drag the Dept field label from the top row of the table and drop it in the first column and then drag the Location field label from the first column and drop it on the first row. Voilá! Excel rearranges the totaled salaries so that the rows of the pivot table show the departmental grand totals and the columns now show the location grand totals.

Try It

Exercise 19-4: Modifying the Structure of a Pivot Table

Use the *Solved19-3.xls* workbook you created in the previous exercise to practice pivoting the row and columns of the basic pivot table as well as modifying the page fields:

1. Exchange the position of the Dept and Location fields in the pivot table by pivoting their fields: Drag the Dept column field and then drop it on top of the Location row field. Then, drag the Location row field up and drop it on cell B4 to the immediate right of the Sum of Salary cell (A4) to make it into the column field.

Note that you change how the fields function in the pivot table by dragging them to new positions in the table. To remove a field from the pivot table, drag it to a cell outside the confines of the table. When you release the mouse button, Excel deletes the field from the table (but not the PivotTable Field List in case you need to add it again somewhere).

2. Drag the Gender field down and drop it on cell C4 to the immediate right of the Location column field to convert it from a page field to a second column field and then select M as the sole criteria to use in displaying the data.

Click the Gender field's drop-down button, remove the check mark from the (All) item, and then put a check mark in the M check box before you select OK.

Note that when the Gender field is added to the column fields, it acts like a subtotaling field so that the pivot table can now display columns with subtotals of the men's and women's salaries as well as the one with their grand total.

3. Add the Years of Service field as a second row field in the pivot table.

In the PivotTable Field List dialog box, click Row Area in the drop-down list, and then click the Years of Service field in the list before you select the Add To button.

Adding Years of Service as a second row field in the pivot table adds another level of subtotals, this time across the rows of the table.

4. Set the criteria of the Gender column field to (Show All) so that pivot table contains the salaries totals for both the men and women.

5. Right-click cell B6 and then select Hide on the shortcut menu.

Hiding a field is another method for removing it from the pivot table because the only way to redisplay the field is to add it from the PivotTable Field List dialog box to the pivot table again.

6. Hide the Gender field in the columns of the pivot table and then add it back to the table as a second page field.

7. Position the cell cursor in cell A1 of the Pivot Table worksheet and then save your modifications to the pivot table in a new workbook file named **Solved19-4.xls** in your Chapter 19 folder in the My Practice Spreadsheets folder. Leave the workbook file open for Exercise 19-5.

Changing the table summary function and adding calculated fields

By default, Excel uses the SUM function to total the values in the numeric field(s) that you assign as the data items in the pivot table. Some data summaries require the use of another summary function such as the AVERAGE or COUNT function. To change the summary function, double-click the label of the field used as a data item or click this label (this label is located at the cell intersection of the first column and row field in a pivot table that has only one data field and uses the default or classic table format). Then, select Field Settings on the PivotTable drop-down list on the PivotTable toolbar to open its PivotTable Field dialog box, where you can select any of the following summary functions in the Summarize By list box:

✔ **Count** to show the count of the records for a particular category (note that Count is the default setting for any text fields that you use as Data Items in a pivot table)

✔ **Average** to calculate the average (that is, the arithmetic mean) for the values in the field for the current category and page filter

✔ **Max** to display the largest numeric value in that field for the current category and page filter

✔ **Min** to display the smallest numeric value in that field for the current category and page filter

✔ **Product** to display the product of the numeric values in that field for the current category and page filter (all non-numeric entries are ignored)

✔ **Count Nums** to display the number of numeric values in that field for the current category and page filter (all non-numeric entries are ignored)

✔ **StdDev** to display the standard deviation for the sample in that field for the current category and page filter

✔ **StdDevp** to display the standard deviation for the population in that field for the current category and page filter

✔ **Var** to display the variance for the sample in that field for the current category and page filter

✔ **Varp** to display the variance for the population in that field for the current category and page filter

After you select the new summary function to use in the Summarize By list box of its PivotTable Field dialog box, click the OK button to have Excel apply the new function to the data presented in the body of the pivot table.

In addition to using various summary functions on the data presented in your pivot table, you can create your own calculated fields for the pivot table. Calculated fields are computed by assigning a formula using existing numeric fields in the data source.

After you finish defining a calculated field to a pivot table, Excel automatically adds its name to the PivotTable Field List dialog box and assigns it as a data item in the data area of the pivot table. The program also adds a new data field and makes it the first column field in the pivot table.

If you want to hide a calculated field from the body of the pivot table, click the data field's drop-down button. Click the name of the calculated field to remove the check mark from its check box before you click the menu's OK button. To add the calculated field back into the pivot table, click its field name in the PivotTable Field List dialog box (by clicking the Show Field List button on the PivotTable toolbar), and then select Data Area in the drop-down list box at the bottom of the dialog box before you select the Add To button.

Try It

Exercise 19-5: Modifying the Summary Functions and Adding a Calculated Field to a Pivot Table

Use the *Solved19-4.xls* worksheet with the modified pivot table you created in the previous exercise to practice modifying the summary function as well as to add a calculated field to your pivot table:

1. Double-click the Sum of Salary cell, A4, in the Pivot Table worksheet to open its PivotTable Field dialog box and then select Average in the Summarize By list box before you select OK.

The body of your pivot table now displays the average salary for each location and department in the company.

2. Change the summary function from AVERAGE to MAX so that the table shows you the highest salaries for each location and department in the company.

3. Restore SUM as the summary function in the table and then, in the PivotTable toolbar, select Formulas⇨Calculated Field on the PivotTable drop-down button to open the Insert Calculated Field dialog box.

Here, you will define the parameters for a Bonus field that calculates bonuses as 2.5% of the employee's salary.

4. Type **Bonus** in the Name text box in the Insert Calculated Field dialog box.

5. Select the Formula text box, delete the 0 (zero) after the = (equal to) sign (which you want to retain), and then click Salary in the Fields list box followed by the Insert Field button.

The Formula text box should now read

```
=Salary
```

6. Type * (asterisk) followed by **0.025** in the Formula text box.

The Formula text box should now contain the complete formula

```
=Salary*0.025
```

7. Select the Add button to add the new Bonus field to end of the fields listed in the Fields list box and then select OK.

As soon as the Insert Calculated Field dialog box closes, you see that Excel has added your Bonus field (as Sum of Bonus) as a data item to the body of the pivot table. You also note that Bonus appears at the very bottom of the list box in the PivotTable Field List dialog box.

8. Position the cell cursor in cell A1 of the Pivot Table worksheet and then save your changes to the pivot table in a new workbook file named **Solved19-5.xls** in your Chapter 19 folder in the My Practice Spreadsheets folder. Close the workbook file.

Creating Pivot Charts

You can spice up your data summaries quite a bit by generating a pivot chart along with a supporting pivot table. To do this, you follow the same procedure as you do when creating a sole pivot table except that you click the PivotChart Report (with PivotTable Report) option button in the PivotTable and PivotChart Wizard - Step 1 of 1 dialog box.

When creating a new pivot chart with a pivot table, Excel always places the pivot chart on a new chart sheet regardless of whether you place the associated pivot table on a new worksheet or elect to place it somewhere on the worksheet that's current when you open the PivotTable and PivotChart wizard. Figure 19-2 shows you how a typical pivot chart appears in its own chart sheet right after you click the Finish button in the PivotTable and PivotChart Wizard - Step 1 of 3 dialog box.

As with the pivot table, you can assign fields to the pivot chart by dragging them to the designated areas in the chart (Drop Page Fields Here, Drop Data Items Here, Drop Series Fields Here, or Drop Category Fields Here). Alternatively, you can click the field name in the Task Pane Field List, select the name of the chart area to which to assign the field in the drop-down list box at the bottom of the Task pane, and finally click the Add To button to its immediate left.

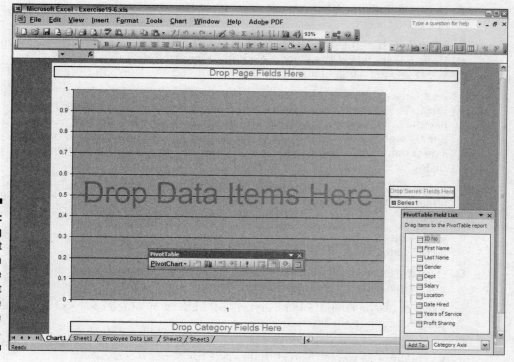

Figure 19-2:
Generating
a new pivot
chart on a
separate
Chart sheet
from the
Employee
Data List.

Although Excel always chooses the Column chart as the basic chart type for each
new pivot chart you generate, you can select another chart type for the pivot chart:
Simply click the Chart Wizard button on the PivotTable toolbar or on the Standard
toolbar to open the Chart Wizard - Step 1 of 4 dialog box. There, you can select a
new chart type from among those types displayed on the Standard Types or the
Custom Types tab. When selecting a new chart type on the Standard Types tab,
be sure that you click the Press and Hold to View Sample button so that you can
see exactly how your pivot chart appears in the selected type. (You may be sur-
prised to see how Excel has to "pivot" the chart's fields to accommodate the
new chart type.)

Try It

Exercise 19-6: Creating a Pivot Chart

Open the workbook *Exercise19-6.xls* in your Chapter 19 folder in the My Practice
Spreadsheets folder on your hard disk or in the Excel Workbook folder on the workbook CD-ROM. This workbook contains a copy of the Employee Data List worksheet
with the data list you will use in creating a pivot table chart:

1. Choose the Data⇨PivotTable and PivotTable Chart Report menu command to
open the PivotTable and PivotTable Wizard – Step 1 of 3 dialog box.

2. Select the PivotChart Report (with PivotTable report) option button under the
heading, What Kind of Report Do You Want to Create? and then select the Next
button.

3. Make sure that Excel has correctly selected the cell range of the Employee
Data List (which should appear in the Range text box as $A$1:$J$33) before

you select the Next button in the PivotTable and PivotTable Wizard – Step 2 of 3 dialog box.

4. Make sure that the New Worksheet button is selected under the heading, Where Do You Want to Put the PivotTable Report? in the PivotTable and PivotTable Wizard – Step 3 of 3 dialog box before you select the Finish button.

    As soon as you select the Finish button to close the PivotTable and PivotTable Wizard – Step 2 of 3 dialog box, Excel adds two new sheets: A Chart1 sheet like the one shown in Figure 19-2 where you build the pivot chart, and a Sheet1 worksheet where Excel builds a pivot table associated with the chart. The program also displays the PivotTable toolbar and the PivotTable Field List dialog box.

5. In the PivotTable Field List dialog box, select the Location field and then, while Category Axis is selected in its drop-down list box, select the Add To button.

    Excel adds the names of the various company sites along the bottom of the chart as the Category Axis titles.

6. Drag the Salary field from the PivotTable Field List dialog box and drop it on chart area with the text, *Drop Data Items Here*.

    Excel draws pale blue columns represented the sum of the salaries for each company location in the chart area.

7. Drag the Gender field from the PivotTable Field List dialog box and drop it on the legend area on top of the text that says, *Drop Series Fields Here*.

    Excel adds purple sections to the columns in the chart to represent the men's salaries, using the pale blue sections for the women's salaries (as indicated by the chart's legend). This chart has now become a Stacked Column chart, visually representing the two data series in a single column.

8. Add the Profit Sharing field as the pages field for this Stacked Column chart.

    You can use this page field to modify the chart so that it represents the sum of all the salaries, the sum of the salaries of just those who are part of the profit-sharing plan, or the sum of the salaries of just those who are not yet part of the plan.

9. Close the PivotTable Field List dialog box and then click the Chart Wizard button on the PivotTable toolbar.

    Excel opens the Chart Wizard – Step 1 of 4 – Chart Type dialog box.

10. Click the thumbnail of the Clustered Column chart in the Chart Sub-Type palette and then select the Finish button.

    Excel redraws the chart as a Clustered Column chart where pale blue columns represent the sum of the women's salaries at different company locations and the purple columns represent the sum of the men's salaries at these sites.

11. Right-click the Value (Y) axis (the vertical one) and then select Format Axis on its shortcut menu to open the Format Axis dialog box.

12. Click the Number tab and then select Currency with 0 (zero) decimal places as the number format for the value axis and select OK.

    The values on the Y-axis of the Clustered Bar pivot chart are now formatted using Currency style format with no decimal places.

13. Rename the Chart1 sheet to **Pivot Chart** and then reposition this sheet so that it follows the Employee Data List worksheet in the workbook.

14. Select the Sheet1 tab and then rename this worksheet tab to **Pivot Table**. Reposition this sheet between the Employee Data List and Pivot Chart sheets in the workbook.

Note that this pivot table created by Excel not only reflects the structure of the Clustered Column pivot chart that you just created but actually forms the basis from which the pivot chart is drawn. This means that any changes that you make to the underlying pivot table immediately affects the structure of the associated pivot chart as well.

15. Select cell A1 on the Employee Data List worksheet and then save your work with the filename **Solved19-6.xls** in your Chapter 19 folder in the My Practice Spreadsheets folder. Close the workbook file as you exit Excel.

Part VI
Excel and the Web

The 5th Wave · By Rich Tennant

"You know kids — you can't buy them just any spreadsheet creation software."

In this part . . .

Like it or not, the Internet is not going away anytime soon. And, as Part VI proves, Excel very much buttresses this amazing online phenomenon through its support of workbook-to-Web-page conversion and Web-page type hyperlinks attached to the cells and graphics in its spreadsheets. Here, you get a chance to try your hand at both converting worksheets to Web pages as well as adding hyperlinks to spreadsheets that instantly connect you to other sheets in the same workbook file, other workbook files on the same disk, as well as to pages and e-mail addresses on the World Wide Web.

Chapter 20

Publishing Spreadsheets as Web Pages

• •

In This Chapter

▶ Saving the worksheet as a static Web page

▶ Saving the worksheet as a Web page with an interactive data table, data list, pivot table, and chart

▶ Exporting data from an interactive Web page to Excel

▶ Adding data from a Web page to a worksheet

• •

With the continuing growth and accessibility to the World Wide Web, HTML (Hypertext Markup Language) and XML (Extensible Markup Language) file formats — once pretty much exclusive to the arena of Web servers — have become more and more common file types understood and used by almost any program running on personal computers. This is so much the case that Excel can now not only save workbooks in the HTML or XML file formats but open them for editing within the program as well.

In this chapter, you get a chance to practice converting Excel spreadsheets to HTML Web pages for use on the Internet or the company intranet. As part of this practice, you not only create static Web pages whose data are frozen but interactive Web pages that users who view the pages with Internet Explorer (version 4.0 or later) can edit online. You also get to practice importing data from Web pages on the Internet directly into your Excel worksheets using the program's Web Query feature.

Saving Worksheets as Web Pages

Converting your favorite spreadsheet into a Web page ready for publishing on the World Wide Web is no more difficult than opening the worksheet and then choosing the Excel File⇨Save As Web Page command from its Menu bar.

However, before you take this simple step, you normally want to see how the spreadsheet appears in the HTML file format when viewed in your default Web browser by choosing the File⇨Web Page Preview command. Doing this launches your computer's default Web browser (usually Internet Explorer, unless you've specifically installed and selected another one) and displays the spreadsheet more or less as it will appear in that browser when saved as an HTML file.

Creating static Web pages

When you open the Save As dialog box after choosing File➪Save As Web Page (shown in Figure 20-1), Excel gives you a choice between saving all the pages of the entire workbook as an HTML file or just the worksheet(s) or chart sheet(s) that you've selected. After designating the name of the new HTML file (with the .htm filename extension), you can simply click the Save button to go ahead and convert the spreadsheet data and create the Web file.

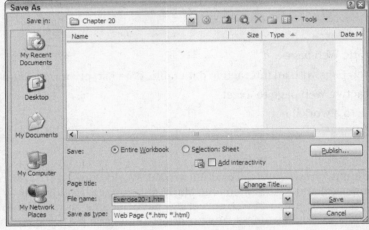

Figure 20-1: The Save As dialog box after choosing the File➪Save As Web Page command.

When you save an entire workbook that contains several sheets of data, Excel saves all the data on each sheet. If you then open the new HTML file in the Internet Explorer, the Web page even retains its original sheet structure and layout.

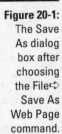

Try It

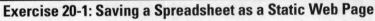

Exercise 20-1: Saving a Spreadsheet as a Static Web Page

If Excel is not currently running, launch the program. Open the workbook *Exercise20-1.xls* in your Chapter 20 folder in the My Practice Spreadsheets folder on your hard disk or in the Excel Workbook folder on the workbook CD-ROM. This workbook contains a version of the CG Media 2006 Sales workbook containing three worksheets — 2006 Sales, 2007 Q1, and Sales Bar Chart — that you will use to practice saving spreadsheets as Web pages:

1. Choose the File➪Web Page Preview menu command to open this workbook in your Web browser.

2. If you use Internet Explorer as your Web browser, click the 2006 Sales, 2007 Q1, and Sales Bar Chart tabs at the bottom of the Explorer window to view all three pages in the preview of the *Exercise20-1.htm* file.

When you view a Web page created from an Excel workbook with multiple worksheets in Internet Explorer, the page contains tabs as well as buttons that you can use to move from sheet to sheet.

3. Close the Web browser window with workbook-as-Web page preview and then, back in Excel, choose the File➪Save as Web Page menu command to open the Save As dialog box.

4. Make sure that the Chapter 20 folder in the My Practice Spreadsheets folder is open in the Save In list box in the Save As dialog box.

5. Accept the default filename *Exercise20-1.htm* and then make sure that the Entire Workbook option button is selected before you select the Save button to create the Web file.

6. Open the Chapter 20 folder on your hard disk in Windows Explorer.

   Click the Start button on the Windows taskbar, select My Documents, and then double-click the My Practice Spreadsheets Folder icon followed by the Chapter 20 folder icon.

   Notice that in addition to adding an *Exercise20-1.htm* file icon, converting the *Exercise20-1.xls* file to HTML has caused Excel to create an Exercise20-1_files folder. This folder contains the all files needed to add the paging tabs to the Web page when viewed with Internet Explorer.

7. Double-click the *Exercise20-1.htm* file icon to open it with your Web browser.

   If you're viewing the Web page with Internet Explorer, use the page tabs to view the data in the 2007 first quarter sales data as well as the bar chart. Note, however, that if you're using Internet Explorer 6.0 to view this Web page, the security settings render the tab navigation buttons inoperable.

8. Close the Web browser and Chapter 20 windows to return to the Excel worksheet and then expand the outline in the spreadsheet table to show all the data on the 2006 Sales worksheet by clicking the three buttons to the left and above the row and column headers.

9. Preview the expanded version of 2006 Sales worksheet as a Web page, and then close the Web browser window and open the Save As dialog box for saving worksheets as Web pages (File⇨Save as Web Page).

10. Select the Selection: Sheet option button and then rename the *Page.htm* suggested filename to **CG Sales 2006.htm** before you select the Save button.

11. Open the new *CG Sales 2006.htm* file in your Web browser and then close all open windows to return to Excel, where you close the *Exercise20-1.xls* workbook file without saving any changes.

Creating interactive Web pages

If you know the users of the spreadsheets you convert to Web pages are going to be viewing them with Internet Explorer (Version 4.0 or later), you can make it possible for them to modify the worksheet data on the Web pages by selecting the Add Interactivity check box in the Save As dialog box when you first save them as Web pages.

Note, however, that before users of one of these later versions of the Internet Explorer can take advantage of the spreadsheet Web page interactivity in Internet Explorer, they must also have installed the Microsoft Office Web Components on their computer. These utilities are not automatically installed when you do a standard installation of Office XP, so you may have to take time out and install them using the Add or Remove Programs Control panel (the Office XP Web Components are part of Office Shared Features group in the Features to Install list box in the Microsoft Office XP Setup dialog box).

Figure 20-2 shows you how a typical interactive data table appears on a new Web page after opening it with Internet Explorer 6.0. Notice that the interactive table is self-contained, with a toolbar at the top and a facsimile of the worksheet row and column header at the top, and vertical and horizontal scroll bars on the right and at the bottom. Notice also that this table uses gridlines to demarcate the cells and sports a sheet tab at the bottom like a regular Excel workbook window.

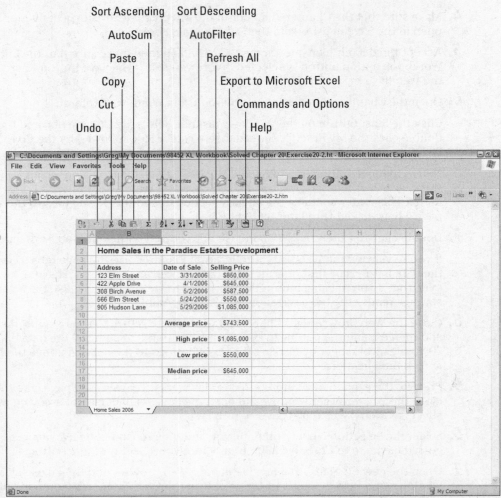

Figure 20-2:
Web page
with an
interactive
worksheet
data table
opened in
Internet
Explorer.

The Office Web Components add a horizontal and vertical scroll bar to the interactive table because you have no way to resize the table. You must use the scroll buttons to bring new parts of the data table into view on the Web page. Likewise, they automatically display the row and column headers to give you a way to widen or narrow the columns and heighten or shorten the rows by dragging the appropriate border of a column letter or row number.

Despite the obvious similarities to the standard workbook window, there are some noticeable differences as well. Most significant is the fact that the interactive spreadsheet table has no Formula bar or Menu bar.

Because there's no Formula bar, you can't tell which values in the table are calculated by formula and which are input as constants. It also means that the only way to edit any of the table cells is by double-clicking the cell and then editing the entry there (at which time, you can immediately tell whether it's a value or formula that you're editing).

Web pages with interactive data tables

When you create interactive Web pages with spreadsheet data tables, users who are running Microsoft Office Web Components on their computer and view the pages with

Internet Explorer can modify the formatting of the table's cell entries as well as edit the contents of their cells. If automatic recalculation is turned on when the interactive Web page is created, the formulas in the spreadsheet table that refer to those modified cells are updated as well.

Try It

Exercise 20-2: Creating a Web Page with an Interactive Data Table

Open the workbook _Exercise20-2.xls_ in your Chapter 20 folder in the My Practice Spreadsheets folder on your hard disk or in the Excel Workbook folder on the workbook CD-ROM. This workbook contains a copy of the Home Sales spreadsheet data table that you will use to practice creating a Web page with an interactive worksheet:

_1._ Choose File⇨Save as Web Page to open the Save As dialog box and there select the Selection: Sheet option button and the Add Interactivity check box before you click the Publish button.

Excel then opens the Publish as Web Page dialog box, where you specify the filename for the interactive Web page as well as make sure that the page is created with interactive spreadsheet functionality.

_2._ Make sure that Items on Home Sales 2006 is selected in the Choose text box, that Sheet with All Contents of Home Sales is highlighted in the list box below, that the Add Interactivity check box is selected, and that Spreadsheet Functionality is selected in the drop-down list box to its right.

_3._ Select the Browse button to open the Publish As dialog box with the Chapter 20 folder selected and then replace _Page.htm_ with **Exercise 20-2.htm** (be sure that you retain the .htm filename extension) before you select OK.

_4._ In the Publish as Web Page dialog box, select the Open Published Web Page in Browser check box and then select its Publish button.

After saving the spreadsheet data table in the _Exercise20-2.htm_ Web page, Internet Explorer opens this new HTML document. In later versions of Internet Explorer, a security message appears on the Information bar at the top of the program. The Window and Security alert dialog box then appears. If this happens, select OK in the alert dialog box. Right-click the Information Bar and click Allow Blocked Content on the shortcut menu followed by selecting Yes in yet another Security Warning dialog box. (There now, don't you feel safe?)

After the Web page opens, note that the interactive spreadsheet data table now contains a toolbar like the one shown in Figure 20-2.

_5._ Click the Commands and Options button on the toolbar to open the Commands and Options dialog box.

This dialog box contains four tabs of options: Format, Formula, Sheet, and Workbook.

_6._ Select the cell range B4:D4 in the data table by dragging through their cells and then click the Italic and Center buttons in the Text Format section of the Format tab.

The table's column headings are now centered in their cells and their text is italicized.

_7._ Select all the cells in the table (A4:D98) and then click the All button in the Border section of the Format tab.

All the cells in the data tab are now outlined with a border.

_8._ Click cell D4 with the Selling Price column heading and then click the Sort Descending button on the toolbar.

All the cells in the table are now sorted by selling price from highest to lowest.

9. Click the Sheet tab in the Commands and Options dialog box and then click the Row Headers, Column Headers, and Gridlines check box to remove their check marks.

   The column and row headings as well as the worksheet gridlines are now removed from the spreadsheet data table.

10. Click the Workbook tab in the Commands and Options dialog box and then click the Sheet Selector check box to remove its check mark.

    The Home Sales 2006 sheet tab is now removed from the spreadsheet data table.

11. Select the Manual option button in the Calculation section on the Workbook tab and then double-click the cell with the selling price of 422 Apple Drive in the table and replace its current 645000 entry with **750000** before you press the Enter key.

12. Select the Calculate button in the Calculation section on the Workbook tab.

    The Web Components now update the Average price, High price, Low price, and Median price cells in the interactive spreadsheet data table.

13. Select the Toolbar check box in the Show/Hide section of the Workbook tab to remove its check mark and then click the Close button in the upper-right corner of the Commands and Options dialog box to close it.

    The interactive toolbar now disappears from the spreadsheet data table.

Note that you can always restore the toolbar by right-clicking any cell in the interactive spreadsheet data table and then selecting Commands and Options on its shortcut menu to reopen the Commands and Options dialog box. From there, you can then reselect the Toolbar check box on the Workbook tab.

14. Choose the File⇨Print Preview Internet Explorer menu command to display the interactive spreadsheet data table in the Print Preview window.

15. If you have access to a printer, click the Print button on the Print Preview toolbar to print the Web page. Otherwise, click the Close button to return to the regular Web page without printing the page.

16. Close the Internet Explorer and then close the *Exercise20-2.xls* workbook in Excel without saving any changes to it.

Web pages with interactive data lists

When you create interactive Web pages with data lists, your users can sort and filter the data in the list as well as modify individual entries in the records and make formatting changes to parts of the list. To filter the data in the Web, users turn on AutoFilter drop-down buttons that work just like those in a regular Excel data list (see Chapter 16).

Try It

Exercise 20-3: Creating a Web Page with an Interactive Data List

Open the workbook *Exercise20-3.xls* in your Chapter 20 folder in the My Practice Spreadsheets folder on your hard disk or in the Excel Workbook folder on the workbook CD-ROM. This workbook contains a copy of the Employee data list that you can use to practice creating a Web page with an interactive data list:

1. Choose File⇨Save as Web Page to open the Save As dialog box. Select the Selection: Sheet option button and the Add Interactivity check box before you select the Publish button.

2. Make sure that Items on Employee Data List is selected in the Choose text box, that Sheet with All Contents of Employee Data List is highlighted in the list box below, and that the Add Interactivity check box and Spreadsheet Functionality in the drop-down list box to its right are selected.

3. Select the Browse button to open the Publish As dialog box with the Chapter 20 folder selected and then replace *Page.htm* with **Exercise 20-3.htm** (be sure that you retain the .htm filename extension) before you select OK.

4. In the Publish as Web Page dialog box, select the Open Published Web Page in Browser check box and then select its Publish button.

After saving the data list in the *Exercise20-3.htm* Web page, Internet Explorer opens the data list complete with a toolbar in the new HTML document.

5. Click the AutoFilter button on the data list's toolbar to add AutoFilter drop-down buttons to each of the fields in the data list.

6. Filter the data list so that only the records of the female employees are displayed in the interactive worksheet.

Click the (Show All) check box in the Gender field's drop-down list to deselect all the check boxes and then click the F check box before selecting OK.

7. Sort the data list alphabetically by department name.

Click the cell with the Dept field name (E1) and then click the Sort Ascending button on the data list toolbar.

8. Use the horizontal scroll bar to display the Profit Sharing field and then filter the list so that only the female employees who participate in the profit-sharing plan are displayed in the data list.

9. Remove the row and column headings, gridlines, sheet tab, and toolbar from the data list and then, if you have a printer available, print the filtered and sorted data.

Deselect the appropriate check boxes on the Sheet and Workbook tabs of the Commands and Options dialog box to remove the row and column headings, gridlines, sheet tab, and toolbar from the interactive data list.

10. Close Internet Explorer and then the *Exercise20-3.xls* workbook in Excel without saving your changes.

Web pages with interactive pivot tables

When you create interactive Web pages with pivot tables, your users can pivot the fields in a table, add new fields to the table, refresh the table data from the external data source (assuming that this source is accessible from the Web page), show details for any of the summarized data in the table, add calculated fields to the table, and page through the summaries using different items in the page fields (see Chapter 19).

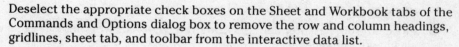

Exercise 20-4: Creating a Web Page with an Interactive Pivot Table

Open the workbook *Exercise20-4.xls* in your Chapter 20 folder in the My Practice Spreadsheets folder on your hard disk or in the Excel Workbook folder on the workbook CD-ROM. This workbook contains a pivot table generated from a copy of the Employee data list that you can use to practice creating a Web page with an interactive pivot table:

1. Choose File➪Save as Web Page to open the Save As dialog box and there select the Selection: Sheet option button and the Add Interactivity check box before you click the Publish button.

2. Make sure that Items on Employee Pivot List is selected in the Choose text box, Pivot Table with PivotTable2 ($A$1:$G$13) is highlighted in the list box below, and that the Add Interactivity check box and PivotTable Functionality in the drop-down list box to its right are selected.

3. Select the Browse button to open the Publish As dialog box with the Chapter 20 folder selected and then replace *Page.htm* with **Exercise 20-4.htm** (be sure that you retain the .htm filename extension) before you select OK.

4. In the Publish as Web Page dialog box, select the Open Published Web Page in Browser check box and then select its Publish button.

After saving the data list in the *Exercise20-4.htm* Web page, the Internet Explorer opens the PivotTable2 worksheet complete with toolbar in the new HTML document.

5. Click the Field List button on the pivot table toolbar (the button immediately to the left of the Help button with the question mark) to display the PivotTable Field List dialog box and then use it to convert the Dept field from the table's column field to its row field.

Select the Dept field in list box in the PivotTable Field List dialog box and then click the Add To button while Row Area is selected in the drop-down list box to its immediate right.

6. In the interactive pivot table, drag the Location row heading to the area marked Drop Column Fields Here to make the Location field the table's sole column field.

7. Close the PivotTable Field List dialog box and then filter the pivot table by selecting M for the Gender page field and No for the Profit Sharing page field.

Deselect the (All) selection on the page field's drop-down list before you select the M or No check box followed by the OK button.

8. Close Internet Explorer and then the *Exercise20-4.xls* workbook in Excel without saving your changes.

Web pages with interactive charts

When you create interactive Web pages with charts, your users can edit the supporting data that is automatically shown beneath the chart as an attached data table and have the chart automatically updated on the page (see Chapter 14).

Try It

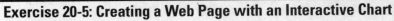

Exercise 20-5: Creating a Web Page with an Interactive Chart

Open the workbook *Exercise20-5.xls* in your Chapter 20 folder in the My Practice Spreadsheets folder on your hard disk or in the Excel Workbook folder on the workbook CD-ROM. This workbook contains a copy of the 2006 Production Schedule data table with an embedded Clustered Column chart immediately beneath it. You will use this embedded chart to practice creating a Web page with an interactive chart:

1. Choose File➪Save as Web Page to open the Save As dialog box and there select the Selection: Sheet option button and the Add Interactivity check box before you select the Publish button.

2. Make sure that Items on 2006 Production is selected in the Choose text box, that Chart with Chart1 (Column) is highlighted in the list box below, and that the Add Interactivity check box and Chart Functionality in the drop-down list box to its right are selected.

3. Select the Browse button to open the Publish As dialog box with the Chapter 20 folder selected and then replace *Page.htm* with **Exercise 20-5.htm** (be sure that you retain the .htm filename extension) before you select OK.

4. In the Publish as Web Page dialog box, select the Open Published Web Page in Browser check box and then select its Publish button.

    After saving the data list in the *Exercise20-5.htm* Web page, Internet Explorer opens the Scheduled Production – 2006 Clustered Column chart with the data table immediately beneath it, complete with toolbar in the new HTML document.

5. Scroll down to display the chart's supporting data table and then make the following changes to the designated cells, noting the changes to the associated columns in the chart above as you update each entry:

    • **350** in cell C3 with production quota for Part 101 in May 2006

    • **380** in cell F3 with production quota for Part 101 in August 2006

    • **650** in cell E5 with production quota for Part 103 in July 2006

6. Close Internet Explorer and then the *Exercise20-5.xls* workbook in Excel without saving your changes.

Exporting an interactive Web page to Excel

Unfortunately, you can't save any of the changes that you make to an interactive Web page in Internet Explorer. The only way that you can save any of the formatting or editing changes you to make to an interactive data table, data list, or pivot table is to export the page back to Excel as an .XML (Extensible Markup Language) file and then save the changes there.

To do this, you click the Export to Microsoft Excel button (the one with the green XL logo with a pencil) on the toolbar at the top of the interactive table or list. Clicking this button launches Excel on your computer and opens the interactive table or list with your edits. (In the case of interactive charts, only the data table attached to the chart opens in Excel, not the chart itself.)

The .XML file that opens in the Excel window is given a temporary filename, something like OWCSheet1.XML (OWC stands for Office Web Components), that appears on the Excel program window's title bar followed by the (Read Only) to indicate that the file is open in read-only mode. This means that you must choose the File⇨Save As command to save the Web page's changes on your disk. In the Save As dialog box, you can save the file by giving it a new filename in the File Name text box (anything's better than OWCSheet followed by a number!) and selecting a new folder (all OWCSheet files are automatically saved in the Temp folder on your hard disk).

Note that Excel automatically saves the file as an .XML file, the type of HTML that enables you to interact with it in the Internet Explorer. If you're not concerned about saving the interactivity and only want to be able to open the edited data table or list in Excel, remember to change the Save as Type setting from XML Spreadsheet (*.xml) to Microsoft Excel Workbook (*.xls).

Exercise 20-6: Exporting the Spreadsheet Data in a Web Page Back to Excel

Open the workbook *Exercise20-2.htm* Web page you created earlier in Exercise 20-2 and saved in your Chapter 20 folder in the My Practice Spreadsheets folder with Internet Explorer. You will use the Home Sales data table in this Web page to practice saving changes made in an interactive Web page back to Excel:

1. Make the same formatting and editing changes to the Home Sales data table that you did in Exercise 20-2 by referring to steps 5 through 12 in this exercise.

2. Close the Command and Options dialog box and then click the Export to Microsoft Excel button to open the formatted and edited Home Sales table in Excel as an XML file with an OWCSheet filename.

3. Choose Tools⇨Options to open the Options dialog box and then select the Gridlines check box on the View menu and the Automatic option button on the Calculation tab before you select OK.

Now you're ready to save the changes you made to the Home Sales table in Internet Explorer as well as the changes you just made in Excel.

4. Choose File⇨Save As to open the Save As dialog box and then click the My Documents button in the left pane.

5. Double-click the My Practice Spreadsheets folder icon in the My Document list box and then double-click the Chapter 20 folder icon in the My Practice Spreadsheets list box.

6. Click the File Name text box and then type **Solved20-6.xml** as the new workbook's filename before you select the Save button.

7. Close your new *Solved20-6.xml* file containing the formatted and edited Home Sales table, but don't exit Excel.

Doing a Web Query

You can use Excel's Web Query feature to extract text or tables (or a combination of the two) from Web pages on the World Wide Web and bring their data into an Excel worksheet. Doing a Web query is a lot like performing the external database query you did in Chapter 16 (with many fewer steps) that extract data from Web pages on the Internet instead of from an external database.

The key to being able to do a Web query is having the URL address of the Web site whose data you want to query (you know, the `http://`-type address that appears on the Address bar of your Web browser when you visit a site). You must have this address handy at the time you start the new Web query because the New Web Query dialog box does not provide a way to search the Internet nor does it give you access to your Web favorites as you have in your Web browser.

 Often the best way to do capture the URL address for the page you want to query is to visit the Web site in your Web browser (using your Web favorites or it search capability), and then select the URL address that appears on the Web browser's Address bar and copy it into the Clipboard with the Edit⇨Copy menu command or Ctrl+C. Then, switch over to Excel, select the text currently displayed in the Address bar of the New Web Query dialog box (refer to the steps that follow), and paste the page's URL address in this text box by pressing Ctrl+V. (You must use this shortcut as you don't have access to the Edit⇨Paste command on the Excel pull-down menus from within a dialog box.)

Exercise 20-7: Importing Web Data into Excel with a Web Query

Open a new workbook in Excel and use it to practice saving data from the World Wide Web in an Excel worksheet:

1. Choose Data⇨Import External Data⇨New Web Query to open the New Web Query dialog box.

When Excel first opens the New Web Query dialog box, it connects you to the Home page set in your Web browser.

2. Type www.yahoo.com in the Address bar and then select the Go button the top of the New Web Query dialog box.

The New Web Query dialog box opens the Yahoo! Home page.

3. Click the Finance link on the Yahoo! Home Page to open the Yahoo! Finance page, and then click the Mutual Funds link on this page.

4. Scroll down and then click the Top Performers link on the Mutual Funds Center page. Next click Overall Top Performers link at the top of the Mutual Fund Top Performers page.

5. Click the yellow button with the right arrow in front of the Top Performers – 3 Month, Top Performers – 1 Year, and Top Performers – 3 Year tables to select them for importing.

6. Select the Import button in the New Web Query dialog box.

As soon as you select Import, the New Web Query dialog box closes and the Import Data dialog box appears. This dialog box gives you a choice between importing the Web data in the current worksheet (stating with the current cell) and a new worksheet.

7. Select the Properties button at the bottom of the Import Data dialog box.

Excel opens the External Data Range Properties dialog box with many settings controlling how the Web data are imported.

8. Replace all in the Name box by entering **3-mo, 1-yr, 3-yr Top Mutual Funds** in this text box before you select OK.

Excel closes the External Data Range Properties dialog box, returning you to the Import Data dialog box.

9. Leave the Existing Worksheet option button selected and =$A$1 in its text box and then select OK in the Import Data dialog box.

10. Excel enters the name of the Web query, 3-mo, 1-yr, 3-yr Top Mutual Funds: Getting Data, in cell A1 and then replaces this query name with the imported data from these three tables on the Yahoo! Mutual Fund Top Performers Web page.

Excel then copies the data from the Yahoo! Top Performers - 3-mo, - 1 Year, and – 3 Year tables into your worksheet. The program also displays the External Data floating toolbar in the worksheet (see Figure 20-3).

11. Click the Edit Query button on the External Data toolbar to open the Edit Web Query dialog box and then click the Save Query button (the one with the Disk icon to the immediate left of the Options button) on the toolbar at the top of the dialog box.

12. Accept the suggested filename, *3-mo, 1-yr, 3-yr Top Mutual Fund.iqy*, as the name for this Web query and then select the Save button.

By saving your Web query in an .iqy file (Internet query), you make it possible to rerun the query with updated data at any later time simply by choosing Data⇨ Import External Data⇨Import Data and then selecting query name (*3-mo, 1-yr, 3-yr Top Mutual Fund.iqy* in this case) in the Select Data Source dialog box before selecting the Open button.

13. Click the Close button in the upper-right corner of the Edit Web Query dialog box.

14. Save your Web query data in a new workbook named **Solved20-7.xls** in your Chapter 20 folder in the My Practice Spreadsheets folder on your hard disk and then close the workbook as you exit Excel.

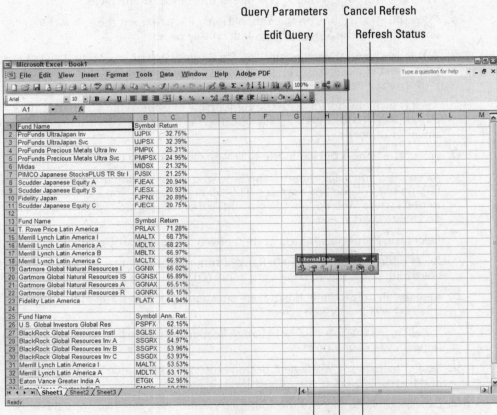

Figure 20-3: Worksheet with data imported from the Yahoo! Mutual Fund Top Performers Web page.

Chapter 21

Adding Hyperlinks to Spreadsheets

Hyperlinks are the kinds of links used on the World Wide Web to take you immediately from one Web page to another or from one Web site to another. In an Excel worksheet, you can attach hyperlinks to text (thus the term, *hypertext*) or to graphics such as buttons or pictures. Worksheet links can take you to a different part of the same worksheet, another worksheet in the same workbook, to another workbook or other type of document on your hard disk, or to a Web page on your company's intranet or on the World Wide Web.

In this chapter, you get a chance to practice creating these different types of hyperlinks and then assigning them to buttons on custom toolbars and to items on custom pull-down menus.

Creating Hyperlinks

To add hyperlinks in an Excel worksheet, you must define two things:

✔ The object on which to anchor the link (this is the object you then click to activate the hyperlink).

✔ The destination to which you go when you activate the link.

The objects onto which you can attach hyperlinks include any text that you enter into a cell or any graphic object that you draw or import into the worksheet (see Chapter 15). The destinations that you can specify for links can be to a new cell or range in the same workbook file or to another file outside of the workbook.

The destinations you can specify for hyperlinks that take you to another place in the same workbook file include

✔ **Cell reference** of a cell on any of the worksheets in the workbook that you want to go to when you click the hyperlink

✔ **Range name** of the group of cells that you want to select when you click the hyperlink — the range name must already exist at the time you create the link

The destinations you can specify for hyperlinks that take you outside of the current workbook include

- **Filename** for an existing file that you want to open when you click the hyperlink — this file can be another workbook file or any other type of document that your computer can open.

- **URL address** of a Web page that you want to visit when you click the hyperlink — this page can be on your company's intranet or the World Wide Web and is opened in your Web browser.

- **New document** that you want to create in Excel or some other program on your computer when you click the hyperlink — you must specify the filename and file extension (which indicates what type of document to create and what program to launch).

- **E-mail address** for a new message that you want to create in your e-mail program when you click the hyperlink — you must specify the recipient's e-mail address and the subject of the new message when creating the link.

Adding links to other sheets in a workbook

Perhaps the most common type of Excel hyperlink is the one that takes you from one sheet to another within the same workbook. You can use these links to move quickly between different tables and lists on the same or different worksheets without having to resort to the sheet tabs or tab scroll buttons.

Try It

Exercise 21-1: Adding Hyperlinks to Other Sheets in a Workbook

If Excel is not currently running, launch the program. Open the workbook *Exercise21-1.xls* in your Chapter 21 folder in the My Practice Spreadsheets folder on your hard disk or in the Excel Workbook folder on the workbook CD-ROM. This workbook contains a 12-Month worksheet with small monthly calendars for all 12 months of 2006. You will practice creating hyperlinks that take you to other sheets in the same workbook by adding links to each of the small monthly calendars on the 12-Month worksheet. Clicking these hyperlinks take you to the worksheet containing a larger version of the calendar for the comparable month:

1. Position the cell cursor in merged cell B2 with the January 2006 heading and then press Ctrl+K (for hyperlinK) or choose the Insert⇨Hyperlink menu command to open the Insert Hyperlink dialog box.

2. Click the Place in This Document button in the pane on the left under the heading *Link To,* and then click 'Jan-06' in the Or Select a Place in This Document list box before you select OK.

As soon as you select OK, Excel closes the Insert Hyperlink dialog box. The text *January 2006* in the merged B2 cell now appears underlined and in blue color, indicating that the text is now hypertext containing a link.

3. Position the mouse pointer somewhere over the *January 2006* hypertext in the merged cell B2 until the mouse pointer becomes a hand with the index finger as its pointer.

When the mouse pointer assumes the hand-with-pointing-finger form, a ScreenTip also appears underneath the pointer. The text in this tip indicates not only the destination of its hyperlink (including the cell and sheet reference and the entire path of the file), but also instructions that to follow the link you click it once, whereas to select the cell, you must click and hold.

4. Click the hypertext in the merged cell B2 to follow it.

As soon as you click the text, its hyperlink takes you to cell A1 on sheet Jan-06 of the *Exercise21-1.xls* practice workbook.

5. Choose the View⇨Toolbars⇨Web menu command to display the floating Web toolbar and then dock it at the bottom of the Excel window.

The Web toolbar contains buttons as well as an Address bar that you can use to navigate the hyperlinks you add to a workbook (see Figure 21-1).

6. Click the Back button on the Web toolbar to return to the merged cell B2 on the 12-Month worksheet.

7. On your own, add hyperlinks to the headings for all the other months (February 2006 through December 2006) on the 12-Month worksheet that take you to cell A1 of the comparable month worksheet in the *Exercise21-1.xls* workbook. For example, clicking the February 2006 link in the merged cell J2 should take you to cell A1 of the Feb-06 worksheet, the March 2006 link in the merged cell R2 should take you to cell A1 of the Mar-06 worksheet, and so on.

8. Check out all 12 hyperlinks that you create on the 12-Month worksheet to make sure that they take you to the correct worksheet in the *Exercise21-1.xls* workbook.

9. Save the version of the workbook with your hyperlinks as new file with the name **Solved21-1.xls** in your Chapter 21 folder in the My Practice Spreadsheets folder and then close the workbook file.

Figure 21-1:
The Web toolbar contains buttons that enable you to navigate hyperlinks in your worksheets as well as Web pages you visit.

Forward

Stop   Start Page   Show Only Web Toolbar

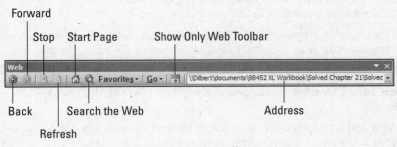

Back   Search the Web   Address

Refresh

Adding links to other documents

Instead of adding hyperlinks that take you to different worksheets in the same workbook, you can just as easily add links that open different files on your computer. These files are often other Excel workbooks that contain related information, but they can just as well be other non-Excel documents whose information you need to use.

When adding hyperlinks that open other non-Excel documents, just keep in mind that you need to have the program that created the other document installed on your computer for the hyperlink to function properly. (In the case of Microsoft Word and PowerPoint Office, however, you can download viewers from the Web that open and print native Word and PowerPoint documents, even if you don't have those programs installed.)

Exercise 21-2: Adding Hyperlinks to Other Documents

Open the workbook *Exercise21-2.xls* in your Chapter 21 folder in the My Practice Spreadsheets folder on your hard disk or in the Excel Workbook folder on the workbook CD-ROM. This workbook contains a copy of the Home Sales 2006 worksheet. In this exercise, you'll add a hyperlink to this worksheet that opens a copy of the 2006 Calendar workbook (complete with hyperlinks from the mini-calendars to the individual calendar sheets) that is also saved in your Chapter 21 folder:

1. Choose the Insert⇨Picture⇨From File menu command to open the Insert Picture dialog box.

2. Click the My Documents button in the pane on the left and then open the Chapter 21 folder in the Insert Figure dialog box by first opening the My Practice Spreadsheets folder.

3. Click the *Calendar.jpg* file icon in the Chapter 21 folder and then select the Insert button.

4. Reposition and resize the calendar graphic object so that it covers the cell range E3:E7 in the Homes Sales 2006 worksheet (your sizing and positioning can be approximate).

5. Right-click the calendar graphic object and then select Hyperlink on its shortcut menu to open the Insert Hyperlink dialog box.

6. While the Existing File or Web Page button is selected in the Link To pane on the left and the Current Folder button selected under Look In, select the workbook file *2006 Calendar with links.xls* in the central list box.

The *2006 Calendar with links.xls* workbook is the one you want opened whenever you click the link you're in the process of attaching to the calendar graphic.

7. Select the ScreenTip button to open the Set Hyperlink ScreenTip dialog box.

8. Type **Open 2006 Calendar workbook** in the ScreenTip Text box before you select OK.

The text you add to this ScreenTip appears beneath the mouse pointer whenever you position it somewhere on the calendar graphic object, letting the user know the destination of the hyperlink you've attached to it.

9. Select the OK button in the Insert Hyperlink dialog box to close it and return to the *Exercise21-1.xls* workbook.

10. Select cell A1 in the Home Sales 2006 worksheet to deselect the calendar graphic object and then save your changes to the workbook with the filename **Solved21-2.xls** in your Chapter 21 folder.

11. Position the mouse pointer over the calendar graphic object now covering the cell range E3:E7 of the Home Sales 2006 worksheet.

Note the ScreenTip, "Open 2006 Calendar workbook," that appears beneath the hand pointer.

12. Click the calendar graphic object to open the *2006 Calendar with links.xls* workbook file.

Depending upon the level of security that is currently in place on your computer, Excel may display an alert dialog box warning that hyperlinks can be harmful to your system. If this is the case, select the Yes button to ignore the warning and continue opening the workbook file.

13. Press Alt+← to return to the *Solved21-2.xls* workbook (this is the equivalent of clicking the Back button on the Web toolbar).

14. Use the hyperlink attached to the calendar graphic to return to the open *2006 Calendar with links.xls* workbook and then close this file.

15. Close the *Solved21-2.xls* workbook without exiting Excel.

Adding links to Web pages

Traditionally, hyperlinks have been associated with making jumps between Web pages on the Internet. Excel enables you to add this kind of traditional hyperlink to text entries and graphic objects in your workbooks as well. In addition to opening Web pages on a corporate intranet site or on the Internet, you can add hyperlinks that open new e-mail messages to important clients and co-workers.

In the next exercise, you get an opportunity to create a hyperlink in a new workbook that takes you directly to my Web site, www.mindovermedia.com, as well as starts a new e-mail message addressed to yours truly.

Note that you must have Internet access in order to be able to successfully complete Exercise 21-3.

Exercise 21-3: Adding Hyperlinks to Web Pages and E-mail Addresses

Open a new workbook in Excel in which you will construct a Mind Over Media worksheet containing a hyperlink to open the Home page of my corporate Web site and a link that opens a new e-mail message addressed to me:

1. Rename Sheet1 to MOM (for Mind Over Media).

2. Choose the Insert⇨Picture⇨From File menu command to open the Insert Picture dialog box.

3. Click the My Documents button in the pane on the left and then open the Chapter 21 folder in the Insert Figure dialog box by first opening the My Practice Spreadsheets folder.

4. Click the *momtrdmk.gif* file icon in the Chapter 21 folder and then select the Insert button.

5. Reposition and resize the Mind Over Media logo graphic object so that its sizing handles cover the cell range B2:D5 in the MOM worksheet (your sizing and positioning can be approximate).

6. Right-click the Mind Over Media logo graphic object and then select Hyperlink on its shortcut menu to open the Insert Hyperlink dialog box.

7. While the Existing File or Web Page button is selected in the Link To pane on the left and the Current Folder button is selected under Look In, click the Browse the Web button (the one to the immediate left of the Browse for File button).

In response, your Web browser opens, displaying your Start page.

8. Click the Address bar in your browser, type **www.mindovermedia.com**, and then press Enter.

The Web browser opens the Welcome page of the Mind Over Media Web site.

9. Close your Web browser and then click the Browsed Pages button under Look In.

Because you just browsed the Home page of the Mind Over Media Web site, Mind Over Media Home now appears at the very top of the Look In list box when the Browsed Pages button is selected.

10. Click Mind Over Media Home at the top of the Look In list box.

The URL address of the Home page of the Mind Over Media Web site, http://www.mindovermedia.com, now appears in the Address text box beneath the Look In list box.

11. Click the ScreenTip button to open Set Hyperlink ScreenTip dialog box and then enter **Greg Harvey's Web site** in the ScreenTip Text box before you select OK.

12. Select the OK button in the Insert Hyperlink dialog box to close it and then click cell A1 to deselect the Mind Over Media logo graphic object.

13. Save your new workbook with the hyperlink to the Home page of the Mind Over Media Web site with the filename **Solved21-3.xls** in your Chapter 21 folder.

14. Position the mouse pointer on the Mind Over Media logo graphic and then click the object after noting the ScreenTip that appears beneath the hand pointer.

As soon as you click the logo graphic, Windows launches your Web browser in which the Home page of the Mind Over Media Web site opens.

15. Press Alt+← to return to the *Solved21-3.xls* workbook and then press Alt+→ to return to the Home page of the Mind Over Media Web site.

16. Close your Web browser.

17. Enter the text **Greg's e-mail** in cell B6 of the MOM worksheet and then use the Bold and Italic buttons on the Formatting toolbar to bold and italicize this text.

18. While cell B6 is selected, press Ctrl+K to open the Insert Hyperlink dialog box and then click the E-mail Address button at the bottom of the Link To pane on the left.

19. Type **gharvey@mindovermedia.com** in the E-mail Address text box.

Note that Excel automatically prefaces the text you enter in this box with mailto: so that the box now contains mailto:gharvey@mindovermedia.com.

20. Click the ScreenTip button and then type **Contact Greg Harvey** in the ScreenTip Text box in the Set Hyperlink ScreenTip dialog box before you select OK.

21. Select OK in the Insert Hyperlink dialog box, and then click cell A1 and save your changes to the *Solved21-3.xls* workbook.

22. Click the Greg's e-mail hypertext in cell B6.

As soon as you click this hyperlink, your e-mail program opens a new message addressed to me at gharvey@mindovermedia with the insertion point located in the Subject field. If you want, go ahead and send me a brief message letting me know how you're doing with the workbook exercises. You can always use this mailto address to give me feedback about the exercises and to ask me questions about anything that isn't clear.

23. Close your e-mail program and then close the *Solved21-3.xls* workbook without exiting Excel.

Editing Hyperlinks

Excel makes it easy to edit any hyperlink that you've added to your spreadsheet. The only trick to editing a link is that you have to be careful not to activate the link during the editing process. This means that you must always remember to click and hold down the mouse button rather than just click the link's hypertext or graphic or, better yet, to right-click the text or graphic to select the link when you want to edit. (Remember that simply clicking only results in activating the link.)

When you right-click a link, Excel displays its shortcut menu. If you want to modify the link's destination or ScreenTip, you click Edit Hyperlink on this shortcut menu. Doing this opens the Edit Hyperlink dialog box with the same options as the Insert Hyperlink dialog box. You can then use the Link To buttons on the left side of the dialog box to modify the link's destination or the ScreenTip button to add or change the ScreenTip text.

Q. How do I delete a link without deleting the graphic object or the contents of the cell to which the link is attached?

A. Selecting the Remove Hyperlink item on the object's or cell's shortcut menu rather than pressing the Delete key gets rid of the link without affecting the graphic, cell contents, or formatting.

Q. I've noticed in the worksheet that Excel automatically displays hypertext (that is, text in a cell to which a hyperlink is attached) in blue underlining that immediately changes to purple underlining after I click the link. Is there any way to change this default hypertext formatting?

A. Yes, but in order to change the appearance of hypertext in the worksheet, you must

change the Font settings for the Hyperlink and Followed Hyperlink styles. To do this, open the Style dialog box (Format➪Style). Select Hyperlink and Followed Hyperlink in the Style Name combo boxes and then click the Modify button. Doing this opens a Format Cells dialog box with a Font tab where you can select any type of formatting you want for the hypertext in your worksheet.

Assigning Links to Toolbars and Menus

Instead of assigning links to text cell entries in the worksheet to graphic objects that you've added, you can assign the links to custom buttons or custom menu items that you add to new or existing toolbars or pull-down menus in Excel. You can then activate the links either by clicking their buttons on the custom toolbar or selecting their items on the custom menus.

Try It

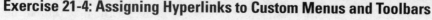

Exercise 21-4: Assigning Hyperlinks to Custom Menus and Toolbars

Open the workbook *Solved21-3.xls* you created in Exercise 21-3 and saved in your Chapter 21 folder in the My Practice Spreadsheets folder on your hard disk. You will use this workbook containing the links to the Mind Over Media trademark graphic and the Greg's e-mail hypertext to create custom menu items for the Help pull-down menu and a custom toolbar containing the same links that you can then use in an Excel workbook:

1. Choose the View⇨Toolbars⇨Customize menu command to open the Customize dialog box.

2. Click the Help pull-down menu to open it.

Insert your custom menu items, Mind Over Media Web Site and Contact Greg, between Customer Feedback Options and About Microsoft Office Excel at the bottom of the Help menu.

3. Click the Commands tab and then click Macros in Categories list box on the left.

As soon as you select Macros in the Categories list box, the Commands list box gives you a choice between a Custom Menu Item and a Custom Button (with a happy face icon) in the Commands list box on the right.

4. Drag the Custom Menu Item to the Help pull-down menu and then, when the horizontal I-beam pointer appears immediately beneath Customer Feedback Options on the Help pull-down menu, release the mouse button.

Excel inserts a Custom Menu Item above About Microsoft Office Excel at the bottom of the Help menu.

5. Right-click the newly added Custom Menu Item on the Help pull-down menu and then select the Name item on the shortcut menu. Drag through the text &Custom Menu Item, replacing it by typing **Mind Over Media &Web Site.** (Make sure that you don't insert a space between the & and Web.)

The placement of the & (ampersand) indicates to Excel which letter in the menu item name to make the hot key. In this case, the W in Web will be underlined in the menu item and made into the hot key so that you can activate this hyperlink by pressing Alt+HW (H to choose the Help menu and W to choose the Mind Over Media Web Site custom menu item).

6. Select Assign Hyperlink⇨Open on the custom button's shortcut menu to open the Assign Hyperlink: Open dialog box.

7. Select the Browsed Pages button and then select the Mind Over Media Home item in the list box to insert `http://www.mindovermedia.com` in the Address text box before you select OK. (You can also type this URL address if Mind Over Media Home no longer appears in the list of your browsed pages.)

8. Add a second custom menu item to the Help menu and place this item in the menu so that its appears immediately beneath the newly added Mind Over Media Web Site menu item (and right above About Microsoft Office Excel).

9. Name this item **Contact Greg** and make the first G in Greg the hot key.

To make a character in the name of a custom menu item the hot key, you must type an & (ampersand) immediately in front of that character.

10. Assign the mailto e-mail address gharvey@mindovermedia.com to the Contact Greg custom menu item.

Select the E-mail Address button in the Assign Hyperlink: Open dialog and then enter **gharvey@mindovermedia.com** in the E-mail Address text box.

11. In the Customize dialog box, click the Toolbars tab and then select the New button to open the New Toolbar dialog box.

12. Type **Links** in the Toolbar Name text box as the name for the new toolbar before you select OK.

Excel opens a new floating toolbar named Links (although the name appears more like Lir in the toolbar until you add buttons to it) that appears above the Customize dialog box.

13. While Macros is selected in the Categories list box on the Commands tab, drag the Custom Button (the one with happy face icon) to the floating Links toolbar.

14. Select Change Button Image on the custom button's shortcut menu and then click the two-page icon on the pop-up palette (the icon at the start of the sixth row of the palette).

15. Assign the Mind Over Media Web site URL address to the first custom button on the Links toolbar.

Click the Existing File or Web Page button in the left panel before you click Browsed Pages button in Look In section of the Assign Hyperlink: Open dialog box. Then select Mind Over Media Home to insert `http://www.mindovermedia.com` into the Address text box. Alternatively, type the URL in this text box yourself.

16. Add a second custom button to the Links toolbar and then assign the ? (question mark) as the button's image and my e-mail address as its hyperlink.

17. Add a third custom button to the Links toolbar using the default happy face image and the Dummies Web site URL (`www.dummies.com`) as its hyperlink.

18. Close the Customize dialog box and then test out the hyperlinks you added to your custom menu items on the Help menu as well as the buttons on your custom Links toolbar.

The great thing about assigning hyperlinks to custom menu items and custom buttons on toolbars is that you can access their links anytime you work on any spreadsheet in Excel. (Of course, in order to be able to use links assigned to custom buttons, their toolbars must first displayed somewhere in the Excel workbook window.)

19. Close the Links custom toolbar and then exit Excel without saving changes to your *Solved21-3.xls* workbook file.

To delete a custom menu item from a pull-down menu or a custom button from a toolbar, open the Customize dialog box and then drag the item off of the menu or toolbar. To move an item or a menu or a button on a toolbar, drag it to a new position. To add a new section by inserting a separator line into the menu or toolbar you're customizing, drag the menu item down or the button to the left or right until the separator appears.

Part VII

Macros and Visual Basic for Applications

The 5th Wave   By Rich Tennant

I don't know—My spreadsheet tells me we should base our overhead budget on sales figures rather than fixed, my plot chart indicates we should escalate our marketing thrust, and my psychoanalysis program tells me I depend too much on outside input and should trust my instincts more.

In this part . . .

Part VII is all about automating routine operations to make your use of the program more efficient. Here, you are introduced to the process of recording sequences of habitual actions in Excel as macros that the program then plays back time and time again in your spreadsheets, much more quickly than you can ever hope to do by hand, and without the slightest deviation. You're also introduced to editing macros with Excel's Visual Basic Editor and using the Visual Basic for Applications programming language to extend their functionality.

Chapter 22

Using Macros

Macros enable you to automate almost any task that you can undertake in Excel. By using Excel's macro recorder to record tasks that you perform routinely, you not only speed up the procedure considerably (as Excel can play back your keystrokes and mouse actions much faster than you perform them manually), but you are also assured that each step in the task is carried out the same way each and every time you perform the task.

In this chapter, you get a chance to practice recording, testing, and playing back macros that you use to automate repetitive tasks required when building and using your Excel worksheets and charts. You also have the opportunity to practice assigning the macros you record to custom menu items and toolbar buttons.

Creating Macros

You can create macros for your Excel spreadsheets in one of two ways:

✔ Use Excel's macro recorder to record your actions as you undertake them in a worksheet

✔ Enter the instructions that you want followed in VBA code in the Visual Basic Editor

Either way, Excel creates a special *module* sheet that holds the actions and instructions in your macro. The macro instructions in a macro module (whether recorded by Excel or written by you) are stored in the Visual Basic for Applications programming language. You can then study the VBA code that the macro recorder creates and edit this code in the Visual Basic Editor, which you open by choosing Data⇨Macro⇨Visual Basic Editor or by pressing Alt+F11 (see Chapter 23).

Using the macro recorder

You can use the macro recorder to create many of the utility-type macros that perform the repetitive tasks necessary for creating and editing your worksheets and charts. When you turn on the macro recorder, the macro recorder records all of your actions in the active worksheet or chart sheet as you make them.

Note that the macro recorder does not record the keystrokes or mouse actions you take to accomplish an action, but only the VBA code required to perform the action itself. This means that any mistakes that you make while taking an action are not recorded as part of the macro. If, for example, you make a typing error and then edit it while the macro recorder is on, only the corrected entry shows up in the macro without the original mistakes and steps taken to remedy them.

The macros that you create with the macro recorder can be stored either as part of the current workbook, in a new workbook, or in a special, globally available Personal Macro Workbook named *PERSONAL.XLS* that's stored in a folder called XLSTART on your hard disk. When you record a macro as part of your Personal Macro Workbook, you can run that macro from any workbook that you have open. (This is because the *PERSONAL.XLS* workbook is secretly opened whenever you launch Excel and, although it remains hidden, its macros are therefore always available.) When you record macros as part of the current workbook or a new workbook, you can run those macros only when the workbook in which they were recorded is open in Excel.

When you create a macro with the macro recorder, you decide not only the workbook in which to store the macro but also what name and shortcut keystrokes to assign to the macro you are creating. When assigning a name for your macro, you use the same guidelines as when assigning a standard range name to a cell range in your worksheet. When assigning a shortcut keystroke to run the macro, you can assign the Ctrl key plus a lowercase letter between a and z, such as Ctrl+q (which is displayed as Ctrl+Q, although you press just Ctrl+q) or the Ctrl key plus an uppercase letter between A and Z as in Ctrl+Q (which appears as Ctrl+Shift+Q because you must press all three keys). You cannot, however, assign the Ctrl key plus a punctuation or number key (such as Ctrl+1 or Ctrl+/) to your macro.

Try It

Exercise 22-1: Recording a New Macro

If Excel is not currently running, launch the program. Use Sheet1 of the new Book1 workbook to practice recording and playing back a new macro that enters the Company Name (Mind Over Media, Inc., in this case) in 12-point bold type and then centers the text across rows A through E with the Merge and Center button:

1. Choose the Tools⇔Macro⇔Record New Macro menu command to open the Record Macro dialog box.

2. Replace the temporary macro name, Macro1, in the Macro Name text box with **Company_Name** (be sure to enter an underscore character between Company and Name and not a space as you would when naming a cell range in the worksheet) and then click the Shortcut Key text box.

3. Type an uppercase **C** so that the Shortcut key appears as Ctrl+Shift+C.

4. Select Personal Macro Workbook on the Store Macro In option's drop-down list.

If you store a macro in the current workbook or a new workbook, you can only use the macro while that particular workbook is open in Excel. When you save a macro in the Personal Macro Workbook, you can use the macro in any workbook you have open.

5. Select the Description text box and then insert the following additional information before the stock *Macro recorded* followed by the current date and *by* followed by your name:

Enter company name in 12-point bold centered across five columns -

6. Select OK to close the Record Macro dialog box.

As soon as the Record Macro dialog box closes, the Stop Recording floating tool-bar appears with only the first two letters and part of third of the toolbar name visible (see Figure 22-1 to identify the two buttons on this tiny toolbar). Also, you notice that Recording appears immediately after Ready on the left side of the Status bar near the bottom of the screen.

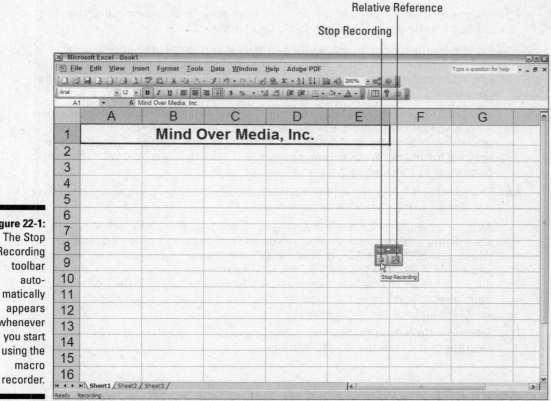

Figure 22-1:
The Stop Recording toolbar auto-matically appears whenever you start using the macro recorder.

7. Type **Mind Over Media, Inc.** in cell A1 and then click the Enter button on the Formula bar (be sure that you don't press the Enter key here).

If you make a typing error when doing this entry, don't worry. Simply delete the incorrect characters and replace them with the correct ones.

8. On the Formatting toolbar, use the Font Size button to increase the point size to 12 and the Bold button to add the boldface attribute to the text.

9. Drag through the cell range A1:E1 to select it and then click the Merge and Center button on the Formatting toolbar.

10. Click the Stop Recording button on the Stop Recording toolbar.

As soon as you click this button, the Stop Recording toolbar is hidden and the Recording status indicator disappears from the Status bar.

11. Position the cell cursor in cell A1 of Sheet2 of the workbook and then press Alt+F8 to open the Macro dialog box.

The Macro dialog box displays a list of all the macros that you defined in the *PERSONAL.XLS* workbook as well as the current workbook. You can use the controls in this dialog box to run or edit a macro, or even to play the macro back a step at a time. (The latter is especially helpful when a macro does something unintended and you want to find out where exactly it went off track.)

12. Click the PERSONAL.XLS!Company_Name macro in Macro Name list box before you select the Run button.

As soon as you select Run, Excel closes the Macro dialog box and runs the Company_Name macro, which enters Mind Over Media, Inc. in cell A1 of Sheet2 in centered 12-point bold text in a merged cell that includes the cell range, A1:E1.

13. Select cell G1 in Sheet3 and then run the Company_Name macro using the short-cut key combination, Ctrl+Shift+C, that you assigned to it.

Excel runs the macro, but this time something unanticipated happens: The program enters the correctly formatted text in cell G1 while still creating the merged cell in the cell range A1:E1 instead of G1:K1 (which would then include the company name).

Excel does this when you run the Company_Name macros in any cell other than A1 of a worksheet because the macro recorder automatically records the cell references in a macro as absolute rather than relative references (unlike when copying formulas). To fix this macro, you will have to rerecord it with relative references in Exercise 22-2.

14. Exit Excel and select the No button when the alert dialog box appears asking you if you want to save your changes to Book1.

As soon as you select No in the first alert dialog box, Excel displays a second alert dialog box, this one prompting you to save changes to the Personal Macro Workbook, *PERSONAL.XLS*, that contains your Company_Name macro. Normally, you would select the Yes button to save your macro for use in other workbooks during other work sessions. However, as you need to rerecord the Company_Name macro using relative references to make it run properly, here you will select No and not bother to save it.

15. Select the No button in the alert dialog box asking if you want to save your changes to the Personal Macro Workbook.

Recording macros with relative cell references

Now you understand why the Stop Recording toolbar contains a Relative Reference button. You need to use this button before you start recording any sequence in a macro that requires relative rather than absolute cell references. Try using this button when rerecording the Company_Name macro in Exercise 22-2 to see what difference it makes when playing the macro back in cells other than A1 in the worksheet.

Try It

Exercise 22-2: Recording a Macro Using Relative Cell References

Launch Excel and then use Sheet1 of the new Book1 workbook to practice rerecording the Company_Name macro, this time using relative cell references:

1. Choose the Tools⇨Macro⇨Record New Macro menu command to open the Record Macro dialog box.

2. Replace the temporary macro name, Macro1, in the Macro Name text box with **Company_Name** (be sure to enter an underscore character between Company and Name and not a space as you would when naming a cell range in the worksheet) and then click Shortcut key text box.

3. Type an uppercase **C** so that the Shortcut key appears as Ctrl+Shift+C.

4. Select Personal Macro Workbook on the Store Macro In option's drop-down list.

5. Select the Description text box and then insert the following additional information before the stock *Macro recorded* followed by the current date and *by* followed by your name:

   Enters company name in 12-point bold centered across five columns -

6. Select OK to close the Record Macro dialog box.

7. Click the Relative Reference button in the Stop Recording toolbar.

   Excel indicates that is recording relative cell references by highlighting the background of the Relative Reference.

8. Type **Mind Over Media, Inc.** in cell A1 and then click the Enter button on the Formula bar.

9. On the Formatting toolbar, use the Font Size button to increase the point size to 12 and the Bold button to add the boldface attribute to the text.

10. Drag through the cell range A1:E1 to select it and then click the Merge and Center button on the Formatting toolbar.

11. Click the Stop Recording button on the Stop Recording toolbar.

12. Position the cell cursor in cell G1 in Sheet1 and then press Ctrl+Shift+C to test the rerecorded Company_Name with relative cell references.

   This time, thanks to relative cell references, the macro works as intended by entering the formatted company name, Mind Over Media, Inc., centered across the merged cell in the range G1:K1.

   Next, record another macro that enters all 12 months (from January to December) in a single row of the worksheet. This macro enters the names of the months, and then makes their names bold and italic and widens their columns with the AutoFit feature. This Twelve_Months macro also requires relative references during recording to ensure that you can use it to successfully the months of the year in any columns of any worksheet.

13. Position the cell cursor in cell A4 of Sheet 1 and then choose the Tools⇨Macro⇨ Record New Macro menu command to open the Record Macro dialog box.

14. Enter **Twelve_Months** as the macro name in the Macro Name text box.

15. Click the Shortcut Key text box and then type an uppercase **M** so that the Shortcut key appears as Ctrl+M.

16. If it's not already selected, select Personal Macro Workbook on the Store Macro In option's drop-down list.

17. Select the Description text box and then insert the following additional information before the stock *Macro recorded* followed by the current date and *by* followed by your name:

   Enters the twelve months of the year from Jan to Dec in bold italic -

18. Select OK to close the Record Macro dialog box and then click the Relative Reference button in the Stop Recording toolbar if necessary.

   Make sure that the background of the Relative Reference button is highlighted and not white before proceeding to step 19.

19. Type **January** in cell A4 and then click the Enter button on the Formula bar.

20. Drag the Fill handle to the right to extend the range to L4 so that all 12 months from January through December are entered in the range A4:L4.

21. Click the Bold and Italic buttons on the Formatting toolbar and then choose the Format⇨Column⇨AutoFit Selection menu command.

22. Click cell A4 to deselect the range A4:L4 and then click the Stop button on the Stop Recording toolbar.

23. Test the Twelve_Months macro by positioning the cell cursor in cell C8 of Sheet1 and then pressing Ctrl+Shift+M.

Excel correctly enters the 12 months of the year in the cell range C8:N8 while at the same time adjusting the widths of columns C to N to suit the length of the month each contains.

24. Exit Excel and select No in the first alert dialog box prompting you to save your changes to the Book1 workbook file, but select the Yes button in the second alert dialog box when prompted to save your macros in the Personal Macro Workbook.

Assigning Macros to Toolbars and Menus

Just as with hyperlinks (Chapter 21), Excel enables you to assign macros you create to the custom buttons that you add to toolbars and to the custom menu items that you add to the Excel pull-down menus. You can also assign macros to any graphic object that you draw or import into Excel. When you assign a macro to a toolbar button, pull-down menu item, or a graphic object, you can then run the macro simply by clicking the button or graphic or by choosing the menu item from its pull-down menu.

Try It

Exercise 22-3: Assigning Macros to Custom Menus and Toolbars

Launch Excel and then use Sheet1 of the new Book1 workbook to practice assigning the two macros that you created in Exercise 22-2 to add custom menu items and tool-bar buttons:

1. Choose the View⇨Toolbars⇨Customize menu command to open the Customize dialog box.

2. Click Insert on the menu bar to open this menu. Click the Commands tab and then click Macros in Categories list box on the left.

3. Drag the Custom Menu Item from the Commands list box to the menu bar and then drop it on the Insert menu to the very bottom of the Insert menu immediately below Hyperlink.

The Custom Menu Item now appears as the very bottom of the Insert pull-down menu.

4. Right-click Custom Menu Item at the bottom of the Insert menu and then, on the shortcut menu that appears, change the Name from &Custom Menu Item to **MOM Compan&y Name.**

Remember that the & (ampersand) character is used in pull-down menu names to define the hot key that the user can press along with the Alt key (Alt+M in this case).

5. Select Assign Macro on the MOM Company Name menu item's shortcut menu to open the Assign Macro dialog box.

6. Click PERSONAL.XLS!Company_Name in the Macro Name list box and then select OK.

7. Select Begin a Group on the MOM Company Name menu item's shortcut menu.

Excel responds by drawing a horizontal separator above the MOM Company Name menu item on the Insert pull-down menu. (You can also insert these kinds of horizontal menu separators by dragging the menu item downward on its menu.)

8. Add a second Custom Menu Item to the bottom of the Insert pull-down menu immediately below the MOM Company Name item. Name this menu item **&Twelve** Months and assign the PERSONAL.XLS!Twelve_Months macro to it.

9. Click the Toolbars tab in the Customize dialog box and then click the Links check box (at the bottom of the list) in the Toolbars list box.

Excel responds by displaying the floating Links custom toolbar you created in Exercise 21-4 in Chapter 21. This toolbar contains three buttons to which hyperlinks are assigned. You will now add a new section to the Links toolbar with custom buttons to which you assign your Company_Name and Twelve_Months macros.

10. Click the Commands tab and then drag the Custom Button from the Commands list box and drop it to the immediate right of the very last button on the custom toolbar with the link to the Dummies Web site.

11. Drag this new custom button slightly to the right until a vertical separator appears between the two buttons with the happy face icons.

12. Right-click the new custom button and then replace &Custom Menu Item with **Company Name** in the Name text box.

The name you assign here becomes the ToolTip for the button, identifying the button's function when you position the mouse pointer over it. Note that there's no need to include an & (ampersand) as part of custom button names as toolbar buttons can only be clicked and therefore have no use for hot keys.

13. Select the pencil icon on the Change Button Image pop-up palette (the fourth one from the left in the fourth row).

14. Select Assign Macro at the very bottom of the new custom button's shortcut menu and then select PERSONAL.XLS!Company_Name in the Macro Name list box before you select OK.

15. Add a second custom button to the end of the Links custom toolbar (to the immediate right of the button with the pencil icon) and then change this button's image to the calculator (the one second from the left in the third row of the Change Button Image pop-up palette). Give it the name **Twelve Months** and, finally, assign the PERSONAL.XLS!Twelve_Months macro to it.

16. Close the Customize dialog box and then test out your two custom menu items on the Insert pull-down menus and two new buttons on the Links custom toolbar.

17. After testing the menu items and buttons, close the Links toolbar and then exit Excel without saving your changes to the Book1 workbook.

Chapter 23

Using the Visual Basic Editor

*V*isual Basic for Applications (usually known simply as VBA) is the official programming language of Excel that you can use to edit as well as to write new macros. The key to editing and writing macros in Visual Basic for Applications is its editing program, the Visual Basic Editor (often abbreviated VBE). The Visual Basic Editor offers a rich environment for coding and debugging VBA code whose interface rivals that of Excel itself in terms of features and complexity.

In this chapter, you get a chance to practice using the Visual Basic Editor to edit macros that you've recorded (see Chapter 22) as well as to enhance their basic functionality through the addition of interactivity. In addition, you get practice using the VBE to create your own custom functions known as user-defined functions (often abbreviated UDF).

Using the Visual Basic Editor

You can open the Visual Basic Editor in one of two ways:

- ✔ Choose the Tools⇨Macro⇨Visual Basic Editor menu command or do the equivalent by pressing the shortcut key combination Alt+F11

- ✔ Click the Visual Basic Editor button on the Visual Basic toolbar (displayed by choosing View⇨Toolbars⇨Visual Basic — shown in Figure 23-1)

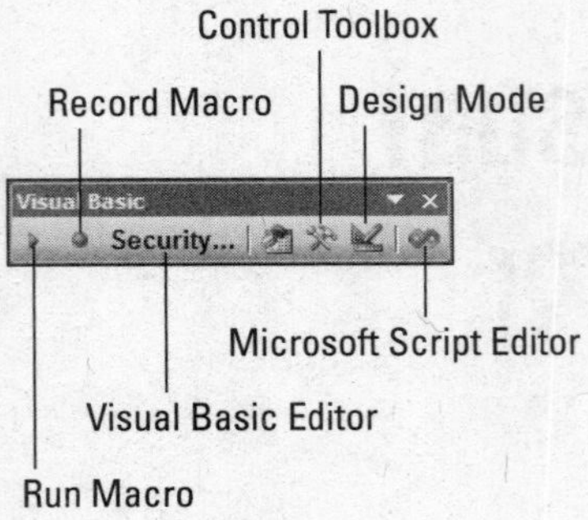

Figure 23-1:
You can use the buttons on the Visual Basic toolbar to record or run a macro as well as to open the Visual Basic Editor.

Control Toolbox

Record Macro   Design Mode

Microsoft Script Editor

Visual Basic Editor

Run Macro

Figure 23-2 shows the arrangement of the typical components of the Visual Basic Editor when you first open it. As you can see, this window contains its own menu bar with a few more menus than the regular Excel window. Beneath the menu bar, you find a Visual Basic Editor Standard toolbar. This toolbar, shown in Figure 23-3 with the names of its buttons called out, contains a number of buttons familiar to you from the Standard toolbar in the regular Excel window.

Beneath the Standard toolbar in the Visual Basic Editor, you find a number of tiled windows of various sizes and shapes. Keep in mind that these are the default windows and their default arrangement. They are not the only windows that you can have open in the Visual Basic Editor (as though it weren't crowded and confusing enough as is), and this is not the only way that they can be arranged.

Project Explorer

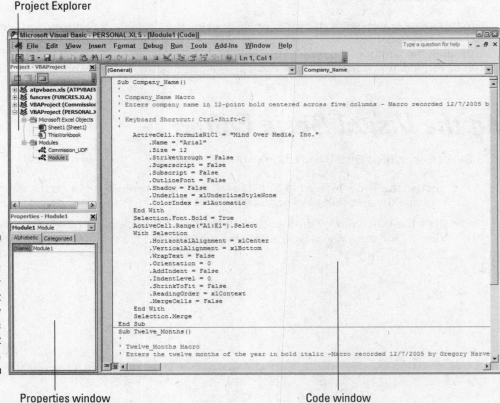

Figure 23-2:
The Visual Basic Editor window as it normally appears when first opened.

Properties window   Code window

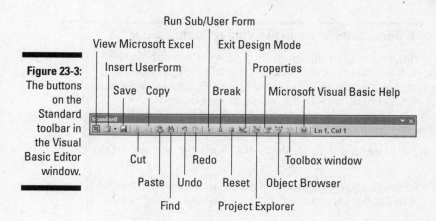

Figure 23-3:
The buttons on the Standard toolbar in the Visual Basic Editor window.

The two most important windows (at least, when you're first starting out using the Visual Basic Editor) are the Project Explorer and the Code window. The Project Explorer window to the immediate left of the Code window (refer to Figure 23-2) shows you all the projects you have open in the Visual Basic Editor and enables you to easily navigate their various parts. Note that in VBA, a _project_ consists of all the code and user forms that belong to a particular workbook along with the sheets of the workbook itself.

Editing a recorded macro

The macros that you record in the workbook as well as any you write for it in the Visual Basic Editor are recorded on module sheets to which Excel assigns generic names such as Module1, Module2, and so forth. The actual lines of VBA programming code for the macro stored on a particular module sheet appears in the Code window when you select its module in the Project Explorer (the Code window appears to the immediate right of the Project Explorer).

If you want to rename a module in your VBA project to something a little more descriptive than Module1, Module2, and so on, you can do this in the Properties window that appears immediately below the Project Explorer. Simply click the name (such as Module1) that appears after the label, (Name), on the Alphabetic tab in the Properties window and replace it with a more descriptive name before you press Enter. When renaming a module, remember that you must use the same naming guidelines as when naming a range name in a worksheet: Begin the module name with a letter, not a symbol or number, and don't put any spaces between words (use under-lines instead).

After you've created a macro, you don't necessarily have to rerecord it to change the way it behaves. In many cases, you may find it more expedient to change its behavior by simply editing its contents in the Visual Basic Editor. Note that if the macro you want to edit is stored in your Personal Macro Workbook (that _PERSONAL.XLS_ file in the XLSTART folder), it's much easier to edit the macro in the Visual Basic Editor by first unhiding the Personal Macro Workbook file in Excel.

Keep in mind that Excel automatically hides the Personal Macro Workbook when you exit Excel. This means that you must use the Windows➪Unhide command to make the _PERSONAL.XLS_ workbook visible if you want to edit its macros directly from this workbook file.

Exercise 23-1: Editing a Recorded Macro in the Visual Basic Editor

If Excel is not currently running, launch the program. You will then unhide the *PERSONAL.XLS* workbook from Sheet1 of this workbook and open the Company_Name macro that you saved as part of your Personal Macro Workbook in Exercise 22-2 in Chapter 21 and edit its commands in the Visual Basic Editor:

1. Choose the Window⇨Unhide menu command to open the Unhide dialog box.

2. While *PERSONAL.XLS* is selected in the Unhide Workbook list box, select the OK button.

Excel opens the *PERSONAL.XLS* workbook (indicated by the appearance of its filename on the Excel program window's title bar) as a seemingly blank workbook.

3. Press Alt+F8 to open the Macro dialog box.

The Macro dialog box displays the Company_Name and Twelve_Month macros you created in Exercise 22-2 (among others, if you've recorded macros in the Personal Macro Workbook on your own).

4. Select the Company_Name macro in the list box before you select the Edit button.

Excel opens the Visual Basic Editor for the Module1 sheet that contains your Company_Name macro. The Code window containing the actual commands in this macro appears less than full size to the right of the Project Explorer and Properties window.

5. Click the Maximize button on the upper-right of the Code window to maximize this window in the Visual Basic Editor.

In the Code window, note that explanatory comments that are not executed as part of the macro are prefaced with apostrophes and appear in green text, whereas all the VBA commands and properties that are executed at the time you run the macro appear in blue and black text.

6. Position the insertion point after the b in Sub in the first line of code at the very top of the Code window and then press F1 to open a Visual Basic Help window with information on the use of the Sub Statement.

Note the first time you try to get online help in the Visual Basic Editor, an alert dialog box appears, indicating that Help is not installed and asking you if want to install it by selecting the Yes button.

After that, you can always get context-sensitive help in the Visual Basic Editor by positioning the insertion point in the command on which you need help and then pressing the F1 Help key.

7. Replace Arial with **Times New Roman** in the Name property that is located immediately under the With Selection.Font statement. Make sure to retain the closed pair of double quotation marks around the font name, as in

```
.Name = "Times New Roman"
```

8. Increase the font size from 12 to **14** points by changing the Size property, as in

```
.Size = 14
```

9. Click the View Microsoft Excel button on the Standard toolbar in the Visual Basic Editor (the very first one with the green XL logo).

Excel closes the Visual Basic Editor window and returns you to the Personal Macro Workbook, *PERSONAL.XLS*.

10. Switch to the Book1 workbook and then test out the changes to the Company_ Name macro by pressing Ctrl+Shift+C.

This time, the macro inserts the Mind Over Media, Inc. company name in the merged cell A1:E1 in 14-point bold using Times New Roman as the font.

11. Close the *Book1.xls* file without saving your changes and then hide the *PERSONAL.XLS* workbook by choosing the Window⇨Hide menu command.

12. Exit Excel, this time selecting the Yes button when prompted to save your changes.

Adding a dialog box that processes user input

One of the biggest problems with recording macros is that any text or values that you have the macro enter for you in a worksheet or chart sheet can never vary thereafter. If you create a macro that enters the heading "Bob's Barbecue Pit" in the current cell of your worksheet, this is the only heading you'll ever get out of that macro. However, you can get around this inflexibility by using the InputBox function. When you run the macro, this Visual Basic function causes Excel to display an input dialog box where you can enter whatever title makes sense for the new worksheet. The macro then puts that text into the current cell and formats this text, if that's what you've trained your macro to do next.

To see how easy it is to use the InputBox function to add interactivity to an otherwise staid macro, follow along with the steps for converting the Company_name macro that currently inputs the text "Mind Over Media" to one that actually prompts you for the name you want entered. The InputBox function uses the following syntax:

```
InputBox(prompt[,title][,default][,xpos][,ypos]
         [,helpfile,context])
```

The many arguments of the InputBox function include

- Prompt, which specifies the message (up to 1024 characters) that appears inside the input dialog box, prompting the user to enter a new value (or in this case, a new company name). To have the prompt message appear on different lines inside the dialog box, you enter the functions Chr(13) and Chr(10) in the text. (Chr stands for Character. The number codes insert a carriage return to start a new line and a linefeed to position the insertion point at the beginning of the line, respectively.)

- Title optional argument, which specifies what text to display in the input dialog box's title bar — if you don't specify a title argument, Excel displays the name of the application on the title bar.

- Default optional argument, which specifies the default response that automatically appears in the text box at the bottom of the input dialog box. If you don't specify a default argument, the text box is empty in the input dialog box.

- Xpos and ypos optional arguments, which specify the horizontal distance from the left edge of the screen to the left edge of the dialog box and the vertical distance from the top edge of the screen to the top edge of the dialog box. If you don't specify these arguments, Excel centers the input dialog box horizontally and positions it one-third of the way down the screen vertically.

- Helpfile optional argument, which specifies the name of the custom Help file that you make available to the user to explain the workings of the input dialog box as well as the type of data its accepts.

- Context optional argument, which specifies the context number assigned to the help topic — note that when you specify a helpfile and context argument, Excel adds a Help button to the custom input dialog box that users can click to access the custom help file in the Help window.

Try It

Exercise 23-2: Making a Recorded Macro Interactive by Adding an Input Dialog Box

Launch Excel to open a new Book1 workbook in the program. You will then unhide the *PERSONAL.XLS* workbook from Sheet1 of this workbook. Open the Company_ Name macro that you edited in the previous exercise in the Visual Basic Editor and add the commands to display a dialog box prompting the user for the worksheet title to enter when the macro is run:

1. Choose the Window⇨Unhide menu command to open the Unhide dialog box.

2. While *PERSONAL.XLS* is selected in the Unhide Workbook list box, select the OK button.

3. Press Alt+F8 to open the Macro dialog box and then select the Company_Name macro in the list box before you select the Edit button.

4. Position the insertion point in the Code window at the beginning of the ActiveCell.FormulaR1C1 statement and press Enter to insert a new line.

5. Press the ↑ key to move the insertion point up the beginning of the new blank line.

Note that the status indicator at the end of the Standard toolbar indicates the insertion point is now located in column 5 of line 8 (Ln 8, Col5).

Now you're ready to create the three variables — InputPrompt, InputTitle, and DefaultText — that contain the values you want used as the *prompt, title,* and *default* arguments of the InputBox function. You create all variables for the code at the beginning of the macro subroutine by declaring their names and setting them equal to the values you initially want used. Then, when you're ready to enter the InputBox function in the code, all you have to do is enter the variable names in the order of the InputBox arguments. Note that by using variables to supply the *prompt, title,* and *default* arguments of the InputBox function, you avoid creating such a long line of code that is not only hard to read but hard to edit as well.

6. Type the following code on line 8 to create the InputPrompt variable and then press the Enter key to start a new line 9:

```
InputPrompt = "Enter the title for this spreadsheet in the
          text box below and then select OK:"
```

7. Type the following code on line 9 to create the InputTitle variable and then press the Enter key to start a new line 10:

```
InputTitle = "Spreadsheet Title"
```

8. Type the following code on line 10 to create the DefaultText variable and then press the Enter key to start a new line 11:

```
DefaultText = "Mind Over Media, Inc."
```

Next, you declare a fourth variable, CompanyName. This variable actually contains the InputBox function using the InputPrompt, InputTitle, and DefaultText variables you just created as its prompt, title, and default arguments.

9. Type the following code on line 11 to create the CompanyName variable that contains the InputBox function:

```
CompanyName = InputBox(InputPrompt, InputTitle, DefaultText)
```

The last step is to the value, "Mind Over Media," in the ActiveCell.FormulaR1C1 property with the CompanyName variable (whose value is determined by whatever is input into the Company Name input dialog box), thus effectively replacing this constant in the macro with the means for making this input truly interactive.

10. Select "Mind Over Media, Inc." in line 12 and replace it with the **CompanyName** variable (with no quotation marks) so that this line contains

```
ActiveCell.FormulaR1C1 = CompanyName
```

11. Carefully check your changes to the code of the Company_Name macro against those in the first five lines shown in Figure 23-4.

12. When everything checks out, choose the File⇨Save PERSONAL.XLS command on the Visual Basic Editor menu bar.

13. Click the View Microsoft Excel button on the Standard toolbar and then activate the Book1 workbook.

14. Test out the interactive version of the Company_Name macro by pressing Ctrl+Shift+C.

A Spreadsheet Title dialog box should appear, prompting you for the name of the spreadsheet.

15. Replace Mind Over Media, Inc. in the Worksheet Title dialog box with **ABC Corp. Sales** and then select the OK button.

The macro now enters ABC Corp. Sales as the worksheet title in 12-point bold type centered over the merged cell A1:E1 in Sheet1 of Book1.

16. Close the *Book1.xls* file without saving your changes and then hide the *PERSONAL.XLS* workbook by choosing the Window⇨Hide menu command.

17. Exit Excel by selecting the Yes button when prompted to save your changes to the Personal Macro Workbook.

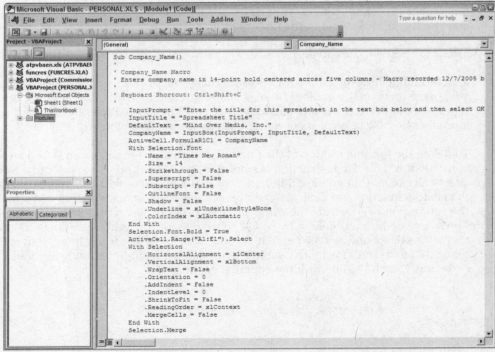

Figure 23-4: Visual Basic Editor Code window after adding new commands to make the Company_Name macro interactive.

Creating User-Defined Functions

One of the best uses of Visual Basic for Applications in Excel is to create custom spreadsheet functions, also known as user-defined functions. User-defined functions are great because you don't have to access the Macro dialog box to run them. In fact, you enter them into your spreadsheets just like you do any of the other built-in spreadsheet functions, either with the Insert Function button on the Formula bar or by typing them directly into a cell.

To create a user-defined function, you must do the four following things:

- ✔ Create a new module sheet where the custom function is to be defined in the Visual Basic Editor by selecting its project in the Project Explorer and then choosing Insert⇨Module on the Visual Basic Editor Menu bar.

- ✔ Enter the name of the custom function and specify the names of the arguments that this function takes on the first line in the Code window. Note that you can't duplicate any built-in function names, such as SUM or AVERAGE, and so on, and you must list argument names in the order in which they are processed and enclosed in parentheses.

- ✔ Enter the formula, or set of formulas, that tells Excel how to calculate the custom function's result using the argument names listed in the Function command with whatever arithmetic operators or built-in functions are required to get the calculation made on the line or lines below.

- ✔ Indicate that you've finished defining the user-defined function by entering the End Function command on the last line.

To see how this procedure works in action, in the following exercise, you create a user-defined function that calculates the sales commissions for salespeople based on the number of sales they make in a month as well as the total amount of their monthly sales (they sell big-ticket items, such as RVs). Your custom Commission function has two arguments — TotalSales and ItemsSold — so that the first line of code on the module sheet in the Code window is

```
Function Commission(TotalSales,ItemsSold)
```

In determining how the commissions are actually calculated, you base the commission percentage on the number of sales made during the month. For five sales or fewer in a month, you pay a commission rate of 4.5 percent of the salesperson's total monthly sales; for sales of six or more, you pay a commission rate of 5 percent.

To define the formula section of the Commission custom function, you set up an IF construction. This IF construction is similar to the IF function you enter into a worksheet cell except that you use different lines in the macro code for the construction in the custom function. An ELSE statement separates the command that is performed if the expression is True from the command that is performed if the expression is False. The macro code is terminated by an END IF statement. To set the custom function so that your salespeople get 4.5 percent of total sales for five or fewer items sold and 5 percent of total sales for more than five items sold, you enter the following lines of code underneath the line with the Function command:

```
If ItemsSold <= 5 Then
    Commission = TotalSales * 0.045
Else
    Commission = TotalSales * 0.05
End If
```

Exercise 23-3: Constructing a Custom Function in the Visual Basic Editor

Open the *Exercise23-3.xls* workbook file in your Chapter 23 folder in the My Practice Spreadsheets folder on your hard disk or in the Excel Workbook folder on the workbook CD-ROM. This worksheet contains an RV Sales worksheet with the sales for three account representatives, Fred, Holly, and Jack, for which you will create the user-defined Commission function:

1. Choose the Window⇨Unhide menu command to open the Unhide dialog box.

2. While *PERSONAL.XLS* is selected in the Unhide Workbook list box, select the OK button.

3. Press Alt+F11 to open the Visual Basic Editor window with a new module sheet from the *PERSONAL.XLS* workbook.

4. In the Projects window in the Visual Basic Editor, click the expand button in front of the Modules folder icon at the bottom of the hierarchy.

5. Select Insert⇨Module on the Visual Basic Editor's menu bar to insert a Module2 in the hierarchy.

6. Select Module2 following (Name) in the Properties window and then replace it with Commission_UDF and press Enter.

Excel renames the Module2 sheet to Commission_UDF and this module name now appears above Module1 in the hierarchy in the Projects window.

7. Click the insertion point in the Code window and then type the following code on Line1:

```
Function Commission(TotalSales, ItemsSold)
```

8. Press Enter to start a new line and Tab to indent; enter the following code on line 2 starting at column 5:

```
If ItemsSold <= 5 Then
```

9. Press Enter to start a new line and then Tab again to indent further, and then enter the following indented code on line 3 starting at column 9:

```
Commission = TotalSales * 0.045
```

10. Press Enter to start a new line and then Shift+Tab to outdent; enter the following indented code on line 4 starting at column 5:

```
Else
```

11. Press Enter to start a new line and then Tab to indent; enter the following indented code on line 5 starting at column 9:

```
Commission = TotalSales * 0.05
```

12. Press Enter to start a new line and then Shift+Tab to outdent; enter the following indented code on line 6 starting at column 5:

```
End If
```

13. Check the lines of code in your custom Commission function against those shown in Figure 23-5. When they check out, proceed to step 14.

14. Choose File⇨Save PERSONAL.XLS on the Visual Basic Editor menu bar to save your custom function.

15. Click the View Microsoft Excel button on the Standard toolbar in the Visual Basic Editor and then hide the Personal Macro Workbook *PERSONAL.XLS* by choosing Window⇨Hide on the Excel menu bar.

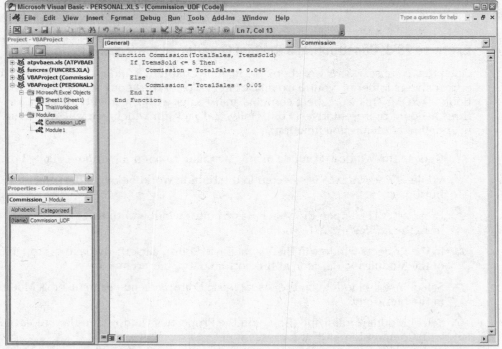

Figure 23-5:
The Visual
Basic Editor
Code
window
after adding
the code
for the
new user-
defined
Commission
function on
its own
module
sheet.

Using a custom function in your spreadsheet

The great thing about custom functions is that they can be inserted into your worksheets with your old friend the Insert Function button on the Excel Formula bar. To
find your custom function in the Insert Function dialog box, you just need to select
User Defined as the function category.

Try It

Exercise 23-4: Building Spreadsheet Formulas with a Custom Function

Switch to the Exercise23-3.xls workbook that you opened at the beginning of the last
exercise and then use its RV Sales worksheet to test out your new Commission
custom function:

1. Position the cell cursor in cell E5 in the RV Sales worksheet and then click the
Insert Function button on the Formula Bar.

2. Select User Defined at the very bottom of the Select a Category drop-down list.

The Select a Function list box now displays the name of your custom function as
PERSONAL.XLS!Commission.

3. While PERSONAL.XLS!Commission is selected in the Select a Function list box,
select OK to open the Function Arguments dialog box for the custom Commission
function.

4. While the insertion point is in the TotalSales argument text box, click cell C4 in
the worksheet that contains Fred's total sales and then press Tab to select the
ItemsSold argument text box below.

5. While the insertion point is in the ItemsSold argument text box, click cell C5 in the worksheet that contains the count of Fred's sales and then select the OK button.

The custom commission function computes Fred's commission as $2,655 (using the 4.5% commission rate because the number of his sales is below five).

6. Use your custom Commission function to compute the sales commissions for Holly in cell E10.

Select cell C9 as the TotalSales argument and cell C10 as the ItemsSold argument for this Commission function.

7. Save your changes to the RV Sales worksheet in a new workbook file named **Solved23-4.xls** in your Chapter 23 folder in the My Practice Spreadsheets folder and then leave the workbook open for Exercise 23-5.

Saving custom functions in add-in files

The only limitation to the user-defined functions that you save as part of a regular workbook files or the Personal Macro Workbook file is that when entering them directly into a cell (without the use of the Insert Function dialog box), you must preface their function names with their filenames. So, for example, if you want to type in the custom Commission function that's saved in the Personal Macro Workbook and you enter the following formula:

```
=Commission(C9,C10)
```

(assuming that cell C9 contains the total sales and cell C10 contains the number of items sold), Excel returns the #NAME? error value to the cell. If you then edit the function to include the Personal Macro Workbook's filename as follows:

```
=Personal.xls!Commission(C9,C10)
```

Excel then calculates the sales commission based on the TotalSales in C9 and the ItemsSold in C10, returning this calculated value to the cell containing this user-defined function.

To be able to omit the filename from the custom functions you create when you enter them directly into a cell, you need to save the workbook file that contains them as an add-in file (with an .xla filename extension). Then, after you've saved the workbook with your user-defined functions as an add-in file, you can start entering them into any worksheet without their filename qualifier after activating the add-in in the Add-Ins dialog box (Tools⇨Add-Ins).

Try It

Exercise 23-5: Saving a Custom Function as an Excel Add-In

Use the *Solved23-4.xls* workbook with the RV Sales commissions that you created in Exercise23-4 to practice saving your custom PERSONAL.XLS!Commission function in an Excel add-in file:

1. Choose the Window⇨Unhide menu command to open the Unhide dialog box.

2. While *PERSONAL.XLS* is selected in the Unhide Workbook list box, select the OK button.

3. Press Alt+F11 to open the Visual Basic Editor window with a new module sheet from the *PERSONAL.XLS* workbook.

4. Choose the Tools⇨VBAProject Properties menu command.

The Editor opens the VBAProject - Project Properties dialog box containing a General and a Protection tab.

5. Click the Protection tab and then select the Lock Project for Viewing check box.

Putting a check mark in this check box prevents other users from viewing the custom functions so that they can't make any changes to them. Next, you add a password that prevents them from removing the view protection status.

6. Click the Password text box and enter **cerrado** (Spanish for closed) as the password there. Then click the Confirm Password text box and reenter **cerrado** as the password exactly as you entered it in the text box above before you select OK.

Now you're ready to return to the worksheet where you can add a title and description for the new add-in file.

7. Click the View Microsoft Excel button on Visual Basic Editor Standard toolbar.

Before saving the *PERSONAL.XLS* workbook as an add-in file, you should add a title and description of the user-defined Commission function it contains (this information then appears in the Add-Ins dialog box whenever you select the add-in file).

8. Choose the File⇨Properties menu command to open the *PERSONAL.XLS* Properties dialog box.

9. Enter **Custom Commission Function** in the Title text box on the Summary tab and then select the Comments text box.

10. Enter the following text in the Comments text box and then select OK:

Computes sales commissions based on the total and number of sales

11. Choose the File⇨Save As menu command and then scroll all the way down to the bottom of the Save as Type drop-down list in Save As dialog box. Click Microsoft Office Excel Add-In (*.xla).

Doing this selects the AddIns folder in the Save In drop-down list box showing the names of any add-in files that you've saved there.

12. Click the File Name combo box and change PERSONAL to **Commission** (without changing the .xla filename extension) before you select the Save button.

After saving your workbook as an add-in file, you're ready to activate the add-in so that you can enter its user-defined functions in any worksheet.

13. Hide the Personal Macro Workbook, *PERSONAL.XLS*, by choosing the Window⇨Hide menu command.

14. Choose the Tools⇨Add-Ins menu command to open the Add-Ins dialog box and there select the Custom Commission Function check box before selecting OK.

15. Position the cell pointer in cell E18 and then type

```
=Commission(
```

16. Click cell C17 with Jack's totals sales to make it the TotalSales argument for the Commission function and then type a , (comma) to separate the TotalSales argument from the ItemsSold argument.

17. Click cell C18 with the count of Jack's sales to make it the ItemsSold argument for the Commission function and then type a) — close parenthesis — before clicking the Enter button on the Formula bar.

18. Enter a formula in cell E19 that sums the sales commissions in cells E5, E10, and E18.

Create a formula that uses the SUM function with these three cell references as its *number* arguments.

19. Select cell A1 and then save your changes to the RV Sales worksheet in a file named **Solved23-5.xls** in your Chapter 23 folder in the My Practice Spreadsheets folder. Exit Excel, being sure to save your changes to the hidden *PERSONAL.XLS* workbook file when prompted to do so during the closing of the program.

Part VIII
The Part of Tens

The 5th Wave — By Rich Tennant

"I told him we were looking for software that would give us greater productivity, so he sold me a spreadsheet that came with these signs."

In this part . . .

The Part of Tens brings together tips and shortcuts galore selected to help you apply your workbook experience to your own work in Excel. Here, you get tips on how to use Excel like a pro, followed by tons of important shortcut keys for entering, formatting, and editing spreadsheets. And for good measure, I've ended this part and the workbook with my own favorite miscellaneous shortcuts.

Chapter 24

Top Ten Tips for Using Excel like a Pro

*P*erforming the exercises in this workbook gives you an opportunity to work with the most important features of the program, especially those related to building and maintaining spreadsheets. To help you make the most of this hands-on experience, this chapter brings together ten of the most important ways to work efficiently and design the best possible spreadsheets as you start to work on your own.

Generate New Workbooks from Templates

Whenever possible, generate new workbooks from templates that are available for Excel. Don't forget the program provides you with a number of useful templates (Balance Sheet, Expense Statement, Loan Amortization, Sales Invoice, and Timecard) all courtesy of Spreadsheet Solutions that you can start using right out of the box. (Select File⇨New, and then click the On My Computer link in the New Workbook task pane and, finally, the Spreadsheet Solutions tab in the Templates dialog box.)

In addition to the Spreadsheet Solution templates that are installed with Excel, you can also go online to the Microsoft Office Templates Home Page (select File⇨New, and then click the Templates On Office Online link in the New Workbook task pane). On the Microsoft Office Templates Home Page, click the Excel link beneath the Microsoft Office Programs heading and then browse the different categories of Excel templates by using their links. After you find a template you want to download, click its thumbnail to open a page showing a larger version of the template along with its rating, number of downloads, and size. To download the template file, click the Download Now button.

After the template is completely downloaded, Excel opens a workbook generated from the template in its program window. You can then customize the workbook as needed before you save the workbook as a template file in your Templates folder by selecting Template (*.xlt) as the file type in the Save as Type drop-down list in the Save As dialog box (File⇨Save As) and removing the number from the temporary filename. Doing this adds the downloaded template to the General tab of your Template dialog box so that you can use it to generate as many new workbooks as you need.

If you can't find a ready-made template online that comes close to generating the type of spreadsheet you need, you can create your own template from a sample worksheet that you build from scratch. In this workbook, you enter the formulas along with all standard headings for the data table(s) that the spreadsheet requires, formatting and securing the tables as needed. Then you save the final workbook as a template file by selecting Template (*.xlt) as the file type in the Save As Type drop-down list in the Save As dialog box (File⇨Save As).

Organize Spreadsheet Data on Different Worksheets

As you know, each new workbook that you open contains three identical blank worksheets into which you can enter the data required for your spreadsheet. Unfortunately, too many times, new spreadsheet designers restrict all data entry to the first worksheet so that they end up with one super-colossal spreadsheet with its data spread far and wide all over the entire worksheet. Although some spreadsheets may require the single-sheet treatment, more often than not, the only reason that every bit of data gets put on one sheet is simply that the spreadsheet designer doesn't even stop to consider using a multi-sheet layout.

By utilizing a multi-sheet layout for your workbook, you not only end up with more manageable worksheets but with one whose data tables and lists are much easier to print individually. Moreover, with just a little forethought, you can set up the data on the successive sheets of the workbook so that when all of them are printed together, the pages of the report naturally present the data and their findings in a clear and cohesive manner.

In designing a spreadsheet that uses a multi-sheet layout, remember that you can add additional worksheets to the workbook (Insert➪Worksheet) as needed — the only restriction to the total number of sheets in a workbook is the amount of computer memory available to keep the workbook open. You can also rearrange the sheets in a workbook simply by dragging their sheet tabs to the desired position in the workbook. You can also rename them with much more descriptive names by double-clicking them.

Keep in mind that you can color-code the worksheet tabs in your workbook. To assign a new color to a sheet tab, right-click the tab and then select Tab Color on its shortcut menu. To select the tab's new color in the Format Tab Color dialog box, click the desired color square in either of its two color palettes before you select OK.

When creating a multi-sheet spreadsheet, consider making the first worksheet a summary worksheet complete with hyperlinks (see Chapter 21) that you or other users of the workbook can use to navigate quickly and directly to important tables and lists on the various worksheets.

Create Data Series with AutoFill

One of the marks of a true Excel pro is her reliance on the AutoFill feature to quickly generate the data series needed in the spreadsheet. Remember that Excel is capable of creating many series such as months of the year, days of the week, and text with numbers (such as Item 100, Gate 200, and the like) simply by entering the first entry in the series in a cell and then dragging the Fill handle down the rows of its column or across the columns of its row to fill out the successive entries in that series (as indicated by the ToolTip that appears beneath the Fill handle).

Also keep in mind that you can use the Fill handle to generate series that use increments other than 1 (which is the default assumed when you use the Fill handle). All you have to do is make two data entries that indicate the increment that the series should use (such as Monday and Wednesday or 50 and 48), and then select both cells before you drag the Fill handle down or across to create the series.

Further, you can define custom data series whose items don't change by a certain increment (such as a series of company locations like Chicago, Pittsburgh, Dallas, and Boston) and then generate the custom series in a spreadsheet by simply entering its first item in a cell and then dragging the Fill handle as you would with any incremented series. To create the custom list, you open the Custom Lists tab of the Options dialog box (Tools⇨Options). There, you type the individual items in the series (terminated by the Enter key) in the List Entries list box in the order in which they are to be generated with the Fill handle and then select the Add button. Alternatively, if this custom series already exists in a cell range somewhere in the spreadsheet, select the cell range in the worksheet after selecting the Import from Cells text box and then select Import.

Use Range Names

The use of range names in a spreadsheet provides several important benefits, perhaps the most important of which is that you can use the range name to both move and simultaneously select the cell range in a flash, no matter where this range is located in the entire workbook. After a range is named, all you have to do to select the range is to choose its range name from the Name box drop-down list on the Formula toolbar.

This method of selecting cell ranges can be a tremendous time-saver when you're dealing with a table or list of data that you find yourself referring to or editing on a regular basis. This is all the more true if the named range's data tables or lists are located in columns and rows in some distant region of a worksheet.

Remember that you can use range names to select cell ranges with data tables or lists that you print on a regular basis. All you have to do is select the cell range with the Name box, and then open the Print dialog box (Ctrl+P) and select the Selection option button in the Print What section before you select the OK button.

The second important use for range names is to define and name a constant (such as a tax rate or interest percentage) whose value you need to refer to in the formulas you're about to build in a data table or list but which you don't want to enter in the worksheet as a separate cell entry. To do this, open the Define Name dialog box (Insert⇨Name⇨Define), and enter the name for the constant in the Names in Workbook text box. Next, set the name equal to the value or the formula that calculates the value you want used in the Refers To text box before you select OK. Then, to refer to the constant in a formula you're building, select its name in the Paste Name dialog box (Insert⇨Name⇨Paste) before you select OK.

The final important use for range names is in documenting the functioning of the formulas in your data tables in a spreadsheet. You can do this by having Excel apply the table's row and column headings to the cells of the table. Simply select the table including the cells with the row and column headings before you open the Create Names dialog box (Insert⇨Name⇨Create) and then select the appropriate check boxes (Top Row, Left Column, Bottom Row, or Right Column) that contain the row and column headings before you select OK. Then, to replace the cell addresses in the formulas in this table with the new range names, open the Apply Names dialog box (Insert⇨Name⇨Apply) and with the Use the Row and Column Names check box selected, select the OK button.

Freeze Column and Row Headings

When it comes to the size of your monitor versus the size of your worksheet, your monitor loses hands down every time. This means that in all except the most concise data tables, the column and row headings that identify the entries in their cells soon disappear from view as you make or edit entries in rows lower and columns further to the right than the original screen can contain. To prevent this from happening by keeping a table's or list's headings on the screen at all times no matter how long or wide the table or list becomes, you need to freeze these headings on the screen. To do this, position the cell cursor in the cell located immediately to the right of the column containing the row headings and immediately below the row with the column headings. Then, choose the Window⇨Freeze Panes menu command.

Don't forget that you can save the frozen panes you set up in a spreadsheet as part of a custom view for the worksheet that you can resume at any time simply by selecting its name in the Custom Views dialog box (View⇨Custom Views).

Prevent Data Entry Errors with Data Validation

Excel's Data Validation feature makes it easy to prevent users from entering the wrong type of data or invalid values in a particular cell range of the spreadsheet. You can also limit data entry errors by using Data Validation to compel the user to select the entry for a cell from only those values you display on the cell's drop-down list.

To restrict data entry for the selected cell, you select the type of entry that is allowed in the cell on the Allow drop-down list (Whole Number, Decimal, List, Date, Time, Text Length, or Custom) on the Settings tab of the Data Validation dialog box (Data⇨ Validation). Depending upon the type of entry you allow, you then restrict the range of allowable values. For example, if you select Date as the allowed entry type, you then specify the start and end dates that the cell entry must be between.

By selecting List as the entry type, you're able to create a cell drop-down list that contains the complete list of allowed entries. That way, the spreadsheet user doesn't have to type anything in order to make the cell entry. This type of cell data validation is perfect when its data entry is restricted to a relatively short list whose values must be consistent and spelled correctly (as when sorting or filtering data).

Note, however, that you must enter the list of allowed entries you want to appear on the cell's drop-down list in a cell range somewhere in a worksheet prior to setting up this kind of List entry in the Data Validation dialog box. You then specify the allowable entries for the cell drop-down list by selecting the Source text box on the Settings tab and then selecting the cell range containing the allowed entries in the worksheet.

When setting up Data Validation for a cell, you can also define an input message displayed when the user selects the cell and an error alert message that is displayed when the user attempts to make an invalid data entry. The input message instructs the user on what range of values are allowed in the cell just as the error alert message informs the user as to why the entry he tried to complete was not allowed.

After setting up Data Validation for a single blank cell, you can then copy the validation settings to an entire range of cells in the spreadsheet using any of the standard copy methods (copy and paste or drag-and-drop).

Trap Error Values in Their Original Formulas

Error values are not only unsightly but, because they spread so easily to other dependent formulas throughout the spreadsheet, they can be difficult to eradicate. The most professional spreadsheet designers, therefore, take steps whenever possible to prevent the spread of error values across the spreadsheet by trapping them at their source. The most famous example of where this kind of error trapping is needed occurs in division formulas where the divisor is a cell reference that at times can be blank. As you remember, blank cells as well as cells with text entries carry a zero (0) value as far as formula computations are concerned so that if they serve as the divisor in a division calculation in a formula, that formula returns the #DIV/0! error value to the cell.

As you found out if you performed Exercise 12-4 in Chapter 12, you can prevent Excel from returning this or any other kind of error value (including #NA) to the cell by making the division calculation itself the value_if_false argument of an IF function that uses the ISERROR logical function in its logical_test argument to test for the return of an error value, and the value 0 (zero) as its value_if_true argument.

So, for example, if cell K7 is the divisor of a division computation and it could be blank at times and therefore cause the division calculation to return #DIV/0!, you could prevent this and block its spread to other formulas dependent upon its result with the addition of the following IF function:

=IF(ISERROR(B7/$K$7),0,B7/$K$7)

In this case, Excel returns zero (0) to the cell in place of any error value, performing the actual division only when it's safe to do so.

You can then use Conditional Formatting (see Chapter 2) to flag all error-trapping formulas that return zero (0) — instead of the desired calculated result — with a special type of color or font. Then, you can use the Find feature (see Chapter 4) to locate all the cells in the worksheet that now sport this special formatting when it comes time to fix their cell references so that their formulas return values other than zero.

Save Memory by Using Array Formulas

In Exercise 6-5 in Chapter 6, you got some experience with constructing array formulas. As you may recall, an *array formula* is one that constructs the same type of calculation in an entire range of cells in a data table at the time you create it. As a result, you don't go through the normal process of first constructing a master formula and then copying to all the other cells in the table that need to perform the same type of calculation.

Array formulas offer two distinct advantages over normal formulas:

✔ Array formulas enable you to create all the duplicate formulas needed in the table in a single operation

✔ Array formulas require a lot less computer memory to store than individual copies of a single master formula

It is actually the latter, memory-related benefit that makes array formulas so useful. By building array formulas, you can save substantial amounts of computer memory (remember that Excel must be able to load every bit of data in a workbook into memory in order to be able to open the file at all — it does not perform like other programs that can load just parts of a document into memory, switching them out as you work). This memory savings is important in really large workbooks as it enables you to add more data to the spreadsheet as well as keep Excel from completely bogging down when you open a spreadsheet for editing or printing.

Controlling the Display of Data in Tables through Outlines

Many of the spreadsheets you create and maintain in Excel require more columns and rows than can possibly fit on a single screen (even with a really large monitor) unless you select a zoom magnification percentage so small that it's impossible to read its data. In some spreadsheets, such as Regional Income and CG Media Sales tables that you worked with in several different exercises, you can easily reclaim some of this screen estate as well as maintain a great degree of flexibility in how much of the data to display by outlining the tables.

When you outline a typical data table (Data➪Group and Outline➪Auto Outline), Excel adds outline buttons to both the rows and columns of the table (that appear in the worksheet's row and column headers). You can then use these outline buttons to control how much of table data is displayed on the screen (accomplished by hiding and unhiding particular rows and columns of the table).

Outlines are perfect for tables such as the Regional Income and CG Media Sales tables, where the monthly income and sales data are naturally summarized by quarterly and annual totals for the various regions and products being tracked. With the help of the level outline buttons, you can quickly collapse the table down the grand totals or quarterly totals and then just as easily completely expand all the monthly income and sales data as well.

Outlining data tables like these makes it a snap to print and chart just a selected part of their data. For example, to create a chart using only the quarterly totals in the regional income table, all you have to do is use the level outline buttons to display only columns with totals in the data table and then select the quarterly data prior to clicking the Chart Wizard button on the Standard toolbar.

Use Compare Side by Side to Work with Two Workbooks

To be a true Excel pro, you need to be comfortable working not only with the spreadsheet data on different sheets of the same workbook but on sheets of different workbooks as well. One way in which Excel facilitates this is through the program's ability to open side-by-side windows on two different workbooks that you have open at a time.

When you're only dealing with two open workbooks (which is most often the case as any more than two open at a time are pretty hard to keep track of), you can create vertical windows (one on top of the other), each displaying a part of a different workbook simply by selecting the Excel Window➪Compare Side by Side With menu command.

What makes this window command so great is that as soon as you choose it, Excel automatically opens a floating Compare Side by Side toolbar containing a Close Side by

Side button that you can use to close the windows as soon as you're done comparing or transferring data between the two.

While the two workbook windows are in open in Excel, you can select different worksheets and scroll to different regions in either one by using its sheet tabs and scroll bars that appear at the edge of the window when you make its workbook active (either by clicking the window's title bar or one of the cells of its worksheets).

To move or copy data between the open workbook files, you have a choice between using the drag-and-drop or copy-and-paste method. To use drag-and-drop, select the data to be moved or copied in the worksheet of the one window and then drag the outline of the cell selection to the desired cell in the worksheet displayed in the other window. If you want to copy the cell selection rather than move it to the workbook in the other window, you must remember to hold down the Ctrl key as you drag its outline to its new position, releasing the Ctrl key only when you're in position and ready to drop the copied data into place.

Chapter 25

Ten (More or Less) Shortcut Keys for Entering Data

. . . .

The key element in entering data in a cell is completing the entry in the cell either by clicking another cell with the mouse pointer, or by using one of the shortcut keys listed below to move the cell cursor. Because most data entry in a spreadsheet is still done with the keyboard (despite Excel's inclusion of voice data entry), it makes sense to be up on the various shortcut keys you can use to complete the data entry, which are shown in Table 25-1. To work as efficiently as possible in constructing new data tables and lists, you need to select the shortcut key that best suits the way you're entering the data. Therefore, you would use the Enter key or the ↓ when entering data down the rows of a single column and the Tab key or the → key when entering data across the columns of a single row (from left to right).

Table 25-1	Data Entry Shortcut Keys
Press	*To*
Arrow keys (←, →, ↑, ↓)	Complete cell entry and move cell cursor one cell in direction of the arrow
Enter	Complete cell entry and move cell cursor down one row
Shift+Enter	Complete cell entry and move cell cursor up one row
Ctrl+Enter	Complete cell entry in all cells in selected range
Alt+Enter	Begin a new line in a cell entry
Tab	Complete cell entry and move cell cursor right one column
Shift+Tab	Complete cell entry and move cell cursor left one column
Esc	Cancel current cell entry
Ctrl+' (apostrophe)	Copy formula in cell above into current cell entry
Ctrl+Shift+" (quotation)	Copy value from cell above into current cell entry
Ctrl+` (accent)	Toggle between displaying cell values and cell formulas in worksheet
Ctrl+;	Insert current date into current cell entry
Ctrl+Shift+;	Insert current time into current cell entry

Chapter 26

Ten (More or Less) Shortcut Keys for Formatting the Worksheet

As you can see in Table 26-1, Excel supports a fair number of formatting shortcut keys. Although many of these shortcut keys duplicate the functions of buttons on Excel's Formatting toolbar, you may find that you prefer the keyboard shortcuts for applying the most common formatting to the cells in the data tables and lists you work with because their use enables you to keep your hands on the keyboard and your attention focused on the spreadsheet itself.

Table 26-1	Formatting Shortcut Keys
Press	*To*
Ctrl+1	Display Format Cells dialog box
Alt+' (apostrophe)	Display Style dialog box
Ctrl+Shift+~ (tilde)	Apply General number format
Ctrl+Shift+$	Apply Currency number format with two decimal places and negative numbers in parentheses
Ctrl+Shift+%	Apply Percent number format with no decimal places
Ctrl+Shift+#	Apply Date number format with day, month, and year, as in 15-Feb-06
Ctrl+Shift+@	Apply Time number format with hour and minute and AM/PM, as in 12:05 PM
Ctrl+Shift+!	Apply Comma number format with two decimal places
Ctrl+B	Add or remove bold
Ctrl+I	Add or remove italics
Ctrl+U	Add or remove underlining
Ctrl+5	Add or remove strikethrough
Ctrl+Shift+&	Apply outline border to current range
Ctrl+Shift+_ (underline)	Remove outline border from current range

Chapter 27

Ten (More or Less) Shortcut Keys for Editing Data

●●

*W*orksheet editing forms a significant part of the work you do in Excel. For that reason, the editing shortcut keys presented in Table 27-1 can go a long way to making your editing work much more efficient. Of all the key combinations in this category, I urge you to become familiar with Ctrl+hyphen (-) to open the Delete dialog box and Ctrl+Shift+plus sign (+) to open the Insert dialog box. The Delete dialog box enables you to remove cells and their contents from tables and lists in the worksheet, while at the same time adjusting the remaining cells in the table or list so that there are no gaps in the data. The Insert dialog box enables you to insert new cells in tables and lists, while at the same time adjusting the remaining cells in the table or list so that they are overwritten.

Table 27-1	Editing Shortcut Keys
Press	*To*
F2	Edit current cell entry and position insertion point at the end of cell contents
Shift+F2	Edit comment attached to current cell and position insertion point in comment box
Backspace	Delete character to left of insertion point when editing cell entry
Delete	Delete character to right of insertion point when editing cell entry: otherwise, clear cell entries in current range
Esc	Cancel editing in current cell entry
Enter	Complete editing in current cell entry
Ctrl+CC	Open Clipboard Task pane
Ctrl+C	Copy cell selection to the Windows Clipboard
Ctrl+X	Cut cell selection to the Windows Clipboard
Ctrl+V	Paste last copied or cut cells from the Windows Clipboard
Ctrl+hyphen (-)	Open Delete dialog box to delete cell selection and shift remaining cells left or up
Ctrl+Shift+plus (+)	Open Insert dialog box to insert new cells and shift existing cells right or down
Ctrl+Z	Undo last action
Ctrl+Y	Redo last action

Chapter 28

Ten (More or Less) Miscellaneous Shortcut Keys

. . . .

The shortcut keys in Table 28-1 are a motley crew, running the gamut from those that enable you to recalculate the worksheet when it's in Manual Calculation mode, to those that hide and unhide rows and columns of the worksheet. Despite their variety, you may well find yourself relying upon them every bit as much as, if not more than, the other shortcut keys that perform the more mundane Excel spreadsheet tasks.

Table 28-1	Various and Sundry Useful Shortcut Keys
Press	*To*
F9	Calculate formulas in all worksheets in all open workbooks
Shift+F9	Calculate formulas in active worksheet
Alt+F8	Open the Macro dialog box to run or edit a macro
Alt+F11	Open the Visual Basic Editor for editing or writing new macros
Ctrl+arrow key (←, →, ↑, ↓)	Move to the edge of the current data region (data range bounded by empty cells or worksheet borders) in the direction of arrow key
Ctrl+Home	Move cell cursor to first cell (A1)
Ctrl+End	Move cell cursor to last cell in the active area (cell in last occupied column and row)
Alt+Page Down	Move cell cursor one screen to the right
Alt+Page Up	Move cell cursor one screen to the left
Ctrl+Page Up	Make the previous worksheet in the workbook active
Ctrl+Page Down	Make the next worksheet in the workbook active
Shift+F10	Display the cell shortcut menu for the current cell
F11 or Alt+F1	Create a chart on its own chart sheet for the data in the current range
Ctrl+Shift+* (asterisk)	Select all the cells in the current pivot table
Ctrl+8	Display or hide outline symbols for outlined worksheet data
Ctrl+9	Hide selected rows
Ctrl+Shift+(	Unhide any hidden rows in selection
Ctrl+0 (zero)	Hide selected columns
Ctrl+Shift+)	Unhide any hidden columns in selection

Appendix A

About the CD

System Requirements

Make sure that your computer meets the minimum system requirements shown in the following list. If your computer doesn't match up to most of these requirements, you may have problems using the software and files on the CD. For the latest and greatest information, please refer to the ReadMe file located at the root of the CD-ROM.

- ✔ A PC with a Pentium or faster processor

- ✔ Microsoft Windows 98 or later

- ✔ Microsoft Excel 2000 or later

- ✔ At least 32MB of total RAM installed on your computer; for best performance, we recommend at least 64MB

- ✔ A CD-ROM drive

- ✔ A sound card

- ✔ A monitor capable of displaying at least 256 colors or grayscale

- ✔ A modem with a speed of at least 14,400 bps

If you need more information on the basics, check out these books published by Wiley Publishing, Inc.: *PCs For Dummies,* by Dan Gookin; or *Windows 98 For Dummies, Windows 2000 Professional For Dummies, Microsoft Windows ME Millennium Edition For Dummies,* all by Andy Rathbone.

Using the CD

To install the items from the CD to your hard drive, follow these steps.

1. **Insert the CD into your computer's CD-ROM drive. The license agreement appears.**

Note to Windows users: The interface won't launch if you have AutoRun disabled. In that case, click Start➪Run. In the dialog box that appears, type **D:\start.exe**.

(Replace D with the proper letter if your CD-ROM drive uses a different letter. If you don't know the letter, see how your CD-ROM drive is listed under My Computer.) Click OK.

2. **Read through the license agreement, and then click the Accept button if you want to use the CD. After you click Accept, the License Agreement window won't appear again.**

The CD interface appears. The interface allows you to install the programs and run the demos with just a click of a button (or two).

What You'll Find on the CD

The following sections are arranged by category and provide a summary of the software and other goodies you'll find on the CD. If you need help with installing the items provided on the CD, refer back to the installation instructions in the preceding section.

Third-party software

Shareware programs are fully functional, free, trial versions of copyrighted programs. If you like particular programs, register with their authors for a nominal fee and receive licenses, enhanced versions, and technical support.

Freeware programs are free, copyrighted games, applications, and utilities. You can copy them to as many PCs as you like — for free — but they offer no technical support.

GNU software is governed by its own license, which is included inside the folder of the GNU software. There are no restrictions on distribution of GNU software. See the GNU license at the root of the CD for more details.

Trial, demo, or *evaluation* versions of software are usually limited either by time or functionality (such as not letting you save a project after you create it).

The CD-ROM contains the following third-party add-ins and utilities, which can help you be more productive as you begin using Excel on your own:

- ✔ Crystal Xcelsius Professional 4, by Business Objects at www.xcelsius.com. This trial version of the Professional edition of Windows-based Crystal Xcelsius uses Macromedia Flash technology to enable you to create truly compelling forms of interactive charts and visual spreadsheet models referred to by Business Objects as *visual analytics*. These visual analytics offer the capability to display worksheet data values simply by positioning the mouse over a portion of the graphic. You can also add sliders to perform ad hoc what-if analysis. They can be easily output to PowerPoint and PDF documents, Outlook messages, and Web pages for sharing with your clients and colleagues.

- ✔ ESQuotes by Gilmore Software at www.esquotes.com. This evaluation version of ESQuotes offers you an easy method for tracking your entire portfolio of stocks and mutual funds in a single Excel workbook.

- ✔ MZ Tools VBA Add-Ins by MZ Tools Software at www.mztools.com. This freeware collection of Visual Basic for Applications add-ins consists of a wide variety of tools designed to help you in developing efficient, error-free Visual Basic code for your Excel workbooks.

✔ Power Utility Pak by JWalk and Associates at `j-walk.com/ss/pup/pup6/` `index.htm`. This trial version of the fifth edition of the ever-popular Power Utility Pak offers you a smorgasbord of add-in tools and custom functions designed to make every aspect of your Excel work a whole heck of a lot easier and more efficient.

✔ Planning Templates Free Sampler by Planning Templates, Inc., at `www.planningtemplates.com`. This freeware sampler consists of a workbook template file containing three worksheets, Net Worth Statement, Budget Worksheet, and Loan Calculator. These worksheets give you a good idea of the type of financial-planning aids you can get from Planning Templates, Inc.

✔ The Spreadsheet Assistant by Macro Systems at `www.add-ins.com`. This 30-day trial version of the popular Spreadsheet Assistant add-in confers a whole range of useful tools to your copy of Excel. These tools are readily available either from the custom Assistants pull-down menu or the Spreadsheet Assistants, File Change, and Sheet Change custom toolbars. Perhaps the most valuable tools in this collection are the custom cell and sheet tab shortcut menus that offer you immediate access to a whole slew of never-before dreamed-of formatting and editing options.

Practice files

This CD-ROM contains practice files that can be used in conjunction with the exercises. All the practice material for the book is all located in a single Excel Workbook folder on the CD-ROM. This Excel Workbook folder contains 22 chapter folders (Chapter 1 through Chapter 21 and Chapter 23 — the exercises in Chapter 22 don't require any practice files) plus a Templates folder.

Before you start working through the exercises in this workbook, I suggest that you copy this Excel Workbook folder to the My Documents folder on your computer's hard disk and then rename the Excel Workbook folder to My Practice Spreadsheets as follows:

1. Insert the CD-ROM into your computer's CD/DVD drive.

2. Click the Start button on the Windows taskbar and then click My Computer on the Start menu to open My Computer in Windows Explorer.

3. Right-click the icon for your CD/DVD drive and select Explore to open its contents in the Windows Explorer window.

4. Click the Excel Workbook folder icon and then press Ctrl+C.

5. Click the My Documents link in the left pane of the Windows Explorer window and then press Ctrl+V.

6. Right-click Excel Workbook folder and then select the Rename option on its shortcut menu.

7. Replace Excel Workbook by typing **My Practice Spreadsheets** and then pressing Enter.

8. Click the Close button in the upper-right corner of the Windows Explorer window to close it.

9. Open the My Practice Spreadsheets folder in My Documents on your hard disk and then open the Templates folder. Select all the files by pressing Ctrl+A and copy them to the Windows Clipboard by pressing Ctrl+C.

10. Open the Microsoft Templates file on your computer's hard disk by double-clicking the My Computer icon on the desktop and then double-clicking the Local Disk (C:) icon followed by the following folders: Document and Settings⇨Your personal folder (as in Greg) ⇨Application Data⇨Microsoft⇨Templates.

If the Application Data folder icon does not appear in your personal folder, you need to choose Tools⇨Folder Options and then select the Show Hidden Files and Folders option button on the View tab before you select OK.

11. Paste the copied the template files into the Templates folder by pressing Ctrl+V.

You are now ready to tackle any of the exercises in the workbook using the practice files saved in the My Practice Spreadsheets folder inside the My Documents folder on your hard disk.

When you're finished doing the exercises and no longer need access to the practice files, go ahead and delete the My Practice Spreadsheets folder and all its contents by dropping it in the Recycle bin on the Windows desktop.

Troubleshooting

I tried my best to compile programs that work on most computers with the minimum system requirements. Alas, your computer may differ, and some programs may not work properly for some reason.

The two likeliest problems are that you don't have enough memory (RAM) for the programs you want to use, or you have other programs running that are affecting installation or running of a program. If you get an error message such as Not enough memory or Setup cannot continue, try one or more of the following suggestions and then try using the software again:

- **Turn off any antivirus software running on your computer.** Installation programs sometimes mimic virus activity and may make your computer incorrectly believe that it's being infected by a virus.

- **Close all running programs.** The more programs you have running, the less memory is available to other programs. Installation programs typically update files and programs; so if you keep other programs running, installation may not work properly.

- **Have your local computer store add more RAM to your computer.** This is, admittedly, a drastic and somewhat expensive step. However, adding more memory can really help the speed of your computer and allow more programs to run at the same time.

Customer Care

If you have trouble with the CD-ROM, please call the Wiley Product Technical Support phone number at (800) 762-2974. Outside the United States, call 1 (317) 572-3994. You can also contact Wiley Product Technical Support at http://support.wiley.com. John Wiley & Sons will provide technical support only for installation and other general quality-control items. For technical support on the applications themselves, consult the program's vendor or author.

To place additional orders or to request information about other Wiley products, please call (877) 762-2974.

Appendix B

Table of Exercises

*T*able B-1 is a handy reference table that lists every exercise in the book, complete with the page number where you can find it.

Table B-1	Table of Exercises
Exercise Name	**Page Number**

(continued)

Table B-1 *(continued)*

(continued)

Table B-1 *(continued)*

(continued)

Table B-1 *(continued)*

John Wiley & Sons, Inc.
End-User License Agreement

READ THIS. You should carefully read these terms and conditions before opening the software packet(s) included with this book "Book". This is a license agreement "Agreement" between you and John Wiley & Sons, Inc. "WILEY". By opening the accompanying software packet(s), you acknowledge that you have read and accept the following terms and conditions. If you do not agree and do not want to be bound by such terms and conditions, promptly return the Book and the unopened software packet(s) to the place you obtained them for a full refund

1. **License Grant.** WILEY grants to you (either an individual or entity) a nonexclusive license to use one copy of the enclosed software program(s) (collectively, the "Software") solely for your own personal or business purposes on a single computer (whether a standard computer or a workstation component of a multi-user network). The Software is in use on a computer when it is loaded into temporary memory (RAM) or installed into permanent memory (hard disk, CD-ROM, or other storage device). WILEY reserves all rights not expressly granted herein.

2. **Ownership.** WILEY is the owner of all right, title, and interest, including copyright, in and to the compilation of the Software recorded on the physical packet included with this Book "Software Media". Copyright to the individual programs recorded on the Software Media is owned by the author or other authorized copyright owner of each program. Ownership of the Software and all proprietary rights relating thereto remain with WILEY and its licensers.

3. **Restrictions on Use and Transfer.**

   (a) You may only (i) make one copy of the Software for backup or archival purposes, or (ii) transfer the Software to a single hard disk, provided that you keep the original for backup or archival purposes. You may not (i) rent or lease the Software, (ii) copy or reproduce the Software through a LAN or other network system or through any computer subscriber system or bulletin-board system, or (iii) modify, adapt, or create derivative works based on the Software.

   (b) You may not reverse engineer, decompile, or disassemble the Software. You may transfer the Software and user documentation on a permanent basis, provided that the transferee agrees to accept the terms and conditions of this Agreement and you retain no copies. If the Software is an update or has been updated, any transfer must include the most recent update and all prior versions.

4. **Restrictions on Use of Individual Programs.** You must follow the individual requirements and restrictions detailed for each individual program in the "About the CD" appendix of this Book or on the Software Media. These limitations are also contained in the individual license agreements recorded on the Software Media. These limitations may include a requirement that after using the program for a specified period of time, the user must pay a registration fee or discontinue use. By opening the Software packet(s), you agree to abide by the licenses and restrictions for these individual programs that are detailed in the "About the CD" appendix and/or on the Software Media. None of the material on this Software Media or listed in this Book may ever be redistributed, in original or modified form, for commercial purposes.

5. **Limited Warranty.**

   (a) WILEY warrants that the Software and Software Media are free from defects in materials and workmanship under normal use for a period of sixty (60) days from the date of purchase of this Book. If WILEY receives notification within the warranty period of defects in materials or workmanship, WILEY will replace the defective Software Media.

(b) WILEY AND THE AUTHOR(S) OF THE BOOK DISCLAIM ALL OTHER WARRANTIES, EXPRESS OR IMPLIED, INCLUDING WITHOUT LIMITATION IMPLIED WARRANTIES OF MERCHANTABILITY AND FITNESS FOR A PARTICULAR PURPOSE, WITH RESPECT TO THE SOFTWARE, THE PROGRAMS, THE SOURCE CODE CONTAINED THEREIN, AND/OR THE TECHNIQUES DESCRIBED IN THIS BOOK. WILEY DOES NOT WARRANT THAT THE FUNCTIONS CONTAINED IN THE SOFTWARE WILL MEET YOUR REQUIREMENTS OR THAT THE OPERATION OF THE SOFTWARE WILL BE ERROR FREE.

(c) This limited warranty gives you specific legal rights, and you may have other rights that vary from jurisdiction to jurisdiction.

6. Remedies.

(a) WILEY's entire liability and your exclusive remedy for defects in materials and workmanship shall be limited to replacement of the Software Media, which may be returned to WILEY with a copy of your receipt at the following address: Software Media Fulfillment Department, Attn.: Excel Workbook For Dummies, John Wiley & Sons, Inc., 10475 Crosspoint Blvd., Indianapolis, IN 46256, or call 1-800-762-2974. Please allow four to six weeks for delivery. This Limited Warranty is void if failure of the Software Media has resulted from accident, abuse, or misapplication. Any replacement Software Media will be warranted for the remainder of the original warranty period or thirty (30) days, whichever is longer.

(b) In no event shall WILEY or the author be liable for any damages whatsoever (including without limitation damages for loss of business profits, business interruption, loss of business information, or any other pecuniary loss) arising from the use of or inability to use the Book or the Software, even if WILEY has been advised of the possibility of such damages.

(c) Because some jurisdictions do not allow the exclusion or limitation of liability for consequential or incidental damages, the above limitation or exclusion may not apply to you.

7. U.S. Government Restricted Rights. Use, duplication, or disclosure of the Software for or on behalf of the United States of America, its agencies and/or instrumentalities "U.S. Government" is subject to restrictions as stated in paragraph (c)(1)(ii) of the Rights in Technical Data and Computer Software clause of DFARS 252.227-7013, or subparagraphs (c) (1) and (2) of the Commercial Computer Software - Restricted Rights clause at FAR 52.227-19, and in similar clauses in the NASA FAR supplement, as applicable.

8. General. This Agreement constitutes the entire understanding of the parties and revokes and supersedes all prior agreements, oral or written, between them and may not be modified or amended except in a writing signed by both parties hereto that specifically refers to this Agreement. This Agreement shall take precedence over any other documents that may be in conflict herewith. If any one or more provisions contained in this Agreement are held by any court or tribunal to be invalid, illegal, or otherwise unenforceable, each and every other provision shall remain in full force and effect.

Index

• D •

● *X* ●

● *Y* ●

● *Z* ●

Notes

Notes

Notes

Notes

Notes

Notes

Notes

Notes

Notes

Notes

Notes

Notes

Apple & Macs

iPad For Dummies
978-0-470-58027-1

iPhone For Dummies,
4th Edition
978-0-470-87870-5

MacBook For Dummies, 3rd
Edition
978-0-470-76918-8

Mac OS X Snow Leopard For
Dummies
978-0-470-43543-4

Business

Bookkeeping For Dummies
978-0-7645-9848-7

Job Interviews
For Dummies,
3rd Edition
978-0-470-17748-8

Resumes For Dummies,
5th Edition
978-0-470-08037-5

Starting an
Online Business
For Dummies,
6th Edition
978-0-470-60210-2

Stock Investing
For Dummies,
3rd Edition
978-0-470-40114-9

Successful
Time Management
For Dummies
978-0-470-29034-7

Computer Hardware

BlackBerry
For Dummies,
4th Edition
978-0-470-60700-8

Computers For Seniors
For Dummies,
2nd Edition
978-0-470-53483-0

PCs For Dummies,
Windows 7
Edition
978-0-470-46542-4

Laptops For Dummies,
4th Edition
978-0-470-57829-2

Cooking & Entertaining

Cooking Basics
For Dummies,
3rd Edition
978-0-7645-7206-7

Wine For Dummies,
4th Edition
978-0-470-04579-4

Diet & Nutrition

Dieting For Dummies,
2nd Edition
978-0-7645-4149-0

Nutrition For Dummies,
4th Edition
978-0-471-79868-2

Weight Training
For Dummies,
3rd Edition
978-0-471-76845-6

Digital Photography

Digital SLR Cameras &
Photography For Dummies,
3rd Edition
978-0-470-46606-3

Photoshop Elements 8
For Dummies
978-0-470-52967-6

Gardening

Gardening Basics
For Dummies
978-0-470-03749-2

Organic Gardening
For Dummies,
2nd Edition
978-0-470-43067-5

Green/Sustainable

Raising Chickens
For Dummies
978-0-470-46544-8

Green Cleaning
For Dummies
978-0-470-39106-8

Health

Diabetes For Dummies,
3rd Edition
978-0-470-27086-8

Food Allergies
For Dummies
978-0-470-09584-3

Living Gluten-Free
For Dummies,
2nd Edition
978-0-470-58589-4

Hobbies/General

Chess For Dummies,
2nd Edition
978-0-7645-8404-6

Drawing
Cartoons & Comics
For Dummies
978-0-470-42683-8

Knitting For Dummies,
2nd Edition
978-0-470-28747-7

Organizing
For Dummies
978-0-7645-5300-4

Su Doku For Dummies
978-0-470-01892-7

Home Improvement

Home Maintenance
For Dummies,
2nd Edition
978-0-470-43063-7

Home Theater
For Dummies,
3rd Edition
978-0-470-41189-6

Living the
Country Lifestyle
All-in-One
For Dummies
978-0-470-43061-3

Solar Power Your Home
For Dummies,
2nd Edition
978-0-470-59678-4

Internet

Blogging For Dummies,
3rd Edition
978-0-470-61996-4

eBay For Dummies,
6th Edition
978-0-470-49741-8

Facebook For Dummies,
3rd Edition
978-0-470-87804-0

Web Marketing
For Dummies,
2nd Edition
978-0-470-37181-7

WordPress
For Dummies,
3rd Edition
978-0-470-59274-8

Language & Foreign Language

French For Dummies
978-0-7645-5193-2

Italian Phrases
For Dummies
978-0-7645-7203-6

Spanish For Dummies,
2nd Edition
978-0-470-87855-2

Spanish
For Dummies,
Audio Set
978-0-470-09585-0

Math & Science

Algebra I
For Dummies,
2nd Edition
978-0-470-55964-2

Biology For Dummies,
2nd Edition
978-0-470-59875-7

Calculus For Dummies
978-0-7645-2498-1

Chemistry For Dummies
978-0-7645-5430-8

Microsoft Office

Excel 2010 For Dummies
978-0-470-48953-6

Office 2010 All-in-One
For Dummies
978-0-470-49748-7

Office 2010 For Dummies,
Book + DVD Bundle
978-0-470-62698-6

Word 2010 For Dummies
978-0-470-48772-3

Music

Guitar For Dummies,
2nd Edition
978-0-7645-9904-0

iPod & iTunes For
Dummies, 8th Edition
978-0-470-87871-2

Piano Exercises
For Dummies
978-0-470-38765-8

Parenting & Education

Parenting For Dummies,
2nd Edition
978-0-7645-5418-6

Type 1 Diabetes
For Dummies
978-0-470-17811-9

Pets

Cats For Dummies,
2nd Edition
978-0-7645-5275-5

Dog Training For Dummies,
3rd Edition
978-0-470-60029-0

Puppies For Dummies,
2nd Edition
978-0-470-03717-1

Religion & Inspiration

The Bible For Dummies
978-0-7645-5296-0

Catholicism For Dummies
978-0-7645-5391-2

Women in the Bible
For Dummies
978-0-7645-8475-6

Self-Help & Relationship

Anger Management
For Dummies
978-0-470-03715-7

Overcoming Anxiety
For Dummies,
2nd Edition
978-0-470-57441-6

Sports

Baseball
For Dummies,
3rd Edition
978-0-7645-7537-2

Basketball
For Dummies,
2nd Edition
978-0-7645-5248-9

Golf For Dummies,
3rd Edition
978-0-471-76871-5

Web Development

Web Design
All-in-One
For Dummies
978-0-470-41796-6

Web Sites
Do-It-Yourself
For Dummies,
2nd Edition
978-0-470-56520-9

Windows 7

Windows 7
For Dummies
978-0-470-49743-2

Windows 7
For Dummies,
Book + DVD Bundle
978-0-470-52398-8

Windows 7 All-in-One
For Dummies
978-0-470-48763-1

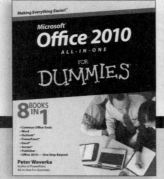

Available wherever books are sold. For more information or to order direct: U.S. customers visit www.dummies.com or call 1-877-762-29
U.K. customers visit www.wileyeurope.com or call (0) 1243 843291. Canadian customers visit www.wiley.ca or call 1-800-567-4797.

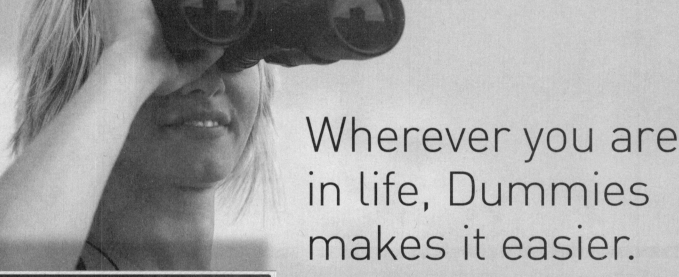

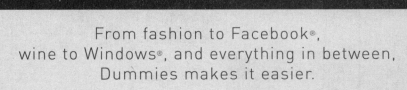

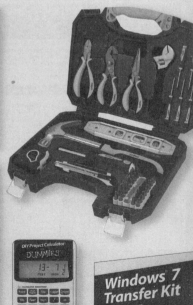

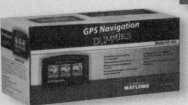